THE MODERN GREEK L[...]

THE
MODERN GREEK
LANGUAGE

A Descriptive Analysis of
Standard Modern Greek

PETER MACKRIDGE

OXFORD UNIVERSITY PRESS
1987

Oxford University Press, Walton Street, Oxford OX2 6DP
London New York Toronto
Delhi Bombay Calcutta Madras Karachi
Kuala Lumpur Singapore Hong Kong Tokyo
Nairobi Dar es Salaam Cape Town
Melbourne Auckland
and associated companies in
Beirut Berlin Ibadan Mexico City Nicosia

Oxford is a trade mark of Oxford University Press

Published in the United States
by Oxford University Press, New York
Paperback edition first published 1987

British Library Cataloguing in Publication Data

Mackridge, Peter
The Modern Greek language: a descriptive
analysis of Standard Modern Greek.
1. Greek language, Modern
I. Title
489'.3   PA1050
ISBN 0–19–815854–8

Library of Congress Cataloging in Publication Data

Mackridge, Peter A.
The Modern Greek language.
Bibliography: p.
Includes index.
1. Greek language, Modern–Grammar.   I. Title.
PA1057.M27   1985   489'.35   84–18934
ISBN 0–19–815854–8

Printed in Great Britain by
Biddles Ltd. Guildford

In memoriam
Irene Pickering Mackridge
(1919–1980)

PREFACE

This book is an attempt to present a fairly comprehensive account of the structure and usage of Standard Modern Greek (SMG), which is defined as the language ordinarily spoken and written at the present day by moderately educated people in the large urban centres of Greece. Today, despite the view frequently expressed by Greeks that the Modern Greek language is in a state of chaos, there is nevertheless a broad consensus about the general principles (and about most of the details) of the language.

The observations contained in this book are based on my own experience of learning to understand and to use the Athenian spoken language since 1965, and on a large amount of spoken and written material collected systematically since 1974, the date at which the military dictatorship fell and the 'language question' suddenly became close to being resolved through the virtual abandonment of what had hitherto been the official language (*katharevousa*). This material consists of articles in newspapers and magazines and recordings both of radio and television broadcasts and of live conversations and discussions. Especially close attention has been paid to the linguistic features employed by people who are speaking naturally and with no intention of impressing by their use of Greek. This is one of the reasons why only a few examples have been taken from creative literature. Most weight has been attached to the utterances of people born and bred in Athens who have completed their high-school education, since these are the chief bearers of SMG; but the speech of Greeks from other areas and from different educational backgrounds has also been studied by way of comparison. Although questionnaires have been employed to elicit which form out of a range of alternatives a speaker uses, and native informants have been consulted as to the acceptability of utterances recorded from other speakers, most of the spoken material was collected from the speech of people who were unaware that their use of the language was being studied. The reason for this is the unreliability of answers to direct questions about what form a Greek speaker uses, since, owing to the highly normative nature of language teaching in Greece, the speaker will usually specify the form which (s)he thinks (s)he uses or ought to use, a response which is often contradicted in practice by his/her use of a different form in informal conversation. Examples taken from written texts are usually assigned a reference (enclosed in brackets); in most cases where such a reference is lacking, the example is either a commonly used phrase or has been noted from oral usage.

This book is not intended in any way to be a grammar. It does not possess any of the kinds of 'adequacy' which, according to Chomsky, are required of a grammar. Instead, it confines itself to an analysis, not without certain generalizations, of a large amount of material, which is not, however, treated as a finite corpus. I should also stress that I have no intention in this book of making any contribution to the study either of linguistic theory or of linguistic universals.

It may be thought presumptuous that someone who is not a linguist in the modern sense, but a 'language-and-literature' man, should write a descriptive analysis of contemporary Greek. As a student of Modern Greek literature as well as language, I am acutely conscious of the fact that certain forms of the language are normally acceptable only in certain situations, and that the gap which separates the grammar of much of Modern Greek literature from that of SMG is sometimes wide. In view of the existence of alternative forms, I feel that close attention must be paid to surface structures (that is, the structure of actual utterances) so that one is fully aware of the possibilities of variation which might not be accounted for in some 'model' of the language. I therefore make no apology for concentrating on the fluid situation which prevails on the surface of Modern Greek rather than attempting to discover the unchanging general principles underlying this surface structure. Although I have been helped tremendously by the writings of modern linguists on Modern Greek, the present book should perhaps be seen as a parallel study to the work of the transformationalists, examining the language in a way which differs from theirs without attempting to vie with it.

Since the language controversy in Greece is an issue that has polarized those who talk and write about Modern Greek, I must make clear where I stand on the matter. As a student of Modern Greek literature, I could hardly be anything but a supporter of demotic in its struggle against *katharevousa*. On the other hand, I can see a danger that demoticists might see this book as being 'reactionary', since it appears to condone the use of a whole host of *katharevousa* elements that are not strictly compatible with the grammar of traditional demotic. Such readers must

bear in mind that this book is an attempt at a descriptive, not a prescriptive, approach to Modern Greek. Thus, when I introduce certain
katharevousa elements I may be far from approving of them; I am
simply stating that such is the usage of at least some educated people.

Hardly ever has there been attempted a description, on a large scale,
of the speech and writing of educated Greeks. Until the last couple of
decades, linguists tended to view Modern Greek as two separate codes,
demotic and *katharevousa*, and to study only the former, dismissing
katharevousa influence on spoken Greek as interference between
codes. The pioneering work of Thumb (1895) was a comprehensive
description of the speech of the less educated; and, although Triandaphyllidis (1941) made many compromises with the language of the
educated in his *Grammar*, the ideological aim of the descriptive and
prescriptive grammarians of Modern Greek has usually been to promote
demotic at the expense of *katharevousa*, as did Mirambel (1959). Now
that *katharevousa* has more or less ceased to exist as a separate code, it
is my task to show just how far it has affected the everyday usage of
educated Greeks, and not to try (as do some demoticists) to revive
'genuine popular forms' which, having been displaced under *katharevousa*
influence, do not appear in that usage.

Nevertheless, Mirambel's book has been a great inspiration to me;
and I have been fortunate in that (as the bibliography to the present
volume indicates) a remarkable amount of highly illuminating work
has been done on Modern Greek since the publication of Mirambel's
Description. I readily admit that much of my own book draws heavily
on the results of this work; thus this book is as much a synthesis of
work done by others as it is based on my own research.

Throughout this book I have borne in mind that readers may not
have a thorough acquaintance with MG. It is for this reason (and because
there is no grammar of the language available to the English-speaking
reader, except Pring (1950)) that I have felt it necessary to include
some sample paradigms in Appendix I.

In the Greek examples I have used the simplified historical orthography. When I have quoted from printed texts I have made the spelling
conform with this system, although I have preserved the original
punctuation. In my English renderings I have attempted to adhere as
closely as possible to the original: in these renderings, square brackets
indicate a word or words which do(es) not appear in the Greek, while
parentheses indicate a word or words which appear(s) in the Greek but
would be omitted in English. In the Greek examples, square brackets

indicate that what appears between them may optionally be deleted. Often, however, English renderings are followed by literal translations: just how literal these are depends on the circumstances.

Outside Chapter 1, neither the International Phonetic Alphabet nor strictly phonemic representations are normally used: when words or parts of words are transliterated, a semi-phonetic transcription is given.

The initial stages of the research for this book were carried out with the assistance of the Hayter Travel Fund, University of London. The bulk of the research was funded by the British Academy. This assistance is gratefully acknowledged.

I would like to express my thanks here to all those who have helped me with material, and especially Mrs Marion Sarafis, who kept me supplied with cuttings from the Greek press; to Dr J. T. Pring and Dr Henry Waring, who read through Chapter 1 and the section on intonation respectively and whose suggestions helped me to avoid many of the pitfalls inherent in Modern Greek phonetics; and to Dr Irene Warburton, who read the completed typescript and alerted me to a number of errors and ambiguities. Needless to say, the responsibility for any shortcomings is entirely my own.

Lastly, I would like to thank my wife, Jackie, both for her advice at various stages of my work on this book and—perhaps more importantly—for her patience and encouragement throughout the long period of research and writing.

PETER MACKRIDGE

CONTENTS

CONTENTS xix

REFERENCES AND ABBREVIATIONS

REFERENCES

And. 1967   = Andriotis (1967).
And. 1976   = Andriotis (1976).
Arg. 1979   Ἀργυρίου, Α., Ἡ ἑλληνική ποίηση, Sokolis, Athens.
Ber. 1973   Μπεράτης, Γ., Τό πλατύ ποτάμι (2nd edn.), Ermis, Athens.
Chr. 1976   = Christidis (1976).
Douk. 1979   Δούκα, Μ., Καρρέ φίξ, Kedros, Athens.
Ely. 1971   Ἐλύτης, Ο., Ἄσμα ἡρωικό καί πένθιμο γιά τόν χαμένο ἀνθυπολοχαγό τῆς Ἀλβανίας (3rd edn.), Ikaros, Athens.
Ely. 1974   Elytis, O., *The Axion esti*, University of Pittsburgh Press, Pittsburgh.
Fra. 1962   Φραγκιάς, Α., Ἡ καγκελόπορτα, Kedros, Athens.
Hadz. 1909   = Hadzidakis (1909).
Hadz. 1976   Χατζής, Δ., Σπουδές, Keimena, Athens.
Ioa. 1976   Ἰωάννου, Γ., Πεζογραφήματα, Ermis, Athens.
Kar. n.d.   Καραγάτσης, Μ., Ὁ κίτρινος φάκελλος, 2 vols. Kollaros, Athens.
Kav. 1963   Καβάφης, Κ. Π., Ποιήματα, 2 vols., Ikaros, Athens.
Kaz. 1958   Καζαντζάκης, Ν., Ἐπιστολές πρός τή Γαλάτεια, Diphros, Athens.
Kaz. 1965   Καζαντζάκης, Ν., Ἀναφορά στόν Γκρέκο (3rd edn.), Eleni Kazantzaki, Athens.
Koum. 1970   Κουμανταρέας, Μ., Τά μηχανάκια (2nd edn.), Kedros, Athens.
Koum. 1978   Κουμανταρέας, Μ., Ἡ κυρία Κούλα, Kedros, Athens.
Kri. 1979   = Kriaras (1979).
Lyp. 1977   = Lypourlis (1977).
Mal. 1938.   Μαλάνος, Τ., Ἕνας ἡγησιακός, Alexandria.
Pla. 1976   Πλασσαρά, Κ., Παρένθεση, Kedros, Athens.
Pla. 1980   Πλασσαρά, Κ., Ἡ τελευταία Ἰθάκη, Philippotis, Athens.
Pol. 1957   Πολίτης, Κ., Κωνσταντίνος ὁ Μέγας, Diphros, Athens.

Pol. n.d.   Πολίτης, Λ., Θέματα τῆς λογοτεχνίας μας, 2η σειρά, Konstandinidis, Salonica.

Pre. n.d.   Πρεβελάκης, Π., Ὁ ἥλιος τοῦ θανάτου, Kollaros, Athens [1959].

Prov. 1977   = Provlimata 1977.

Sef. 1969   Seferis, G., Collected Poems 1924–1955 (tr., ed., and introd. by E. Keeley and P. Sherrard), Cape, London.

Sef. 1973   Σεφέρης, Γ., Μέρες τοῦ 1945–51, Ikaros, Athens.

Sef. 1977   Σεφέρης, Γ., Μέρες Δ΄, Ikaros, Athens.

Sid. 1959   Σιδερίδου-Θωμοπούλου, Ν., Ἀντρέας Καρκαβίτσας. Athens.

The. 1940   Θεοτοκάς, Γ., Λεωνῆς, Pyrsos, Athens.

Tsa. 1973   Τσάτσου, Ι., Ὁ ἀδερφός μου Γιῶργος Σεφέρης, Kollaros, Athens.

Tsi. 1970   Τσιφῶρος, Ν., Ἑλληνική μυθολογία, Ermis, Athens.

Tsi. 1973   Τσίρκας, Σ., Ἀριάγνη (4th edn.), Kedros, Athens.

Vaf. 1970   Βαφόπουλος, Γ. Θ., Σελίδες αὐτοβιογραφίας, Vol. 1, Kollaros, Athens.

Ven. 1969   Βενέζης, Η., Ὥρα πολέμου (2nd edn.), Kollaros, Athens.

Vik. 1882   Βικέλας, Δ., Σαικσπείρου Τραγῳδίαι μεταφρασθεῖσαι ἐκ τοῦ ἀγγλικοῦ ὑπό . . . Μέρος Ε: Ἁμλέτος, Koromilas, Athens.

Vra. 1953   Βρανούσης, Λ., Ρήγας (Vasiki Vivliothiki 10), Aetos, Athens.

A   Αὐγή (daily).

AI   Ἀθλητική Ἠχώ (weekly).

D   Διαβάζω (fortnightly).

E   Ἐλευθεροτυπία (daily).

FD   Τό Φῶς τῆς Δευτέρας (weekly).

K   Καθημερινή (daily).

N   Τά Νέα (daily).

NE   Νέα Ἑστία (bi-monthly).

P   Ὁ Πολίτης (monthly).

R   Ριζοσπάστης (daily).

T   Ταχυδρόμος (weekly).

V   Τό Βῆμα (daily; weekly from September 1982).

OTHER ABBREVIATIONS AND SYMBOLS

A   adjective; (in Appendix II) accusative

acc.	accusative
act.	active
Adv.	adverb
AG	Ancient Greek
C	consonant
D	demotic
E	English
F	French; (in Appendix II) feminine
f.	feminine
fem.	feminine
G	German; (in Appendix II) genitive
gen.	genitive
impf.	imperfective
intrans.	intransitive
It.	Italian
K	*katharevousa*
L	Latin
lit.	literally
m.	masculine
masc.	masculine
MG	Modern Greek
N	noun; (in Appendix II) neuter; nominative
n.	neuter
neg.	negative
nom.	nominative
n-p	non-past
O	object
P	(in Appendix II) plural
pass.	passive
pers.	person
pf.	perfective
pl.	plural
R	Russian
S	subject; (in Appendix II) singular
sg.	singular
sing.	singular
SMG	Standard Modern Greek
Sp.	Spanish
T	Turkish
trans.	transitive

ult.	ultimately
V	verb; vowel; (in Appendix II) vocative
v.i.	intransitive verb
v.t.	transitive verb
Ven.	Venetian dialect
voc.	vocative
[. . .]	phonetic transcription (but see Preface)
/. . ./	phonemic transcription
{. . .}	morpheme
<	etymologically derived from
>	etymologically produces
←	morphologically or syntatically derived from
→	morphologically or syntactically produces
*	(before word(s) or form(s)) unacceptable
?	(before word(s) or form(s)) of doubtful acceptability

INTRODUCTION

1 THE SPEAKERS OF GREEK

Modern Greek is spoken by about 12 to 13 million people. It is the sole official language of the Republic of Greece and one of the two official languages of the Republic of Cyprus. Since 1981 it has also been one of the official languages of the European Community. It is spoken as sole mother tongue by more than 95 per cent of the population of Greece (which totals about 10 million) and by half a million of the 600,000 or so inhabitants of Cyprus. It is also spoken by a significant number of people of Greek origin (perhaps 2 or 3 million) who are resident in many parts of the world, chiefly North America, Australia, Germany, and the United Kingdom.

The almost total linguistic homogenization of Greece has been a phenomenon of the past seventy years, which have seen a remarkable increase in the proportion of Greek speakers to the speakers of other languages (which in 1928 were, in descending order of numbers, Turkish, Macedonian Slav and Bulgarian, Ladino, Armenian, Koutsovlach, Albanian, Romany, and others: I am indebted to Angelopoulos (1979) for some of the information contained in these paragraphs). The same period has also seen the concentration within Greece of a large number of Greek speakers formerly resident in Asia Minor and Istanbul, the Ukraine and the Caucasus, Egypt, Bulgaria, and elsewhere in the Balkans and the Near and Middle East. Most of this change has come about through a series of population exchanges and of other mass movements, the most important of these being exchanges between Greece, Bulgaria, and Serbia/Yugoslavia in the period 1913-19, the repatriation of Greeks from the Soviet Union in 1919, the exchange between Greece and Turkey in 1923, the almost total annihilation of the Ladino- (Spanish-) speaking Jews during the Axis Occupation, the exodus of Greeks from Egypt during the Nasser regime, and, lastly, the gradual departure of almost the entire Greek minority of Istanbul.

Since the first Greek national census to include a question about mother tongue was that of 1928 and the last was that of 1951, it is impossible to know the precise numbers of people with mother tongues other than Greek in Greek territories either in 1913 or in 1983. In addition, the figures given in these censuses may well underestimate the actual numbers of people whose mother tongue was anything other than Greek. Today there are still well over 100,000 Turkish speakers in Thrace, and speakers of Koutsovlach (Arumanian) may be encountered in large numbers in Epirus and Macedonia; while speakers of Albanian and Macedonian Slav still remain too, in less significant numbers (the former scattered in various parts of Epirus, Attica, Boeotia, and the Peloponnese, the latter in Macedonia). My own impression, based on travels in various parts of Greece, is that all these minority languages (with the exception of Turkish) will have practically died out in Greece during the course of the next generation. One must bear in mind that most of the speakers of these languages are in fact bilingual in their mother tongue and in Greek (as was also the case to a large extent in the past); and that no education is officially available in Greece in any of these languages except Turkish, nor is any material published in Greece in any of the minority languages but Turkish and Armenian.

2 THE DEVELOPMENT OF THE GREEK LANGUAGE

Modern Greek is the sole descendant of Ancient Greek and as such is a member of the Indo-European group of languages.

After the end of the Golden Age of Classical Greece (i.e. after the late fourth century BC) the Greek language underwent some rather radical changes in a relatively short period. The ancient dialects were for the most part superseded by the *koine* ('common language'), which was based largely on the Attic dialect of Athens, but with some features taken from other dialects. The *koine* spread throughout the Greek world (which included much of the Middle East and southern Italy as well as Greece and Asia Minor) and underwent a process of simplification as it was spoken and written as a lingua franca by a large number of geographically dispersed people, many of whom did not have Greek as their mother tongue. Thus by the time Constantinople was founded (AD 324), many of the changes that have occurred in the Greek language between Classical and modern times had already taken place, particularly in the sphere of pronunciation, but also in morphology, syntax, and vocabulary. (For a detailed survey of the linguistic changes which took place, see Browning 1983.)

Meanwhile, although such texts as the Septuagint (the Greek translation of the Old Testament carried out by seventy Jews in Alexandria in the third century BC) and the New Testament (most of which was originally written in Greek) display many of the characteristics of the Greek actually spoken at the time, most serious writing was done in a language which attempted to approximate to Attic or some other Classical dialect. After Greek became the official language of the Eastern Roman (Byzantine) Empire in the sixth century AD, the continued existence of schools of Greek, in which the Classical language was studied as a model for contemporary usage, ensured that the Greek used for official purposes throughout the Byzantine period was of a more or less archaic variety. Some Byzantine authors actually wrote in Attic Greek, while others (especially hymnographers and chroniclers) used a heterogeneous range of varieties of Greek which were largely based on the Hellenistic *koine*, but which sometimes included more modern features.

The spoken language did not fully make its appearance in writing, however, until the twelfth and thirteenth centuries, when the central administration of the Byzantine Empire was weak, and especially after the conquest of Constantinople by the Fourth Crusade in 1204. It is during these centuries that texts began to be written in a language which is recognizably Modern Greek, even though their authors often introduce archaic elements into what is otherwise perhaps a fair representation of the language spoken at the time. The fact that most of these late Byzantine vernacular texts cannot be localized geographically according to the linguistic forms they employ suggests either that the MG dialects had hardly begun to diverge from each other, or that these authors were deliberately writing in a new *koine*, a new 'common' language. The modern Cretan and Cypriot dialects, however, are well represented in literary and non-literary texts from the thirteenth to the seventeenth centuries, that is, during a period between the end of Byzantine control over these islands and the beginning of the Turkish occupation.

Nevertheless, by the time the Greek state was founded, about 1830, the spoken language (at least in many of its chief dialects) had moved remarkably little away from the late Byzantine *koine*, which in turn was still relatively close to the Hellenistic *koine*. It is quite astounding not only how little the spoken Greek language had altered from Classical to modern times (even in comparison with the changes that took place between Latin and Italian, for instance), but that it should have survived at all despite Arab incursions and mass settlements by Slavs during the

Byzantine period, followed by conquests by Crusaders, Venetians, and Turks. The fact is that although it was only a tiny cultural élite that preserved a consciousness of Hellenic continuity from Classical times, Greek remained a prestige language because of the Byzantine Empire and the Eastern Orthodox Church. Greek was, after all, the original language of most of the New Testament, and it was the language in which church services were conducted in all the areas controlled by the Patriarchate of Constantinople. In addition, at the very centre of the Ottoman Empire, Greeks were entrusted by the Sultan with key administrative posts, including the government of Wallachia and Moldavia (from the early eighteenth century), so that, well after the fall of the Byzantine Empire in 1453, a knowledge of Greek was still highly prized in the Balkans as well as in other areas in the Eastern Mediterranean.

3 THE STANDARD LANGUAGE AND THE DIALECTS

There is hardly any correspondence between the dialects of MG and those of the ancient language. The MG dialects developed during medieval times but, considering the difficulties of access to some of the regions in which Greek was spoken, the dialects remained remarkably close to each other. The one that is, linguistically speaking, furthest removed from the core is Tsakonian, a descendant of the ancient Doric dialect, spoken in an inaccessible region of the south-eastern Peloponnese. All the other MG dialects are derived from the Hellenistic *koine*. Of these, the ones that diverged furthest from the *koine* were those of the Pontic-Cappadocian group (formerly spoken in Asia Minor), and those of southern Italy (where there are still Greek speakers today). (For an examination of the MG dialects, see Kondosopoulos 1981, and Newton 1972b.)

Just as the minority languages of Greece are fast disappearing, so are the dialects, which have gradually been giving way to a standard language since the Greek War of Independence (1821-9), and especially during the twentieth century. It was a convenient coincidence that the Peloponnese constituted the bulk of the territory liberated by the Greeks from the Turks during the War of Independence, since the dialects of the Peloponnese (with the exception of Tsakonian) were among those which remained phonologically and morphologically closest to the written language. When Athens became the capital of the Greek kingdom in 1834, it was settled in large part by Peloponnesians, whose dialects soon superseded the rather different 'old Athenian' spoken by the inhabitants of pre-Independence Athens. (The only feature of the 'old Athenian' dialect that survives in Standard Modern Greek seems to be the verb τσουλάω 'I roll' and its derivatives, < AG κυλίνδω, later κυλίω.) At the same time, a significant proportion of the administrative and intellectual élite was composed of Greeks from Istanbul, whose dialect, despite a few northernisms, was remarkably close to those of the Peloponnese; and the cultural superiority of Greeks from the Ionian Islands (especially Corfu) resulted in features of their dialects (which were again close to Peloponnesian) entering the language of Athens. During the twentieth century the influx of Greek speakers from various areas outside Greece and the influence of universal education, the press, broadcasting, and compulsory military service, together with improved land, sea, and air communications, have made Greece (and especially Athens and Salonica) into a melting-pot in which speakers of various kinds of Greek have gradually sunk their linguistic differences; and the language which gradually developed out of this situation in the speech of the prestigious urban élites was Standard Modern Greek.

So far we have been talking about the spoken language. Meanwhile, from the foundation of the Greek state onwards, the written language for most purposes was *katharevousa*, which phonologically and morphologically did not stray very far from the Hellenistic *koine*. Although the written language was not the *origin* of SMG (in contrast with the situation with standard languages in many other countries), it none the less helped to produce the norms of the language through the amalgamation of some of its characteristics with those of the Peloponnesian and Istanbul dialects.

Today the speakers of SMG constitute the dominant speech community in Greece. Although it must be borne in mind that persons who have completed high-school education make up only 10 per cent of the population of Greece (see Petrounias 1978: 202) and that perhaps more than 50 per cent of the 3 million inhabitants of the Athens–Piraeus conurbation were not born there (see *D* 49. 51), it is especially in Athens (and Salonica) and among moderately educated people that SMG has developed, spreading geographically and socially to such an extent that it has largely displaced local dialects and special parlances. Today the speech (even the pronunciation) of moderately educated people from all parts of Greece tends to be hardly distinguishable from that of an Athenian. The Salonican (or northerner in general) may give himself away by the use of the accusative instead of the genitive for the indirect object, or by his 'dark' *l*; the Cretan by his substitution of palato-alveolars for palatalized velars (e.g. [tʃ] for [c]); the Corfiote by his 'sing-song' intonation; and (especially) the Cypriot by his double consonants and by his addition of final *n* to certain forms; but all these are rather small details, and one can speak today of a genuinely standard form of MG.

4   THE GREEK LANGUAGE QUESTION

Diglossia (the contemporaneous existence of two different varieties of the same language used for different purposes) has been a feature of the Greek language since the end of the fourth century BC, when the spoken language began to diverge perceptibly from the old norms which were being adhered to by writers. The situation in which at least some writers use a variety of the language which differs markedly from the spoken has continued until the present day. This does not mean that the written language has remained the same from a certain date onwards: on the contrary, despite intermittent reactions during which authors have attempted to return to the alleged purity of Attic or Hellenistic Greek, the written language has developed through a fairly constant process of compromise with the spoken. Meanwhile the spoken language (at least until the nineteenth century) has continued along its own path, undergoing developments which are partly potentialities within the Greek language itself and partly the result of influence from other languages (particularly Latin, Italian, and Turkish).

Between Hellenistic and modern times there were fairly well-defined areas within which each variety of the language functioned, even though there was no official codification involved. Thus for most of the Byzantine period the spoken language was tacitly excluded from writing. But the boundaries between the areas in which the different varieties were used were subject to alteration, and in the late Byzantine period it became acceptable for certain types of secular verse (chiefly romances) to be composed in the spoken language. With the end of the Byzantine Empire rather more areas of writing were opened up to the spoken language, although it tended to be confined (apart from *belles-lettres*) to works deliberately intended for a popular audience.

Until the eighteenth century, then, because of a general agreement about which variety of language was suitable for each type of use, there

was no overt language question in Greece. The controversy really began
in the late eighteenth century, when, under the influence of the French
Enlightenment, Greek intellectuals began to publish significant numbers
of secular works of an educational nature, in an effort to revive the arts
and sciences which they perceived as being sadly lacking in Greece. In
so doing they were (some consciously, others unconsciously) preparing
the ground for the political independence of Greece. Some of these
scholars believed that a Greek cultural rebirth was possible only through
a return to Ancient Greek language and culture: they saw it as a prerequisite for this rebirth that the Greek people should learn not only to
read but also to write and speak Ancient Greek, to such an extent that
AG would actually supersede the 'vulgar' and 'debased' language spoken
by their countrymen. Others felt that the Greek people could be enlightened only through the use of the spoken language in serious writing.
(At that time spoken Greek was usually known as ρωμαίικα 'Romaic',
as opposed to ἑλληνικά 'Greek', which referred to the ancient language;
by 1821 however ἑλληνικά was being used for both languages, a fact
which has been the source of some confusion.) But these two groups
were by no means the largest: the majority of the Greek Enlighteners
(the most influential of these being A. Korais) preferred to use a variety
of language which, while largely based on the structure of the spoken
language, contained a large number of elements from Classical and Hellenistic Greek, but also (although its proponents never admitted this)
owed much to French turns of phrase. Each of these groups—the archa-
ists (or Atticists), the vulgarists, and the compromisers—set about
defending their own chosen variety of the language and attacking those
who supported any other variety, in a host of polemical books and
articles.

The terms δημοτική ('the people's language') and καθαρεύουσα
('the purifying language') were hardly used at this time (i.e. the half-
century leading up to the Greek War of Independence of 1821), even
though the latter was first used in 1796 and the former in 1818, as far
as I can ascertain: they became current in the late nineteenth century.
Nevertheless, the variety of language supported by the compromisers
became what we know as *katharevousa*. This is not to say that Korais
and his like-minded intellectuals actually invented *katharevousa*: the
variety of Greek which they proposed as the language of the state and
of education already existed, but more as a result of haphazard juxta-
positions of ancient and modern elements than as a methodically
planned compromise.

The establishment of the Greek state (*c.* 1830) saw the institutional-ization of *katharevousa* as the language of all governmental and ad-ministrative business, education, and the press. All other writing outside poetry also came to use *katharevousa*, while poets were divided: some wrote entirely in demotic, others entirely in *katharevousa*, and yet others sometimes in one variety and sometimes in the other. The official language gradually moved further away from the spoken between 1830 and 1880, as intellectual leaders called for increasingly more 'purification', which meant the arbitrary imposition of archaic features on to what was still a basically modern structure, without any attempt to assimilate these features to the essential rules of the modern language. By the 1850s, the gradual move towards a more archaic language was generally seen as 'progressive', the language of Korais being viewed as 'old-fashioned'.

As Mirambel (1964: 415) points out, rather than rejuvenating old words, *katharevousa* 'vieillit des mots neufs' by adding ancient in-flexions and other features to neologisms. A good example is μπόμπα (*bômba*) 'bomb', which became (and has remained) βόμβα (*vómva*) for two reasons: (a) initial μπ did not occur in Ancient Greek; and (b) Western European *b* was in any case transliterated into *katharevousa* as β (pronounced *v*) because Ancient Greek β (pronounced *b*) was trans-literated into Western European languages as *b*! The advocates of *katharevousa*, blinding themselves to sound-changes which had taken place since Classical times, ignored the fact that the sequence *mv* was non-existent not only in words of demotic origin, but in Classical Greek too (Classical μβ was pronounced *mb*, as is Modern Greek μπ). The result is that this loanword was dressed up to *look* like an ancient word, while each letter was given its modern pronunciation, irrespective of the fact that this gave rise to a sequence of sounds which had been excluded, by natural processes, from the language.

The fact is, however, that spoken Greek is so close to Ancient Greek that the temptation to bridge the small gap which separated them was widespread. But, as Mirambel (1964: 417) points out, whereas the Hellenistic purists wrote in a particular dialect which had been alive at a particular time (viz. Classical Attic), the modern purists tended to accept any elements of post-Homeric Greek that did not smack of demotic.

During this period (1830–80) the language question was more or less dormant. The reaction against the increasing archaism of *katharevousa* came first from the poets, who saw the impossibility of writing true poetry in such an artificial language, and then from the literary prose-writers and dramatists (in the 1880s and 1890s), who in their turn realized that they could not write stories and plays about everyday Greek life when most of the vocabulary associated with that life was excluded from writing. The conversion of Greek prose fiction and drama from *katharevousa* to demotic occurred with great rapidity. Having won literature over to their side, the demoticists went on, especially from the first decade of the twentieth century onwards, to demand that *katharevousa* be abolished altogether. Reaction against the threat of domination by demotic (often known as μαλλιαρή, or 'hairy language' since its proponents were reputed to have long hair) some-times took a violent form. Riots broke out in Athens in 1901, when A. Pallis published his demotic translation of the New Testament, and again in 1903, when the National Theatre put on a performance of Aeschylus in a semi-demotic translation. In view of these incidents, and particularly because of the demoticists' insistence that demotic should become the official medium of education, a clause was included for the first time in the Constitution of 1911 declaring *katharevousa* to be the official language of the state and making it a punishable offence to attempt to alter this situation.

Despite this, demotic texts were introduced for the first time into primary-school readers in 1913, chiefly as a result of pressure from a demoticist lobby known as the Educational Society, founded in 1910, and demotic became the chief language of primary education between 1917 and 1920. But for some years thereafter, the situation was fluid, with successive governments increasing or decreasing the use of demotic in primary schools. For the most part, secondary schools and the University of Athens remained unaffected by demoticism: indeed, no Modern Greek of any sort, not even *katharevousa*, was taught in secondary schools until 1909; before this there was a total official disregard for Modern Greek culture. By this time, the language question had become an overtly political issue. Already, in the first decade of the century, demoticists were accused of involvement in a Russian plot to take over Greece, and the Russian Revolution only served to make such accusations all the more emotive. The proponents of both *katharevousa* and demotic now used the term 'national language' to refer to their own variety of Greek, accusing their opponents of attempting to jeopardize the unity of the nation. The controversy reached such a level of fanaticism that in 1941, during the Axis Occupation, a distinguished Classical scholar was dismissed from his teaching post at Athens

University for publishing an article printed according to the 'single-accent system'.

Also in 1941, however, the cause of demotic made an historic step forward with the publication of the *Modern Greek Grammar* by Trianda-phyllidis and others (Triandaphyllidis was one of the founder members of the Educational Society). The authors had been commissioned to write the grammar by the dictator Metaxas, who foresaw its use as an official grammar of demotic. Although the Axis Occupation meant that the grammar had considerably less impact than it should have done, it is nevertheless looked to as a more or less authoritative guide to morphology (it does not deal with syntax).

In 1964 the ruling Centre Union Party put demotic on an equal footing with *katharevousa* as the language of education. But this reform was short-lived, since the military dictatorship of 1967–74 confined the teaching of demotic to the first four grades of primary school. One of the beneficial consequences of the military regime was the anti-*katharevousa* reaction that followed it. Law 309 of 1976 instituted Νεοελληνική (Δημοτική) as the language not only of education but of the administration, while the 1975 Constitution sensibly made no mention of an 'official language'. The determination of the government of the time that Greece should join the EEC perhaps helped to expedite the process of demoticization. Efforts were made to train civil servants in the use of demotic, but naturally the process has been a gradual one, many bureaucrats being slow to come to terms with the change.

The situation in 1983 was that SMG was used throughout the education system and the administration, in almost all newspapers and all weekly magazines, and throughout the broadcasting system. *Katharevousa* was still used to some extent in the law, in the army, and in the Church. The official text of the Constitution was still in *katharevousa* (although there is also a—privately published—translation in demotic), while almost all laws were formulated in *katharevousa* and there was still much resistance among lawyers against demotic. The Church still used the Byzantine liturgy; the only authoritative text of the New Testament which could be used in church services was the original Greek one; and most documents issued by the Church of Greece were still in *katharevousa*. Nevertheless, the Archbishop of Athens delivered his Christmas message in demotic for the first time in 1981. Apart from this, much scholarly writing on the law, medicine and theology was still being done in *katharevousa*.

After the electoral victory of the socialist PASOK party in 1981, moves were made to introduce the monotonic system not only into schools, but into the administration. For schoolchildren this was generally felt to result in a great saving of time: it had been estimated that out of the 12,000 hours which the average child spent on grammar during twelve years' schooling, 3,000 were spent on learning how to use the accents and breathings. Outside the daily and weekly press, however, most printing was still being done in 1983 according to the simplified historical system.

Alexiou (1982: 172-3) presents an interesting case history of a typical Greek born in 1952 who graduated from Athens University in 1974. The language that he learned at home began to be 'corrected' as soon as he went to school at the age of six, when he encountered schoolbooks whose 'demotic' was in reality a hybrid variety designed to make it easier for pupils subsequently to learn *katharevousa*. In 1964 he was faced with new textbooks in true demotic; but in 1967 he had to revert to textbooks in *katharevousa*. At University, even if he had studied literature, he would have found that, although many of the texts he studied were in demotic, all lectures and all written work were presented in *katharevousa*. He would have emerged with a clear and thorough knowledge of neither demotic nor *katharevousa* (nor Ancient Greek, for that matter), but would perhaps have been most at home writing in a variety of Greek which contained features of all three. Worst of all, though, the inherent verbosity of *katharevousa* would probably have seriously affected his thought processes. What Labov (1970: 202) has written about Standard English is even more true of *katharevousa*: 'It is this verbosity which is most easily taught and most easily learned, so that words take the place of thought, and nothing can be found behind them.'

5 STANDARD MODERN GREEK

Since 1976 Modern Greek diglossia has more or less ceased to exist, and there is for most purposes a single, unified Greek language. In Standard Modern Greek the Greek language has come closer to developing a set of universally accepted norms than at any other stage in its history. We must however examine (a) what relation SMG bears to demotic and *katharevousa*, and (b) to what extent it is actually standardized.

In this book the term Standard Modern Greek is being used to refer to the language normally written and spoken today by moderately educated Greeks in the urban centres. Although 'demotic' is often defined as 'spoken Greek', this term (or 'traditional demotic') will be used to refer to the language spoken by ordinary Greeks before the influence of *katharevousa* became pronounced. This demotic was characterized by a remarkable phonological and morphological coherence and homogeneity, and the demoticists of the 1880s and 1890s (led by Psycharis) attempted to enrich the language by means of new coinages, based on Ancient Greek roots, which were made to conform with the demotic rules. This attempt, however, met with widespread resistance, and educated speakers (whose spoken usage had traditionally diverged from the purity of demotic) appear to have preferred to use internal borrowings from AG with the minimum of adaptation to demotic rules. (For K features in SMG phonology, see 1.5.1; for morphology, see especially 4.5.1.2 and generally the whole of Chapter 5.) Thus the ordinary spoken language of educated Greeks became a mixture of demotic and *katharevousa* features, a mixture reflected in varieties of written Greek known as μικτή ('mixed') and γλώσσα τῶν ἐφημερίδων ('language of the newspapers'); each of these comprised a fairly arbitrary mixture of K and D features. Meanwhile, although these written varieties contained many K features that were not normally used in speech, the spoken language of educated Greeks was gradually evolving into one which, although it lacked the symmetry of traditional D, had its own coherence. The outcome of this process was the variety of MG known as καθομιλουμένη ('the widely spoken language'); and, now that D and καθομιλουμένη are together established as the official language of Greece, one is entitled to designate them Standard Modern Greek. (There is no MG adjective corresponding to 'standard', and certain Greek linguists call this variety of the language Κοινή Νεοελληνική 'Common Modern Greek'.)

In its written form, SMG has evolved out of the use of D in progressively wider fields. As D has moved into each domain which was hitherto occupied by K, it attracted to itself certain features of K (particularly vocabulary and fixed expressions, but also some concomitant phonological, morphological, and syntactical features) which have seemed indispensible to any discourse in the field concerned.

There has developed a common linguistic sense which has processed the various linguistic features suggested to it by the proponents of the different varieties of Greek, and has accepted some and rejected others.

The result is that, in the present situation, 'demotic' (strictly defined as the homogeneous traditional spoken language unaffected by K) is, paradoxically, primarily a *written* language. It is an ideal construct, codified by Triandaphyllidis' *Grammar* (1941), which, despite its author's professed aims (p. xxi), is more normative than descriptive. In so far as it is descriptive, the *Grammar* is based not on the spoken language but on the MG folk songs and on literature (p. xxii). The syntax and usage of D have been further codified in hortative books and articles produced over a period of years (e.g. *Nea Ikonomia* 1965, Mesevrinos 1978, and Kriaras 1979: Tzartzanos's *Syntax* (1946–63) is in fact more descriptive, but this author too mostly confines himself to a study of folk songs and literature). It is with the rules of this 'ideal' demotic that many conscientious writers attempt to conform, avoiding πολυτυπία (the use of more than one surface realization of the same underlying form) and using the minimum of K grammatical features.

Clearly, literary demotic based on Triandaphyllidis's *Grammar* is part of SMG, but it is not coextensive with it. Since SMG is not an ideal language, but a real one, it contains many features that are not sufficiently accounted for by Triandaphyllidis, including alternative grammatical forms and much K influence. The idealist demoticists, in their desire to achieve the ideal demotic, often counsel the avoidance of K elements which are now firmly established in the spoken and written language of most educated people. They sometimes even go so far as to recommend the use of alleged synonyms for words of K origin, even though the items in question differ in meaning. They thus show that they value conformity to type above precision in expression, and hence they are reminiscent of the advocates of K: they are the purists of demotic. SMG, then, is a very broad category which covers a range of varieties, including both demotic and καθομιλουμένη.

It has been said that SMG is not a correct term, since MG presents a diversity of both free and conditioned variants. But 'a standard language is by no means what common usage would call a standardized language' (Pride and Holmes 1972: 8). There seem in fact to be two chief criteria which a standard language has to fulfil: codification (minimal variation in form) and elaboration (maximal variation in function) (Haugen 1966: 107). As far as the second of these is concerned, 'the definitive seal of approval as a fully recognized standard is dependent on the use of a language in two functions: fully official (governmental) and bellettristic' (Hall 1972: 150). Since SMG began to be used for all official purposes as recently as 1976, one cannot expect it to be totally standardized; codification will gradually come about as Greeks become more and more accustomed to using it for every form of communication.

There is already evidence that certain alternative forms are rapidly predominating over certain others. Since the introduction of SMG into all levels of education and the administration, people who were inhibited by social pressures from using certain D forms now feel free to use them; and it has become fashionable, especially for young people, to eschew forms which are perceived as smacking of K. Fashion, therefore, as an integral part of social mores, may accelerate the process of standardization.

Unlike K, many of whose advocates actually saw it as an extension of AG, the official language of Greece today is not a parasite depending on AG for its existence: it is an autonomous language (just as traditional demotic was in its day) which is nevertheless free to use the resources of vocabulary provided by the ancient language.

This is not to say, however, that all Greeks are satisfied with the linguistic situation that prevails today. There is in some Greeks who claim to want to protect the language from various assaults (including the invasion of new loanwords) a hankering after diglossia: one feels that they would prefer administrative and scientific writing to be done in K, with D being preserved unsullied for everyday conversation and for poetry. It seems to me, however, that the official introduction of SMG into all walks of life has made it at last possible for Greeks to make *stylistic* choices from the wealth of alternative words and forms: thus a new set of registers suitable for various situations is developing within this one language, where before there existed simply the invidious choice between K, D, and μικτή.

1

THE SOUNDS AND ORTHOGRAPHY OF MODERN GREEK

1.1 THE SOUND SYSTEM

The sound system of Modern Greek is economical, consisting as it does of twenty-three distinctive sounds (according to Table 1.1). These twenty-three phonemes, and their various phonetic realizations, correspond quite closely to the sounds of Spanish, which possesses twenty-seven phonemes.

TABLE 1.1

Vowels	Consonants	
a	p	t
e	b	d
i	f	θ
o	v	ð
u	k	m
	g	n
	x	s
	γ	z
		l
		r

This list (which corresponds to that of Setatos 1974: 14) is neither a definitive nor a universally accepted list of the MG phonemes. Some scholars (e.g. Koutsoudas 1962: 11) treat /j/ as a separate phoneme. For different treatments see Warburton (1970b: 16–17) and Ruge (1976: 17 and 24).

1.2 THE ALPHABET

Modern Greek has precisely the same twenty-four letters as Classical
Greek. Table 1.2 gives each letter in upper and in lower case, followed
by its Greek name and its most usual pronunciation(s).

TABLE 1.2

A α	ἄλφα	[a]	Ξ ξ	ξί	[ks]
Β β	βῆτα	[v]	O o	ὄμικρον	[o]
Γ γ	γάμμα	[ɣ], [j]	Π π	πί	[p]
Δ δ	δέλτα	[ð]	P ρ	ρό	[r]
Ε ε	ἔψιλον	[e]	Σ σ	(ς at end of word)	
Z ζ	ζῆτα	[z]		σίγμα	[s], [z]
Η η	ἦτα	[i]	T τ	ταύ	[t]
Θ ϑ	ϑῆτα	[θ]	Υ υ	ὔψιλον	[i]
I ι	γιῶτα	[i], [j], [ç]	Φ φ	φί	[f]
Κ κ	κάπα	[k], [c]	Χ χ	χί	[x], [ç]
Λ λ	λάμδα	[l]	Ψ ψ	ψί	[ps]
Μ μ	μί	[m]	Ω ω	ὠμέγα	[o]
Ν ν	νί	[n]			

Double consonants (ββ, κκ, λλ, μμ, νν, ππ, ρρ, σσ, ττ) are normally
pronounced as if they were single; an exception is γγ, for which see
1.4.2.2.

For αι, ει, οι, υι, ου, see 1.4.1.

For μπ, αυ, ευ, see 1.4.2.1.

For γγ, γκ, γι, γυ, γει, see 1.4.2.2.

For ντ, τζ, see 1.4.2.3.

(Some of the letters have alternative colloquial names, the vowels
being called simply by their sound—e.g. ἄ, ἔ—and the consonants by
the consonant sound followed by -u—e.g. βού, γού.)

1.3 DIACRITICS

Throughout this study a distinction is made between stress, accent, and
emphasis. Stress, which belongs to the phonetic domain, is defined in
1.8. An accent is one of the marks written over a vowel, usually (but
not always) in order to indicate stress. Emphasis is a semantic concept,
referring to the special importance attached to a certain word or words
by the speaker/writer.

In the simplified historical orthography adopted in the present book, each initial vowel has one of the two so-called *breathings* written over it: when a word begins with a sequence of two written vowels which constitute a single vowel sound (or a vowel sound + -*f*- or -*v*-), the breathing is placed over the second written vowel. These breathings have no synchronic value, but simply show whether the vowel was pronounced in Classical Greek with a preceding aspirate /h/ (in the case of the rough breathing or δασεία (‘)), or without (in the case of the smooth breathing or ψιλή (’)). In addition, all words of two or more syllables (and most monosyllables) carry an accent. In words of two or more syllables, the accent is placed over the stressed vowel, while in monosyllables the accent over the vowel serves no phonetic function. The accent is written over the second vowel of a two-vowel sequence pronounced as a single sound (or as vowel sound + -*f*- or -*v*-); if the stressed vowel is represented by a capital letter, the accent and breathing are written before this letter. When αι, ει, οι, ου, αυ, or ευ represent two vowels pronounced separately, the second carries a diaeresis (¨) unless the first bears an accent or breathing (for further details, the examples of Greek words and sentences throughout this book can be observed). The accents are of two kinds, each of which has the same function: the acute (ὀξεία (’)) and the circumflex (περισπωμένη (˜)).

Since the position of the stress in MG is rather unpredictable, and because it is a significant bearer of meaning, close attention has to be paid to its position; and it is advisable (especially for pedagogical purposes) that the use of the accent mark should not be discontinued (see also 1.7 and Appendix II).

1.4 PHONETICS

Having looked at the theoretical basis of the SMG sound system and at the alphabet and diacritics, we shall now examine in some detail the realization of each phoneme in speech, and its representation in the orthography. According to modern linguistic practice, the phonemic representation is given between solidi (slashes), while the phonetic representations, in the International Phonetic Alphabet, are enclosed in square brackets. Not all the subtleties of the IPA are being used here: [ʎ] stands for what may be either a palatalized dental (or alveolar) lateral or a palatal lateral, [ɲ] for a palatalized dental (or alveolar) nasal or a palatal nasal, and [n] and [l] for sounds which may sometimes be dental and sometimes alveolar.

1.4.1   VOWELS

The five vowel sounds of SMG are the following (the orthographic representation is shown in the right-hand column):

[a] low central   α
[e] mid front   ε, αι
[i] high front   η, ι, υ, ει, οι, υι
[o] mid back   ο, ω
[u] high back   ου

Their relative positions of articulation may be represented thus:

i   u

e   o

a

The vowel sounds of SMG are remarkably pure in quality. Vowel length is not a distinctive feature: it is fairly constant, each vowel being pronounced somewhere between English short and long vowels in length, but closer to the long vowels. A stressed vowel in SMG retains the same quality as, and is usually only slightly longer than, an unstressed vowel, the chief component of stress being extra loudness (see also 1.8).

Nevertheless, when unstressed /i/ precedes a vowel (except in words of learned origin and except when preceded by consonant + /r/), it is realized as one of the following: (a) the palatalization of a preceding velar consonant or of /l/ or /n/; (b) [j] if it is not preceded by a consonant, or if it is preceded by a voiced consonant (including /r/); or (c) [ç] if it is preceded by a non-velar voiceless consonant in the same word. (As will be seen below, [j] and [ç] are the palatalized counterparts of [γ] and [x] respectively, the first of each pair being voiced and the second voiceless.) The palatalization of a consonant slightly affects the quality of the preceding vowel, although this is not shown here in the phonetic representation.

(a)	κιάλια	'binoculars'	/kiália/	[ˈcaʎa]
	γκιώνης	'scops owl'	/giónis/	[ˈɟonis]
	χιόνι	'snow'	/xióni/	[ˈçoni]
	γιαλός	'shore'	/ɣialós/	[jaˈlos]
	πανιά	'sails; cloths'	/paniá/	[paˈɲa]
(b)	γιατρός	'doctor'	/iatrós/	[jaˈtros]
	παιδιά	'children'	/peðiá/	[peˈðja]

	σιτάρια	'wheat' (pl.)	/sitária/	[si'tarja]
	(but ἄγρια	'wildly'	/áɣria/	['aɣria])
(c)	μάτια	'eyes'	/mátia/	['matça]
	ποιός;	'who?'	/piós/	[pços]

In words of learned origin, unstressed /i/ before a vowel often retains its vocalic value. But the situation is unstable, and unstressed /i/ in this context varies as to length and amount of friction. Examples of pairs of words which are, however, normally distinguished by the presence of [i] or of [j] or [ç] are the following (the first of each pair being of learned origin):

(a)	σκιάζω	{'I shade' 'I scare'}	/skiázo/	{[sci'azo] ['scazo]}
(b)	λόγια	{'learnèd' (f.sg.:/n.pl.) 'words'}	/lóɣia/	{['lojia] ['loja]}
	Μήδεια μύδια	Medea' 'mussels'	/míðia/	['miðia] ['miðja]
(c)	-ποιῶ πιῶ	'-ify' 'I drink'	/pió/	[pi'o] [pço]

(For further examples of the [i]/[j]/[ç] alternation, see 1.4.2.2 and 1.5.)

Apart from the normally obligatory realizations of /i/ as shown above, the high vowels /i/ and /u/ (and /e/ in certain positions) are often reduced in unstressed position in fast speech, although such reductions are avoided by those who make a deliberate effort to 'speak well'. When one of these vowels is reduced before or after a voiceless consonant, it is devoiced. If a reduced /i/ or /e/ follows a velar consonant, it may disappear, leaving the palatalization of the velar as the only sign of its underlying presence (see Theophanopoulou-Kontou 1972-3). For vowel elision, see 1.5.2.

1.4.2 CONSONANTS

1.4.2.1 Labials

There are four labial consonant phonemes in MG, in addition to the nasal /m/ (for which see 1.4.2.4):

p	[p]	voiceless bilabial stop	π
b	[b]	voiced bilabial stop	μπ, π
f	[f]	voiceless labio-dental fricative	φ, (a)υ, (ε)υ
v	[v]	voiced labio-dental fricative	β, (a)υ, (ε)υ

Brackets round Greek letters in the last column indicate that the letter outside the brackets is pronounced in the manner indicated when it is preceded by the letter within brackets.

Like /k/ and /t/, the voiceless stop /p/ is unaspirated; and, like them, it is voiced after a nasal (becoming [b], [g], and [d]). The combination of letters μπ at the beginning of a word (and often medially) represents the voiced stop [b], just as γκ represents [g] and ντ [d]. The digraphs αυ and ευ are pronounced [af] and [ef] respectively at the end of a word (unless the following word begins with a voiced consonant) and before a voiceless consonant, and [av] and [ev] before a voiced consonant (including /l/ and /r/), or before a vowel within the same word; but before /f/ and /v/ they simply become [a] and [e], on the principle that double consonants are pronounced as single.

ἱπποδρόμιο	'racecourse'	/ipoðrómio/	[ipo¹ðromio]
πόλεμος	'war'	/pólemos/	[¹polemos]
στόν πόλεμο	'in the war'	/stombólemo/	[stom¹bolemo]
λάμπα	'lamp'	/lámba/	[¹lamba]
μπαμπάς	'daddy'	/babás/	[ba¹bas]
ἄνευ ὅρων	'unconditional(ly)'	/ánef óron/	[ane¹foron]
αὐτοκίνητο	'car'	/aftokínito/	[afto¹cinito]
αὔριο	'tomorrow'	/ávrio/	[¹avrio]
Εὔα	'Eve'	/éva/	[¹eva]
εὔφορος	'fertile'	/éforos/	[¹eforos]
Εὔβοια	'Euboea'	/évia/	[¹evia]

1.4.2.2 Velars

Each of the four velar consonants has a palatalized and an unpalatalized realization. In their unpalatalized form they correspond precisely in voicing and manner of articulation to the four labials and the four dentals.

k	[k]	voiceless velar stop	}	κ
	[c]	voiceless palatalized velar stop		
g	[g]	voiced velar stop	}	γκ, γγ, κ
	[ɟ]	voiced palatalized velar stop		
x	[x]	voiceless velar fricative		χ
	[ç]	voiceless palatalized velar fricative		χ, ι
γ	[ɣ]	voiced velar fricative		γ
	[j]	voiced palatalized velar fricative		γ, ι, γι, γυ, γει

The velars are palatalized before the front vowels /e/ and /i/. Although [j] is often designated as a glide, it is probably more correct to call it a voiced palatalized velar fricative. The letter γ may represent [ɣ], [j], [ŋ] (before γ, χ, or κ), or else [g] or [ʝ] (after γ). The digraphs γκ and γγ represent [g] or [ʝ] at the beginning of the word, [ŋg], [ŋʝ], [g], or [ʝ] medially.

ἐκκλησία	'church'	/eklisía/	[ekliˈsia]
καρπός	'fruit; wrist'	/karpós/	[karˈpos]
στόν καρπό	'on the wrist'	/stongarpó/	[stoŋgarˈpo]
κέρασα	'I treated (to a drink)'	/kérasa/	[ˈcerasa]
τόν κέρασα	'I treated him (to a drink)'	/tongérasa/	[toŋˈʝerasa]
ἄγχος	'Angst'	/ánxos/	[ˈaŋxos]
χέρι	'hand; arm'	/xéri/	[ˈçeri]
γάμος	'wedding; marriage'	/ɣámos/	[ˈɣamos]
γερός	'strong, robust'	/ɣerós/	[jeˈros]
καράβια	'ships'	/karávia/	[kaˈravja]
γιαλός	'shore'	/ɣialós/	[jaˈlos]
γυαλιά	'glasses'	/ialiá/	[jaˈʎa]
γειά σου	'hello; goodbye'	/ɣiásu/	[ˈjasu]
γκρίνια	'complaining'	/grínia/	[ˈgriɲa]
ἀνάγκη	'need; necessity'	/anángi/	[aˈnaŋʝi]
κάλος	'corn (callous)'	/kálos/	[ˈkalos]
κι ἄλλος	'and another'	/kiálos/	[ˈcalos]
χώνει	'he thrusts'	/xóni/	[ˈxoni]
χιόνι	'snow'	/xióni/	[ˈçoni]
ράφια	'shelves'	/ráfia/	[ˈrafça]
γκιώνης	'scops owl'	/giónis/	[ˈʝonis]

It will be noticed that [j] may derive from /i/ or from /ɣ/, and [ç] from either /i/ or /x/.

1.4.2.3 Dentals

There are four dental consonants, in addition to the nasal /n/ (for which see 1.4.2.4).

t	[t]	voiceless dental stop	τ
d	[d]	voiced dental stop	ντ, τ
θ	[θ]	voiceless dental fricative	ϑ
δ	[ð]	voiced dental fricative	δ

The digraph ντ represents [d] initially and [nd] or [d] medially. The digraphs τσ and τζ represent the voiceless and voiced affricates [ts] and [dz] respectively.

περιττός	'superfluous'	/peritós/	[peri¹tos]
τρόπος	'way, manner'	/trópos/	[¹tropos]
τόν τρόπο	'the way' (acc.)	/tondrópo/	[ton¹dropo]
πάντα	'always'	/pánda/	[¹panda]
νταντά	'wet-nurse'	/dadá/	[da¹da]
θέλω	'I want'	/θélo/	[¹θelo]
εἶδα	'I saw'	/ída/	[¹iδa]
τσακίζω	'I snap'	/tsakízo/	[tsa¹cizo]
τζάκι	'hearth'	/dzáki/	[¹dzaci]

1.4.2.4 Nasals

There are two nasal phonemes in Modern Greek. They have the following realizations:

m	[m]	voiced bilabial nasal	}	μ, ν
	[ɱ]	voiced labio-dental nasal		
n	[n]	voiced dental (or alveolar) nasal	}	ν
	[ɲ]	voiced palatalized dental (or alveolar) nasal or palatal nasal		
	[ŋ]	voiced velar nasal		ν, γ

(i) Normally, when /m/ and /n/ precede a vowel they are pronounced [m] and [n] respectively. When palatalized (i.e. when followed by a weakened /i/ + vowel) /m/ becomes [mj] or (in some idiolects) [mɲ] (this last may occur even before stressed /i/); /n/ is palatalized to [ɲ] not only before weakened /i/ + vowel, but (in some idiolects) before the full vowel [i]. The pronunciation [mɲ] and the palatalization of /n/ before /i/ (like that of /l/ in the same position) are not normally considered to be a sign of careful pronunciation, even though it is a feature of most of the chief Modern Greek dialects.

(ii) When a nasal precedes a consonant in Modern Greek various phenomena may occur: (a) the nasal may become assimilated in its place of articulation with the following consonant; (b) it may voice a following voiceless stop; (c) it may disappear as a separate sound, but nasalize the previous vowel; or (d) it may disappear altogether. These four phenomena are not all mutually exclusive, but which of them occur(s) at any given point depends on the nature of the following consonant, on the individual speaker (geographical provenance, education, etc.), and sometimes on the etymology of the word. Nevertheless, (a), i.e. the assimilation of the nasal, is a normal characteristic of standard speech. Before consonants, the nasals are conditioned variants, agreeing in place of articulation with the following consonant: the dental [n] appears before dentals, [m] before bilabials, [ŋ] before velars, and [ɱ] before labio-dentals.

(i)	πράγμα	'thing'	/práɣma/	[ˈpraɣma]
	βλέμμα	'gaze'	/vléma/	[ˈvlema]
	Νάσος	'Nasos' (name)	/násos/	[ˈnasos]
	Ἄννα	'Anna'	/ána/	[ˈana]
	τζάμια	'window-panes'	/dzámia/	[ˈdzamja] or [ˈdzamɲa]
	μπετονιέρα	'cement-mixer'	/betoniéra/	[betoˈɲera]
	φωνή	'voice; shout'	/foní/	[foˈni] or [foˈɲi]
(ii)	(a/b) Ἀντρέας	'Andrew'	/andréas/	[anˈdreas]
	(a/b) κάμπος	'plain'	/kámbos/	[ˈkambos]
	(a/b) ἀνάγκη	'need'	/anángi/	[aˈnaŋɟi]
	(a) συμφωνία	'agreement; symphony'	/simfonía/	[simfoˈnia] or [simfoˈɲia]
	(a) τῶν φίλων	'of the friends'	/ton fílon/	[tomˈfilon]

In traditional demotic, a nasal could occur only before a vowel or one of the voiced stops [b], [g], or [d] (which themselves were often underlying voiceless stops voiced by the preceding nasal, as in στόν πόλεμο, τόν κέρασα, and τόν τρόπο in examples already given). The influence of *katharevousa* phonology (which, briefly, entailed the wholesale introduction of all or most of the possible AG consonant clusters, but pronounced letter by letter in the Modern Greek manner) and the influx of foreign words into the language have led to the possibility of a nasal being followed by any one of the following: the voiceless fricatives [f], [x], and [θ], the voiced fricatives [v], [ɣ], and [ð], the sibilants [s] and [z], and the liquids [l] and [r]. Not all such combinations commonly occur within words, but the genitive plural of the definite article (τῶν) and the masculine accusative singular of the third-person proclitic pronoun (τόν) may be followed by any of these sounds.

To begin with the combinations of nasal + consonant that existed in traditional demotic, some dialects always pronounced the nasal fully, others always omitted it completely, while others displayed a certain variety. Grammarians, on the other hand, have taught that these combinations should be pronounced with or without the nasal according to whether or not the nasal was present in an earlier version of the word in question: thus AG κόμβος > κόμπος 'knot' [ˈkombos]; T *tempel* > τεμπέλης 'lazy' [temˈbelis]; but T *soba* > σόμπα 'stove' [ˈsoba]. This rule may have been well motivated as far as some dialects were concerned, since their speakers pronounced the voiced stops with or without a preceding nasal, just as they found them, with no interference from writing. With the rise of literacy, however, speakers have usually treated every instance of μπ, ντ, or γγ/γκ alike, that is, either always with or always without the nasal, according to each speaker's idiolect. Furthermore, it cannot be expected that speakers will know the etymological origin of all the words they use. The situation today, at least in Athens, is that the absence of the nasal in such cases has become widespread, even in the speech of highly educated people, but especially among the young, the male and the less educated (this is phenomenon (iid) above). Those who pride themselves on their careful speech, however, still keep to the grammarians' etymologically based rule.

Nevertheless, it is common to hear speakers uttering hypercorrect forms in loanwords in which etymologically there was no nasal, e.g. μοντέρνος 'modern' as [monˈdernos] instead of [moˈdernos], and βεντέτα as [venˈdeta] in both its meanings, i.e. 'star' (< F *vedette*) and 'vendetta' (< It.), despite the grammarians' precept that the two meanings should be distinguished in pronunciation.

The truth is that the presence or absence of a nasal before a voiced stop never makes a semantic distinction (with perhaps the single exception of βεντέτα). Despite this, however, the suppression of the nasal in this position when its presence is etymologically motivated is still regarded by many as a sign of slovenly speech.

στόν Πόρο	'to Poros'	[stomˈboro] or [stoˈboro]
κάμπος	'plain'	[ˈkambos] or [ˈkabos]
δέν τέλειωσα	'I haven't finished'	[ðenˈdeʎosa] or [ðeˈdeʎosa]
πέντε	'five'	[ˈpende] or [ˈpede]
στόν κόσμο	'in the world'	[stoŋˈgozmo] or [stoˈgozmo]
'Αγγλία	'England'	[aŋˈglia] or [aˈglia]

On the other hand, one should beware of believing that the nasal is either present or not: between these extremes there appears in reality to be a continuum of possibilities which include a slight pre-nasalization of the stop or a slight nasalization of the preceding vowel, or both.

It is common, at least in Athenian speech, for the subjunctive markers *νά* and *θά* to voice the /t/ of a following proclitic pronoun; this phenomenon is not usually indicated in the orthography (e.g. *νά τό πῶ* 'I should say' [nado¹po]; *θά τό 'λεγα* 'I would say' [θa¹doleɣa]).

In loanwords there are certain combinations of nasal + voiceless stop which, at least in some idiolects, resist the tendency towards voicing: thus one may hear, e.g. *κουμπανία* 'folk-song band' as [kumpa¹nia], or *ντοκουμέντο* 'document' as [doku¹mento]. In addition, when they have resulted from elision, such combinations normally resist voicing, the most common example being *κάντε* (< *κάνετε*) 'do!' (imperative) [¹kante].

Some combinations of three sounds require some comment: namely a nasal followed by underlying /pt/, /kt/, /ps/, /ks/, or /ts/. In the case of /pt/ and /kt/, which occur only in words of non-demotic origin, voicing does not normally take place, and often the /k/ or /t/ is omitted in speech:

> *Πέμπτη* 'Thursday' [¹pempti] or [¹pemti] (cf. traditional demotic *Πέφτη*, formed by dissimilation of /p/ before /t/ followed by deletion of the nasal before the fricative /f/; but contrast SMG *πάμφτωχος* 'very poor', pronounced in full as [¹paɱftoxos])
> *σαλπιγκτής* 'bugler' [salpiŋ¹ktis]

The clusters /ps/, /ks/, and /ts/ are normally voiced only when they stand at the beginning of a word after a preceding nasal:

τόν τσάκ ωσα 'I caught him'	[ton¹dzakosa] or [to¹dzakosa]
στήν ψυχή	'in the soul'	[stim¹bziçi] or [sti¹bziçi]
λάμψη	'flash'	[¹lampsi]
δέν ξέρω	'I don't know'	[ðeŋ¹gzero] or [ðe¹gzero]
Σφίγξ	'Sphinx'	[sfiŋks]

To turn now to fricatives after nasals: these sounds were never preceded by nasals in traditional demotic, and many speakers have difficulty in coping with nasals in such positions. It is probable that in some MG dialects an AG nasal before a voiceless fricative did not simply drop without trace, but nasalized the preceding vowel, at least in some words (e.g. [¹āθropos], AG and SMG *ἄνθρωπος*). Today, despite intensive pronunciation drills in Greek schools over many decades, many speakers either omit a nasal where it is written before a fricative, or nasalize the preceding vowel instead of pronouncing the nasal (these are phenomena (iid) and (iic) respectively).

In traditional demotic (and according to the precepts of most grammars), the final /n/ of the following words is dropped when the next word in the phrase begins with any sound except a vowel or a stop: the negatives δέν and μήν, the definite articles τόν and τήν, certain pronouns (cf. 4.5.3.1), and the indefinite article and numeral έναν. (One might add, for old demotic, the conjunction άν 'if' and the conjunction and preposition σάν 'when; like', which are normally written and spoken with the final /n/ (ν) in all environments today.) Careful writers of demotic will usually take care to abide by these rules, although in practice the /n/ is often written or pronounced even where it is superfluous. The following are examples of the rule:

δέν έρχομαι	'I'm not coming'
δέ θά 'ρθω	'I won't come'
μήν τό λές	'don't say it'
μή λές τίποτα	'don't say anything'
τόν μπαμπά	'daddy' (acc.)
τό θεῖο	'uncle' (acc.)
τήν Καίτη	'Katy' (acc.)
τή Ρένα	'Rena' (acc.)
έναν άνθρωπο	'a person' (acc.)
ένα μήνα	'a month' (acc.)

1.4.2.5 Sibilants

Modern Greek has two sibilant phonemes:

s [s]   voiceless alveolar fricative   σ, ς
z [z]   voiced alveolar fricative   ζ, σ, ς

These sounds are alveolar rather than dental, and, since there is normally no semantic distinction in MG between alveolar and palato-alveolar fricatives, they may be articulated by some speakers so far back as to be almost indistinguishable from [ʃ] and [ʒ] respectively. Other speakers, however, especially those who have had close contact with languages such as English or French, sometimes make a distinction in loanwords between those which originally contained [ʃ] and [ʒ] and those which contained [s] and [z]. The following are examples of this phenomenon.

σοκάκι	'alley'	(< T sokak)	[soˈkaci]
σόκ	'shock'	(< F choc)	[sok] or [ʃok]
ζέστη	'heat'	(< AG ζέω)	[ˈzesti]
ζελέ	'jelly'	(< F gelée)	[zeˈle] or [ʒeˈle]

Such distinctions should by no means be considered to be either wide-spread or counselled by grammarians; rather, they are instances of speakers attempting to imitate the sounds of a foreign language; the same is true of pronunciations such as [blœ] or [blǿ] for [ble] (μπλέ 'blue' < F bleu), or [ˈʃokiŋ] for [ˈsokin] (σόκιν risqué' < F < E shocking), or [ʒãˈbō] for [zamˈbon] (ζαμπόν 'ham' < F jambon). Nevertheless, some dialects of Modern Greek distinguish between alveolar and palato-alveolar fricatives.

The sound [s] is represented by the letter σ (written ς in word-final position), which is always pronounced [s] before vowels or voiceless consonants, and before a pause; [z] is represented by ζ before vowels and by σ/ς before voiced consonants ([z] does not occur before voiceless consonants, according to the principle of 'identity of voice': see below, 1.5). There is some variation among speakers between [s] and [z] before the liquids /l/ and /r/. As has been seen above, /l/ and /r/ are treated as voiced when they follow the digraphs αυ and ευ. Nevertheless, σ/ς is normally pronounced [s] before /l/, but as [z] before /r/, although some speakers display the opposite phenomenon: in fact, the pronunciation [sl] may be influenced by spelling.

ἄσσος	'ace'	/ásos/	[ˈasos]
εἶσαι	'you are' (sing.)	/íse/	[ˈise]
κομμουνιστής	'communist'	/komunistís/	[komuniˈstis]
κομμουνισμός	'communism'	/komunizmós/	[komuniˈzmos]
Σλάβος	'Slav'	/slávos/	[ˈslavos]
τῆς Λίτσας	'of Litsa'	/tislítsas/	[tiˈslitsas]
Ἰσραήλ	'Israel'	/izraíl/	[izraˈil]

1.4.2.6 Liquids

There are two liquid phonemes:

l	[l]	dental (or alveolar) lateral	} λ
	[ʎ]	palatalized dental (or alveolar) lateral or palatal lateral	
r	[r]	alveolar flapped	ρ

(ὁ) κάλος	'corn (callous)'	} /kálos/	[ˈkalos]
(τό) κάλλος	'beauty'		
μαλλί	'wool'	/malí/	[maˈli] or [maˈʎi]
μαλλιά	'hair (of head)'	/maliá/	[maˈʎa]
ὄρος	'term; condition'	/óros/	[ˈoros]
ὀρρός	'serum'	/orós/	[oˈros]

While Setatos (1974: 14) designates these sounds as voiced, other linguists class them as 'neutral as regards voice' (e.g. Warburton 1970b: 16–17). While they may or may not voice the preceding underlying /s/ (see 1.4.2.5), they always voice the preceding labial fricative in words spelled with αυ and ευ (see 1.4.2.1). Nevertheless, /l/ and /r/ may be preceded by either a voiced or a voiceless consonant:

σταυρός	'cross'	/stavrós/	[staˈvros]
αβρός	'courteous'	/avrós/	[aˈvros]
but αφρός	'foam'	/afrós/	[aˈfros]

Table 1.3 summarizes the chief features of the SMG consonants.

TABLE 1.3

	Bilabial	Labio-dental	Dental	Alveolar	Palatal	Velar
Stop	p b		t d			k g
Fricative		f v	θ ð	s z		x γ
Nasal	m	ɱ	n	n	ɲ	ŋ
Lateral			l	l	ʎ	
Flapped				r		

Where the symbols are paired, the first is voiceless, the latter voiced.

1.5 SEQUENCES OF SOUNDS IN WORDS OF POPULAR AND LEARNED ORIGIN

In traditional demotic there were certain constraints regarding possible sequences of sounds, irrespective of whether these sequences might occur within words or across word boundaries. The most general of these were that

(i) there could be no instances of double consonant or vowel sounds;

(ii) in any sequence of obstruents (i.e. stops or fricatives), all the consonants were either voiced or voiceless.

More particular rules were the following:

(iii) [i] could not occur before another vowel (thus /i/ + V → [j] or [ç] + V): if the /i/ was originally stressed, then the stress was transferred to the vowel (thus /í/ + V → [j] or [ç] + V́).

(iv) two voiceless stops or two voiceless fricatives could not co-occur: such combinations were dissimilated to become voiceless fricative + voiceless stop (or, in the case of fricative + /s/, vice versa). Thus the following sounds were changed from Ancient to Modern Greek:

κτ or χϑ → χτ [xt]
πτ or φϑ (also αυϑ/ευϑ) → φτ [ft]
αυχ or ευχ → αυκ [afk] or ευκ [efk]
αυσ or ευσ → αψ [aps] or εψ [eps]
σϑ → στ [st]
σχ → σκ [sk]

Exceptions were the combination σφ [sf], and the sequence [pt] in the apocopated preposition ἀπ' followed by the definite article, both of which remained unchanged.

(v) a nasal could be followed only by a vowel or voiced stop; thus voiceless stops and voiced fricatives were converted to voiced stops after nasals, and nasals were deleted before voiceless fricatives:

μπ and μβ → μπ [mb]
ντ and νδ → ντ [nd]
γκ → γκ [ng]
μφ → φ [f]
νϑ → ϑ [θ]
γχ → χ [x]

(vi) a voiced fricative could not precede a nasal. Here the fricative was deleted:

γμ → μ [m]
αυμ or ευμ → αμ [am] or εμ [em]

Nevertheless the combination σμ [zm] remained.

In addition, there were numerous other sequences of sounds in Ancient Greek which dropped out of the spoken language.

Under the influence of *katharevousa*, many ancient or pseudo-ancient sequences of sounds entered the written, and consequently the spoken language, even within the boundaries of the same word. In the following examples of words of *katharevousa* origin which are now found in SMG, it will be noticed that sometimes there are doublets, or pairs of words which derive from the learned and the popular tradition respectively, preserving the phonology of each of the historical forms of MG, namely *katharevousa* and demotic:

(i) double vowels:

/oo/	πρόοδος	'progress'	[ˈprooðos]
/ii/	ποιητής	'poet'	[piiˈtis]

(ii) /ns/   ρύπανση   'pollution'   ['ripansi]
(the sequence /ns/, which is absent from Classical Greek, except across morpheme boundaries in compound words, also contravenes (v))
/kδ/   ἐκδρομή   'excursion'   [ekδro'mi] (also non-standard [egδro'mi] and [eγδro'mi])
(iii) /io/   στοιχεῖο   'element; feature'   [sti'çio]
(cf. στοιχειό   'ghost'   [sti'ço])
(for further examples see 1.4.1)
(iv) /kt/   ἔκταση   'extent'   ['ektasi]
/xθ/   ἐχθρός   'enemy'   [ex'θros]
/pt/   λεπτά   'minutes'   [le'pta]
(cf. λεφτά   'money'   [le'fta])
/fθ/   φθίνω   'I decline'   ['fθino]
(cf. φτύνω   'I spit'   ['ftino])
/fx/   εὐχαριστῶ   'thank you'   [efxari'sto]
/fs/   καύσιμο   'combustible' (n. sing.)   ['kafsimo]
(cf. κάψιμο   'burning'   ['kapsimo])
/sθ/   μισθός   'salary'   [mi'sθos]
/sx/   σχέδιο   'plan; pattern'   ['sçeδio]
(v) /mv/   βόμβα   'bomb'   ['vomva]
/nδ/   Ἀλέξανδρος   'Alexander'   [a'leksanδros]
/mf/   συμφωνῶ   'I agree'   [simfo'no]
/nθ/   πένθος   'mourning'   ['penθos]
/nx/   ἐλέγχω   'I check; I control'   [e'leŋxo]
/nγ/   συγγραφέας   'author'   [siŋγra'feas]
(vi) /γm/   τάγμα   'battalion'   ['taγma]
(cf. τάμα   'vow'   ['tama])
/vm/   ρεῦμα   'current'   ['revma]
(cf. ρέμα   'torrent'   ['rema])

In practice, there is some variation in the extent to which *katharevousa* sequences are fully pronounced. As has already been said, many speakers fail to pronounce a full nasal before a consonant. Similarly, /kt/ in many words of learned origin is commonly pronounced [xt] (e.g. πρακτικός [praxti'kos]); strangely, this pronunciation seems more widespread (and thus more acceptable to the speakers' linguistic sense) than, for instance, [ft] for /pt/ or [sk] for /sx/ (e.g. λεπτοδείκτης [lepto'δiktis] or [lepto'δixtis] 'minute hand', but not *[lefto'δixtis]; κοπτοραπτού [koptora'ptu] 'seamstress, dressmaker', not *[koftora'ftu];

σχολεῖο [sxoˈlio] or σχολειό [sxoˈʎo] 'school', not ?[skoˈʎo]). Conversely, some speakers pronounce certain perfectly ordinary demotic words according to *katharevousa* phonology (e.g. φθάνω [ˈfθano] for [ˈftano] 'I arrive'; χθές [xθes] for [xtes] 'yesterday'; even λεπτά [leˈpta] for [leˈfta] 'money'). The pronunciations [ft] for /fθ/ and [xt] for /xθ/ are very frequently (but not exclusively) found in the perfective passive stems of verbs (e.g. συμβουλεύτηκα [ft] 'I consulted', στηρίχτηκα [xt] 'I supported myself', but φθινόπωρο [fθ] 'autumn', ὄχθη [xθ] 'river-bank').

As for the opposition between [i] and [j] or [ç] before a vowel, again there is a certain variation among speakers. While most words of demotic origin with /i/ before a vowel will be pronounced with [j] or [ç], words of learned origin vary according to their frequency of use, the most common tending to be pronounced with [j] or [ç], the less common with [i], or with either in free variation:

ἄδεια | (adj.) 'empty' (f. sing. or n. pl.) [ˈaðja]
| (noun) 'licence; permission' [ˈaðia] or [ˈaðja]

In the case of the noun here, the former pronunciation is likely to be used when the speaker is on his/her best linguistic behaviour, the latter when (s)he is talking more casually. (It is however noteworthy that when followed by a possessive pronoun, the noun is pronounced with [i], never [j]: ἡ ἄδειά μου 'my licence' [iaðiˈamu].) Some words have different pronunciations according to their meaning and context, e.g. διάθεση [ˈðjaθesi] 'mood, humour', [ðiˈaθesi] '(syntactical) voice'. In some words, both [i] and [j] or [ç] may co-occur, e.g. Χατζηκυριάκειο [xadziciˈrjacio] (name of an institution in Piraeus): here the *katharevousa* suffix -ειο(ν) has been attached to a demotic name (Χατζηκυριάκος).

1.5.1 DIPHTHONGS

Two vowel sounds in sequence are usually pronounced more or less as a diphthong in words of demotic origin: there may be greater stress on the first or on the second vowel, or both may be unstressed; the unstressed vowel(s) of a diphthong are reduced in length. The second vowel is most often [i] or [u]: γάιδαρος [ˈɣaiðaros] 'donkey', κλαίει [ˈklei] '(s)he cries', ἐξηγήσεων [eksiˈjiseon] 'explanations' (gen.), ρολόι [roˈloi] 'clock; watch', πάω [ˈpao] 'I go', ναοῦ [naˈu] 'temple; church', ταΐζω [taˈizo] 'I feed', τάισε [ˈtaise] '(s)he fed' (but cf. imperative τάισέ με [taiˈseme] 'feed me', in which /taise/ is considered to consist of three syllables: cf. the last paragraph of 1.7).

1.5.2 FURTHER REMARKS ON SEQUENCES OF SOUNDS WITHIN AND ACROSS WORD- (AND MORPHEME-) BOUNDARIES

As has been indicated, in MG there is in principle no distinction between the pronunciation of sequences of sounds within words (or within morphemes) and their pronunciation across word- (or morpheme-) boundaries. This applies especially to the voicing of voiceless stops after a nasal, to the voicing of /s/ before a voiced consonant, and to the degemination of double consonants; these phenomena occur especially between the article and its noun and between a pronoun or negative and the verb:

ὁ καιρός	'time' (nom.)	/okerós/	[oceˈros]
τόν καιρό	'time' (acc.)	/tongeró/	[tonɟeˈro]
τῆς Ἄννας	'Anne's'	/tisánas/	[tiˈsanas]
τῆς Μαρίας	'Mary's'	/tizmarías/	[tizmaˈrias]
τῶν νόμων	'of the laws'	/tonómon/	[toˈnomon]

(pronounced the same as τῶν ὤμων 'of the shoulders')

τῆς στροφῆς   'of the turn'   /tistrofís/   [tistroˈfis]

(pronounced the same as τῆς τροφῆς 'of the food')

In view of the possibility of ambiguity in certain cases, many trained speakers (such as broadcasters and public speakers in general) deliberately avoid running words together in this way, and one may hear utterances such as ἡ δική μας ζωή 'our own life' [iðiˈcimas zoˈi] (which resists the voicing of /s/ to [z] and then the latter's degemination) and τήν τροπή 'the turn (of events)' (acc.) [tintroˈpi] (to avoid confusion with τήν ντροπή 'shame' (acc.) [tindroˈpi]). Sometimes speakers pronouncing nasal + voiceless stop across word boundaries may fail to assimilate the nasal, or fail to voice the stop; e.g. ὅταν περάσω 'when I pass' [otanbeˈraso], δέν ξέρω 'I don't know' [ðeŋˈksero]. Similarly, one may even hear a glottal stop between vowels, as in ὁ καιρός θά εἶναι αἴθριος 'the weather will be fine' [oceˈros θaˈine ˈʔeθrios].

Educated speakers often pronounce double consonants separately within a word when the first instance of the consonant occurs at the end of a prefix of learned origin and the second at the beginning of the root word. This applies to the prefixes {pan}, {sin} and {en} (especially before /γ/) and {ek}:

παμμέγιστος	'very large'	[pamˈmejistos]
παλλαϊκός	'of all the people'	[pallaiˈkos]

συγγραφέας	'author'	[siŋɣraˈfeas]
ἐγγράμματος	'literate'	[eŋˈɣramatos]
ἐκκεντρικός	'eccentric'	[eccendriˈkos]

There is no doubt that such people are influenced both by the spelling and by the etymology of the words concerned.

There are many instances in which vowel sounds may (or must) be deleted. One case of obligatory deletion is that of /e/ in the preposition σέ before the definite article. The /u/ of the proclitic second-person-singular pronoun σοῦ may optionally be deleted before a third-person pronoun; the /e/ of εἶναι '(s)he/it is; they are' may optionally be elided, especially before a word beginning with a vowel or /t/; the /o/ of ἀπό 'from' may be elided before a definite article; and the final /e/ of certain imperative singular forms may be dropped before a clitic pronoun (φέρε το → φέρ' το). The vowel /i/ in particular is often omitted in casual speech in especially common words (such as the definite article):

τῆς Ἰταλίας	'of Italy'	[tisitaˈlias] or [tsitaˈlias]
στίς ἐφημερίδες	'in the newspapers'	[stisefimeˈriðes] or
		[stsefimeˈriðes]
εἰκοσιτρία	'twenty-three'	[ikosiˈtria] or [ikoˈstria]
περισσότερο	'more'	[periˈsotero] or [perˈsotero]
πέρυσι	'last year'	[ˈperisi] or [ˈpersi]
σημερινός	'today's'	[simeriˈnos] or [simerˈnos]

In each of the above cases, the word in question is usually spelled as it is shown here, and it is the first of the two pronunciations which is considered to be correct.

Elision and prodelision are particularly frequent phenomena in MG when two vowel sounds meet at the end and beginning of two words which are closely connected with each other semantically and syntactically. (In the following paragraphs 'elision' refers to the deletion of a vowel at the end of a word, 'prodelision' to the deletion of an initial vowel.) Particularly susceptible to these phenomena are (a) the prepositions μέ, σέ and ἀπό and the definite article before nouns and adjectives, and (b) the particles θά and νά, the relative pronoun πού and proclitic pronouns before verbs. Much attention has been paid by linguists to the *hierarchy of vowels* in MG: this is the system of prevalence of one vowel over another. If the two vowels are identical, they may simply become degeminated; if they are different, one may prevail over the other according to the following system (> here = 'prevails over'): /a > o > u > e or i/ (/i/ sometimes prevails over /e/, sometimes vice versa). Stress is irrelevant to which vowel disappears, and so is the order in which the vowels appear. Such elision or prodelision is so common in speech (although it is never obligatory) that the words are often written with the elision indicated by an apostrophe; in less colloquial styles of writing, however, the words are normally written in full.

/aa/ → /a/	τά ἄλλα or τ᾽ ἄλλα 'the others' (neuter)
	τά ἄκουσα or τ᾽ ἄκουσα 'I heard them' (neuter)
	θά ἀναφέρω or θ᾽ ἀναφέρω 'I will mention'
/oo/ → /o/	τό ὄνομα or τ᾽ ὄνομα 'the name'
	τό ὀνειρεύτηκα or τ᾽ ὀνειρεύτηκα 'I dreamed (of) it'
/uu/ → /u/	τοῦ οὐρανοῦ or τ᾽ οὐρανοῦ 'of the sky'
/ee/ → /e/	(σέ ἐμένα) σέ μένα or σ᾽ ἐμένα 'to me' (emphatic)
/ii/ → /i/	τί εἶναι; or τί ᾽ναι; 'what is it?'
/oa/ → /a/	ἀπό ἄκρη σέ ἄκρη or ἀπ᾽ ἄκρη σ᾽ ἄκρη 'from one end to the other; right across'
/ua/ → /a/	μοῦ ἀρέσει or μ᾽ ἀρέσει 'I like it'
/ae/ → /a/	τά ἔλεγε or τά ᾽λεγε '(s)he used to say them'
/oe/ → /o/	τό ἔχω or τό ᾽χω 'I have it'
/oi/ → /o/	τό εἶχα or τό ᾽χα 'I had it'
/ue/ → /u/	αὐτός πού ἔρχεται or αὐτός πού ᾽ρχεται 'the one who comes'
/ui/ → /u/	σοῦ εἶχα πεῖ or σοῦ ᾽χα πεῖ 'I'd told you'
/ei/ → /i/	σέ εἶδα or σ᾽ εἶδα 'I saw you'

(Note that τά ᾽χανε may be reduced from either τά εἴχανε 'they had them' or τά ἔχανε '(s)he lost them'.)

Prodelision never takes place in nouns or adjectives (although it may with the numeral or indefinite article ἔνας: τό ἔνα → τό ᾽να). Prodelision of the augment in verbs is extremely common, as it is also with certain other frequently used verb forms beginning with /e/ or /i/ (namely εἶμαι, ἤμουν, ἔχω, εἶχα, ἔρχομαι, ἔρθω, εἶπα, ἤπια and ἤθελα, in both numbers and in all three persons).

In some idiolects there are certain exceptions to these rules, especially when ἀπό is followed by /e/ or /a/, e.g. ἀπ᾽ ἐδῶ for ἀπό ᾽δῶ 'from here', or ἀπό ᾽φτά for ἀπ᾽ αὐτά 'from these'.

Finally, some remarks should be made about vowel sequences across morpheme boundaries in compound words. In Classical Greek and in some varieties of katharevousa, hiatus between vowels in such circumstances was avoided by elision (e.g. κατά + ἔρχομαι → κατέρχομαι) or crasis (the running together of two vowels to produce a third sound, e.g. πρό + ἔβαλα → προὔβαλα), while in traditional demotic similar phenomena occurred (mainly prodelision, e.g. ξανά + ἔρχομαι → ξανάρ-χομαι 'I come again'). Nevertheless, the tendency in recent times has been to preserve the full form of each word in a compound. This means that side by side with ancient or archaizing or traditional demotic formations, there are modern formations which do not follow the same rules. One of the ancient rules which is rarely observed in new forma-tions is that which transforms a voiceless stop into a fricative before a vowel written with the rough breathing. Here are just a few examples of the modern tendency (with some ancient or modern counter-examples):

/ae/ καταεκνευρισμένος 'extremely irritated'
        (cf. κατά + ἔνα → καθένας 'each one')
/ai/ παραοικονομία 'the "black economy" '
        (cf. παρά + οἰκία → παροικία 'foreign colony')
/ao/ ἡ μεταομηρική ἐποχή 'the post-Homeric period'
        (cf. μετά + ὅριον → μεθόριος 'of the border')
/ie/ ἀντιαισθητικός 'unsightly'
        (cf. ἀντί + ἐλληνικός → ἀνθελληνικός 'un-Greek; anti-Greek')
/ii/ ἀντιοικονομικός 'uneconomic(al)'
        (cf. ἀντί + ἠχῶ → ἀντηχῶ 'resound')
/oa/ ὑποανάπτυκτος 'underdeveloped'
        (cf. the more learned formation ὑπανάπτυξη 'underdevelop-
        ment')
/oe/ δυτικοευρωπαϊκός 'West European'
        (cf. τό + ἐλάχιστον → τουλάχιστον 'at least')
/oo/ ὑποομάδα 'subgroup'

Across word boundaries too there is a dual system operating on the sequence of vowels between ancient prepositions and their nouns or adjectives. While no one will say *ὑπ᾽ ἀνάπτυξιν (which would be a correct formation in Ancient Greek) for ὑπό ἀνάπτυξιν 'under develop-ment; developing', the phrase καθ᾽ ὅλη τή διάρκεια 'for the whole duration (of), throughout' (as a more emphatic variant of κατά τή διάρκεια 'for the duration (of), during') is still used, although it should properly be seen as a fixed expression which bears traces of an older system rather than as a living example of this system at work.

1.6 HOMONYMS

True homonyms (i.e. words written and pronounced identically) are rare in MG. They are mostly confined to monosyllables, e.g. σέ (preposition and pronoun) νά (modal and deictic particle), although there are some longer homonyms, e.g. τά σάλια 'saliva' and 'shawls'; πάντα 'everything' or 'always'; ρόδα 'wheel' or 'roses'; and πόντος 'centimetre' or 'Pontus'. Other examples are given elsewhere in this chapter.

Homographs (words spelled identically but pronounced differently) are even rarer, the difference in pronunciation normally being that between the vocalic or non-vocalic /i/: e.g. λόγια and σκιάζω (see 1.4.1; see also 1.7 for words distinguished by stress position).

Homophones (words pronounced alike but spelled differently) are more numerous, but not nearly so common as in French. They include: μέρη 'places; parts' and Μαίρη 'Mary'; βάζο 'vase' and βάζω 'I put'; πιάνο 'piano' and πιάνω 'I catch'; φιλάω 'I kiss' and φυλάω 'I keep'; οἱ ἀδερφοί 'the brothers' and ἡ ἀδερφή 'the sister'; κλείνω 'I close' and κλίνω 'I incline; I decline'; γείρω 'I lean' (perfective); γύρο 'turn' (acc.) and γύρω 'around'; (οἱ) τοῖχοι 'walls (of house)', (τά) τείχη 'walls (of city)', (ἡ) τύχη 'luck' and τύχει 'happen' (perfective); κρητικός 'Cretan' and κριτικός 'critic(al)'; ἀκριβός 'expensive' and ἀκριβῶς 'precisely'; and even phrases such as τούς Ἕλληνες 'the Greeks' (acc.) and τούς ἔλυνες 'you were untying them (masc.)'. Some homophones are distinguished only by their breathings (and thus are not distinguished in the monotonic system), e.g. τά ἄρματα 'arms' and τά ἅρματα 'chariots; tanks'; and (ὁ) ὅρος 'term, condition' and (τό) ὄρος 'mountain'.

1.7 STRESS AND ACCENT

In MG a word may be stressed only on one of its last three syllables. There is practically no variation (as there is in English) in stress in certain words according to idiolect; and stress is a semantically significant feature in MG (as it is not in French). The position of the stress is in many cases the only distinguishable feature in the pronunciation of two different words: e.g. γέρος 'old man' and γερός 'robust'; νόμος 'law' and νομός 'department, prefecture'; τζάμι 'window-pane' and τζαμί 'mosque'; ἄλλα 'others' (neuter) and ἀλλά 'but'; ἡ μέρα 'the day' and ἥμερα 'tame' (n. pl.); ὅρων 'terms; conditions' and ὡρῶν 'hours' (both gen. pl.); διπλωμάτων 'diplomas' and διπλωματῶν 'diplomats' (both gen. pl.); κουράστηκες 'you have got tired' and κουραστικές 'tiring' (fem. pl.); χαλί 'carpet' and χάλι '(bad) state'; παίρνω 'I take' and περνώ 'I pass'; τό χαρτί 'the paper' and τό χάρτη 'the map' (acc.). Nevertheless, there are a few non-standard pronunciations which differ from the norm in stress alone, e.g. ἀερό-πλανο for ἀεροπλάνο 'aeroplane', and κινηματόγραφος for κινηματο-γράφος 'cinema'.

All verbs and many nouns (but not normally adjectives) shift their stress from one syllable to another in conjugation and declension, according to fairly fixed rules (see chapters 4 and 5 and Appendix I). There are certain underlying historical principles which have contributed to the present situation. In order to understand these rules one must realize that in AG certain vowels were pronounced long and others short (in MG, as has been mentioned, all vowels are more or less equal in length, and vowel length is not a distinctive feature): some written vowels were always pronounced long (η, ω, and all vowel sounds represented by more than one letter, e.g. ου, αι, αυ, ευ: each of these last two examples is considered for the purposes of breathings and accents as consisting of two vowels); some were always short (ε and ο); while others were sometimes long and sometimes short (α, ι, and υ). At the ends of words, however, -αι and -οι were short (although -αις and -οις were long). The basic rules for the position of accents were as follows:

(a) no word could be accentuated more than two syllables from the end;

(b) those words which ended in a long syllable could not be accentuated more than one syllable from the end.

In traditional Greek orthography (which was in use in most printed matter till recent years), there were three different accent marks, each of which however in MG indicated the same thing, i.e. which syllable was stressed. Additional rules concerning the type of accent included the following:

(c) the circumflex (περισπωμένη [̑]) could be placed only over a long vowel and only when that vowel was the penultimate or final in the word;

(d) only the acute (ὀξεία [́]) could be placed over the penultimate vowel if the last vowel was long;

(e) the grave (βαρεία [̀]), and not the acute, could be placed over the last vowel of a word unless that word was followed by a punctuation mark or by an unaccentuated word (except the article ὁ or ἡ), in which case the acute could be used.

One consequence of rule (b) is that all verbs (which end in -ω) are stressed on the penultimate or final syllable in the imperfective non-past (present) active. The same rule accounts for certain morphologically motivated stress-shifts in nouns (e.g. ὁ ἄνϑρωπος 'person' (nom.), but τοῦ ἀνϑρώπου (gen.): in the nominative the -o- is 'short' according to AG rules, while, in the latter, the -ου is 'long'). Nevertheless, there are some contraventions of rule (b) in certain MG forms of nouns and adjectives (e.g. μπακάληδων 'grocers' (gen.), ἡ κυρία Καρπόζηλου 'Mrs Karpozilos', ἀδύνατου 'weak' (masc. and neuter gen. sing.): in all these forms the last vowel is 'long'); by the time declensions of this kind entered the language, this rule (together with the distinction between vowel-lengths) had ceased to operate. Most of those nouns of AG origin which displayed stress-shift retained the shift, while the learned tradition also influenced many new nouns to conform with the ancient pattern.

It is rule (a) that explains the shift of stress when a word normally stressed on the antepenultimate syllable is followed by an enclitic pronoun (with which it forms a single phonological word): ὁ δάσκαλος [oˈðaskalos], but ὁ δάσκαλός μας [oðaskaˈlozmas] 'our teacher'; ἄνοιξε τό παράϑυρο [ˈanikse topaˈraθiro] 'open the window', but ἄνοιξέ το [aniˈkseto] 'open it'.

1.8 INTONATION

Research into Modern Greek intonation and related prosodic features was limited and impressionistic until Waring's (1976) thorough investigation of the subject.

Assuming three basic pitch levels (high, mid, and low), Waring identifies four basic tones (fall, rise, rise–fall, and fall–rise): and in addition to these latter he specifies a special raised fall (fall to mid-pitch).

A striking feature of MG intonation is the tendency for changes in pitch to occur with sudden jumps rather than with a gradual ascent or descent. Moreover, the intonation of Athenians tends to be more monotonous (that is, with fewer and less extreme changes of pitch) than that of speakers from certain other areas of Greece, particularly the Ionian and Aegean islands. The most common neutral intonation patterns are the rise at the end of a clause which is not the end of a complete utterance, and the fall at the end of a complete utterance; for example:

		Clause-end (non-final)	Utterance-end
(1) μιλᾶς	'you speak'	2 13 milás	2 31 milás
(2) μ' ἀρέσει	'I like it'	2 13 marési	2 3 1 marési
(3) διάβασες	'you read' (past)	1 3 ðjávases	3 1 ðjávases

(Numbers over vowels or placed initially refer to pitch levels, '1' being the lowest. MG utterances do not usually end in more than two unstressed syllables.) Normally a change of pitch takes place (or begins) on a stressed syllable. However, if there is to be a fall–rise or rise–fall, the second element of each may occur (or begin) on an unstressed syllable (as, for example, in (5) below).

Waring has been able to make certain broad correlations between intonation and meaning. These correlations are the following (the tones are given in descending order of frequency):

(a) *falling*: no special implication; but if it is marked (e.g. by reaching very low pitch), then conclusion, finality, definiteness;

(b) *rising*: incompletion or continuation, including non-final phrases, many questions, encouraging remarks, invitations and some other imperative types;

(c) *falling–rising*: as (b), or to express doubt, uncertainty, or qualification of what is said;

(d) *rising–falling*: contrast, such as that of insistently polar questions (Waring 1982: 25).

A particular characteristic of MG is that yes/no questions are very often distinguished from statements only by intonation (or by a question-mark in the orthography). In many cases, the particular intonation for yes/no questions (and never used except for such questions) is what Waring calls the 'raised fall', i.e. a final fall to mid position, which, because the voice does not descend to low pitch at the end of the fall, gives the impression of a deliberately unfinished fall:

(4) φτάσαμε(;)	(a) statement	(b) question
	31	3 2
	ftásame	ftásame
	'we've arrived'	'have we arrived?'

Another typically Greek question intonation is the rise-fall, the use of which, according to Waring, is the clearest indication that a speaker can give that (s)he is asking a question:

1 3   1

(5) φτάσαμε;   ftásame

The pattern 131, observed in (5), may be found also with words stressed on the penultimate or even the final syllable:

1 31

(6) ... είσαι; '... are you?'   íse

2   131

(7) ... μετρό; '... metro?'   metró

In the case of the final stress in (7), a rise-fall may be observed on a single syllable.

MG rhythm tends to be *syllable-timed* rather than *stress-timed*: this often gives Greek speech a staccato effect (Waring 1976: 280–1). Stress is defined by Waring (ibid.: 266) as 'the sort of prominence on a syllable—particularly on the syllable nucleus—which to a native speaker may suggest (usually unconsciously) that one or other of the tones [mentioned above] is either fully realised or begun on that syllable'. Stress is usually also marked by extra length and loudness. The difference in length between stressed and unstressed syllables is not so great in Athenian speech as it is in some island speech (ibid.: 280); and the difference in loudness between stressed syllables with tones of various prominence and between stressed and unstressed syllables is generally less than that which may be observed in English, Russian, or German (ibid.: 354), although the changes that do occur may be quite sudden. There are even instances in which a stressed syllable may not be as long as the following unstressed syllable (as in (6)).

1.9 ORTHOGRAPHIC REFORMS

In recent years attempts have been made to simplify the orthography of MG. While a literate Greek speaker has no difficulty in pronouncing an unknown word when it is presented to him/her in written form (unlike the situation in English), the converse is not true: even educated Greeks have perennial problems with orthography, the most difficult being the accents, the breathings, the spelling of the /i/, and the double consonants. Up to 1982, when the so-called 'monotonic' (single-accent) system was officially introduced, certain minor simplifications had been made, including the following:

(i) the grave accent is replaced by the acute (this was a recognition of the status quo in handwriting and typing).

(ii) the circumflex is replaced by the acute in penultimate position unless both the following conditions apply: (a) that the penultimate syllable contains a vowel which can *only* be 'long' (i.e. any vowel or combination of vowels except *a, ε, ι, o, υ*) *and* (b) that the final syllable contains a vowel which can *only* be 'short' (i.e. ε, o or final αι or ει). There are certain exceptions, e.g. that the final -*a* of neuter nouns and adjectives is considered to be 'short' (thus γλώσσα, ωραία (f.), but ωραία (n. pl.), γραφεία, χώμα); and that the penultimate vowel of certain verb inflections is considered 'long' and the final vowel 'short' (thus, αγαπούσα, κομάμαι).

(iii) a single consonant can replace a double consonant in many words of non-Greek origin (e.g. καπέλο 'hat' < It. *capello*).

(iv) the spelling -η- in the 'subjunctive' verb endings is replaced by -ει- (as for 'indicative').

(v) the diaeresis, which distinguishes a true diphthong from a digraph, may be omitted when the first of the two vowels of the diphthong bears an accent or breathing (e.g. γάιδαρος 'donkey', but γαϊδάρου (gen.)).

This is the basis of the simplified historical orthography used throughout this book. (For details of the monotonic system see Appendix II.)

1.10 PUNCTUATION

Little need be said about punctuation conventions in MG. They follow the European pattern, except that (·) stands for a semicolon and (;) for a question mark. In practice, punctuation tends to occur where one might pause in speech or reading aloud. Thus a comma is often placed between a subject and the immediately following verb, particularly if the subject consists of a lengthy phrase. For the same reason a comma may be placed even between a verb and its object; while the presence or absence of commas before and/or after a relative clause does not always correspond to a distinction between non-defining and defining clauses (which are not usually distinguished in Greek speech by a pause or absence of pause).

Various conventions are used for the quoting of direct speech. In prose fiction, the normal practice is to introduce a piece of direct speech at the beginning of a paragraph simply by a dash, with no indication of where the speech ends and the narrative begins:

—Δυστυχῶς, μοῦ εἶπε, ἦρϑες ἀργά ' "Unfortunately," (s)he said, "you've come too late." '

In journalism, however, direct speech is normally enclosed within εἰσαγωγικά (« »), which are also used generally for the quoting or pointing out of individual words or phrases, or for indicating that the word(s) is/are being used metaphorically.

Some typefaces do not have the equivalent of italics (κυρτά στοιχεῖα), their place being taken by the spacing out of the letters of the word(s) to be stressed.

Much use is made by comic writers of ἀποσιωπητικά (. . .), usually to lead up to the 'punch-line' of a story, or to some other word or phrase to which the writer attaches particular importance.

2

GENDER, CASE, NUMBER, AND PERSON

Before examining the morphology of the MG nominal and verbal systems, we shall look at some of the basic categories underlying these systems. (Attention is drawn, however, to the tables of inflection in Appendix I.) Gender and case concern the nominal system alone; number represents the meeting point of noun and verb; while person is shared by personal pronouns and the verbal system.

2.1 GENDER

There are three genders in MG: masculine, feminine, and neuter.

2.1.1 GENDER AND HUMAN SEX

It would be as well to investigate first of all how native Greek speakers conceive of grammatical gender in relation to themselves and their fellow humans. The most basic concept is that while masculine nouns may be applied to females as well as males, feminine nouns also to males, and neuters to either, the masculine is generally thought of as not necessarily marked for gender when referring to persons (similarly, the neuter is unmarked with reference to inanimates): the masculine may cover both males and females, whereas the feminine normally refers only to females. Thus while 'man (male)' is ἄντρας (masc.) and 'woman' γυναίκα (fem.), 'person' or 'human being', whether it refers to a male or to a female, is ἄνθρωπος (masc.).

The best way of testing this concept in reality is to study the use of the interrogative ποιός 'who', which is inflected for gender, number and case (Kazazis 1980). If a woman telephones someone and wants the recipient of the call to guess her identity, she may say,

   (1) ξέρεις ποιά είμαι; 'do you know who (fem.) I am?'; or
   (2) ξέρεις ποιός είναι; 'do you know who (masc.) it is?'

Similarly, the recipient of the call may ask,

(3) ποιά είσαι; 'who (fem.) are you?'; or

(4) ποιός είναι; 'who (masc.) is it?'

From these examples it would appear that there is a correlation between person and gender: in these circumstances, the feminine goes with the first or second person and the masculine with the third. The recipient of the call (who would be less polite if (s)he used the feminine and the second person than if (s)he used the more impersonal masculine and third person) is in effect saying, in (3), 'You are a woman (probably known to me): who are you?', and, in (4), 'You are a person: who are you?'

The rule appears to be that 'when the sex and number of the referent of ποι- are contextually presupposed', gender and number agreement must be applied to that pronoun (Kazazis ibid.: 255). Now, in the first and second persons, sex and number are taken for granted, since in the first the speaker knows which sex (s)he is, while in the second (s)he is assumed to know the sex of the addressee. In the third person, gender and number agreement of ποιός is usually necessary only when a predicate is stated (ποιά είναι αὐτή; 'who's she/that (fem.)?'), or if the gender and number are obvious from the context (ποιός παντρεύτηκε; 'who (masc. sing.) got married?', because the answer may refer to one man, to one woman, or to a man and a woman together; but ποιάν παντρεύτηκε ὁ Νίκος; 'whom (fem. sing.) did Nick marry?', because the answer can refer only to one female; similarly, a bus conductor may say, γιά ποιούς είναι τά εἰσιτήρια; 'for whom (masc. pl.) are the tickets?', since the plurality of the tickets shows that there must be more than one person involved, though the speaker is unaware of their sex). On the other hand, it is possible to say to a little girl as a sign of endearment,

(5) ποιός είναι καλό κορίτσι; 'who's (masc.) [a] good girl (neuter)?',

in which the pronoun is masculine, the noun neuter, and the referent female!

There is a parallel with all these situations, in which usage in the first and second persons differs from that in the third: in MG the subject of a verb in the first or second person is stated (as a pronoun) only when that subject is emphasized in opposition to any other possible subject, while in the third the subject has either to have been stated at some time or to be inferrable by other means (such as the speaker pointing at the referent). The third person is thus felt to be vaguer and more neutral than the first and second.

Similarly, one might say,

(6) πάω σήμερα στό γιατρό 'I'm going to the doctor['s] (masc.) today',

even if one knows that the doctor in question is a woman, and despite the fact that in other contexts, in which her sex is significant, the use of ἡ γιατρός (with feminine article) or of some feminine derivative (ἡ γιατρίνα, ἡ γιάτρισσα, ἡ γιατρέσσα) is possible. Again, a woman might say,

(7) ἔχω δυό φίλους στόν κόσμο 'I have two friends (masc.) in the world',

even though both these friends may be female: if she said δυό φίλες or δυό φιλενάδες (the feminine forms), she would mean 'two *female* friends', which might suggest that she had other friends who were male. A shopkeeper might say,

(8) οἱ γυναῖκες εἶναι οἱ καλύτεροι πελάτες μου 'women are my best customers (masc.)',

since if he had used the feminine καλύτερες πελάτισσες he would have been saying 'women are my best *female* customers', which is nonsense. Thus it can be seen that in many nouns which can refer to either men or women it is only the feminine version (if it exists at all) which clearly indicates gender.

In traditional demotic the gender of nouns was inextricably linked with their inflexion, and a noun could not change gender without altering its declension (that is to say, there were no nouns of common gender in traditional demotic). For this reason, many speakers are hesitant to use feminine articles and adjectives with nouns that decline like masculines. Thus nouns with masculine form but referring to women are much more frequently used as complements (without article or adjective) than as subjects or objects. Such a noun used as a complement is quite acceptable:

(9) ἡ κυρία Λάμπρου εἶναι βουλευτής 'Mrs Lambrou is [a] Member of Parliament (masc.)';

while phrases such as

(10) ἡ νέα βουλευτής κυρία Λάμπρου 'the (fem.) new (fem.) Member of Parliament (masc.) Mrs (fem.) Lambrou',

although frequent in the press, are not so commonly heard in normal speech, where the feminine noun βουλευτίνα is more likely (even though this particular feminine has a slightly comic ring about it). It is in fact difficult to determine to which grammatical gender a noun belongs in certain utterances, when a noun which can apply to men or women is used as a complement:

(11) ἡ κυρία Μακρῆ εἶναι ἱδρυτής καί πρόεδρος τῆς ἐταιρείας 'Mrs Makri is [the] founder and chairman of the company'.

In (11), are the nouns grammatically masculine or feminine (both ἱδρυτής and πρόεδρος have common gender, i.e. they may be used with a masculine or a feminine article, and there is no commonly used feminine form)? The answer is immaterial until an adjective has to be applied to the noun, and here one observes some variety. There are certain professional and other areas which women have entered in large enough numbers for them to be widely acceptable. Thus one finds:

(12) ἡ Ἄννα εἶναι δημοτική σύμβουλος or κοινωνική λειτουργός 'Anna is a town councillor' or 'social worker',

in which each adjective is feminine, suggesting that each noun is also feminine here (both the nouns in question are of common gender). On the other hand, there are rigidly fixed collocations, such as in the following:

(13) ἦρθε καί ἀνέλαβε τά καθήκοντά της ἡ Μαρία Παυλοπούλου ὡς γενικός ἐπιθεωρητής μέσης ἐκπαιδεύσεως 'Mary Pavlopoulos has come and taken up her duties as general (masc.) inspector of secondary education';

here the noun has to be taken as masculine, even though in other contexts one might find ἡ ἐπιθεωρητής 'the (fem.) inspector' (but not *ἡ γενική ἐπιθεωρητής 'the general (fem.) inspector'). The situation is complicated, and the idea that gender might inhere in a given noun in MG is seen to be not always valid. (It is possible that constructions such as that in (13), which are undoubtedly of *katharevousa* origin, are influenced by French constructions such as *le nouveau professeur*, which may refer to a male or a female.)

On the other hand, where there are separate forms for masculine and feminine (e.g. ὁ φοιτητής (masc.), ἡ φοιτήτρια (fem.) 'student'), complications can still arise. If one wants to say, 'Helen is the only student of mine who failed (in) the examinations', one cannot say,

(14) ἡ Ἑλένη εἶναι ἡ μόνη φοιτήτριά μου πού ἀπέτυχε στίς ἐξετάσεις,

unless all one's students are female (since the sentence would mean '. . . the only (female) student of mine . . .'); the masculine ὁ μόνος φοιτητής μου would be impossible in any circumstances, since Helen is not a male; so that one has to say something such as,

(15) ἡ Ἑλένη εἶναι ἡ μόνη ἀπ' ὅλους τούς φοιτητές μου πού ἀπέτυχε στίς ἐξετάσεις 'Helen is the only [one] (fem.) of all my students (masc.) who failed (in) the examinations.'

Again, in an article about a Greek business enterprise, a journalist could write,

(16) ὁ διευθυντής τῆς ἑταιρείας ἦταν γυναίκα 'the managing director (masc.) of the company was a woman',

and then proceed to talk of her as ἡ διευθύντρια (fem.) 'the managing director (fem.)'. Although the journalist knew when he was writing that the person in question was a woman, it would have been tautologous to begin (16) with ἡ διευθύντρια . . . 'the (female) managing director was a woman'. In (16), despite the use of the definite article, reference is made not so much to a specific person as to a title, while the feminine noun in subsequent sentences refers to the already specified person. Clearly, then, there are contexts in which the use of the feminine noun serves to emphasize that the person referred to is female, but others where its use for a female referent is obligatory.

In order to stress the unusual fact of a woman doing what has traditionally been a man's job, two techniques can be resorted to. One may use a feminine article or adjective to show that the person concerned is female:

(17) ἡ πρώτη ἐπαγγελματίας πιλότος ἀεροπλάνων 'the (fem.) first (fem.) professional aircraft pilot' (i.e. 'the first professional woman aircraft pilot'),

in which the words for 'professional' and 'pilot' are masculine in form but do not indicate sex (contrast the use of the masculine article and adjective ὁ πρῶτος . . ., which would make the phrase mean simply 'the first professional aircraft pilot'). Alternatively, one may place γυναίκα 'woman' before the noun in question: οἱ γυναῖκες πιλότοι 'women pilots' (contrast οἱ πιλοτίνες '(female) pilots', which would not stress their femininity but would simply correspond grammatically to their sex: 'pilots who happen to be female').

Table 2.1 gives examples of various gender–sex correlations in MG nouns referring to persons.

TABLE 2.1

		Gender	Sex
ὁ ἄντρας	'man'	masc.	male
ἡ προσωπικότητα	'personality'	fem.	either
ὁ/ἡ πρόεδρος	'president'	common	either
ὁ ποιητής	} 'poet' {	masc.	either
ἡ ποιήτρια		fem.	female
τό παιδί	'child'	neuter	either
τό ἀγόρι	'boy'	neuter	male
τό κορίτσι	'girl'	neuter	female

2.1.2 THE GENDER OF NOUNS

Although gender in MG usually corresponds with the sex of animate referents, it is assigned fairly arbitrarily, more often than not as the result of an historical accident (e.g. the gender of the word in AG, or in its donor language in the case of a loanword). Gender does not inhere in a given word (or, more precisely, in a given lexeme: see Lyons 1968: 197): there are nouns, for instance, which alter their gender from singular to plural (4.5.1.3), and gender is often changed through the addition of some derivational suffix, such as a diminutive or augmentative ending (4.6.1). Some words are found with two different genders and two sets of inflections, e.g. ὁ σωλήνας 'pipe, tube' (the standard form, which is masculine) and ἡ σωλήνα (a less frequent feminine form): this is perhaps partly because the nominative plural, which is the same for both forms, (οἱ σωλῆνες) does not indicate its gender. Thus gender is neither constant within a word, nor is it fixed in relation to the referent (e.g. the standard πετσέτα (fem.) 'towel; napkin', and the dialectal προσόψι (neuter) 'towel'). A symptom of this is that mistakes are sometimes made in gender, especially in the plural of feminine nouns in -ος (e.g. one finds infrequently used nouns such as παράμετροι 'parameters' or πυραυλάκατοι 'missile ships', both strictly feminine, used with masculine adjectives, even though the same speakers might use feminine adjectives with the same words in the singular). There is certainly much truth in the statement that 'morphologically, a noun in Demotic Greek is masculine, feminine or neuter for no other reason

[than] that it occurs with a definite set of inflectional morphemes and not another set' (Sotiropoulos 1972: 37); but one has to make an exception for feminines in -ος.

Nevertheless, male humans are normally referred to by masculine nouns, and females by feminines (with the provisos noted above, 2.1.1), even though a woman may be a καλός ἄνθρωπος 'nice person' or a καλλιτεχνικός τύπος 'artistic type' (in which both nouns and adjectives, and articles if used are masculine), a man may be an ὀρντιπάντσα (fem.) '(mil.) batman' or μιά προσωπικότητα (fem.) 'a personality', e.g.

(1) ὁ Χρῆστος γίνεται μιά προσωπικότητα πού θέλει νά σταθεῖ στά πόδια της 'Christos [name of a child] is becoming a personality who wants to stand on [his] own feet',

in which the possessive pronoun της is feminine, in agreement with προσωπικότητα: usually, pronominal gender in MG is syntactically, not semantically based. It is perhaps because Greeks do not expect a strict correlation between gender and sex that the burgeoning women's movement seems to be making little or no effort to alter the language, unlike its counterparts in English-speaking countries.

It is possible to make a few statements about general principles underlying the semantic aspect of the assignment of gender to nouns. Most abstract concepts are referred to by feminine nouns; so much so that if a speaker hesitates while searching for the suitable abstract noun, (s)he will invariably utter a feminine article before (s)he has found the right noun. The fact that most abstract nouns are feminine has made it easy for Greek poets to personify abstract concepts, apostrophizing them as if they were idealized women: and, even in everyday life, the phrase θέλω τήν 'Ελευθερία may mean 'I want Liberty' or 'I want [a woman called] Eleftheria'! There is a tendency for names of fruit-trees to be feminine, while their fruit is neuter (ἡ μηλιά 'apple-tree', τό μῆλο 'apple'), suggesting that the feminine may have connotations of fecundity. Names of rivers are masculine, historically because ποταμός 'river' is masculine, but also no doubt because their flow into the sea (θάλασσα, feminine) has masculine connotations. When a speaker does not know the gender of an inanimate object, (s)he will refer to it in the neuter (e.g. τί εἶναι αὐτό; 'what's that?'); the neuter of numerals is also used when counting (i.e. when the numerals are not adjectival: e.g. ἡ σελίδα τρία 'page (fem.) three (neuter)', but τρεῖς σελίδες 'three (fem.) pages (fem.)'). The neuter is also used for quoting words in the metalanguage (e.g. τό λέξη 'the word "word"', cf. ἡ λέξη 'the word'), and for titles of literary works, etc., which do not consist simply of noun phrases (e.g. τό "Περιμένοντας τόν Γκοντό" ' "Waiting for Godot" ').

Names of animals vary according to whether they have a single form for both sexes, two separate forms (one of them unmarked for sex, the other marked), or three forms (one unmarked for sex, the other two marked). The last usually refer to animals which are familiar in the home or the field, such as γαϊδούρι (neuter) 'donkey' (sex unspecified), γάιδαρος (masc.) 'male donkey', γαϊδούρα (fem.) 'she-donkey'; πρόβατο (neuter) 'sheep' (neutral), κριάρι (neuter) 'ram', προβατίνα (fem.) 'ewe' (together with ἀρνί (neuter) 'lamb'). Two-term appellations also refer to familiar animals: ἄλογο (neuter) 'horse' (neutral), φοράδα (fem.) 'mare' (together with πουλάρι (neuter) 'foal': 'stallion' is βαρβάτο ἄλογο literally 'uncastrated horse'); γάτα (fem.) 'cat' (female or neutral), γάτος (masc.) 'tom-cat'. Other animals have a single term, such as ἀλεπού (fem.) 'fox' and ἐλέφαντας (masc.) 'elephant'. In cases where sex needs to be specified, the word can be preceded by the adjectives ἀρσενικός 'male' or θηλυκός 'female', which follow the gender of the noun, not the sex of the animal. Some creatures have words in two forms and two genders, which do not refer to sex, e.g. τζιτζίκι (neuter) or τζίτζικας (masc.) 'cicada' and κοτσύφι (neuter) or κότσυφας (masc.) 'blackbird': the masculine version is normally used only in the singular, and perhaps shows a personifying familiarity on the speaker's part.

Names of boats are conventionally used indeclinably with the neuter article (ἦρθε τό Ἕλλη; 'has the *Elli* arrived?', εἶναι ὁ καπετάνιος τοῦ Κρήτη 'he's the captain of the *Kriti* (Crete)', whereas both names are feminine when not applied to boats), although boats with familiar masculine or feminine names are often affectionately personified (νά ἡ Ἕλλη! 'there's the *Elli*!', which in other contexts could mean 'there's Elli [woman's name]!'). Similar to the neuter with names of boats (the neuter noun πλοῖο 'ship' being presumably understood) is the use of the feminine article with names of companies, the name itself being indeclinable and the noun ἐταιρεία 'company' being understood (ὁ διευθυντής τῆς Πετρόλα 'the managing director of Petrola', ἡ Παπαστράτος '(the) Papastratos [company]', ἡ Ἰντεάλ Στάνταρντ 'Ideal Standard').

Names of makes generally follow the gender of the word for the product concerned: μιά (fem.) ὀλιβέτι 'an Olivetti' (sc. γραφομηχανή (fem.) 'typewriter'), μιά (fem.) πολαρόωτ 'a Polaroid' (sc. φωτογραφική μηχανή (fem.) 'camera'), but ὁ (masc.) *Ronson* 'the Ronson' (sc.

ἀναπτήρας (masc.) 'cigarette lighter'). With makes of cars and motor-cycles, the gender seems to bear some relation to the size of the engine: larger models tend to be assigned feminine gender (compare the pre-ponderance of feminine suffixes in augmentatives, 4.6.1), while smaller ones are neuter. Here the fact that αὐτοκίνητο 'car' is neuter and μοτο-συκλέτα 'motorcycle' is feminine has no bearing (but cf. κούρσα (fem.) '(de luxe) car'): ἡ Ρόλς-Ρόυς 'Rolls-Royce', ἡ Μερσεντές 'Mercedes [-Benz]', and ἡ BMW (pronounced beemvé) 'BMW (car or motorbike)' are feminine, but τό Φίατ 'Fiat', τό ντεσεβό '[Citroën] 2CV', and τό Χόντα 'Honda' are neuter. There are, however, exceptions, especially where a small machine has a name which resembles a Greek feminine (e.g. ἡ βέσπα (feminine) 'Vespa', by analogy with Greek feminines in -a).

There has been a marked tendency over the past decades for Greek to borrow large numbers of nouns from foreign languages (particularly French and English) without providing them with Greek inflectional suffixes and therefore without their gender being predictable from their endings. Nevertheless, every noun in MG must have gender, and the distribution of indeclinable loanwords among the gender categories is a complex matter. Nouns referring to humans usually follow in gender the sex of the referent (ὁ or ἡ στάρ (masc. or fem.) 'star (actor or actress)'), but not always (τό μανεκέν (neuter) 'fashion model' < F mannequin (masc.)). Words which are feminine in French usually remain feminine in Greek, while French masculines (and English nouns) referring to non-humans generally become neuter: ἡ πλάζ (fem.) < F plage (fem.); τό καμουφλάζ (neuter) < F camouflage (masc.). With some words, however, an analogical process relating them with exist-ing Greek words has given them a different gender in Greek from that which they possessed in French: thus argot (masc.) became ἡ ἀργκό (fem.) 'slang' under the influence of γλώσσα (fem.) 'tongue; language', while sac de voyage (masc.) became ἡ σάκ-βουαγιάζ (fem.) 'travelling bag', by analogy with βαλίτσα (fem.) 'suitcase' or τσάντα (fem.) '(hand-)bag'. In other cases a change of gender is perhaps due to the word having been brought into common use by people who did not know French well, but who simply urgently needed a word for an object (e.g. τό ντουί (neuter) 'light socket' < F douille (fem.)). Analogy with Greek words is sometimes used in titles, such as οἱ Κυρια-κάτικοι Τάιμς (masc. pl.) 'The Sunday Times', by analogy with οἱ χρόνοι or οἱ καιροί 'times', both masculine, although Le Monde (masc.) becomes ἡ Μόντ (fem.) in Greek, by analogy with ἐφημερίδα (fem.) 'newspaper'.

Many indeclinable names of foreign countries and towns are feminine, either because they end in -a or because of the existence of feminine nouns such as χώρα 'country' and πόλη 'town': thus ἡ Ναμίμπια (indecl.) 'Namibia', ἡ Λυών 'Lyon', ἡ Οὐάσιγκτον 'Washington': cf. ὁ Οὐάσιγκτον (masc.) '[George] Washington'. Names of foreign football teams tend to be feminine (cf. ὁμάδα (fem.) 'team'), even if the same name is used as a neuter to refer to their place of origin: ἡ Λίβερπουλ (fem.) 'Liverpool (team)', but τό Λίβερπουλ (neuter) 'Liverpool (town)'.

As to the number of MG nouns in each gender, the neuter is the most frequent, followed by the feminine, then the masculine. Mirambel (1959: 84) gives the following figures for gender out of a random sample of about 600 nouns: neuter 240, feminine 195, masculine 149; if one takes a count in various texts the gap between feminine and neuter sometimes narrows, but the masculine always lags well behind. This disparity has come about partly because a large number of nouns which were masculine and feminine in AG have become neuter after having had neuter diminutive suffixes added to them and then having their diminutive force removed. In the modern language, where in colloquial speech diminutives are frequent, diminutive suffixes tend to be neuter and feminine rather than masculine, which tends to reduce the incidence of masculine nouns in everyday usage. In a text which employs many abstract nouns, the proportion of feminines will rise at the expense of neuters and masculines. As has been seen, more new loanwords are assigned to the neuter than to the other genders (very few except those referring to men are masculine at all); and this serves to reinforce a tendency, present in the language for several centuries, to increase the proportion of neuters to the other genders.

2.1.3 GENDER CONCORD

Articles, pronouns, and adjectives agree in gender and number with the nouns to which they refer rather than with their referent, as we have seen:

(1) ἡ Μαρία εἶναι καλός ἄνθρωπος 'Mary is a nice (masc.) person (masc.)';

(2) ὁ ᾽Ελύτης εἶναι μιά ἀπό τίς ἐπιβλητικότερες φυσιογνωμίες τῆς σύγχρονης ἑλληνικῆς ποίησης 'Elytis is one (fem.) of the most imposing (fem.) figures (fem.) in contemporary Greek poetry.'

On the rare occasions when a lack of gender agreement is found, the disparity can usually be explained by the fact that although a neuter noun has been used to refer to a human, the speaker feels it more natural to switch to the masculine or feminine when employing an adjective to qualify that noun (although this can happen only if the adjective is a postmodifier):

(3) ἀπό τά παιδιά πού γνώρισες, πόσοι εἶναι ἔτοιμοι νά πάρουν ναρκωτικά; 'of the kids (neuter) that you've met, how many (masc.) are prepared (masc.) to take drugs?';

(4) τό ξενοδοχεῖο εἶχε πολλά γκαρσόνια ξένους 'the hotel had many (neuter) foreign (masc.) waiters (neuter)' (in which 'foreign' comes after the noun).

In (3) the subject of conversation was in fact not children (for whom the neuter might have been natural throughout) but young adults; in (4), the neuter ξένα 'foreign' might have been ambiguous (it could have meant 'from other hotels'), and in addition the masculine ξένος is so frequently used as a noun ('foreigner') that the sentence could be rendered, 'the hotel had many waiters who were foreigners'.

When an adjective (or some other word inflected for gender) refers to two or more nouns of differing genders, there is some variety in usage. Generally, if the nouns refer to humans, the adjective will be masculine. In other cases, the adjective might agree with the nearest noun:

(5) μέ πολλή ἀνιδιοτέλεια καί ζῆλο 'with great (fem. sing.) disinterestedness (fem.) and zeal (masc.)';

(6) μέ ἀλόγιστο θυμό καί λύσσα 'with incalculable (masc. sing.) anger (masc.) and rage (fem.)';

or it might be put into the neuter plural: the latter phenomenon is especially found where the adjective is separated from the nouns by a copula (i.e. where the adjective is used predicatively rather than attributively), and often occurs even when both nouns are feminine:

(7) τό περιβάλλον καί ὁ τρόπος πού δούλεψε ἦταν ἰδανικά 'the environment (neuter) and the way (masc.) [in] which he worked were ideal (neuter pl.)';

(8) οἱ αἰσθητικές ἀναζητήσεις κι ἡ ἐπεξεργασία τοῦ στίχου εἶναι καθορισμένα ἀπ' τήν ποίηση τῆς ἐποχῆς του 'the aesthetic aspirations (fem. pl.) and the elaboration (fem.) of the verse are determined (neuter pl.) by the poetry of his time.'

As these examples suggest, the kind of construction in which one adjective qualifies two nouns belongs more to literary styles than to colloquial speech.

2.2   CASE (SEE ALSO APPENDIX I)

Almost all nouns, adjectives, and pronouns, and certain numerals, are inflected for case in MG. There are said to be four cases: nominative, vocative, accusative and genitive. That statement means that (at least in certain words) each of these cases may be realized as a separate form. In practice, this occurs only with one class of nouns (non-neuters in *-os*, see Class 2A, 4.1.2) and the adjectives and pronouns that decline like them, and then only in the singular. Most nouns have only two or three separate forms in each of the two numbers; feminines in *-a* have a single form for the nominative, vocative, and accusative plural, and some cannot be used in the genitive plural at all; while some nouns lack both genitives. Nevertheless, since each of the four cases may be realized as a separate form, it is sensible to state whether, for example, παιδί 'child' (nom./voc./acc. sing.) is syntactically nominative, vocative, or accusative in a given context.

The nominative and accusative are by far the most frequently used cases, the genitive being used perhaps less than half as frequently as either of these. The vocative is the least frequently used case, being usable only in a limited number of circumstances. There is wide variety in the use of the genitives, according to speaker, linguistic context, and the type of word concerned. While the genitive is extremely common in clitic personal pronouns, it is used in nouns with human referents more than in others, and in the singular more often than in the plural. It tends to be found more frequently in discourse of a more complicated kind than it is in colloquial speech. Less-educated speakers tend to avoid the genitive of nouns as much as possible, and some will hardly ever use the genitive at all except when referring to humans (in fact, in some dialects this case does not exist in the plural). Many of the uses of the genitive in SMG today have been influenced by Western European languages and by *katharevousa*.

2.2.1   THE NOMINATIVE

The nominative is usually considered to be the basic case, and nouns (including proper nouns), adjectives, pronouns, and numerals appear in dictionaries in the nominative singular (if they have a singular), and hence they are talked about in this case (e.g. ἡ λέξη ἄνϑρωπος 'the

word "man" ', τό φαινόμενο πόλεμος 'the phenomenon [of] war', τό
χωριό Περαχώρα 'the village [of] Perachora', τό ξενοδοχεῖο Ἑλλάς
'Hotel Hellas', even if the preceding word is in a case other than the
nominative). The nominative is also used in most circumstances where
the sentence has no verb, such as exclamations, but not including invo-
cations (τί βλάκας! 'what a fool!', νά ἡ Μαρία! 'there's Mary!'), but also
in some exclamations which contain verbs: εἶδες ὁ Γιῶργος! 'there!
I told you what would happen to George' (lit. 'did you see George
(nom.)?'), or κοίτα ἡ τύχη της! 'how's that for luck!' (lit. 'look at her
luck (nom.)').

Syntactically, the nominative is used for the subjects of verbs and
for words which refer to the existential subject in the same clause, i.e.
subject complements and words in apposition to the subject:

(1) ὁ Γιάννης εἶναι γιατρός 'John (nom.) is [a] doctor (nom.)';
(2) ὁ Κώστας ἔγινε σπουδαῖος δικηγόρος 'Kostas (nom.) became
    [an] excellent (nom.) lawyer (nom.)';
(3) ἦρθε ἡ φίλη μου ἡ Νίκη 'my friend (nom.) Niki (nom.) came/
    has come'.

Note also the following uses of the nominative after prepositions
(which are normally followed by the accusative: see 6.2), in circumstances where the noun or adjective after the preposition is really
a subject complement:

(4) ἀπό φτωχός πού ἦταν ἔγινε ὁ πλουσιότερος Ἕλληνας ἐφο-
    πλιστής 'from being poor [lit. 'from poor (nom.) that he was']
    he became the richest Greek shipowner';
(5) πάει γιά βουλευτής '(s)he's standing for parliament' (lit. '(s)he's
    going for Member of Parliament (nom.)');
(6) ἦρθαν πάνω ἀπό διακόσιοι ἄνθρωποι 'more than two hundred
    (nom.) people came' (the accusative would also be acceptable
    here);
(7) ὡς κι ὁ Γιάννης ἦρθε στό πάρτυ 'even John came to the party'
    (lit. 'until and John (nom.) came . . .').

The nominative may also be used after ἀπό in its distributive sense,
where the noun is the subject:

(8) δεξιά κι ἀριστερά ὑπάρχει ἀπό ἕνας τοῖχος 'there's a wall on
    either side' (lit. 'right and left exists from one (nom.) wall
    (nom.)').

2.2.2 THE VOCATIVE

The MG vocative is used to call or address someone or something. It is used

(a) on its own, or preceded by ἔ, to call someone's attention: Πέτρο! 'Peter!', ἔ, χοντρέ! 'hey, fat [man]!', κύριε! 'sir!';

(b) at the beginning, middle, or end of a clause, to show affection or respect (or contempt) for the person addressed: τί θέλεις, χρυσέ μου; 'what do you want, my darling? [lit. 'my golden (masc. voc. sing.)']'), ἐπιτρέψτε μου νά διαφωνήσω μαζί σας, κύριε καθηγητά 'permit me to disagree with you, (Mr) professor', τί χαζεύεις, ρέ βλάκα; 'what are you gawping at, you fool?' (ρέ, or βρέ, is an unceremonious term of exclamation or address, used on its own or in front of a noun, adjective, or pronoun: cf. ρέ σύ! 'hey you!');

(c) on its own, when abusing someone in an exclamation: δολοφόνε! 'murderer!', ἠλίθιε! 'idiot'.

As may be seen from some of the examples, the vocative is regularly used with the second person, while the other cases have no particular connection with any person.

Morphologically, the vocative has a separate form from the other cases only in the singular of Class 2A nouns and adjectives; and in these and other masculine nouns the nominative is often used for the vocative, especially by less-educated speakers or in circumstances such as roll-calling.

2.2.3 THE ACCUSATIVE

Despite what has been said about the nominative at the beginning of 2.2.1, it could be argued with some justification that in MG the accusative is the prime (unmarked) case. There is only one class of nouns (2A) in which the accusative has a different form from both the nominative and the genitive. With the exception of this class, the accusative singular has the same form as either the nominative (feminines and neuters) or the genitive (masculines), while in the plural the accusative of all genders is the same as the nominative. Furthermore, the accusative singular of *all* masculine and feminine nouns (and most neuters) ends in a vowel, being formed by deleting the final -s of either the nominative (masculines) or the genitive (feminines). Lastly (again with the exception of Class 2A), the accusative singular and plural is identical to the vocative: thus, in more formal terms, the singular ending without -s marks the form as non-nominative for masculines and non-genitive for feminines. (Note also, in respect of gender, that masculine-singular nouns stand out in MG from both feminines (except the few in 2A) and neuters in that they alone display a morphological distinction according to whether they function as subject or as object.)

The accusative in MG is used for the direct objects of almost all transitive verbs and of most prepositions. In fact, traditional demotic had no verbs or prepositions whose direct objects were not in the accusative, but *katharevousa* influence has led to the objects of certain words being in the genitive. (In northern Greece the indirect object of a verb regularly appears in the accusative.)

The accusative is used after certain other parts of speech in addition to verbs and prepositions. The adjectives γεμάτος 'full (of)' and ὅλος 'all' can be followed by a noun in the accusative, although the former is sometimes used with the preposition μέ 'with' or ἀπό 'from':

(1) τό πρόσωπό του ἦταν γεμάτο σπυριά 'his face was covered [in] spots (acc.)';

(2) εἶμαι ὅλος αὐτιά 'I'm all ears (acc.).'

The accusative is also used after certain nouns, adverbs, and particles, especially in exclamations: e.g. the noun ἀνάθεμα 'curse' (often in the form πανάθεμα < πού ἀνάθεμα: lit. 'who curse') after a clause in which the 'object' of this word has already been referred to:

(3) πού 'σαι, πανάθεμά σε; 'where are you, damn you?';

and the noun κρίμα(ς) 'pity, shame':

(4) κρίμα(ς) τά λεφτά πού ξοδέψαμε! 'all that money paid out for nothing!' (lit. 'pity (noun) the money (acc.) which we spent').

The exclamatory word καλῶς (originally the adverb 'well') is used with the accusative of a clitic pronoun or a noun as a familiar expression of greeting or welcome (καλῶς τον 'hello, welcome', lit. 'well him (acc.)'; καλῶς τά παιδιά 'hello, lads', lit. 'well the children (acc.)'). The particles νά (sometimes) and μά (always) are followed by the accusative; the former (a deictic particle which has no etymological connection with the subjunctive marker νά, for which see 9.4.2 ff.) is followed by a clitic pronoun or noun (νά με 'here I am', νά τή Μαρία 'there's Mary'), although it is also sometimes found with a nominative or even a combination of the two cases (νά με τώρα μόνος 'here I am now alone', in which the pronoun is accusative but the adjective nominative); μά is followed only by a noun phrase containing a definite article + noun, and is normally used to invoke divine beings as witness to the truth of a statement (μά τό Θεό 'by God' or 'as God's my witness').

Apart from the instances in which the accusative is conditioned by the presence of another word in a phrase or clause, its most common use is probably its adverbial function in expressions of time, place, and measurement. Duration (time) and distance (place) are expressed in the same way:

$$
(5) \quad \text{περπατήσαμε}
\begin{cases}
τρεῖς ὦρες \\
τρία χιλιόμετρα \\
\text{[for] three hours (acc.)'} \\
\text{three kilometres (acc.)'.}
\end{cases}
$$
'we walked'

Nevertheless, whereas point in place is expressed by σέ 'in' + accusative, point in time is most often expressed by a bare accusative: νύχτα 'at night', τή νύχτα 'during the night' (but with σέ for clock-time: στίς ὀχτώμιση 'at half past eight', lit. 'at-the eight-half'), τή Δευτέρα 'on Monday', τήν πρώτη Σεπτεμβρίου 'on the first of September' (but σέ + plural of the cardinal for any date above 'first': στίς δεκαπέντε Αὐγούστου 'on the (fem. pl.) fifteen[th] of August'), τήν περασμένη ἑβδομάδα 'last week', τό Μάρτιο 'in March', τό 1983 'in 1983', τόν περισσότερο χρόνο 'most of the time/year', τό Πάσχα 'at Easter', τήν προπολεμική ἐποχή 'in the pre-war period', τόν εἰκοστό αἰώνα 'in the twentieth century', δυό φορές 'twice'.

Expressions of measurement are various. Here more colloquial usage prefers the accusative, while in some instances more formal styles employ the genitive. The various ways of saying, 'this house is ten metres high' are: αὐτό τό σπίτι ἔχει δέκα μέτρα ὕψος (lit. 'this house has ten metres (acc.) height (acc.)') or αὐτό τό σπίτι εἶναι δέκα μέτρα ψηλό (which corresponds exactly to the English); in both constructions the word order can be altered to ὕψος δέκα μέτρα or ψηλό δέκα μέτρα respectively. In more formal style, the rendering would be: . . . ἔχει ὕψος δέκα μέτρων (lit. '. . . has height (acc.) of ten metres (gen.)').

Other nouns may stand instead of those denoting dimension (ἦταν δέκα χιλιόμετρα ποδαρόδρομος 'it was ten kilometres (acc.) footslogging (nom.)'). Expressions of time may take a similar form:

(6) καταδικάστηκε σέ δέκα χρόνια κάθειρξη 'he was sentenced to ten years (acc.) imprisonment (acc.)';

(or, more formally, σέ δέκα χρόνων κάθειρξη: lit. 'to ten years' (gen.)

imprisonment'). Note that such expressions as (6) are grammatically the converse of apparently similar ones examined below (2.2.5), in which more formal language uses the genitive not for the numeral but for the other term.

A phrase such as 'a table two metres wide' can be ἕνα τραπέζι δυό μέτρα φαρδύ (which corresponds precisely to the English, with δυό μέτρα in the accusative), in which φαρδύ can be replaced by τό φάρδος (lit. 'the breadth'), in the nominative or accusative. Again, the word order may be different, the last word(s) changing places with δυό μέτρα. In more official styles, two genitives are used: ἕνα τραπέζι πλάτους δύο μέτρων (lit. 'a table of-width (gen.) of two metres (gen.)': τό πλάτος is more formal than τό φάρδος). Similar to such constructions are those expressing measure of comparison with comparative adjectives (ἡ Χριστίνα εἶναι ἕνα χρόνο μεγαλύτερη ἀπό τόν Παῦλο 'Christine is one year (acc.) older than Paul') or with adverbs of place or time (place: ἕνα χιλιόμετρο μακριά 'a kilometre (acc.) away', δυό δρόμους παρακάτω 'two streets (acc.) further down'; time: ἕνα χρόνο μετά 'a year (acc.) later').

To complete this account of the accusative in expressions of measurement, its distributive meaning of 'per' should be noted: δυό δραχμές τό κιλό 'two drachmas per kilo (acc.)', τρεῖς φορές τήν ἡμέρα 'three times a day (acc.)'.

Finally, there are many assorted idiomatic uses of the accusative. There are certain reduplicated expressions of the accusative in adverbial use: a noun in the accusative repeated with a definite article in the middle (χρόνο τό χρόνο 'year by year': lit. 'year (acc.) the year (acc.)'), or without the article, expressing the idea of 'along' (γιαλό-γιαλό 'along the shore'). There are expressions in which some word is presumably understood, such as λόγο τιμῆς '[on my] word of honour', with perhaps μά 'by' understood; or ὁ Γιάννης τό βιολί του or τό χαβά του 'John keeps harping on the same old tune' (lit. 'John his violin (acc.)' or 'his tune (acc.)'), in which the verb παίζει 'plays' is presumably understood. There are also the invariable expressions ἕνα σωρό 'a lot' (lit. 'a pile (acc.)'), as in ἦρθαν ἕνα σωρό γυναῖκες 'a lot of women came', and ἕνα-δυό or καναδυό (the latter a contracted form of κανένα δυό) 'one or two', which vary neither in case nor in gender, as in πῆγα καναδυό φορές 'I went a couple of times' (φορές is feminine).

There is also an exclamatory use of the accusative in a verbless clause (e.g. τόν καημένο τό Δημήτρη! 'poor Dimitris!'), referring either to the person addressed or to a third person. Such an exclamation, if it is abusive, is often preceded by βρέ or ρέ, in which case it can refer only to a third person (βρέ τόν πούστη! 'the bastard!').

2.2.4   THE GENITIVE

The genitive in MG normally has an inherently semantic role, while the nominative and accusative are conditioned by the syntactic context. The genitive presents more difficulties of description than do the other cases in MG. This is because (a) some words lack a genitive completely; (b) many do not have a genitive plural; (c) many less-educated speakers tend to avoid the genitive (especially in the plural) even of those nouns that are not defective; and (d) the fairly clearly circumscribed uses of the genitive in traditional demotic have been radically increased under the influence of AG and modern European languages, particularly French.

In traditional demotic, the genitive was used almost exclusively either to express possession or to realize an underlying dative or ablative. By the very nature of these uses, the genitive was normally confined to nouns, adjectives, pronouns, articles, and numerals denoting animate referents, particularly humans:

(1) τά σπίτια τῶν Τούρκων 'the houses of the Turks';
(2) ἡ γυναίκα μου 'my wife';
(3) πές τοῦ Κώστα πώς θά 'ρθω 'tell Kostas (gen.) that I'll come';
(4) νά σοῦ δώσω τίποτα πορτοκάλια; 'shall I give you some oranges?';
(5) σοῦ ἔχω φράουλες σήμερα 'I've got strawberries for you today';
(6) μοῦ πῆρες τό τουφέκι 'you've taken my gun' (lit. 'of-me you-took the gun');
(7) τοῦ 'σπασα τό κεφάλι 'I broke his head' (lit. 'of-him I-broke the head'.

In these examples, (1) and (2) show a strictly possessive use, (3)–(5) a dative (= 'to' or 'for'), (6) an ablative (= 'from') and (7) an ethic dative (which denotes the interested party in an action, i.e. the person for whose benefit or to whose disadvantage the action is carried out).

To express concepts such as 'the leg of the chair' or 'the setting of the sun' (the former a possessive but without an animate referent, the latter not a possessive at all), traditional demotic either used ἀπό with the accusative (cf. Romance de or di, originally 'from', to express the genitive), as in

(8) τό πόδι ἀπ' τήν καρέκλα (lit. 'the leg from the chair'),

or compound nouns, such as καρεκλοπόδαρο 'chair-leg' or ἡλιοβασίλεμα 'sunset'.

These uses of the genitive remain in SMG (in which, since, e.g., καρέκλα has no genitive plural, it is still necessary to say τά πόδια ἀπ' τίς καρέκλες for 'the legs of the chairs'), but have been joined by others, with the result that, in addition to its traditional uses, the genitive of nouns in MG is now used in a similar way to that in other modern European languages, not only after nouns and verbs, but after other parts of speech. Nevertheless, the genitive of clitic pronouns still has wider uses than that of nouns.

One of the chief reasons for the relative infrequency of the genitive of nouns compared with that of clitic pronouns is that the genitive of nouns, unlike other cases, can often be avoided by means of paraphrases consisting of preposition + noun, while the genitive of clitic pronouns cannot normally be readily paraphrased. There was clearly a tendency in traditional demotic for the genitive of nouns to disappear, a tendency which the influence of the learned language has definitely reversed. In our account of the genitive we shall point to the influence of the learned language and, in addition, give examples of switches from pronouns to nouns and vice versa.

2.2.4.1 The genitive with verbs

As has been said already, the prime uses of the genitive with verbs in traditional spoken Greek are in dative and ablative senses. In the former, a clitic pronoun in the genitive corresponds to a noun in the accusative preceded by σέ 'to' or γιά 'for' (that is, it expresses the indirect object):

(1a) τῆς ἔδωσα τήν ἐφημερίδα 'I gave her the newspaper';
(1b) ἔδωσα τήν ἐφημερίδα στήν Ἑλένη 'I gave the newspaper to Helen';
(2a) τοῦ ἔφτιαξε καφέ '(s)he made him [some] coffee';
(2b) ἔφτιαξε καφέ γιά τό Μιχάλη (or στό Μιχάλη) '(s)he made Michael [some] coffee.'

Nevertheless, the fact that the genitive of pronouns is used in such contexts may influence the speaker to put the noun in the genitive too:

(1c) ἔδωσα τήν ἐφημερίδα τῆς Ἑλένης (= 1b);
(2c) ἔφτιαξε καφέ τοῦ Μιχάλη (= 2b).

In fact, if a noun is used together with a genitive proclitic pronoun referring to the same referent, the use of the genitive in that noun is obligatory:

> (1d) τῆς Ἑλένης τῆς ἔδωσα τήν ἐφημερίδα (= 1b, but with emphasis either on 'gave' or on 'newspaper');
>
> (2d) τοῦ Μιχάλη τοῦ ἔφτιαξε καφέ (= 2b, but again with emphasis on either the verb or the direct object).

Since, however, there may be some ambiguity in sentences where the genitive of a noun is used without a corresponding pronoun (examples (1c) and (2c) could mean 'I gave Helen's newspaper' and 'I made some of Michael's coffee' (Kazazis 1967)), such a construction is not normally used outside colloquial speech. (It is perhaps possible to see the origin of the 'dative' genitive in MG as being precisely that the genitive indicates possession: the consequences of χάρισα τό βιβλίο τοῦ Γιάννη 'I gave the book [as a present] to John' is τό βιβλίο εἶναι τοῦ Γιάννη 'the book is John's.')

On the other hand, there are idiomatic constructions in which the genitive is mandatory because a noun cannot be used without an accompanying pronoun:

> (3) τῆς Στέλλας τῆς ἦρθε νά κλάψει 'Stella felt like crying' (lit. 'of-the Stella of-her it-came to she-cry');
>
> (4) τοῦ Γιώργου θά τοῦ εἶναι δύσκολο νά ἔρθει 'it will be difficult for George to come' (lit. 'of-the George will of-him it-is difficult . . .').

Certain constructions using what might be termed the *ethic genitive* can have only pronouns as indirect objects:

> (5) φίλησέ μου τήν Καίτη 'give my love to Katy' (lit. 'kiss of-me the Katy');
>
> (6) τί μοῦ γίνεσαι; 'how are you?' (lit. 'what of-me you-become');

in (6) the μοῦ is optional, and adds an element of affection for the person addressed.

A clitic pronoun in the genitive in ablative use corresponds to a noun preceded by ἀπό 'from':

> (7a) τοῦ κρύψαμε τό μυστικό 'we hid the secret from him';
>
> (7b) κρύψαμε τό μυστικό ἀπό τό δάσκαλό μας 'we hid the secret from our teacher.'

Again, however, if a pronoun is used as well as the noun, the genitive must be used:

(7c) *τοῦ κρύψαμε τό μυστικό τοῦ δασκάλου μας* (= 7b, with emphasis on the verb, or—less likely—on the direct object).

There are instances in which a genitive used with a verb could be taken
as either dative or ablative depending on the extra-linguistic context: thus,

(8) *θά σοῦ πάρω ἕνα μπουκάλι κρασί*

might mean 'I shall get a bottle of wine for you' if I am setting off for
the shops, but 'I shall take a bottle of wine from you' if I am rum-
maging through your larder.

There are circumstances in which the genitive of a pronoun used as
an ethic dative actually denotes possession: these are those in which the
pronoun could be transferred to the subject or object of the verb without changing the meaning of the clause (cf. also examples (6) and (7)
in 2.2.4):

(9a) *μοῦ κόπηκε ἡ ἀναπνοή* 'my breath was taken away' (lit. 'of-
me was-cut the breath');
(9b) *κόπηκε ἡ ἀναπνοή μου* (subject);
(10a) *τοῦ βγάλανε τό πουκάμισο* 'they took off his shirt' (lit. 'of-
him they-took-off the shirt');
(10b) *βγάλανε τό πουκάμισό του* (object).

In (10a) the genitive of the pronoun could appear twice: both with the
verb and after the direct object.

There are in addition certain verbs, originally introduced through
katharevousa, which may take a genitive, although their use with clitic
pronouns is not frequent. Nowadays, however, there is a tendency to
replace the genitive with *ἀπό* or *σέ* + accusative. Thus in the following
examples,

(11) *τῆς δεξιώσεως προηγήθηκε συνδιάσκεψη μεταξύ τῶν ἡγετῶν*
'the reception was preceded by a conference among the
leaders' (lit. 'of-the reception preceded conference . . .': the
verb *προηγοῦμαι* is deponent), and
(12) *τό συνέδριο, τοῦ ὁποίου προεδρεύει ὁ κ. Φλῶρος, γίνεται στό
Χίλτον* 'the conference, which is chaired by Mr Floros, is
taking place at the Hilton' (lit. 'the conference, of-the which
chairs the Mr Floros . . .'),

the genitives may be replaced by *ἀπό τή δεξίωση* and *στό ὁποῖο* respectively.

There are also certain expressions in which εἶμαι 'I am' is followed by a noun in the genitive, many of which again originated in *katharevousa*:

(13)　αὐτό τό θέμα δέν εἶναι τῆς δικαιοδοσίας μου 'this subject is not within [lit. 'of'] my jurisdiction';

(14)　δέν εἶναι τῆς ὥρας νά συζητήσουμε γι' αὐτό τό ζήτημα 'it is not the time [lit. 'of-the hour'] (for us) to discuss this matter.'

2.2.4.2　The genitive governed by nouns

From being used almost exclusively of possession in traditional demotic, the genitive governed by nouns has come to be used in SMG for a wide range of figurative meanings which are difficult to categorize. We shall attempt to deal with the chief senses here, but our survey will by no means be complete. One general observation which should be made is that a pronoun can be substituted for a noun in the genitive only in uses (a), (b), and, less often, (c) below, but not in the other uses.

(a) *Possession*. Still the most frequent use of the genitive after nouns is the *adnominal possessive*: the referent of the word in the genitive (almost always animate) 'possesses' the referent of the other word (almost always a person or thing), the whole phrase being normally susceptible of being paraphrased by a more or less equivalent phrase using a relative clause containing the verb ἔχω 'I have' (in contrast to the situation in other uses of the genitive). Thus:

(1a)　τό ρολόι μου 'my watch';

(1b)　τό ρολόι πού ἔχω 'the watch which I have';

(2a)　οἱ ἐχθροί τῆς Ἑλλάδας 'the enemies of Greece';

(2b)　οἱ ἐχθροί πού ἔχει ἡ Ἑλλάδα 'the enemies which Greece has'.

A figurative adnominal possessive is less common in MG than in English; thus, the sentence 'the significance of this crisis for the history of Greece' will normally be rendered,

(3)　ἡ σημασία πού ἔχει αὐτή ἡ κρίση γιά τήν ἱστορία τῆς Ἑλλάδας 'the significance which this crisis has . . .'.

The possessive μου 'my' is also used with the vocative to indicate affection or familiarity: Βασίλη μου 'my [dear] Basil', κύριε Δημητράκο μου 'my [dear] Mr Dimitrakos'.

(b) *Subjective genitive*. Here the underlying structure of the phrase containing the genitive may be said to consist of subject + (usually intransitive) verb, the former corresponding to the word in the genitive in the surface structure, the latter to the noun which governs it (and which always denotes a process). Thus the phrase,

(4a) τό σφύριγμα τοῦ τραίνου 'the whistling of the train',

is connected with the phrase,

(4b) τό τραῖνο σφυρίζει 'the train whistles';

while the version,

(4c) ?τό σφύριγμα πού ἔχει τό τραῖνο 'the whistling which the train has',

would make sense only in limited circumstances; τό σφύριγμά του 'its whistling' is also perfectly acceptable.

(c) *Objective genitive.* This is the converse of (b): the underlying structure may be said to consist of transitive verb + direct object, the former corresponding to the head noun, the latter to the word in the genitive. The head noun again denotes a process. Thus,

(5a) ἡ δημιουργία αὐτῆς τῆς κατάστασης 'the creation of this situation',

is connected with the phrase,

(5b) δημιούργησαν αὐτή τήν κατάσταση 'they created this situation' (or, alternatively, δημιουργήθηκε αὐτή ἡ κατάσταση 'this situation was created').

The use of the pronoun, in ἡ δημιουργία της, would be acceptable, but not the version,

(5c) *ἡ δημιουργία πού ἔχει αὐτή ἡ κατάσταση 'the situation which this situation has'.

Often a genitive is ambiguous, in that it might be interpreted as being either subjective or objective. Thus,

(6a) ἡ ὑποστήριξη τῆς οἰκογένειάς του 'the support of his family',

might be subjective (connected with

(6b) (αὐτός) ὑποστηρίζει τήν οἰκογένειά του 'he supports his family'),

or objective (connected with

(6c) ἡ οἰκογένειά του τόν ὑποστηρίζει 'his family supports him');

although in the absence of evidence to the contrary the genitive will normally be interpreted as objective since the verb ὑποστηρίζω is transitive. Also note:

(7) χωρίς τήν ὑποστήριξή του ἀπό τήν οἰκογένειά του 'without-the support of his family' (lit. 'without his support by/from his family': the possessive pronoun after ὑποστήριξη could be replaced by a noun in the genitive).

This is one of the arguments put forward by purist demoticists who argue against the over-use of abstract nouns and of genitives (see 11.1.2.2): example (6a) can be rendered unambiguous if one says,

(6bi) ἡ ὑποστήριξη πού δίνει στήν οἰκογένειά του 'the support which he gives to his family', or

(6ci) ἡ ὑποστήριξη πού τοῦ δίνει ἡ οἰκογένειά του 'the support which his family gives him'.

It is even possible to have a subjective and an objective genitive in the same clause, although the former must be a pronoun and the latter a noun:

(8a) ἡ γνώση του τῆς ξένης γλώσσας 'his knowledge of the foreign language'; cf.

(8b) (αὐτός) ξέρει τήν ξένη γλώσσα 'he knows the foreign language'; but not

(8c) *ἡ γνώση τοῦ Νίκου τῆς ξένης γλώσσας 'Nick's knowledge of the foreign language'.

(d) *Genitive of place or time.* The genitive in MG is often used to express place or time at or from. Thus:

(9) ἡ ναυμαχία τῆς Ναυπάκτου 'the (sea-)battle of Lepanto' (= the battle which took place *at* Lepanto);

(10) οἱ Γάλλοι τοῦ δέκατου ἔνατου αἰώνα 'the French of the nineteenth century' (= those who lived *in* the nineteenth century);

(11) ἐλιές Καλαμάτας 'Kalamata olives' (= olives *from* Kalamata');

(12) σαρδέλες τοῦ κουτιοῦ 'tinned sardines' (lit. 'sardines of-the box').

In these cases the nouns in the genitive cannot be replaced by pronouns: οἱ ἐλιές της would mean 'its [Kalamata's] olives' (i.e. possession). There is, however, a genitive of origin in which a pronoun can be used:

(13) ἕνα γράμμα τοῦ πατέρα μου 'a letter of/from my father' (cf. ἕνα γράμμα του 'one of his letters' or 'a letter from him');

(14) ποιήματα τοῦ Σεφέρη 'poems of/by Seferis' (cf. ποιήματά του 'poems of his' or 'poems by him').

In both these examples, either possession or origin may be implied.

(e) *Genitive of quality.* In phrases such as,

(15) πατέρες καλοῦ χαρακτῆρος 'fathers of good character',

which are definitely of learned origin, the underlying structure is the opposite of that which underlies phrases containing genitives of possession: here it is the referent of the head noun that possesses the quality referred to by the noun in the genitive. Many of these phrases are stereotyped, having been translated from foreign languages:

(16) ξενοδοχεῖο πολυτελείας 'de luxe hotel' (lit. 'hotel of luxury');

(17) προβλήματα αὐτοῦ τοῦ εἴδους 'problems of this kind';

(18) πολίτες δεύτερης κατηγορίας 'second-class citizens'.

Sometimes these genitives are equivalent to adjectives (e.g. πολυτελές ξενοδοχεῖο 'luxurious hotel').

A subcategory of genitives of quality consists of genitives of measurement:

(19) μιά τηλεόραση δεκεννέα ἰντσῶν 'a nineteen-inch television' (lit. 'a television of-nineteen inches');

(20) δρόμος ἐκατό μέτρων 'hundred-metres race';

(21) παιδί πέντε χρονῶν 'a five-year-old child' (lit. 'child of-five years').

As we have already seen, most genitives of measurement (but *not* those referring to the age of persons) are commonly replaced in colloquial usage by accusatives. Most genitives of quality may be detached from their head-nouns to become complements of verbs:

(15a) αὐτός ὁ ἄνθρωπος εἶναι καλοῦ χαρακτῆρος 'this man is of good character';

(16a) τό ξενοδοχεῖο πού μείναμε δέν ἦταν πολυτελείας 'the hotel we stayed at wasn't de luxe';

(19a) ἡ τηλεόρασή μας εἶναι μόνο δεκαεννέα ἰντσῶν 'our television is only [a] nineteen-inch [one]';

(21a) ὁ γιός μου εἶναι πέντε χρονῶν 'my son is five years old.'

(f) *Genitive of cause or purpose.* Examples of such uses are:

(22) ὁ καημός τοῦ χωρισμοῦ 'the sadness of parting' (= γιά τό χωρισμό 'because of parting');

(23) ἕνα ποτήρι τοῦ κρασιοῦ 'a wine-glass' (lit. 'a glass of-the wine', = γιά τό κρασί 'for wine'; cf. ἕνα ποτήρι κρασί 'a glass [of] wine').

(g) *Genitive of content and partitive genitive.* Other uses of the genitive include that of content, in which the noun in the genitive denotes that which the referent of the first noun consists of; and the partitive–genitive construction, where the referent of the head word represents a portion of the referent of the genitive word. Informal usage prefers an appositional construction (see 2.2.5) or one with ἀπό.

(24) (μιά) σειρά μαθημάτων 'a series/course of lessons' (= μιά σειρά [ἀπό] μαθήματα);

(25) δυό ἑκατομμύρια δολλαρίων 'two million dollars' (lit. 'two millions of-dollars', = δυό ἑκατομμύρια δολλάρια).

2.2.4.3 *The genitive after pronouns, numerals, and adjectives*

There are various uses of the genitive after pronouns, numerals, and adjectives, according to whether (a) the word in the genitive can only be a clitic pronoun or (b) it can only be a noun. Only the former type belongs to traditional demotic.

(a) *Clitic pronouns only.* Certain pronouns, numerals, and adjectives can take a 'clarificatory genitive' (Tzartzanos 1946: 113) which specifies the person(s) or thing(s) to which the first word refers. Sometimes the pronoun in the genitive intensifies the first word, as with μόνος 'alone': μόνος μου '(all) by myself', in the double sense of 'without company' and 'without help' (in its latter sense it may be preceded by ἀπό):

(1) ἔμεινε μόνη της 'she was left [lit. 'she remained'] all alone';

(2) τό ἔκαναν [ἀπό] μόνοι τους 'they did it all by themselves';

(3) σκοτώθηκε μόνος του 'he killed *himself*' (as opposed to his being killed by anyone else).

Some words can be followed by a clitic pronoun in the genitive or by an emphatic pronoun or a noun after ἀπό:

(i) *Numerals.* Ἕνας μας 'one of us' (cf. ἕνας ἀπό μᾶς (same meaning), (ὁ) ἕνας ἀπό τούς Γερμανούς 'one of the Germans'); δυό τους 'two of them', οἱ δυό τους 'the two of them', κι οἱ δυό τους 'both of them' (cf. δυό ἀπ' αὐτούς 'two of them', δυό ἀπ' τούς ἄντρες 'two of the men').

(ii) *Pronouns and adjectives*. Κάποιος τους 'one of them' (cf. κάποιος ἀπ' αὐτούς (same meaning), κάποιος ἀπ' τούς βουλευτές 'one of the members of parliament'); κανένας μας 'any/none of us' (cf. κανένας ἀπό μᾶς (similar meaning, but stronger), καμιά ἀπ' τίς καρέκλες 'any/none of the chairs'); ὁ καθένας μας 'each of us' (ὁ καθένας ἀπό μᾶς 'each one of us', ὁ καθένας ἀπ' τούς στρατιῶτες 'each one of the soldiers'); ὁ πρῶτος τους 'the first of them' (ὁ πρῶτος ἀπ' αὐτούς (same meaning), ὁ πρῶτος ἀπ' τούς ἀστυνομικούς 'the first of the policemen'); ἄλλοι τους (ἄλλοι ἀπ' αὐτούς) 'others of them' (cf. ἄλλοι ἀπ' τούς συνέδρους 'others of the delegates').

With some of these words, the clitic pronoun is not so commonly found as ἀπό + the emphatic pronoun (κάποιος, πρῶτος, ἄλλος), with others the emphatic pronoun conveys a more intense meaning than the clitic. The quantifier ὅλος 'all' is used in a similar way, except that it cannot be followed by ἀπό: ὅλοι σας 'all of you'.

The genitive of the clitic pronoun is always used with the possessive adjective δικός (μου etc.) '(my) own' (when used attributively with a noun) or 'mine' (when used predicatively):

(4) ἔχει δικό της αὐτοκίνητο 'she has her own car' (or 'a car of her own');

(5) αὐτά τά βιβλία εἶναι δικά τους 'these books are theirs'.

The genitive of the clitic pronoun is sometimes found after a comparative or superlative (otherwise ἀπό + accusative):

(6) ἡ Ἰσμήνη εἶναι δυό χρόνια μεγαλύτερή του 'Ismene is two years older than him' (cf. μεγαλύτερη ἀπ' αὐτόν);

(7) ὁ Λίνος εἶναι ὁ καλύτερός μας 'Linos is the best of us' (cf. ὁ καλύτερος ἀπό μᾶς).

Finally, there are a few adjectives sometimes constructed with a genitive clitic (otherwise with μέ 'with'):

(8) δέ βρήκαμε τόν ὅμοιό του 'we haven't found his like' (cf. ὅμοιος μέ 'similar to');

(9) ὁ Χρῆστος εἶναι συνομήλικός της 'Christos is the same age as her [lit. 'contemporary of-her']' (cf. συνομήλικος μέ τή Βάσω 'the same age as Vaso').

(b) *Nouns only.* Certain adjectives may be followed by nouns in the genitive, although most such constructions belong to formal styles.

There are some deverbal adjectives found with genitives, where the underlying structure consists of the relevant verb and its object:

(1) τέτοιες ἐνέργειες εἶναι ἀντιπροσωπευτικές τῆς νοοτροπίας τῆς ἀντιπολίτευσης 'such actions are representative of the mentality of the [political] opposition' (cf. τέτοιες ἐνέργειες ἀντιπροσωπεύουν τή νοοτροπία . . . 'such actions represent the mentality . . .').

Other genitives after adjectives can sometimes be paraphrased by the preposition γιά 'for, about':

(2) εἶναι ἔνοχος/ἀθῶος τοῦ ἐγκλήματος 'he is guilty/innocent of the crime' (cf. γιά τό ἔγκλημα);

(3) θά σᾶς κρατήσω ἐνήμερο τῶν ἐξελίξεων 'I shall keep you informed of (the) developments' (cf. γιά τίς ἐξελίξεις);

(4) ἕνας ποιητής ἄξιος τοῦ ὀνόματος 'a poet worthy of the name'.

The genitive in the phrase ἔγκυος ἔξη μηνῶν 'six months pregnant' (lit. pregnant of-six months') is probably to be equated with genitives of measurement (2.2.4.2 (e)), such as ἔνα μωρό ἔξη μηνῶν 'a six-month-old baby'.

The genitive of a noun is sometimes found after a noun phrase containing an adjective in the superlative:

(5) τό ψηλότερο κτίριο τοῦ κόσμου 'the tallest building in [lit. 'of'] the world'.

The genitive here may well be the result of French influence (cf. *le bâtiment le plus haut du monde*), and is often replaced by σέ + accusative (τό ψηλότερο κτίριο στόν κόσμο).

2.2.4.4 The genitive with adverbs

There are many adverbs of place which, when constructed with a preposition (+ noun or disjunctive pronoun), form a kind of composite preposition (see also 6.2): πάνω στό τραπέζι 'on (top of) the table', πάνω ἀπό τό τραπέζι 'above the table', etc. If a clitic pronoun is used instead of a noun, then the preposition proper is dropped and the pronoun appears in the genitive. Thus: κοντά στίς ρίζες 'close to the roots', κοντά σέ σένα 'close to *you*' (emphatic), but κοντά σου 'near you'; μέσα στό σπίτι 'inside the house', μέσα σ' αὐτο 'inside *it*' (emphatic), but μέσα του 'inside it'.

Two adverbs of time can be constructed with clitic pronouns but not with disjunctive pronouns or nouns. These are ποτέ '(n)ever': ποτέ μου '(n)ever in my whole life'; and πάντα 'always': πάντα μου 'forever' (the first is far more frequent than the second):

(1) ποτέ μου δέ θά σέ ξεχάσω 'I shall never forget you as long as I live.'

Finally there are certain de-adjectival adverbs and certain adjectives and nouns used adverbially which are constructed with the genitive. These include: ἀναλόγως 'according to, proportionately to' (ἀναλόγως τῶν περιστάσεων 'according to the circumstances': frequently translated into demotic as ἀνάλογα μέ τίς περιστάσεις), and χάριν 'for the sake of' (almost exclusively in παραδείγματος χάριν 'for example', cf. demotic λόγου χάρη).

2.2.4.5 The genitive after prepositions

There are several prepositions, all of them of *katharevousa* origin, which take the genitive. They will be examined in 6.2.6.

2.2.4.6 The genitive in exclamations

There are various greetings, wishes, and other exclamations in which a clitic pronoun in the genitive may be present. Such are: καλημέρα σας 'good morning to you'; μπράβο της! 'good for her!'; περαστικά του 'I hope he gets well soon'; γειά σου! 'hello; goodbye' (here the pronoun is omitted only among people who are on very familiar terms, and then only as a farewell or a toast: 'cheers'); ντροπή τους! 'shame on them!'; ἀλίμονό σου! 'woe betide you!'.

The exclamatory words νά and ὁρίστε may be followed by a genitive clitic in an 'ethic' sense: νά σου τον 'there he is, you see'; νά τα μας! or ὁρίστε μας! 'what a [shameful] situation!'

2.2.4.7 Idiomatic genitives of nouns

In colloquial Greek there are some genitives of nouns, used with their definite articles, which have various metaphorical adverbial or adjectival uses. Some examples are given here in suitable contexts:

(1) δέ βρῆκα φούστα τῆς προκοπῆς 'I didn't find [any] skirt [that was] any good' (προκοπή 'industriousness, success');

(2) ἔγινε τῆς κακομοίρας or τῆς τρελῆς 'there was a terrible commotion' (lit. 'it-became of-the unfortunate woman/madwoman');

(3) ἡ ὀρχήστρα ἔπαιζε τοῦ ξεκουφαμοῦ 'the orchestra was playing deafeningly loud' (ξεκουφαμός 'a complete deafening');

(4) ἔχει πέσει τοῦ θανατᾶ '(s)he's at death's door' (lit. '(s)he's fallen of-the death-merchant');

(5) τά κοντά μαλλιά ἔγιναν τῆς μόδας 'short hair has become fashionable' (μόδα 'fashion');

(6) ἔφαγε τοῦ σκασμοῦ '(s)he ate fit to burst' (σκασμός 'bursting');

(7) κάνει τοῦ κεφαλιοῦ του 'he goes his own way' (lit. 'he does of his head').

More common than all these, however, and not confined to colloquial use, is the genitive of χρόνος 'year' in τοῦ χρόνου in its meaning of 'next year' (also 'of the year').

In some of its uses the genitive is governed by another word which has been deleted. In expressions such as 'to/at someone's house', the words τό σπίτι may be omitted: στοῦ Μάρκου 'to/at Mark's house' (for στοῦ Μάρκου τό σπίτι, which preserves the older demotic word-order, in which genitives normally preceded the nouns which governed them). There are also several areas of Athens which were originally named after persons and which are normally used only in the genitive, irrespective of their syntactic function in the clause: τοῦ Φιλοπάππου 'Philopappou', τοῦ Σκαραμαγκᾶ 'Skaramanga' (presumably a noun such as γειτονιά 'neighbourhood' or συνοικία 'quarter' is understood). When talking about the times of buses, trains, etc., one can say:

(8) θά πάρω τῶν ἐντεκάμιση 'I shall catch the 11.30' (lit. 'I shall catch [the bus, train, etc.] of-the eleven-half').

Saints' days (which are still important in the Greek calendar because of the institution of name-days) are often expressed by the genitive of the saint's name:

(9) τοῦ ἁγίου Δημητρίου πήγαμε ἐκδρομή στήν Πάρνηθα 'on St. Demetrius' day [26 Oct.] we went [on an] excursion to [Mount] Parnes' (lit. 'of-the saint Demetrius . . .').

From phrases of a biblical nature such as τό ἅγιο τῶν ἁγίων 'the holy of holies' there have arisen some similar constructions like τῶν ἀδυνάτων ἀδύνατον 'absolutely impossible' (lit. 'of-the impossible (neuter gen. pl.) impossible (neuter sing.)'), which is often shortened simply to τῶν ἀδυνάτων:

(10) εἶναι τῶν ἀδυνάτων νά ἔρθω 'it's absolutely impossible for me to come'.

Other examples of genitives arising through deletion are those in which the deleted word has already been uttered:

(11) μάτια πράσινα σάν φιδιού 'green eyes like [those] of [a] snake',

in which μάτια is understood before φιδιού; or

(12) ὁ ἐξοπλισμός τους εἶναι καλύτερος ἀπό τῶν Γερμανῶν 'their equipment is superior to [that] of the Germans',

in which τόν ἐξοπλισμό is understood before τῶν Γερμανῶν (in the last example some writers would prefer ἀπό ἐκεῖνον τῶν Γερμανῶν, which however would strike many Greeks as foreign).

2.2.5 APPOSITIONAL CONSTRUCTIONS

There are numerous circumstances in which two nouns are placed together in the same case (either nominative or accusative according to syntactic context). The chief constructions concerned are expressions of content or measurement (see also 2.2.3). In some of these types of expression the second noun is found in the genitive in more formal usage.

(1) ἕνα κουτί σπίρτα 'a box [of] matches';
(2) δυό κιλά πατάτες 'two kilos [of] potatoes' (in such constructions, when the definite article is used, it may be repeated: τά δυό κιλά οἱ πατάτες 'the two kilos [of] (the) potatoes');
(3) πλῆθος γυναῖκες 'many women' (lit. 'crowd women': but cf. ἕνα πλῆθος ἀπό γυναῖκες or ἕνα πλῆθος γυναικῶν (gen.) 'a crowd of women');
(4) χιλιάδες Ἕλληνες 'thousands [of] Greeks' (but cf. χιλιάδες λαοῦ 'thousands of people (gen.)');
(5) δυό ἑκατομμύρια δραχμές 'two million drachmas' (or δραχμῶν (gen.));
(6) ἕνας μικρός ἀριθμός ἐπισκέπτες 'a small number [of] visitors' (more formally, ἐπισκεπτῶν (gen.)).

Other types of appositional construction include the following:

(7) εἴκοσι χρόνια Ἐπίδαυρος 'twenty years of the Epidaurus Festival' (lit. 'twenty years Epidaurus');
(8) εἶναι ὀδοντίατρος τό ἐπάγγελμα '(s)he's [a] dentist [by] profession';
(9) ἦρθε ἕνας γέρος, Μιχάλης τό ὄνομα 'an old man came, Michael [by] name';

(10) τί εἶδος ἄνθρωπος εἶναι; 'what sort [of] man is he?' (cf. the even more colloquial τί σόι ἄνθρωπος . . .;—more formally τί εἴδους (gen.) ἄνθρωπος . . .;).

2.2.6 CASE AGREEMENT

Adjectives agree in case with the nouns or pronouns they modify, as they do in gender and number. Similarly, two or more nouns and pronouns syntactically governed by the same word also appear in the same case. As with gender, however, one occasionally finds sentences that display a lack of case agreement, or provide examples of anacolouthon (the latter usually as a result of attraction into a case other than the strictly logical one).

Lack of case agreement between a noun and its premodifier is found in extremely restricted circumstances: the lack of agreement is only apparent, since the premodifier is really an indeclinable word, e.g. ἕνα-δυό συνάδελφοι 'one or two colleagues', in which, while the noun is in the nominative, the numeral appears to be in the accusative (the same premodifier does not inflect for gender either).

In utterances where a noun or pronoun is not in what would appear to be the grammatically correct case, the speaker/writer has either deliberately changed his/her mind about the syntax of the utterance in mid-sentence, or unconsciously changed tack. The former phenomenon often occurs in lists whose items should logically be in an oblique case, but which appear in the nominative:

(1) εἶδα τή θέα πού ἀπλωνόταν ἀμφιθεατρικά: ὁ Ὑμηττός, ὁ Φιλοπάππος κι ἡ Ἀκρόπολη 'I saw the view which spread out amphitheatrically: Hymettus, Philopappus, and the Acropolis' (Kar. n.d.: II 123):

although the three locations are what the speaker saw, they appear in the nominative. Repetition of a genitive is often avoided in a list:

(2) ἀποστολές γάλακτος γιά τά μωρά, βιταμίνες καί φάρμακα γιά ἔγκυες γυναῖκες 'consignments of milk (gen.) for babies, vitamins (nom./acc.) and medicines (nom./acc.) for pregnant women' (P 29.41).

A prescriptive grammarian would say that the use of the nom./acc. of βιταμίνες and φάρμακα is incorrect, but it was probably motivated by the writer's reluctance to use the genitive plural of βιταμίνη, which is, admittedly, infrequently used.

The genitive is sometimes avoided when the word in question is in apposition to another genitive:

(3) ἡ συνειδητοποίηση τῆς γυναίκας ὡς φύλο 'the consciousness of woman (gen.) as [a] sex (nom./acc.)' (*P* 29.43).

Such a construction as (3) is condemned by grammarians; on the same page of the same article, however, the 'correct' construction is found (despite the rather garbled thinking):

(4) ἡ τοποθέτηση τοῦ γυναικείου κινήματος ὡς ζωντανοῦ μέλους στό σῶμα τῶν ποικίλων κοινωνικῶν μεταλλαγῶν 'the placing of the women's movement (gen.) as [a] living member (gen.) in the body of the various social changes.'

More frequent than these constructions are those in which the verb demands an object in the accusative or genitive, whereas a noun or pronoun governed by that verb appears in the 'wrong' case. This is often heard in speech, where the speaker changes tack having embarked on a sentence:

(5) ἐγώ . . . δέ μέ εἶδε κανείς 'I (nom.) . . . no one saw *me*' (ἐγώ for ἐμένα);

(6) τά παιδιά τούς ἀρέσει νά τσαλαβουτᾶνε μέ τό κουτάλι 'children like to slop their food around with their spoons' (lit. 'the children (nom./acc.) of-them it-pleases to they-splash-around with the spoon').

Strictly speaking, in (6), 'children' should be in the genitive, to agree with the pronoun τούς, but it is put into the nominative/accusative partly because 'children' is at least the subject of the second verb.

Anacoloutha involving nominal and adjectival relative clauses will be examined elsewhere (8.1.1 and 8.2.1).

2.3 NUMBER

Modern Greek has two numbers: singular and plural. There are no traces of the ancient dual, nor are there survivals of ancient words referring to two terms (cf. E *both*), except for a tiny number of rarely used learned words such as ἀμφότεροι 'both (adj.)' (only used in the plural).

Most nouns have both singular and plural. Most nouns denoting substances (*mass-nouns*) have plural as well as singular, the former (if it refers to a liquid) regularly denoting a (usually large) quantity of the substance: τό αἷμα 'blood' (the substance *in abstracto*, or in the body), pl. τά αἵματα 'blood' (a quantity of blood, e.g. pouring from a body or spilled on the ground). Many mass-nouns referring to solids have two meanings in the singular—the substance and an object made of that substance—only the latter having a plural: ἡ πέτρα 'stone (substance); the stone (object)', μιά πέτρα 'a stone', pl. οἱ πέτρες '(the) stones'; τό ψωμί 'bread (substance); the loaf', ἕνα ψωμί 'a loaf of bread', pl. τά ψωμιά '(the) loaves'.

Many abstract nouns are similarly both countable and uncountable, depending on their meaning: τό φῶς 'light (substance); the light (= lamp)', ἕνα φῶς 'a light', pl. τά φῶτα '(the) lights'; ἡ δυσκολία 'difficultness; the difficulty', μιά δυσκολία 'a difficulty', pl. οἱ δυσκολίες 'the difficulties'; τό σαμποτάζ 'sabotage; the act of sabotage', τά σαμποτάζ '(the) acts of sabotage'. There are few uncountable collective nouns: compare the following with their uncountable English equivalents: τά ἔπιπλα 'furniture' (sing. ἔπιπλο 'piece of furniture'); τά ροῦχα 'clothes' (sing. ροῦχο 'article of clothing'); τά παντελόνια 'trousers' (sing. παντελόνι 'pair of trousers'); οἱ πληροφορίες 'information' (sing. πληροφορία 'piece of information').

Nevertheless, many abstract nouns are normally uncountable: e.g. ἡ γαλήνη 'calm, serenity', ἡ εἰρήνη 'peace'. Other nouns with singular only include ὁ νοῦς 'mind', and most names of places (although in poetry one occasionally finds plurals of singular place-names: also cf. the colloquial ἄσε με μέ τίς Εὐρῶπες σου 'stop going on at me about Europe': lit. 'leave me with your Europes').

Few nouns in MG exist only in the plural. There are very few *summation plurals* such as τά κιάλια 'binoculars'. Most nouns that have no singular are either place-names (οἱ Δελφοί 'Delphi', οἱ Σπέτσες 'Spetses', τά Γιάννινα 'Yannina'), or denote celebrations (τά γενέθλια 'birthday', τά Χριστούγεννα 'Christmas', τά ἐγκαίνια 'inauguration'); but note τά ἀνάκτορα '(royal) palace'. Many nouns have a different (or additional) meaning in the plural, including some mentioned in another chapter (4.5.1.3); other examples: ἡ διακοπή 'interruption, break', pl. οἱ διακοπές 'interruptions, breaks; holidays'; ἡ ἀρχή 'beginning; principle', pl. οἱ ἀρχές 'beginnings; principles; the authorities' (also note that οἱ ἀρχές, τά μέσα, and τά τέλη 'beginning', 'middle', and 'end'—all plural —are regularly followed by a genitive denoting a year, month, etc.); τό γράμμα 'letter (of alphabet, or item of correspondence)', pl. τά γράμματα 'letters (both meanings); reading, writing, learning'.

Just as the masculine of pronouns and some animate nouns is unmarked for gender, and the feminine marked, so the singular is unmarked for number and the plural marked. Thus, *κάποιος φωνάζει* 'someone's calling/shouting' or *ποιός είναι;* 'who is it?' may refer to one or more persons. The singular is frequently used for the plural in general statements:

(1) *ὁ ἄνθρωπος εἶναι μαλακός καί διψασμένος σάν τό χόρτο* 'man is soft and thirsty as grass' (Sef. 1967: 306);

(2) *ὁ Ἕλληνας τρώει πιό πολλά μακαρόνια ἀπ' τόν Ἰταλό* 'the Greek(s) eat(s) more macaroni than the Italian(s)';

(3) *περισσότερο μοῦ ἀρέσει τό ἄλογο παρά τό μουλάρι* 'I like horses (or 'the horse') better than mules (or 'the mule')';

(4) *ἡ ντομάτα ἔχει τριάντα δραχμές τό κιλό* 'tomatoes are thirty drachmas a kilo.'

In the first three examples, the singular may be taken to refer either to a specific instance or to a general truth; in (4), tomatoes are recategorized as a substance.

Syntactically, an adjective agrees in number with the noun or pronoun it modifies, and the verb agrees with the number of its subject(s). In practice, however, there are some exceptions, particularly when a word agrees with the number of its referent rather than with the relevant word in the clause.

A prime example of this is found in words modifying the subject of a verb (or its associated personal pronouns) in the polite plural, where this subject is a single person. The second person plural of the verb and personal pronoun may be used when addressing more than one person, or as a polite address of one person. The polite plural is not used as frequently in MG as it is in French, but is regularly found in the conversation of educated adults. Children hardly use it, and young people tend to avoid it except when being especially polite (e.g. to a teacher). Middle-class adults, on the other hand, use it regularly among themselves unless and until they have passed beyond a threshold of familiarity, which may happen at any time (even during their first meeting), or not at all. Usage depends very much on the individual, and some adults have a habit of addressing anyone younger than themselves in the singular from the beginning of their first meeting; it is also quite common to find a person using a singular to a collocutor who is addressing him/her in the plural. The second person singular is used not only as an informal address between people, but also by advertisers who want to reach a popular audience; for smarter products, advertisers address potential customers in the second plural (with either singular or plural adjectives). The general trend is towards the retrenchment of the polite plural as relations among people in middle-class Greek society become more informal. Linguistically, any word that modifies the subject of a polite plural or its associated pronouns agrees with the number and sex of the person addressed:

(5) εἶστε Ἕλληνας ὑπήκοος; 'are you (pl.) [a] Greek (masc. sing.) subject (masc. sing.)?';

(6) εἶστε πολύ καλή 'you are (pl.) very good/kind (fem. sing.)';

(7) σᾶς βλέπω κουρασμένο σήμερα 'you look tired today' (lit. 'I see you (pl.) tired (masc. sing.) today.'

Other exceptions to the agreement rule arise when there is (or is felt to be) more than one noun modified by the adjective, or more than one subject of the verb.

We have already mentioned the problem of the agreement of an adjective with more than one noun when examining gender (2.1.3). As far as number is concerned, two nouns may cause the adjective to appear in the plural (especially when the adjective does not immediately precede the nouns), or, alternatively, the adjective may agree with the noun closest to it:

(8) ἑλληνική μουσική καί τραγούδια 'Greek (fem. sing.) music (fem. sing.) and songs (neuter plural)'.

In the converse case, where two adjectives modify one noun, the noun is normally singular when it would have been singular if modified by one adjective:

(9) ὁ δέκατος ὄγδοος καί ὁ δέκατος ἔνατος αἰώνας 'the eighteenth (sing.) and (the) nineteenth (sing.) centuries (sing.)' (= ὁ δέκατος ὄγδοος αἰώνας καί ὁ δέκατος ἔνατος αἰώνας);

(10) τό ἀριστερό καί τό δεξί χέρι 'the left (sing.) and (the) right (sing.) hand[s] (sing.)'.

A different phenomenon is exemplified by phrases such as:

(11) ἔγραψε περισσότερα ἀπό ἔνα καλά ποιήματα '(s)he wrote more (pl.) than one (sing.) good (pl.) poem (pl.)',

in which the noun and its accompanying adjective are in the plural (despite the numeral 'one') because of the plural adjective 'more' and because in reality there were at least two poems.

Attraction of a verb into a different number by the referent of its subject is found in the utterance,

(12) θά φύγουν ὁ κόσμος 'people (sing.) will leave (pl.)',

which is normally considered to be less correct than φύγει (sing.): in (12), the verb is plural because the speaker thinks of 'people' as consisting of many persons. One does not find many examples of such usage in MG (contrast British English 'the government are', 'the police are', etc.). Nevertheless, other instances of attraction are frequent. Examples of grammatically singular subject and plural verb are the following:

(13) ὁ Ἕλληνας καί ὁ Τοῦρκος ἀντιπρόσωπος πρότειναν ἕνα κοινό σχέδιο 'the Greek and the Turkish representative[s] (sing.) have proposed (pl.) a joint plan' (← Ὁ Ἕλληνας ἀντιπρόσωπος καί ὁ Τοῦρκος ἀντιπρόσωπος πρότειναν ...);

(14) τό ἕνα ἐργοστάσιο μετά τό ἄλλο τό ἐπιβεβαίωσαν 'one factory (sing.) after the other (sing.) has (pl.) confirmed this' (← πολλά ἐργοστάσια τό ἐπιβεβαίωσαν) (P 33.106);

(15) τό 90% τῶν προβλημάτων περιέχουν τήν ἴδια τή λύση τους '(the) 90 per cent (sing.) of (the) problems contain (pl.) their own solution' (← τά περισσότερα προβλήματα περιέχουν ... 'most problems contain ...').

All these examples are felt to be quite acceptable.

Sometimes two subjects may be attached to a singular verb; this construction is especially frequent when the verb precedes:

(16) ἦρθε ὁ Πέτρος κι ὁ Παῦλος 'Peter and Paul came (sing.)';

but it is occasionally found with a following verb:

(17) ἡ ἀγωνία καί ἀνησυχία ἔγινε μόνιμο σύνδρομο τῶν βουλευτῶν τῆς Νέας Δημοκρατίας 'anxiety and worry have become (sing.) a permanent syndrome of the deputies of New Democracy [political party]' (T 9 Aug. 1979, 8).

Example (16) is quite normal; in (17) a plural verb could have been used, but then the definite article would probably (but not necessarily) have been inserted before the second noun: as it is, 'anxiety-and-worry' is clearly being considered as a composite unit. The converse of this is

found in utterances where two or more singular subjects separated by
ἤ 'or' or οὔτε 'nor' have a plural verb:

(18) οὔτε ὁ Τάκης οὔτε ὁ Θάνος δέν ἦρθαν 'neither Takis nor
Thanos came (pl.)';

(19) κάποιος ἤ κάποια ἀποφάσισαν ὅτι . . . (lit. 'someone (masc.) or
someone (fem.) decided (pl.) that . . .': a kind of construction
often used by feminist speakers).

With οὔτε a singular verb would be unusual; with ἤ it would be quite
common.

Occasionally one finds sentences in which a collective noun is the
subject of two or more verbs, the first being in the singular and subsequent verbs being in the plural, the speaker by this time having
abandoned the grammatical number of the subject for the sake of the
number of real referents:

(20) τό ζευγάρι ὁδηγήθηκε χθές στόν Εἰσαγγελέα καί ἀντιμετω-
πίζουν τίς κατηγορίες 'the couple (sing.) was brought (sing.)
yesterday before the magistrate, and they face (pl.) the charges.'

2.4 PERSON

There are three persons in MG, the first person plural denoting a combination of first and second, first and third, or all three; and the second
person plural being used when addressing more than one person or
for a combination of second and third persons, but also when talking
politely to a single person (see 2.3).

Apart from its chief use, the second person singular of the verb is
used colloquially when the subject is indefinite, being replaced in more
formal usage by the third person singular + κανείς 'one' (cf. French on),
which in this meaning is always grammatically masculine:

(1) ἄν πᾶς στό Παρίσι θά βρεῖς ὅ,τι σοῦ ἀρέσει 'if you go to Paris
you'll find whatever you like',

which could mean,

(1a) ἄν πάει κανείς στό Παρίσι θά βρεῖ ὅ,τι τοῦ ἀρέσει 'if one goes
to Paris one will find whatever one [lit. 'he'] likes.'

The use of the emphatic forms of the second-person pronoun ἐσύ,
ἐσένα would however preclude the possibility of impersonal meaning.

The third person plural of the verb is also used impersonally, especially in circumstances where the agent is unknown or simply unspecified:

(2) πῶς κρατοῦν τή ρακέτα; 'how does one hold the racket?';
(3) τόν πιάσανε 'he's been caught/arrested' (lit. 'they've caught him': see further 3.1.2.1).

The third person of the verb can be used, as has been seen, in questions of the kind, ποιός εἶναι; 'who is it?'. It is also used as a sign of politeness by waiters, shop assistants, etc.:

(4) τί θέλει ὁ κύριος; 'what does the gentleman want?'.

The first person plural of the verb is often used in recipes:

(5) παίρνουμε 250 γρ. ἀλεύρι καί μισό κιλό γάλα, τά ἀνακατεύ-ουμε . . . '(we) take 250 g. of flour and half a kilo of milk, (we) stir them . . .';

this is an alternative to the plural of the imperative. It is also used by heads of state to refer to themselves, in which case adjectives modifying the subject are singular if the referent is a single person (as with polite plurals, 2.3). There is also a 'first person plural of community' (Tzartzanos 1946: 54), used in addressing someone, to express either solidarity with the addressee or a slight reprimand (it is also a useful way of avoiding a sometimes difficult choice between second singular and second plural):

(6) τί κάνουμε σήμερα; 'how are you [lit. 'we'] today?';
(7) δέν ντρεπόμαστε λιγάκι; 'aren't you ashamed?' (lit. 'aren't we ashamed a little?');
(8) μπήκαμε τώρα; 'have you got it [i.e. understood] now?' (lit. 'have we entered now?').

Verbs in the first or second person may have nouns as their overt subjects: these nouns in fact stand in apposition to the (unstated) pronoun subjects:

(9) γιά τήν ἐκπομπή αὐτή συνεργαζόμαστε εἰκοσιδύο ἄνθρωποι 'there are/were twenty-two of us working on this/that [TV] programme' (lit. '. . . we-collaborate(d) twenty-two people (nom.)').

On the other hand, with a verb in the first or second person plural, the speaker may state the third-person subject(s) but not the first/second, which has to be understood from the verb:

(10)   στό φοῦρνο δουλεύαμε ὁ μπάρμπα-Στάθης, μιά λεύτερη κόρη
        του, ἡ Βιργινία, κι ὁ μικρότερος γιός του, ὁ Φίλιππος 'old
        Stathis, an unmarried daughter of his, Virginia, (and) his
        youngest son [and I] worked (first pl.) at the bakery' (Ven.
        1969: 197).

And often one of the existential subjects of a plural verb may be placed in a prepositional phrase introduced by μέ 'with' (see 3.1.2.3, example (9a)).

There is a choice between first/second and third persons in relative clauses in sentences of the type 'I am the first/only (person) who . . .': contrast (11) and (12):

(11)   εἶμαι ὁ πρῶτος πού ἦρθε 'I am the first [one] who came (3rd
        person)' (Ber. 1973: 128);

(12)   ἔτυχε νά εἶμαι ὁ πρῶτος πού τό ἀνακοίνωσα 'I happened to be
        the first to announce it' (lit. 'it-happened to I-am the first
        who it I-announced' (B 19 Oct. 1979).

2.4.1 IMPERSONAL VERBS

Exclusively impersonal verbs (i.e. those which exist only in the third person singular) are few in MG: e.g. πρέπει 'it is necessary', χιονίζει 'it snows', πρόκειται 'it is a question (of); be about (to)'. Phrases consisting of copula + neuter singular adjective should be added to these: e.g. εἶναι δυνατόν 'it is possible'. There are other verbs which exist only in the third person, but which may form a plural: e.g. συμβαίνει 'it occurs', συμβαίνουν 'they occur'.

Verbs which may be used impersonally, but have other persons too are far more numerous. A few verbs are normally used impersonally, but may be used personally in the same meaning: one of these is τυχαίνει 'it happens (that)'; compare example (12) in 2.4. with the following:

(1)   δέν ἔτυχα νά δῶ αὐτό τό ἔργο 'I didn't happen (1st pers.) to
       see that play'.

Other verbs vary in meaning according to whether they are used personally or impersonally: βρέχω 'I moisten', βρέχει '(s)he/it moistens; it rains'; μπορῶ 'I am able', μπορεῖ '(s)he/it is able; it may be'; γίνομαι

'I become'; γίνεται '(s)he/it becomes; it happens; it is done' (in the last meaning, which is not impersonal, the plural may be used); φαίνομαι 'I appear (+ complement); I am visible'; φαίνεται '(s)he/it appears; (s)he/it is visible; it seems'.

In fact, Warburton (1979) has shown that certain of these verbs are impersonal only in the sense that they have a clause rather than a person as their subject (πρέπει, συμβαίνει, μπορεῖ, γίνεται, φαίνεται). In this respect the impersonal μπορεῖ contrasts syntactically with the personal μπορῶ, in that the latter has the νά-clause as its object. Warburton also argues convincingly that the impersonal μπορεῖ, φαίνεται, etc., should be treated as quite separate verbs from the personal μπορῶ, φαίνομαι, etc. For instance, personal μπορῶ requires an animate subject, and the verb(s) in the νά-clause must have the same subject; impersonal μπορεῖ can be followed by a νά-clause with a verb in any person and with an animate or inanimate subject. Again, personal φαίνομαι (in which the speaker describes someone's or something's appearance) normally requires the existential subject to be present at the time of utterance; while impersonal φαίνεται has no such requirement, and simply expresses the speaker's impression (which may or may not be based on the existential subject's appearance).

Because of the flexibility of MG word order, the subject of a subordinate clause following an impersonal verb may appear before the main verb and seem to be its subject; if this subject is anything but singular and third person, it will appear not to agree with the main verb:

(2a) πρέπει νά φύγουν τά παιδιά, or
(2b) τά παιδιά πρέπει νά φύγουν 'the children must leave.'

The difference in meaning between these two sentences is that in (2a) the emphasis falls on the subject, while in (2b) it falls on the verb of the subordinate clause. In (2b) the subject of the second verb has been placed before πρέπει, but is not its subject. This becomes clearer if μπορεῖ is substituted for πρέπει in (2b):

(3a) τά παιδιά μπορεῖ νά φύγουν,
(3b) τά παιδιά μποροῦν νά φύγουν 'the children may leave.'

In (3a), in which the impersonal (singular) μπορεῖ is used, the speaker is expressing the *possibility* that they may leave; in (3b), which contains the personal μποροῦν (plural), (s)he is suggesting either that the children are *allowed* to leave or that they are *capable* of doing so.

This explains the apparent lack of concord between subject and verb (or between noun and adjective) in sentences such as the following:

(4) οἱ Σοβιετικοί φαίνεται νά τηροῦν τούς κανόνες 'the Soviets seem (sing.) to be observing (pl.) the rules';

(5) οἱ γυμνιστές ἀπαγορεύτηκε νά πλησιάζουν πιά στίς ἀμμουδιές τοῦ 'Σαλάντι Μπήτς' 'the nudists were forbidden [or, 'have been forbidden'] (sing.) to approach (pl.) the beaches of the Salandi Beach [Hotel] in future' (T 25 June 1981, 16) (ἀπαγορεύω 'I forbid' does not take an animate direct object);

(6) ὑπῆρχαν πολλά πού ἄξιζε νά διατηρηθοῦν 'there were many that were worth preserving' (lit. '. . . which it-was-worth to they-be-preserved');

(7) ἡ ὁμάδα του εἶναι γνωστό πόσο ἀναμείχθηκε σ' αὐτή τήν ὑπόθεση 'it is known (neuter) how much his team (fem.) was involved in this affair.'

Finally it should be mentioned that certain verbs which in the active may be used only in the third person singular (ξημερώνει 'it dawns, day breaks', βραδιάζει 'evening falls', νυχτώνει 'night falls') may be used in the passive with animate subjects:

(8) νυχτωθήκαμε σ' ἕνα ὀρεινό χωριό 'night found us [lit. 'we were benighted'] at a mountain village';

There is also a compound deponent verb ξημεροβραδιάζομαι:

(9) αὐτός ξημεροβραδιάζεται στό καφενεῖο 'he spends all his day [i.e. from dawn to dusk] at the café.'

3

VOICE, ASPECT, AND TENSE

Throughout this chapter, reference may be made to the inflection tables in Appendix I.

3.1 VOICE AND TRANSITIVITY

Voices are distinguished formally in the MG verb: active and passive (the latter is often labelled 'medio-passive', since it combines morphological and semantic characteristics of the AG middle and passive voices). As happens in other languages, however, the morphological categories (*voice*) do not always coincide with the semantic categories (*diathesis*), and there are active verbs in MG which do not denote action on the part of the subject, just as there are so-called 'deponent' verbs which, while they exist only in a passive form, have an active meaning; there are also verbs which, although their active forms take a direct object, do not form a passive; while other transitive verbs form a passive with a different meaning. Let us examine first the most normal uses of the two morphological voices.

3.1.1 THE ACTIVE

Generally speaking, the subject of an active verb is the agent or experiencer of the action or state denoted by the verb:

(1) ἔφαγα τά μακαρόνια 'I ate the spaghetti' (agent);
(2) ἔνιωσα μιά λαχτάρα 'I had [lit. 'felt'] a fright' (experiencer).

But the grammatical subject of an active verb is often the object or *patient* of the action denoted by the verb:

(3) γκρέμισε τό σπίτι 'the house collapsed' (cf. passive γκρεμίστηκε τό σπίτι 'the house collapsed', or 'the house was demolished');

(4) λέρωσε (act.) or λερώϑηκε (pass.) τό σακκάκι μου 'my jacket
     got dirty';
(5a) ξεβιδώνει (act.) 'it unscrews (= can be unscrewed)'; cf.
(5b) ξεβιδώϑηκε (pass.) 'it has come unscrewed'.

Unlike the utterances in which the subject is the agent, those in which
the grammatical subject is the experiencer, object, or patient can
usually be paraphrased by sentences in which the subject has become
the grammatical object:

(2a) μέ πῆρε μιά λαχτάρα (lit. 'a fright took me');
(3a) τό γκρεμίσανε τό σπίτι 'they demolished the house';
(5c) τό ξεβίδωσα 'I unscrewed it.'

(See also 3.1.3.)

With certain verbs, the active may have a *factitive* meaning:

(6) έκοψα τά μαλλιά μου 'I cut my hair' or 'I had my hair cut'
     (= ό κουρέας μοῦ έκοψε τά μαλλιά 'the barber cut my hair');
(7) ό Περικλῆς έχτισε τόν Παρϑενώνα 'Pericles built the Par-
     thenon' (i.e. 'had it built').

3.1.2 THE PASSIVE

A verb in the morphological passive, unless it belongs to one of the
types mentioned in 3.1.4.2 and 3.1.4.3, may be used with one or more
of the following meanings: (a) truly passive (i.e. the grammatical subject is the object or patient of the action and the sentence may be
replaced by an active one without change of meaning), (b) reflexive, or
(c) reciprocal.

3.1.2.1 The true passive

It has been observed (e.g. by Warburton 1970b: 79–84; and 1975) that
the true passive in MG is used most often when the agent is not explicitly
stated (1a). If an agent is expressed, it is more likely to be inanimate or
abstract (2a), and when an animate agent is specified, it is most likely
to be indefinite (3a). If an animate agent is definite, it is more likely to
be in the plural (4a); and the least likely use of the true passive is where
a single animate agent is explicitly specified (5a). This last kind of
sentence is more commonly found in official and journalistic styles
(under *katharevousa* influence) than in everyday speech. In most cases
a true passive can be replaced by an active which may be more acceptable in normal usage (1b–5b):

(1a) ὁ Γιάννης σκοτώϑηκε στόν πόλεμο 'John was killed in the war';

(1b) τό Γιάννη τόν σκοτώσανε στόν πόλεμο (lit. 'they killed John in the war');

(2a) τά δέντρα ξεριζώϑηκαν ἀπό τόν ἄνεμο 'the trees were uprooted by the wind';

(2b) τά δέντρα τά ξερίζωσε ὁ ἄνεμος 'the wind uprooted the trees' (an abstract noun as subject here would be less likely);

(3a) ἡ Μαρία φιλήϑηκε ἀπό πολλούς 'Mary has been kissed by many [men]';

(3b) τή Μαρία τή φίλησαν πολλοί 'many [men] have kissed Mary';

(4a) ὁ Γιάννης σκοτώϑηκε ἀπό τούς Γερμανούς 'John was killed by the Germans';

(4b) τό Γιάννη τόν σκοτώσανε οἱ Γερμανοί 'the Germans killed John';

(5a) ?τό δέντρο κόπηκε ἀπό τό Γιάννη 'the tree was cut [down] by John';

(5b) τό δέντρο τό ἔκοψε ὁ Γιάννης 'John cut [down] the tree'.

Warburton further points out that ἀπό before an inanimate or abstract agent (as in (2a)), is more instrumental or causative than agentive: this explains why ἀπό may be replaced by μέ in many utterances:

(6) ἡ Κόρινϑος ἐκπροσωπήϑηκε παλιότερα μέ τόν Παγκορινϑιακό 'Corinth was represented formerly by [lit. 'with'] Pancorinthiakos [football team]' (*T* 27 Sept. 1979),

and especially after verbs expressing emotion:

(7) εὐχαριστήϑηκα ἀπό/μέ 'I was pleased by', or

(8) συγκινήϑηκα ἀπό/μέ 'I was moved by'.

Often the passive in MG is *process orientated* rather than *agent orientated*:

(9) αὐτό τό δωμάτιο ζεσταίνεται εὔκολα 'this room heats [lit. 'is heated'] easily'.

3.1.2.2 The passive with reflexive meaning

Although reflexive action may, when the subject is animate, be expressed by means of an active verb with τόν ἑαυτό (μου etc.) as direct object (e.g.

(1a) θεωρεῖ τόν ἐαυτό του ἁρμόδιο 'he considers himself competent':
cf. passive form,

(1b) θεωρεῖται ἁρμόδιος 'he is considered competent'),

with certain common verbs, and only when the context is unambiguous, the passive form may be used instead:

(2a) κοιτάχτηκε στόν καθρέφτη '(s)he looked at himself/herself in the mirror'; but cf.

(2b) πῆγε στήν Ἀθήνα νά κοιταχτεῖ '(s)he went to Athens to be looked at [by a doctor]';

(3) ντύσου καί πλύσου 'get dressed and washed'.

There are some verbs whose passive form can only have a reflexive meaning (e.g. σηκώνω 'I lift', pass. σηκώνομαι 'I get up'). On the other hand, a passive verb which would normally be interpreted as reflexive might be interpreted as factitive in the appropriate context (e.g. ξυρίζομαι 'I shave [myself]', but ξυρίζομαι στόν κουρέα 'I am shaved by the barber, I have a shave at the barber's'). One way of making the reflexive meaning unambiguous is to add μόνος (μου) 'by (my)self':

(4) σκοτώθηκε μόνη της 'she killed herself'.

Alternatively, the prefix αὐτο- may be attached to a passive verb (e.g. αὐτοκαταστρέφεται '(s)he's destroying him/herself').

Another way of expressing reflexive action, which is however rare, is confined to verbs of perception or φαντάζομαι 'I imagine':

(5) δέν μπορῶ νά μέ φανταστῶ νά δουλεύω σέ μιά δουλειά πού δέ θά μοῦ ἄρεσε 'I can't imagine myself working in a job I didn't [lit. 'wouldn't'] like':

here the clitic pronoun is used for τόν ἐαυτό μου.

3.1.2.3 The passive with reciprocal meaning

Subjects which perform an action on each other may take a passive verb (usually in the plural), as long as the context is clear:

(1) κοιταχτήκαμε στά μάτια 'we looked into each other's eyes';

(2) θά τηλεφωνηθοῦμε 'we'll phone each other' (despite the fact that τηλεφωνῶ is intransitive and takes only an indirect object).

The singular may be found with a collective noun as subject:

(3)   τό ζευγάρι φιλήθηκε 'the couple kissed'.

The interpretation put on a verb with passive form is often independent of the context, but is conditioned by the verb itself: e.g. βλέπεστε will hardly be interpreted as meaning anything but 'you see each other', while ἀκούγεστε will be understood to mean 'you can be heard'. Reciprocal meaning may be made unambiguous by the use of μεταξύ τους 'between/among them' after an active or passive verb (active if the verb is intransitive, passive if not), or by means of the reciprocal prefix ἀλληλο- (sometimes ἀλληλ- before vowels):

(4)   μοιάζουν μεταξύ τους 'they resemble each other';
(5)   ἀλληλοπειραζόμαστε (or πειραζόμαστε μεταξύ μας) 'we tease each other' (cf. πειραζόμαστε 'we are [easily] teased/annoyed').

The prefix ἀλληλο- is normally used only with verbs of moderately learned origin, and almost always with verbs in the passive (but cf. active ἀλληλοεπιδροῦν 'they interact'); again, it is normally used with verbs which in the active are transitive (but cf. ἀλληλοεξαρτῶνται 'they are interdependent'). Alternatively, the expression of reciprocation may be achieved by means of a singular or plural verb in the active followed by ὁ ἕνας τόν ἄλλον (lit. 'the one the other'), in the appropriate cases:

(6)   κοίταξε ὁ ἕνας τόν ἄλλον (or κοιτάχτηκαν [μεταξύ τους]) 'they looked at one another';
(7)   πλησιάζουν ὁ ἕνας τόν ἄλλον (or πλησιάζουν μεταξύ τους) 'they're approaching one another';
(8)   δέ μιλᾶνε ὁ ἕνας μέ τόν ἄλλον (or δέ μιλᾶνε μεταξύ τους) 'they don't talk to each other'.

When two or more agents in a reciprocal sentence are specified, the normal construction is one in which the verb is plural, and one of the agents is given after μέ 'with':

(9a)   συναντηθήκαμε στό δρόμο μέ τόν Κυριάκο 'Kyriakos and I met in the street'; cf.
(9b)   συνάντησα τόν Κυριάκο στό δρόμο 'I met Kyriakos in the street'.

In journalistic style, the singular is often used in a reciprocal sense:

(10)   ὁ πρωθυπουργός συναντήθηκε χθές μέ τόν κ. Σμίτ 'the Prime

Minister yesterday met [lit. 'was-met with'] Mr Schmidt'
(the active συνάντησε would imply a chance meeting).

3.1.3 TRANSITIVITY

Although something has so far been said in passing about transitive and
intransitive verbs, it is necessary to examine transitivity in MG in
greater detail. The situation is especially complex in that there is a considerable fluidity in this area of semantics and syntax; speakers and
writers often feel free to produce new variations on the constructions
that are normally found with a given verb.

Theoretically, MG verbs can be placed in the various categories that
have been applied to English, according to the most frequent construc-
tion(s) found with each verb. In practice, however, there is so much
variation that such categorization may seem futile. Nevertheless, let us
begin by making some broad distinctions.

There are verbs in MG which are normally intransitive and others
which are normally transitive. The intransitive verbs (those which take
neither object nor complement) include ὑπάρχω 'I exist', ἔρχομαι
'I come', κρυώνω 'I am/get/catch cold', κοντεύω 'I come close', πέφτω
'I fall', φέγγω 'I shine', βήχω 'I cough', ἀκινητῶ 'I am motionless', etc.

Transitive verbs include those which take complements (*intensive
verbs*) and those which take direct objects (*extensive verbs*). The former
include not only copulas such as εἶμαι 'I am', but also certain verbs
which may otherwise be intransitive or extensive: e.g. μαθαίνω 'I learn'
(normally extensive): μαθαίνω κομμώτρια 'I'm learning [to be a] hair-
dresser'; δηλώνω 'I state, declare' (normally extensive): δήλωσε
γιατρός '(s)he stated [that (s)he was a] doctor' (e.g. on his/her pass-
port); ἀναλαμβάνω 'I undertake, take on/up' (normally extensive):
ἀνέλαβε ναύαρχος τοῦ στόλου 'he took up [his post as] admiral of the
fleet'; δουλεύω 'I work' (normally intransitive): δουλεύω τζαμάς
'I work [as a] glazier'.

Extensive transitive verbs include those which in most circumstances
must be used with a direct object (e.g. κλέβω 'I steal', ἀγγίζω 'I touch',
ἀγοράζω 'I buy'), and those whose object may be deleted (e.g. φοβᾶμαι
'I fear; I'm afraid', λυπᾶμαι 'I pity; I'm sorry', τρώω 'I eat; I'm eating',
διαβάζω 'I read; I'm reading', and verbs of perception, such as ἀκούω
'I hear; I listen (to)'). Nevertheless, even those verbs which normally
require a direct object may be used without if the object is readily
understood from the linguistic or situational context: if two people are
playing ball, one may shout to the other, 'ρίξε!' (lit. 'throw!'), the

object 'the ball' being understood. Some of these transitive verbs must be accompanied by an adverbial, others not; some verbs may alter their meaning according to whether an adverbial is present or not: e.g. βάζω 'I put; I put on':

(1a) ἔβαλα τό καινούριο κοστούμι μου στήν ντουλάπα 'I put my new suit in the wardrobe';

(1b) ἔβαλα τό καινούριο κοστούμι μου 'I put on my new suit'.

There are a few verbs in MG which take two direct objects. One of these is διδάσκω 'I teach':

(2) ἡ Κολέτ μέ δίδαξε γαλλικά 'Colette taught me French'.

When both the objects are expressed by clitic pronouns, however, one of them must appear in the genitive (according to the rules concerning clitics: see 6.3.1.1):

(2a) ἡ Κολέτ μοῦ τά δίδαξε 'Colette taught me it [lit. 'them']'.

In the following examples, (3) may be passivized in two different ways, with either of the objects becoming the subject of the passive sentence (as in English: Warburton 1977b: 280):

(3) διδάσκουν τά παιδιά γραμματική 'they are teaching the children grammar' (or, in another context: 'the children are teaching grammar');

(3a) διδάσκεται γραμματική στά παιδιά 'grammar is being taught to the children';

(3b) τά παιδιά διδάσκονται γραμματική 'the children are being taught grammar.'

Other verbs taking two direct objects include κερνάω 'I treat' (which cannot be passivized):

(4) μέ κέρασε ἕνα οὐζάκι '(s)he treated me [to] an ouzo'.

A number of verbs are *ditransitive*, i.e. they take both a direct and an indirect object (e.g. δίνω 'I give'). The same kind of construction often occurs with κάνω 'I make, I do' (of which the passive version is γίνομαι, with the direct object of κάνω becoming the subject):

(5a) τοῦ ἔκαναν πλύση ἐγκεφάλου 'they brainwashed him' (lit. 'of-him they-made washing of-brain');

(5b) τοῦ ἔγινε πλύση ἐγκεφάλου 'he was brainwashed' (lit. 'of-him it-happened washing of-brain').

Some transitive (including ditransitive) verbs are used with object complements (such usages should not be confused with double direct objects):

(6) τήν πῆραν πωλήτρια 'they took her [on as a] salesgirl' (simple transitive);

(7) ἡ MOULINEX σᾶς κάνει δῶρο καί μιά ζυγαριά WAY-MASTER 'Moulinex also gives you a free Waymaster weighing machine' (ditransitive: σᾶς is the indirect object, δῶρο the direct object, with μιά ζυγαριά as object complement).

Another construction which resembles the double direct object is the direct object followed by a noun used adverbially in the accusative:

(8) τό γέμισε λάδι '(s)he filled it [with] oil';

(9) θά πάω τά παιδιά περίπατο 'I'll take the kids for a walk' (lit. 'I'll go the children walk') (cf. (16b)).

Similar constructions are found with the same verbs in intransitive use:

(8a) γέμισε λάδι 'it became full [of] oil' (cf. γεμάτο λάδι 'full [of] oil');

(9a) θά πάω περίπατο 'I'll go for a walk.'

The fact that neither of the adverbial nouns (λάδι, περίπατο) may be replaced by clitic pronouns in any of these examples indicates that they are not objects of the verbs. Similarly, in

(10) ἀδυνάτισα ἐφτά κιλά 'I've lost seven kilos' (lit. 'I-became-thin seven kilos'),

ἐφτά κιλά is an accusative of measurement, not a direct object of the verb.

We have already mentioned some verbs which may be used transitively or intransitively. There is a large number of such verbs, and various types of relationship exist between their transitive and intransitive uses. Verbs such as γκρεμίζω and λερώνω (3.1.1, examples (3) and (4)) may be used transitively (with patient as object) or intransitively (with patient as subject), and also possess a passive (whose meaning is hardly different from the intransitive active); others (such as ξεβιδώνω: 3.1.1, example (5)), have a transitive or an intransitive (potential) meaning in the active, and also possess a true passive.

The largest group of verbs which may be used either transitively or intransitively consists of those which do not have a passive and in which, without the real situation necessarily being altered, the object of the transitive verb (the patient) may become the subject of the intransitive. The action of the transitive verb is causative, that of the intransitive is passive or reflexive:

(11a) ἄνοιξα τήν πόρτα 'I opened the door' ('I caused it to open');

(11b) ἄνοιξε ἡ πόρτα 'the door opened' ('it was caused to open', 'it opened itself');

(12a) ἄναψα τή λάμπα 'I lit the lamp';

(12b) ἄναψε ἡ λάμπα 'the lamp lit up';

(13a) σταμάτησα τό τραῖνο 'I stopped the train';

(13b) σταμάτησε τό τραῖνο 'the train stopped';

(14a) ἄδειασα τό μπουκάλι 'I emptied the bottle';

(14b) ἄδειασε τό μπουκάλι 'the bottle emptied out';

(15a) ξύπνησα τό γιό μου 'I woke up my son';

(15b) ξύπνησε ὁ γιός μου 'my son woke up.'

Most such verbs have a past passive participle (e.g. ἀναμμένος 'lit, alight') or a passive verbal adjective (e.g. ἀνοιχτός 'open'), or both.

In the following verbs the intransitive sense is felt to be the more normal, and it is possible to coin *ad hoc* transitive constructions with many other normally intransitive verbs:

(16a) ἡ Ρένα πῆγε στό νοσοκομεῖο 'Rena went to the hospital';

(16b) πῆγα τή Ρένα στό νοσοκομεῖο 'I took Rena to the hospital';

(17a) μεγάλωσα στή Θήβα 'I grew up in Thebes';

(17b) μέ μεγάλωσε ἡ γιαγιά μου 'I was brought up by my grandmother'.

In both (18a) and (18b) the verb is transitive, its sense altering according to whether its object refers to a person or to a subject of study:

(18a) σπούδασα θεολογία στή Θεσσαλονίκη 'I studied theology at Salonica';

(18b) μέ σπούδασε ἕνας θεῖος μου 'an uncle of mine paid for my education.'

With other verbs the non-causative/causative correspondence is achieved with the use of different prefixes or suffixes: e.g. ὁμολογῶ 'I confess, acknowledge', ἐξομολογῶ 'I confess (of priest)'; ἐξασθενῶ 'I become weak', ἐξασθενίζω 'I weaken, enfeeble'.

There are other normally intransitive verbs which have a more specific idiomatic use when transitive:

(19a) πέθανε ἀπό καρκίνο '(s)he died of cancer';

(19b) τόν πέθαναν στό ξύλο 'they gave him a terrible beating' (lit. 'him they-died to-the wood');

(20a) τόν ἔχασα ἀπό τά μάτια μου 'I lost him from sight';

(20b) ἡ Ἀφροδίτη στέλνει ἕνα σύννεφο, τόν χάνει ἀπό τά μάτια του 'Aphrodite sends a cloud and makes him [Paris] disappear from his [Menelaus'] sight' (Tsi. 1970: 248);

(21a) ὡς τότε, τρέχαμε ἀπό παιδίατρο σέ παιδίατρο 'up to then we had been going [lit. 'were running'] from paediatrician to paediatrician';

(21b) ὡς τότε τό τρέχαμε ἀπό παιδίατρο σέ παιδίατρο 'up to then we had been taking him [lit. 'were running it'] from paediatrician to paediatrician' (T 27 May 1982, 100).

In some other verbs the object of the transitive version (the patient) may not be convertible into the subject of the intransitive version, since the intransitive verb may have quite a different meaning:

(22a) ἔκαψα τά ξύλα 'I burnt the wood';

(22b) καίει τό σίδερο 'the iron's burning hot';

(23a) πέταξα τά χαρτιά 'I threw away the papers';

(23b) πέταξε τό πουλί 'the bird has flown';

(24a) ἔδεσα τό σκύλο 'I tied up the dog';

(24b) ἔδεσε τό γιαούρτι 'the yoghurt has set.'

The verb αἰσθάνομαι 'I feel' may be transitive (taking as object a noun phrase or noun clause) or intransitive (in which case it has a so-called 'middle' meaning):

(25a) ξαφνικά αἰσθάνθηκα τό πόδι μου μουδιασμένο 'suddenly my foot/leg felt numb' (lit. '. . . I felt my foot/leg numb');

(25b) δέν αἰσθάνομαι καλά 'I don't feel well.'

Some other verbs have various different meanings according to whether they are intransitive or transitive (and sometimes, in the latter case, whether they have an animate or inanimate subject). Some examples are given below:

(26a) ἔγραψε τήν ἱστορία τῆς Ἑλλάδας '(s)he wrote the history of Greece';

(26b) θά μέ γράψει ἡ ἱστορία 'I'll go down in history' (lit. 'history will write me');

(26c) βλέπεις τί γράφει ἡ ταμπέλα; 'can you see what the sign says [lit. 'writes']?';

(27a) πλήρωσα τό κρασί 'I paid [for] the wine';

(27b) πλήρωσα τά λεφτά 'I paid the money';

(27c) πλήρωσα τόν ὑπάλληλο 'I paid the assistant/employee';

(28a) χωρίσαμε τούς δυό ἀντιπάλους 'we separated the two opponents';

(28b) θά χωρίσω τήν περιουσία μου στά παιδιά μου 'I shall divide up my property among my children';

(28c) μέ χώρισε ὁ Κυριάκος 'Kyriakos has divorced me';

(28d) χωρίσαμε μέ τό Στέλιο 'Stelios and I have separated/divorced';

(28e) χωρίζονται μεταξύ τους ἀπό μιά ὁριζόντια γραμμή 'they are separated from each other by a horizontal line';

(29a) ὁ Δημήτρης πέρασε ἀπό τό σπίτι μου 'Dimitris dropped in on me';

(29b) πέρασα τή γέφυρα 'I crossed the bridge';

(29c) τήν πέρασα ἀπό τή γέφυρα 'I took her across the bridge';

(29d) θά περάσετε τίς σανίδες πολλά χέρια παρκετίνη 'you will coat the boards with many layers of parquet polish' (*T* 28 May 1981, 48).

In (29d) there is only one true object of the verb (namely, τίς σανίδες), πολλά χέρια παρκετίνη being an adverbial phrase (cf. (8) and (9)) which includes a noun (παρκετίνη) in apposition to the previous noun.

Such examples could be multiplied almost infinitely. We shall finally confine ourselves however to mentioning two further phenomena: the active use of a normally deponent verb (30), and a group of verbs which SMG has inherited from *katharevousa* and which were traditionally constructed with the genitive (31)–(32):

(30) ὁ ὑπουργός δέν παραιτήθηκε, τόν παραίτησαν 'the minister didn't resign, he was fired [lit. 'they resigned him']' (Hadz. 1909: 79)

(compare a similarly comic transitive use of a normally intransitive verb:

(30a) δέν αὐτοκτόνησε, τόν αὐτοκτόνησαν 'he didn't commit suicide, he was "suicided" ');

(31) εἶχα κυριαρχηθεῖ ἀπό τό πνεῦμα τοῦ θανάτου 'I had been overcome by the spirit of death' (Vaf. 1970: 350) (κυριαρχῶ

usually takes the genitive: perhaps the author intended to write κυριευτεῖ);

(32) δέ θέλουμε νά στερηθοῦμε τήν εὐχαρίστηση νά . . . 'we don't want to be deprived of the pleasure of . . .' (στερῶ was formerly used with the accusative of the animate and the genitive of the inanimate object).

Such flexibility as we have observed in the transitivity or otherwise of verbs results in a breadth of choice of expression for the speaker/ writer. Creative writers in particular have availed themselves of the opportunity of producing new metaphorical structures by using normally intransitive verbs with direct objects. But in everyday speech too there is a considerable number of formerly intransitive verbs that have changed their nature by becoming transitive, and transitive verbs which have changed through being able to take a different class of object than they were found with traditionally.

3.1.4 CORRESPONDENCE BETWEEN ACTIVE AND PASSIVE

Some examples have already been given of possible switches from active to passive and vice versa. We shall now examine some further examples of correspondence and non-correspondence between the morphological voices.

3.1.4.1 *Verbs with no passive form*

Verbs which are intransitive in their active form do not have a passive. But there are many common verbs which, though they are active in form, and transitive, do not form a passive. These include κάνω 'I do', ἔχω 'I have', ξέρω 'I know', θέλω 'I want', περιμένω 'I wait for'. (Most verbs which lack a passive naturally do not form a past passive participle; but κάνω has καμωμένος 'made (of)'; and see below, 3.1.5.) A periphrasis can be used to form the equivalent of the passive of most of these verbs: γίνεται 'it is done', εἶμαι γνωστός 'I am known', ἀναμένεται '(s)he/it is awaited' (the last rather formal). Other verbs have passive forms which are not normally used in a true passive sense: e.g. κοιτάζω 'I look at' (see above, 3.1.2.2), βλέπω 'I see', τρώω 'I eat' (τρώγονται 'they are edible' or 'they quarrel', but not normally 'they are eaten').

3.1.4.2 *Verbs with no active form*

These are the so-called *deponent* verbs, some of which are transitive and others intransitive. The following are among the transitive deponents:

λυπᾶμαι 'I am sorry (for)' (but cf. active λυπῶ 'I sadden', far less common), φοβᾶμαι 'I am afraid (of)' (cf. active φοβίζω 'I frighten'), θυμᾶμαι 'I remember' (cf. θυμίζω 'I remind'), καταριέμαι 'I curse', αἰσθάνομαι 'I feel', βαριέμαι 'I am bored (with)', ντρέπομαι 'I am ashamed (of)'. Intransitives include ἔρχομαι 'I come' (with active forms only in the perfective), κοιμᾶμαι 'I sleep' (cf. active κοιμίζω 'put to sleep'), παραπονιέμαι 'I complain', κάθομαι 'I sit' (with active forms only in the perfective: cf. also active καθίζω 'I sit' (transitive)), στέκομαι 'I stand; I stop', διαμαρτύρομαι 'I protest'. There are also the copulas γίνομαι 'I become' (with active forms only in the perfective) and φαίνομαι 'I seem'.

Some transitive deponents may have corresponding periphrases to express their passive meaning: e.g. δέχομαι 'I receive' → γίνομαι δεκτός 'I am received'; παραδέχομαι 'I accept' → εἶμαι παραδεκτός 'I am accepted/acceptable'; ἀντιλαμβάνομαι 'I perceive' → γίνομαι ἀντιληπτός 'I am perceived/perceptible'; μᾶς ἐπιτέθηκε ὁ ἐχθρός 'the enemy attacked us' → δεχτήκαμε ἐπίθεση ἀπό τόν ἐχθρό 'we were attacked by the enemy' (lit. 'we received attack from/by the enemy'). Occasionally one encounters a deponent being used for its own passive: such usage is not normally considered correct, although the phrase τά ἐπικαλούμενα ἀποδεικτικά στοιχεῖα 'the invoked elements of proof' is a normal term in legal parlance (from normally deponent ἐπικαλοῦμαι 'I invoke').

3.1.4.3 Verbs with different meanings in active and passive

These verbs, which cannot be changed from one voice to the other without a complete change of meaning, include συμβουλεύω 'I advise' → συμβουλεύομαι 'I consult', δανείζω 'I lend' → δανείζομαι 'I borrow', μοιράζω 'I distribute' → μοιράζομαι 'I share', ὁρκίζω 'I conjure, put on oath' → ὁρκίζομαι 'I swear', ξεφορτώνω 'I unload' → ξεφορτώνομαι 'I get rid of', δέ μέ νοιάζει 'I don't mind' (lit. 'it doesn't worry me') → νοιάζεται τό μαγαζί '(s)he minds the shop'. In most cases what is called passive here is in fact a relic of the ancient middle meaning, and the subject is the agent of the action; in each case the verb is transitive.

Certain other verbs may also remain transitive in their passive form: e.g.

(1a) περιέβαλε τά πάντα μέ μιάν ἀτμόσφαιρα ἀμεριμνησίας '(s)he/ it surrounded everything with an atmosphere of carefreeness' →

(1b) τά πάντα περιβλήθηκαν μιάν ἀτμόσφαιρα ἀμεριμνησίας

'everything was surrounded [with] an atmosphere of care-freeness' (Kar. n.d.: I 176);

(2a) μέ πληροφόρησαν γιά τή δολοφονία του 'they informed me about his assassination' →

(2b) πληροφορήθηκα τή δολοφονία του ἀπό τήν τηλεόραση 'I was informed [of] his assassination on [lit. 'from the'] television';

(3a) τῆς ντύσανε τό καινούριο της φόρεμα 'they dressed her in her new dress' (lit. 'of-her they-dressed her new dress') →

(3b) ντύθηκε τό καινούριο της φόρεμα 'she put on [lit. 'dressed'] her new dress';

(4a) φορτώσανε τά τρόφιμα στά βαγόνια 'they loaded the provisions into the [railway] trucks' →

(4b) τά βαγόνια ἦταν φορτωμένα τρόφιμα 'the trucks were loaded [with] provisions.'

3.1.4.4 'Από in agentive, causative, or instrumental sense after active verbs

The close semantic links between the active and the passive in MG are shown by the fact that ἀπό can be used with either voice to express agent, cause, or instrument (translatable into English as 'by', 'from', 'because of', 'by means of', 'through', etc.). Thus one may easily find pairs of sentences such as the following:

(1a) τά γαλλικά τά ἔμαθα ἀπό τόν κ. Βαλμά 'I learned French from Mr Valmas';

(1b) τά γαλλικά τά διδάχτηκα ἀπό τόν κ. Βαλμά 'I was taught French by Mr Valmas',

in which only the verbs are different, one being active and the other passive (or, strictly, middle), but each with the same meaning and each followed by ἀπό + agent (the English rendering of ἀπό in two different ways in the above sentences disguises the fact that the constructions are identical).

The following examples illustrate various uses of active verb + ἀπό + agent (which is not necessarily animate):

(2)   ἡ ΑΕΚ ἔχασε μέ 1–0 ἀπό τόν Παναθηναϊκό 'ΑΕΚ [football team] lost (by) 1–0 to Panathinaikos';

(3)   πολλοί ἐπαγγελματίες θά χάσουν τίς δουλειές τους ἀπό τούς ξένους 'many professionals will lose their jobs to foreigners';

(4)   τό περιοδικό βγαίνει ἀπό τούς φοιτητές τῆς Φιλοσοφικῆς Σχολῆς

'the magazine is put out [lit. 'comes out'] by the students of the Arts Faculty' (= ἐκδίδεται 'is published');

(5) ἀνησυχῶ ἀπό τήν ἀπουσία του 'I'm worried [lit. 'I worry'] by his absence.'

In some cases, the active verb could be replaced by its own passive (cf. 3.1.1):

(6) ἡ κυκλοφορία παρέλυσε ἀπό τό χιόνι 'the traffic was paralysed by the snow' (= παραλύθηκε);

(7) τό ἔργο ζωντανεύει ἀπό ἀρκετά πραγματικά στοιχεῖα τῆς ἐποχῆς 'the work/play/film is enlivened [lit. 'comes to life'] by several real elements of the time' (= ζωντανεύεται).

3.1.5 SEMANTIC ANOMALIES OF THE PAST PASSIVE PARTICIPLE

The regular situation with the so-called past passive participle as regards semantic voice (diathesis) is that a transitive verb in active form possesses a past passive participle with passive meaning (e.g. δένω 'I tie' → δεμένος 'tied', i.e. 'in a state of having been tied'). In fact, some of these participles may have a reciprocal rather than passive meaning: e.g. ἡ ἀγαπημένη μου κόρη 'my beloved daughter' (passive), but ἕνα ἀγαπημένο ἀντρόγυνο 'a loving couple' (reciprocal). But there are three other possible situations, in which (a) an intransitive active-form verb has a past passive participle with active meaning; (b) a transitive active-form verb has the participle with active meaning; and (c) a transitive passive-form (deponent) verb with active meaning has a past passive participle with passive meaning. In addition, there are also many transitive verbs which lack a past participle altogether: these include both active-form verbs (e.g. ἔχω, θέλω, ξέρω, περιμένω, ἐλπίζω 'I hope', ρωτῶ 'I ask', νομίζω 'I think', βρίζω 'I swear at') and passive-form verbs (e.g. αἰσθάνομαι, θυμᾶμαι).

(a) Intransitive active verb → active participle

There is a large number of verbs of this nature: e.g. διψάω 'I'm thirsty' → διψασμένος 'thirsty', πεινάω 'I'm hungry' → πεινασμένος 'hungry', πέφτω 'I fall' → πεσμένος 'fallen', κρυώνω 'I am cold; I catch cold' → κρυωμένος 'suffering from a cold', γερνάω 'I grow old' → γερασμένος 'grown old', σκύβω 'I bend down' → σκυμμενος 'stooping' (cf. the active verbal adjective σκυφτός 'bent'), πεθαίνω 'I die' → πεθαμένος 'dead'. None of these has any finite passive form. Some verbs have a negative verbal adjective in -τος (which usually has a passive sense with transitive verbs) even without forming a past passive participle: e.g. διστάζω 'I hesitate' → ἀδίστακτος 'unflinching'. Sometimes however the semantic voice of the participle may differ from that of the verbal adjective: e.g. γελάω 'I laugh; I fool' → γελασμένος 'fooled', but γελαστός 'laughing'.

(b) Transitive active verb → active participle

A much smaller number of transitive verbs may form a participle of this kind with active meaning; but since these verbs all have optional object deletion, they are not very different from the previous group. English often presents a similar phenomenon. Examples: διαβάζω 'I read' → διαβασμένος 'well-read (of person)' (also, of pupil, 'having done homework', negative ἀδιάβαστος; but cf. ἔνα πολυδιαβασμένο βιβλίο 'a much-read book', in passive meaning), τρώω 'I eat' → φαγωμένος 'having eaten' (in the plural, and in the appropriate context, the participle could mean 'having quarrelled', from the reciprocal sense of the passive τρώγονται), πίνω 'I drink' → πιωμένος 'drunk (person)', ἀποφασίζω 'I decide' → ἀποφασισμένος 'decided, determined (person)' (negative ἀναποφάσιστος 'indecisive', and a positive active-form adjective ἀποφασιστικός 'decisive'). As is clear from some of the examples quoted so far, the past passive participle of a particular verb may belong to more than one semantic voice category (active, passive, reciprocal, etc.). This is especially applicable to verbs which in the active may be either transitive or intransitive, or to transitive verbs which may take two different kinds of object (or no object at all). Thus:

(1a) δέν μπορῶ νά συνηθίσω τή ζέστη 'I can't get used to the heat' (trans.) →

(1b) δέν εἶμαι συνηθισμένος στή ζέστη 'I'm not accustomed to the heat' (active);

(2a) δέ συνηθίζεται αὐτή ἡ χρήση 'this usage is not customary' →

(2b) αὐτή ἡ χρήση δέν εἶναι συνηθισμένη (same meaning, with participle in passive sense: negative ἀσυνήθιστη);

also χτυπῶ '(trans.) I hit, beat; (intrans.) I hurt myself' → χτυπημένα αὐγά 'beaten eggs', but ἦταν χτυπημένος ἄσχημα 'he was badly hurt'; and while κερδίζω 'I earn; win; beat (an opponent)' and χάνω 'I lose' have adjectival participles κερδισμένος 'won' and χαμένος 'lost' in passive senses, these may be substantivized as ὁ κερδισμένος and ὁ χαμένος in games of chance etc. to mean 'the winner' and 'the loser' in an active sense. An apt example of the semantic subtleties of past passive participles is the phrase περασμένα ξεχασμένα 'let bygones be bygones' (lit. 'past forgotten (neuter pl.)'), which represents an underlying phrase in which one verb is active in meaning and the other passive (πέρασαν καί ξεχάστηκαν 'they have passed (act.) and they have been forgotten (pass.)').

(c) Deponent verb → passive participle

While intransitive deponents preserve their semantic voice (i.e. active) in the past passive participle (e.g. παραπονιέμαι 'I complain' → παραπονεμένος 'plaintive'), many transitive deponents possess a past participle with passive meaning: e.g. ὀνειρεύομαι 'I dream (of)' → ὀνειρεμένος 'dreamed-of' (cf. verbal adjective ὀνειρευτός with same sense), καταριέμαι 'I curse' → καταραμένος '(ac)cursed', ἐγγυῶμαι 'I guarantee' → ἐγγυημένος 'guaranteed'. A similar situation obtains with δανείζομαι 'I borrow': despite the existence of the active δανείζω 'I lend', the meaning of the participle δανεισμένος 'borrowed' might be said to derive from the passive, which could be regarded as a deponent: consider

(1) ἄλλοι στίχοι δανεισμένοι ἀπό προγενέστερα δημοσιεύματα 'other verses borrowed from [not 'lent by'] earlier publications' (Vra. 1953: 214).

As in the other two groups, some deponent verbs form verbal adjectives which are anomalous with respect to semantic voice: e.g. παραδέχομαι 'I accept' → παραδεκτός 'accepted; acceptable' (neg. ἀπαράδεκτος 'unacceptable'); and others mentioned in 3.1.4.2.

3.1.6 VOICE IN NOUNS AND ADJECTIVES

Finally, the fact that voice applies to deverbal adjectives and nouns as well as to verbs has already been implied without being made explicit. In the example, ἡ ὑποστήριξη τῆς οἰκογένειάς του, as we have seen (2.2.4.2), the first noun may be taken in an active or a passive sense, according to whether it is his family that supports him or he that supports his family (the first interpretation viewing the noun as active and the second as passive). While such abstract nouns (in -si) may denote either of the voices according to context, concrete nouns in -της usually denote the active voice (they are *agent nouns*).

Equally, deverbal adjectives may indicate voice: those in -τος usually (but not always, as we have seen) denote passive, while those in -τικός usually denote active voice.

3.2   ASPECT

The categories of tense and aspect, and the interplay between them, are among the facets of MG which have attracted the greatest scholarly attention during the last half century, and since the debate between Tzartzanos (1932, 1934) and Andriotis (1932, 1934) about whether or not the subjunctive exists in MG, a number of linguists have tended to push aside the distinction between the indicative and the subjunctive moods (which seemed to be valid for AG) in favour of that between the perfective and imperfective aspects, which certainly works better when applied to the modern language; and in several books and articles Mirambel (e.g. 1942: 28) has stressed that the aspectual distinction overrides not only mood but tense as well: he claims (1956: 219) that on the hierarchical scale of values in the MG verb, aspect occupies the top rank, followed by voice and mood, with tense at the bottom. The aspectual distinction in MG is one that comes so naturally to the native speaker that (s)he is normally unable to explain it (and books of grammar and syntax for Greek readers are usually more or less silent on the matter[1]); but aspect is probably the most difficult concept for the learner of MG to master, and even those non-native speakers who can speak MG almost perfectly are often given away as foreigners by their mistakes in aspect. The tense distinctions, on the other hand, are less difficult to grasp.

For the purposes of aspect and tense we shall examine first what distinctions are made explicitly in the morphology of the verb, and we shall use the terminology that has become acceptable among modern linguists, giving the traditional terms alongside them. It is unfortunate that there is much similarity among the various terms, which may give rise to confusion.

3.2.1   THE VERB FORMS

Although a neat matrix can be made of a bipartite division of the MG verb into imperfective and perfective aspects, it is more faithful to the true linguistic situation to include the perfect as a third aspect: it should be borne in mind, however, that the perfect is not as crucial to the distinctions of aspect as are the imperfective and perfective, quite

---

[1] It is significant that there is no satisfactory term for 'aspect' in MG: neither τρόπος 'way' (Triandaphyllidis 1941: 312 ff.) nor ποιόν ἐνεργείας (Babiniotis-Kondos 1967: 146–8) is helpful, and neither is in wide use. I would humbly suggest ὄψη as a direct translation of the Russian *vid* (from which the term 'aspect' has itself been translated).

apart from the fact that it is always expressed periphrastically, and that the two elements which form it are not 'uninterruptible' (e.g. they may be separated by an adverb of time or even by a whole nominal or adverbial phrase).

Table 3.1 contains the finite active forms of ἀγαπῶ 'I love' (in the first person singular) with their modern labels: there is of course an exactly corresponding matrix for the passive.

TABLE 3.1

		Aspect		
		Imperfective	*Perfective*	*Perfect*
Tense	Non-past	ἀγαπῶ	ἀγαπήσω	ἔχω ἀγαπήσει
	Past	ἀγαπούσα	ἀγάπησα	εἶχα ἀγαπήσει

Each of the forms given in the table represents the intersection of tense and aspect.

The term used here for each of these forms is:

Imperfective non-past (= 'present indicative' and 'present subjunctive');
Imperfective past (= 'imperfect');
Perfective non-past (= 'aorist subjunctive');
Perfective past (= 'aorist indicative');
Perfect non-past (= 'perfect');
Perfect past (= 'pluperfect').

Some verbs lack one or more aspects. Those which lack the imperfective alone are extremely few, being confined to certain fixed expressions (e.g. *χρηματίζω: ἐχρημάτισε δήμαρχος '(s)he served as mayor'); nevertheless, a number of verbs are less commonly used in the imperfective than in the other aspects, either because of their semantic function (e.g. ἀποκοιμιέμαι 'I fall asleep'), or because the formation of the imperfective is morphologically problematic (e.g. κορεσ- 'satiate', imperfective κορεννύω, διαγνωσ- 'diagnose', imperfective διαγι(γ)νώσκω).

There is, however, an important group of verbs which exist only in the imperfective: since the 'perfect formant' (see 3.2.4.1) is formed from the perfective stem, it follows that verbs which do not have a perfective do not have a perfect either. Such verbs include εἶμαι 'I am', ἔχω 'I have', ἀνήκω 'I belong', ξέρω 'I know', περιμένω 'I wait for', πρέπει 'it is necessary', πρόκειται 'it is a question of; be about to' (impersonal) and χρωστάω 'I owe'.

3.2.2 INDICATIVE AND SUBJUNCTIVE

The terms 'indicative' and 'subjunctive' are not used in our morphological terminology, since they are differentiated not formally (within the verb form) but according to syntactical context. The only moods that have distinct forms from those given in Table 3.1 are the imperative and the participles: other moods are expressed by the use of any of the finite forms preceded by the particles νά, θά, or ἄς, or by a variety of other 'grammatical words', which will be examined under the name of *subjunctive markers* in Chapter 9. Nevertheless, in view of the fact that the perfective non-past, alone of all the forms, may not be used absolutely, two semantic categories of modality (in addition to the imperative and the participle) will have to be posited for finite forms of the verb: indicative (unmarked for mood) and subjunctive (marked for mood).

The only formal difference between the indicative and the subjunctive modalities in MG is that the former excludes the use of the perfective non-past (hence the traditional appellation of this form as 'subjunctive': it is almost always a *bound form*), while the latter does not; and, syntactically, the subjunctive is always preceded by a *subjunctive marker*. 'Subjunctiveness', then, does not inhere in a particular verb form, but is a function of the subjunctive markers. (For further details about distinctions between the indicative and the subjunctive and for a full treatment of subjunctive clauses, see Chapter 9.)

3.2.3 ASPECTUAL DISTINCTIONS: PERFECTIVE AND IMPERFECTIVE

Futurity is not expressed in MG by its own verb form but is just one of several semantic functions of the modal particle θά (see 9.1). Thus we can talk about the existence of two tenses in MG, namely non-past and past, which exist for each of the three aspects, imperfective, perfective, and perfect. This categorization is reinforced by the morphology of the MG verb, which has similar endings for most of the non-past paradigms, and an identical set of endings for most of the past forms (see 5.3.1 and 5.3.2).

Aspect in MG concerns not the *location* of the action or state in time, but the speaker's attitude to its 'temporal distribution or contour'

(Hockett, in Lyons 1968: 315). It is this subjective nature of aspectual distinctions which makes them so difficult to master for one who is not a native speaker. On the other hand, it would be quite wrong to suggest that the distinction in each case is purely dependent on the whim of the speaker: once the speaker has decided what (s)he means the hearer to understand, there is hardly ever any choice in the matter.

The most basic concepts behind MG aspect are the following: in using a verb in the *perfective*, the speaker is viewing the action (or series of actions) as a single, completed whole (neither progressive nor habitual); with the *imperfective*, (s)he sees the verb as referring to a series of repeated actions not viewed as a whole (iterative) or to a continuous action in progress (progressive or durative). Thus the verbs in the Greek equivalents of (1) 'I went to the University yesterday' (single action) and (2) 'I studied [= carried out my studies] at Salonica University' (repeated visits plus various related activities, all viewed as a completed whole) are equally perfective:

(1) χτές πῆγα στό Πανεπιστήμιο,
(2) φοίτησα στό Πανεπιστήμιο Θεσσαλονίκης.

On the other hand, in (3) 'When I was young I went [= used to go] to church every week' (iterative), and (4) 'As I was going to church yesterday I met Catherine' (progressive), the verb 'go' is imperfective in MG:

(3) ὅταν ἤμουν μικρός πήγαινα στήν ἐκκλησία κάθε βδομάδα,
(4) χτές, τήν ὥρα πού πήγαινα στήν ἐκκλησία, συνάντησα τήν Κατερίνα.

It is not the *actual* nature of the action that is crucial, but the way in which it is viewed by the speaker at the time of the utterance: the journey to the university in (1) may have lasted exactly the same length of time as the journey to the church in (4); what conditions the use of the imperfective in (4) is the fact that something is expressed as having occurred *during* the journey. When a speaker uses the perfective, (s)he tends to stand at a distance from the action, seeing it as a completed whole, irrespective of whether it occurs in the past or the future; when using the imperfective, the speaker's mental standpoint is not the time of speaking but the time of the action expressed by the verb. In (4) the journey to the church has begun but has not been completed by the time the speaker meets Catherine: the journey here constitutes the circumstances of the single event (the meeting), which is expressed by a verb in the perfective. (Clearly, since the imperfective may express the iterative or the progressive, it is immaterial whether each action in an iterative series is viewed as completed or in progress.)

In expressions of past or future action, the perfective is the unmarked aspect, in the sense that a verb in the perfective does *not* specify whether the action is progressive or iterative or neither: it may simply state that something happened or will happen (e.g. νά μοῦ γράψεις (perfective) 'write to me (once or more than once)', but νά μοῦ γράφεις (imperfective) 'write to me (regularly or often)'). Thus in past or future reference the perfective is the most frequently used aspect: it is the natural aspect for the verb to be in unless there are clear grounds for using the imperfective (i.e. that the action is considered as durative or repeated). This, coupled with the fact that morphologically the perfective stem is diachronically and synchronically more stable than the imperfective (i.e. the perfective stem of a large number of verbs has not changed since classical times, while their imperfective has; and with some verbs speakers who use the same perfective stem may differ in their usage of the imperfective: cf. Mirambel 1959: 141, and Ebbesen 1979: 65-6), has led some grammarians to see the perfective as the basic stem of the MG verb. (Nevertheless, it is always the imperfective stem that appears in dictionaries.)

3.2.3.1 Aspect and adverbials

The perfective is typically accompanied by adverbials denoting *point in time* (e.g. αὔριο 'tomorrow', στίς ἕξη 'at six o'clock; on the sixth', τό 1983 'in 1983', etc.), unless these co-occur with *imperfective adverbials* and unless the verb denotes an action which expresses the background to another action. The imperfective adverbials, i.e. those that are typically found with verbs in the imperfective, tend to refer to *frequency* (e.g. κάθε τόσο 'every so often', καθημερινά 'daily', πάλι καί πάλι 'again and again', καμιά φορά 'occasionally', τακτικά 'regularly'), or *duration* (e.g. μέρα μέ τή μέρα 'as the days go/went by', ὅλο (καί) 'all the time'); the imperfective also typically co-occurs with another verb, of which it acts as the background (as in example (4) in 3.2.3).

It should not be thought, however, that the perfective cannot be used with adverbials denoting number of times: on the contrary, δυό φορές 'twice', χίλιες φορές 'a thousand times', πολλές φορές 'many times', even ἀμέτρητες φορές 'innumerable times' (but not καμιά φορά) are always used with the perfective (unless there is some other factor in the context which conditions the imperfective, as there is in δυό φορές τό μήνα 'twice a month'), since each of these adverbials is considered as indicating a completed series consisting of a specified number of times.

By contrast, συχνά 'often' is more usually found with the imperfective, although it may be used with the perfective. It is only in this limited area within aspect that subjective choice is possible. The following pair of sentences (Newton–Veloudis 1980b: 32) may refer to the same actual situation, but in them it is clear that 'aspect is determined by what sentences assert, not by what they imply':

(1a) γιά ἕνα χρόνο ἐρχόταν κατά μέσον ὄρο μιά φορά τό μήνα 'for a/one year (s)he came (used to come) on average once a month' (imperfective);

(1b) ἕνα χρόνο ἦρθε δώδεκα φορές 'one year (s)he came twelve times' (perfective).

3.2.3.2 Aspect in present or timeless reference

Where the time of the action in an indicative sentence is neither specifically past nor specifically future (i.e. the time of utterance and the time of action partially coincide), the imperfective will clearly be the correct aspect, since the speaker's viewpoint will necessarily be the time of the action. This explains the lack of a perfective form in MG for declarations concerning the present (in other words, it explains why the perfective non-past cannot be used outside subjunctive clauses): statements about the present or statements with timeless reference necessarily refer to durative or iterative actions or states. Consider the following exchanges:

(1a) —Τί δουλειά κάνεις;—Γράφω. ' "What work do you do?" "I write." ';

(1b) —Τί κάνεις τώρα;—Γράφω. ' "What are you doing now?" "I'm writing." '

In (1a) the reference is timeless, and the action either durative or (more likely!) iterative; in (1b) the reference is present and the action is durative. Both sentences employ the imperfective in MG. In fact, a completed action in the present is practically a logical impossibility, and the occasions when the imperfective non-past is used to refer to a completed action are of three types: (a) the *historic* or *narrative* present, used in narrating stories (e.g. γυρίζει καί μοῦ λέει . . . 'he turns round and says to me . . .'); (b) broadcast commentaries (e.g.

ὁ Μπουμπλῆς σουτάρει ἀλλά δέν πετυχαίνει τό γκόλ 'Boublis shoots, but doesn't reach the goal'), which could also be classed as a historic present, since the comment almost inevitably *follows* the action (except perhaps in cricket!); and (c) performative declarations (e.g. συνημμένα σᾶς στέλνω τό ἔγγραφο . . . 'attached I send you the document').

One anomalous idiomatic use of the perfective, in which it refers to *habitual* actions, is the 'consuetudinal future' (Ben-Mayor 1980: 157-8):

(2) κάθε Τετάρτη, στίς ἐφτάμιση ἀκριβῶς, θά ἔρθει (perf.) ἐδῶ, νά μοῦ κάνει καί νά τοῦ κάνω συντροφιά 'every Wednesday, at 7.30 precisely, he's in the habit of coming here so we can keep each other company' (Kar. n.d.: II 125) (lit. '. . . to of-me he-makes and to of-him I-make company').

The imperfective non-past without θά would be more commonly used here than θά + perfective.

3.2.3.3 Potential meaning of the imperfective

In addition to its progressive and iterative meanings, the imperfective also has a *potential* sense, i.e. it may indicate that the subject is capable of acting (or being acted upon) in the manner designated by the verb:

(1) κόβει ἐκεῖνο τό μαχαίρι; 'does that knife cut?' (i.e. 'is it sharp?');
(2) δέν ἔκοβε τό μαχαίρι 'the knife wouldn't cut';
(3) αὐτό τό κρέας δέν κόβεται 'this meat is uncuttable.'

The passive is frequently used idiomatically in this way:

(4) ἐσύ δέ διορθώνεσαι 'you're incorrigible' (lit. 'you are not corrected');
(5) τό τί τράβηξα δέν περιγράφεται 'what I suffered defies description' (lit. 'the what I-pulled is-not-described').

3.2.3.4 Coincidence, scope, and scenario

Most of what has been said with regard to aspect in the last pages applies equally to verbs in main and subordinate clauses, irrespective of whether or not the verbs are preceded by subjunctive markers such as those which will be examined in Chapter 9.

The situation is sometimes more complex, however, in subjunctive subordinate clauses than in main clauses, and something must be said about the concepts of *coincidence*, *scope*, and *scenario*.

3.2.3.4.1 Coincidence

The concept of 'coincidence' was applied to the aspect of MG verbs in subordinate clauses by Seiler (1952) and was refined by Bakker (1970). The principle is that the imperfective aspect of a subordinate verb in a subjunctive clause indicates that the action it denotes coincides temporally with that of the verb in the main clause (i.e. the two actions occur at the same time); the perfective, by contrast, indicates a lack of temporal coincidence (the action of the subordinate verb is completed before, or commences after, that of the main verb). Thus the verbs ἀρχίζω 'I begin', ἐξακολουθῶ and συνεχίζω 'I continue', παύω and σταματῶ 'I stop' (but cf. (22b)) are followed by νά + imperfective, since the beginning, continuing, or finishing is seen as coinciding with an (albeit infinitesimal) portion of the other action: e.g. ἄρχισα νά τρέχω 'I started running', ἐξακολούθησα νά περπατάω 'I went on walking', σταμάτησε νά βρέχει 'it('s) stopped raining'. It could be said that this usage conforms with the basic rules stated earlier, in that the action of the second verb in each example is by definition seen by the speaker as durative, since it has a beginning, middle, or end.

The imperfective is usually used, especially after verbs of perception, in a νά-clause which stands as a complement to the direct object of the main verb: e.g.

(1) τήν ἄκουσα νά τραγουδάει 'I heard [or 'listened to'] her singing';
(2) τούς εἴδαμε νά περνᾶνε τό δρόμο 'we saw them crossing the road';
(3) σέ φαντάστηκα νά χάνεις τό δρόμο σου 'I imagined you losing your way'.

(These might be considered as corresponding to sentences in which one verb denotes an action, another the background to that action:

(1a) τήν ὥρα πού τραγουδοῦσε, τήν ἄκουσα 'while she was singing (imperfective), I heard her (perfective)' etc.,

in which case the verbs in the imperfective are necessarily being viewed as durative.)

The imperfective is also normally used after verbs such as ξέρω 'I know (how to)', συνηθίζω 'I get used (to)', μαθαίνω 'I learn (how to)', (μοῦ) ἀρέσει '(I) like', where the subordinate verb suggests an iterative action: e.g. ξέρεις νά ὁδηγᾶς; 'do you know how to drive (imperfective)?'; ἔχω συνηϑίσει νά κοιμᾶμαι τό μεσημέρι 'I've got used to sleeping (imperfective) in the middle of the day'.

The perfective is found typically after verbs or phrases such as the following (provided that the second action is not viewed as habitual or progressive): κοντεύω 'I get near (to)', εἶμαι ἔτοιμος 'I'm ready', περιμένω 'I expect', φοβᾶμαι 'I'm afraid (to)', ἐλπίζω 'I hope', παρακαλῶ 'I beg', προφταίνω 'I have time (to)'; e.g.

(4) κόντεψα νά σκοτωϑῶ 'I almost got killed';
(5) εἶστε ἔτοιμοι νά φύγετε; 'are you (pl.) ready to leave?';
(6) περιμένω νά ἔρϑεις 'I'm waiting for you to come';
(7) φοβόμουνα νά πάω 'I was afraid to go';
(8) ἐλπίζω νά μέ πάρεις τηλέφωνο 'I hope you'll phone me';
(9) τόν παρακάλεσα νά μέ βοηϑήσει 'I asked him to help me';
(10) δέ ϑά προφτάσουμε νά τελειώσουμε 'we shan't have time to finish.'

In each of the above examples, the action of the main verb is viewed as being completed before the action of the subordinate verb begins; so much so that (while this is by no means a necessary precondition of a perfective non-past) the action of the subordinate verb may never occur. Certainly (outside expressions referring to future time), in cases where the action of the subordinate verb has not occurred, the imperfective non-past is usually excluded: in example (4), for instance, I was clearly *not* killed, while in (7) the speaker could have gone on to say, 'so I didn't go', and in (9) the sentence could have continued, 'but he refused'. In all these cases, there is a lack of coincidence between the actions. For the same reasons, the conjunctions (and subjunctive markers) πρίν and προτοῦ 'before' are almost always followed by the perfective non-past:

(11) τόν ξεπάστρεψα πρίν μέ πάρει χαμπάρι 'I finished him off before he got wind of me';

clearly here, as in other πρίν-clauses, there is a lack of coincidence between the actions.

The perfective is often used after the universal relatives ὅποιος 'whoever', ὅ,τι 'whatever', ὅπου 'wherever', ὅποτε 'whenever', ὅσο(ς) 'however much' and ὅπως 'however', in future or timeless reference:

(12) ὅποιος ἔρϑει, πές του νά περιμένει 'whoever comes, tell him to wait';
(13) ὅ,τι πεῖς δέ ϑά σέ πιστέψω 'whatever you say, I shan't believe you';

(14)   ὅπου καί νά ταξιδέψω ἡ Ἑλλάδα μέ πληγώνει 'wherever
       I travel, Greece wounds me' (Sef. 1969: 106);
(15)   φεύγουν ὅποτε τούς καπνίσει 'they leave whenever they feel
       like it' (lit. 'whenever of-them it-smokes');
(16)   οἱ καλλικάντζαροι ἀπειλοῦν ὅσα παιδιά γεννηθοῦν τά Χριστού-
       γεννα 'the goblins threaten those children who are born at
       Christmas';
(17)   γράφει ὅπως τοῦ κατέβει 'he writes however he likes' (lit.
       '. . . however of-him it-descends').

In all these cases, it seems, the action of the verb governed by the conjunction is viewed as having been completed before the other action
begins, even though the action of the subordinate verb is potentially
iterative. In these cases, lack of coincidence appears to overrule progressivity and iterativeness (contrast 9.4.4.4 (8)).

The semantic difference between the aspects in instances where
either is grammatically acceptable may be illustrated by the following
pairs of sentences (taken from Bakker 1970):

(18a) τόν ἄφησα νά κλαίει (imperfective) 'I left him crying; I let
       him go on crying' (progressive; coincidence);
(18b) τόν ἄφησα νά κλάψει (perfective) 'I let him cry' (non-
       progressive, non-iterative; ?coincidence);
(19a) μ' ἐμπόδιζε νά ὁδηγῶ (imperfective) '(s)he was hindering
       my driving (but I was driving)' (progressive; coincidence);
(19b) ἐμπόδιζε τή σκέψη νά γυρίσει (perfective) 'it was preventing
       the thought from returning (so it didn't return)' (non-
       progressive, non-iterative; no coincidence);
(20a) μπορεῖ νά λείπουν (imperfective) 'maybe they're away (now)'
       (progressive; coincidence);
(20b) μπορεῖ νά λείψουν (perfective) 'maybe they'll be away (in
       the future)' (progressive; non-coincidence—the lack of
       coincidence overrides the progressivity);
(21a) πρέπει νά θυμᾶστε (imperfective) '(surely) you must remem-
       ber' (inferential; progressive; coincidence);
(21b) πρέπει νά θυμηθεῖτε '(please) you must remember' (obli-
       gative; non-progressive; non-coincidence).

As can be seen, in certain instances a difference in aspect in the subordinate verb may alter the meaning of the first or the second verb, or
both: compare the two meanings of ἀφήνω ((18a) and (18b)), of
ἐμποδίζω ((19a) and (19b)), of πρέπει and of θυμᾶμαι ((21a) and

(21b): in the former, ϑυμᾱμαι refers to an (involuntary) state, in the latter to a (voluntary) action of recollection). Notice too the two meanings of σταματῶ in the following:

(22a) σταμάτησα νά τρώω σουβλάκια (imperfective) 'I ['ve] stopped eating *souvlakia*' (coincidence);

(22b) σταμάτησα νά φάω σουβλάκια (perfective) 'I stopped (in order) to eat *souvlakia*' (no coincidence)

(in (22b), νά could be preceded by γιά, but not in (22a)).

Sometimes, however, when the reference is unambiguously to future time (e.g. when the verb is accompanied by a future adverbial), progressivity or iterativeness may overrule non-coincidence:

(23a) μπορεῖ νά γυρίζουν στό μέλλον (imperfective) 'maybe they'll return in the future' (iterative or progressive);

(23b) μπορεῖ νά γυρίσουν στό μέλλον (perfective) (same translation, but no implication of iterativeness or progressivity).

The same sentences, but without στό μέλλον, will normally be taken to refer to the present (23a) and the future (23b) respectively (Ben-Mayor 1980: 97–8). Thus a rule could be posited that in a subjunctive subordinate clause, where non-coincidence is explicitly expressed (e.g. by an adverbial), aspect may differentiate between a statement and a non-statement of iterativeness or progressivity; but where temporal reference is not explicit, aspect may distinguish between a statement or non-statement that the two actions coincide temporally (but cf. 9.4.4.5).

3.2.3.4.2 Scope

When dealing with sentences containing a subjunctive subordinate clause, one should observe carefully which verb is covered by certain elements (such as negatives and adverbials), i.e. their *scope*. Compare the following (brackets have been inserted to indicate the coverage or scope of the adverbial):

(1a) θέλω (νά σοῦ γράφω κάθε μέρα) (imperfective) 'I want (to write to you every day)';

(1b) (ἔχω μεγάλη διάθεση νά γράψω) κάθε ὥρα (perfective) 'every hour (I have [a] great desire to write)' (Tsats. 1973: 93).

In (1a) the speaker says that (s)he wishes to write at least one letter each day, while in (1b) it is not the writing but the desire that occurs every hour (for this reason the word order has been altered in English to make the meaning clearer). The scope of the adverbial covers the verb γράφω in (1a), but the phrase ἔχω διάϑεση in (1b).

There is a tendency for a verb governed by an iterative verb to be in the perfective, as in the following (both examples from Bakker 1970):

(2) κάϑε φορά πού τέλειωνα (impf.) ἕνα σχέδιο (βιαζόμουνα (impf.) νά βάλω (pf.) ἐμπρός κάτι ἄλλο) 'every time I finished one pattern (I used to be in a hurry to start something else)';

(3) κάϑε φορά πού (ἐπρόκειτο (impf.) νά ἐπισκεφτῶ (pf.) τό γιατρό) ἡ μέρα μου πήγαινε (impf.) χαμένη 'every time (I was to visit the doctor), my day was wasted'.

In each sentence there are two non-subjunctive verbs in the imperfective, whose iterative aspect is reinforced by the adverbial κάϑε φορά. One of these verbs in each sentence governs a subjunctive verb in the perfective. The perfective is used because the scope of the adverbial covers only the non-subjunctive verbs: each time the speaker in (2) hurried to start a new pattern, she started a new pattern *only once*; similarly, each time the speaker in (3) was due to visit the doctor, she visited him *only once*. (There may also be a lack of coincidence, since on some occasion the pattern might not have been started, and the visit to the doctor might not have been made; nevertheless, the imperfective could be used in the subjunctive verb if the action was viewed as progressive, or if the verb referred to an action that was repeated habitually for every single occasion referred to in the verb which governs it.)

The negative may also affect aspect: compare the following:

(4a) ἤξερε νά κολυμπάει '(s)he knew how to swim';

(4b) δέν ἤξερε νά κολυμπήσει (pf.) '(s)he didn't know how to swim.'

In (4a) the imperfective is used because on any occasion the person's ability to swim might have coincided with his/her swimming; in (4b) the person's inability to swim could never coincide with his/her swimming.

3.2.3.4.3 Scenario

Another way of approaching the examples (4a) and (4b) above is according to the concept of *scenario expressions* (Newton, 1979a and 1979b). A scenario expression is one which contains an explicit or implicit statement of certain conditions under which an action takes place. In (4a) these conditions are something like, 'whenever there is a convenient stretch of water available'. In (4b) there is no such scenario.

(The same distinction would have held if the main verb had been μπορῶ 'I can' instead of ξέρω.) It is in scenario expressions that the imperfective is used, while the perfective is used where the performance (or non-performance) of the action does not depend on certain conditions: the imperfective is used to refer to actions considered as being *relative* to others, as we have seen when discussing coincidence, while the perfective is used for actions considered as being *absolute* or independent.

Consider the following pairs of sentences, in which a scenario expression is used with a modal (here μπορῶ in the deontic sense of 'I am permitted'):

(5a) μπορεῖς νά 'ρθεῖς (pf.) ὅποτε θέλεις,
(5b) μπορεῖς νά 'ρχεσαι (impf.) ὅποτε θέλεις.

(Newton 1979a: 33). Both these sentences may be rendered in English as, 'you may come whenever you like'. But (5a) implies 'at whatever time you like, you may come once' (i.e. either once and for all, or once each time, with specific permission being given for each occasion); while (5b) implies, 'on whatever occasions you like, you may come however many times you like' (with standing permission being given for an indefinite number of visits). In (5a) the verb [νά] 'ρθεῖς is not covered by the scenario expression ὅποτε θέλεις, whereas the verb [νά] 'ρχεσαι in (5b) is. Thus the examples could be explained thus: (5a) 'whenever-you-like, you may come'; (5b) 'you may-whenever-you-like come-whenever-you-like'. This is shown more clearly in sentences concerning actions which by their nature do not admit of repetition:

(6a) μπορεῖς ὅποτε θέλεις ν' αὐτοκτονήσεις (pf.),
(6b) *μπορεῖς ὅποτε θέλεις ν' αὐτοκτονεῖς (impf.) 'you may commit suicide whenever you like.'

Here only the perfective is possible, since the action denoted by the subordinate verb is performable only once: the adverbial covers the main verb but not the subordinate.

The perfective (referring as it does more to specific actions than does the imperfective) may distinguish a definite from an indefinite subject. Consider the following:

(7a) οἱ κοπέλες πρέπει νά παντρεύονται (impf.) μικρές 'girls should marry young';
(7b) οἱ κοπέλες πρέπει νά παντρευτοῦν (pf.) μικρές '*the* girls should marry young'.

(Newton 1979b: 158–9). The Greek sentences are distinguished by
a difference in aspect, the English by the absence or presence of the
definite article. In (7a), although the speaker is probably thinking of
each girl marrying once, the imperfective is used because they are
considered as marrying one after another (or else there is a scenario:
'whenever girls exist . . .'); in (7b), there is no scenario, and the specific
girls are considered to be getting married on particular occasions. The
interplay between aspect and specificness can be further illustrated in
the following pair of sentences, in which it is the object of the verb that
is in question:

(8a) μπορεῖς νά σκοτώνεις (impf.) τίς κότες 'you may/can kill
hens';

(8b) μπορεῖς νά σκοτώσεις (pf.) τίς κότες 'you may/can kill *the*
hens' (Newton 1979b: 164).

There is no grammatical difference here between the deontic (permission) and physical (ability) meanings of μπορεῖς: but, in (8b) as in (7b),
the perfective aspect leads the hearer to interpret the noun as referring
to specific objects, rather than to a scenario ('whenever hens exist . . .').

It should not be thought, however, that the foregoing remarks about
scenario expressions hold true in all cases. It is not difficult to find
counter-examples, such as the following:

(9) κάθε φορά πού καλέστηκε (pf.) στά ὅπλα καινούρια κλάση,
πολλοί τό ἔκοψαν (pf.) ποδάρι γιά τίς ράχες 'every time a new
class was called to arms, many [men] made for the hills'
(Pre. n.d.: 331);

(10) γιατί δέ μ' ἄφηνες (impf.) νά φύγω (pf.) ὅσες φορές τό προ-
σπάθησα (pf.); 'why didn't you let me leave on all the occasions when I wanted to?' (Pla. 1976: 137);

(11) κάθε φορά πού τόν συναντήσω (pf.), μελαγχολῶ 'every time
I meet him I get depressed' (Sef. 1977: 300).

In (9) we have a scenario expression which structurally differs little
from (2) and (3), except that here both verbs are in the perfective:
there seems no reason why they should not be imperfective. In (10) we
have a mixed structure, in which one main verb is imperfective, the
other perfective: again, the perfective is hard to explain (although the
subordinated perfective νά φύγω follows the same pattern as in (2) and
(3)). In (11) we have a sentence with timeless reference, in which the
subordinated verb is in the perfective, following the pattern which has

already been observed after universal relatives (3.2.3.4.1): in this case, κάθε φορά πού is equivalent to ὅποτε 'whenever'. In this last example, the perfective is quite regular: thus it must be borne in mind that sentences with non-temporal (general) or future reference may differ in aspect from those with past reference (see also 9.4.4.4). In (9) and (10), on the other hand, where the verbs refer to the past, the imperfective would perhaps have been more normal than the perfective. In (9) the divergence from the norm may be a matter of dialect (the writer is Cretan, and uses such constructions frequently): in (10) it is clearly a matter of style (the writer is Athenian). Very little work has been done on differences in aspectual usage according to dialect and style, and it is clear that more research is needed.

3.2.4 THE PERFECT ASPECT

More will be said about the perfective and imperfective aspects when we come to examine tense and mood in greater detail. Before that, however, we should look at the perfect aspect.

The perfect has been termed an aspect rather than a tense, since it consists of two tense-forms (traditionally called the 'perfect' and the 'pluperfect') and can be used, like each of the other two aspects, in the various moods (including, of course, the future, but not the imperative). The perfect differs from each of the other aspects, however, in that it always refers to a time anterior to another time (whether the latter be the time of utterance or the time of another verb in the same linguistic context). It stands on its own also by virtue of the fact that its use is hardly ever obligatory: it can normally be replaced by another aspect (normally the perfective) without any real change of meaning except to disambiguate a potentially ambiguous utterance. Kahane and Kahane (1958: 458) suggest that the use or otherwise of the perfect is a matter of idiolect; but it is to be doubted that this means more than that some speakers use it more than others (see further 3.3.1.3).

The nature of the perfect is that it combines reference to two times (e.g. past and present, past and more-past, or future and less-future). It is used in describing a completed action (thus resembling the perfective), and it is not used where there is a coincidence of actions, nor where an action is considered as progressive or iterative.

The perfect non-past, when used indicatively (i.e. without a subjunctive marker), is used to denote an anterior action or series of actions whose present (or future) result is stressed: thus it is used in conversational speech far more than in, e.g., written narrative. It may be used not only for actions which have occurred a number of times (or never) within a period ending in the present or future (1), but also for actions which happened once and for all in the past (2), and for a series of actions which stopped happening some time ago (3):

(1) ἀπό τό 1961 ἔχω πάει δέκα φορές στό Λονδίνο 'since 1961 I have been to London ten times' (i.e. from 1961 to the present);

(2) ἔχω γεννηθεῖ τό 1946 'I was born in 1946';

(3) ὁ Καζαντζάκης ἔχει γράψει δέκα μυθιστορήματα 'Kazantzakis wrote ten novels' (though K. is long since dead!);

but in (2) and (3) and similar constructions the action must have some consequence in the present (e.g. that I am alive, and that K.'s novels are there to be read).

Despite (2) and (3), the difference in meaning between the perfect and the other verb forms in MG is much more like English than it is like French (in which the difference between the perfect and the past historic is one of register); on the other hand, it may be that spoken French has influenced some Greek speakers to use the perfect more than is necessary, and in (2) and (3) the perfective past would be preferred by many speakers to the perfect non-past.

It is however sometimes useful to distinguish the perfect non-past from the perfective past. Imagine two people in the Museum at Olympia. If one says to the other,

(4a) τόν Ἑρμή τοῦ Πραξιτέλη τόν ἔχεις δεῖ;

(s)he means, 'have you [ever] seen the Hermes of Praxiteles?' (i.e. once or more during the period from your birth to the present), the implication being that they have not yet reached the statue on their present visit. By contrast, a speaker who asks,

(4b) τόν Ἑρμή τοῦ Πραξιτέλη τόν εἶδες;

will most probably be asking, 'did you see the Hermes of Praxiteles?', implying that the statue has already come into sight and then disappeared again (i.e. the speaker is asking whether the other person saw it on a specific occasion). Although the perfective past could be used for both meanings, the use of the perfect non-past would be advisable in the first case so that ambiguity should be avoided. The perfect non-past could not be used in the second meaning, however: although the perfect is usually replaceable by another aspect (normally the perfective), the converse is not true.

3.2.4.1 The form of the perfect

Something should be said about the various ways of expressing the perfect aspect. The standard version consists of the relevant form of ἔχω 'I have' followed by the *perfect formant*,[1] which is identical to the third person singular of the perfective non-past of the relevant voice: e.g. ἔχω δέσει 'I have tied', ἔχω δεθεῖ 'I have been tied'; εἶχα δέσει 'I had tied', εἶχα δεθεῖ 'I had been tied'. Thus it shares characteristics with the other two aspects: its first element (ἔχω) is imperfective, its second (the perfect formant) is formally perfective. There is, however, an alternative (but less common) active form when a direct object is present, consisting of ἔχω followed by the past passive participle, which agrees in number, gender, and case with the object: e.g. τόν ἔχω δέσει (or δεμένο) τό γάιδαρο 'I have tied up the donkey'. For the passive, εἶμαι 'I am' may be followed by the same participle: e.g. εἶχε δεθεῖ ὁ γάιδαρος 'the donkey had been tied up', ἦταν δεμένος ὁ γάιδαρος 'the donkey was tied up'. Note that with some verbs εἶμαι + passive participle is equivalent to ἔχω + active perfect formant: e.g. ἔχω πεινάσει 'I have become hungry', εἶμαι πεινασμένος 'I am hungry' (cf. 3.1.5).

In each case, however, the version which employs the perfect formant does not mean precisely the same as that which uses the participle: while the former emphasizes the action, the latter emphasizes its result. Also, in ἔχω + participle, the verb ἔχω normally retains its meaning of possession, while it does not do so in ἔχω + perfect formant (hence, τόν ἔχω δεμένο τό γάιδαρο would be better rendered as 'I've got the donkey tied up'). (This is the situation in SMG, though in many dialects ἔχω + participle does not necessarily retain the idea of possession: thus the geographical provenance of a speaker may affect his/her way of forming the perfect.)

3.2.5 THE ASPECT OF THE PARTICIPLE

The question of which aspect is displayed by the past passive participle was left unanswered by Seiler (1952: 39). Kahane and Kahane (1958)

---

[1] There is no satisfactory term for this form, either in English or in Greek, as far as I am aware. Greek linguists often call it ἀπαρέμφατο 'infinitive' (which, while justifiable historically, is synchronically misleading); Hesse (1980: 13) calls it 'aorist participle'.

place it under perfect aspect. This is probably generally speaking correct, in view of its appearance in composite forms which are equivalent to the perfect tenses (e.g. ἔχει γραφεῖ 'it has been written' = εἶναι γραμμένο 'it is written').

Nevertheless, the situation is rather complex. The only participle about whose aspect there can be no doubt is the present passive, which is always imperfective, since it refers to a progressive action: e.g., in its purely adjectival (attributive) use,

(1) ἡ ἀπαιτούμενη κριτική ἀκρίβεια 'the requisite critical precision',

where it corresponds to the imperfective ποὺ ἀπαιτεῖται 'which is required'. This action may coincide with that of another verb: e.g., in verbal use,

(2) ἐπισκεπτόμενοι τὴν Ἀκρόπολη θά δεῖτε . . . 'while visiting the Acropolis, you will see . . .',

where the participle does not correspond precisely to the perfective ὅταν ἐπισκεφτεῖτε 'when you visit': the participle stresses coincidence, whereas its paraphrase in finite form does not.

The present active participle, which cannot be used adjectivally, is also normally imperfective (e.g. ἔφυγε τρέχοντας 'he ran away', corresponding to ἔφυγε ἐνῶ ἔτρεχε 'he left while he was running') because it displays progressivity and coincidence (the present active participle (usually) and the present passive participle (always, when used non-attributively) have the same subject as the main verb); but it may sometimes correspond to a perfective past: e.g.

(3) φτάνοντας στήν πόρτα, χτύπησε 'arriving at the door, (s)he knocked' (corresponding to ὅταν ἔφτασε 'when (s)he arrived'),

in which case it presumably functions as a perfective (or at least a perfect), since the action is considered to be non-progressive and does not coincide with the other. This is probably what gave rise to the *perfect participle* (e.g. ἔχοντας φτάσει 'having arrived'), which does not have a long history, and is considered by many speakers to be an unwelcome intrusion from French or English (the perfect participle also exists in the passive: e.g. ἔχοντας πληροφορηθεῖ 'having been informed'). Note that, like the present passive participle of a transitive deponent, while the perfect active participle of a transitive verb may have a noun as an object, it may not govern a clitic pronoun, which suggests that neither has become completely established in the normal language (e.g. *ἔχον-τάς το λύσει 'having solved it' is impossible and ?μεταχειριζόμενός το 'using it' is of doubtful acceptability).

To make matters more confusing, some so-called past passive participles are not necessarily past at all (e.g. συλλογισμένος 'pensive' = πού συλλογίζεται 'who is thinking', or πού συλλογιζότανε 'who was thinking': this verb has no commonly used present participle form); while some verbs have three participles with active meaning (e.g. σκύβοντας 'bending', σκυμμένος 'bent' and ἔχοντας σκύψει 'having bent').

Table 3.2 shows the characteristics of the five participles according to whether they may be used adjectivally, whether they refer to an action (where '-' corresponds to 'result'), whether they are active in meaning (cf. 3.1.5), whether they refer to an action anterior to that of the main verb, and whether their aspect is perfective or imperfective, or neither.

TABLE 3.2

	Syntactic function		Voice	Time	Aspect	
	Adjective	Action	Active	Anterior	Perfective	Perfect
Present act.	–	+	+	– (+)	– (+)	–
Present pass.	+	+	– (+)	–	–	–
Perfect act.	–	+	+	+	–	+
Perfect pass.	–	+	– (+)	+	–	+
Past pass.	+	– (+)	– (+)	+ (–)	–	+

Despite the highly asymmetrical nature of this table, which would suggest a degree of redundancy, the only pair of participles which are truly interchangeable are the present and perfect active (and then only when the former expresses non-progressivity and non-coincidence). Each of the others has its own particular function which cannot be performed by any of the rest.

As has been seen, many verbs are lacking in one or more participle forms. The functional oppositions between each pair of participles may differ according to which forms exist for a particular verb. A verb which possesses all participle forms (e.g. σχεδιάζω 'I plan') displays the most regular set of oppositions. Thus (omitting the perfect participles):

(4) σχεδιάζοντας αὐτό τό κτίριο εἶχα ὑπόψη μου τά ἐξῆς ζητήματα
. . . '[in/when] designing this building, I bore in mind the
following considerations . . .'.

Here the action of the participle took place at the same time as that of
the main verb; the action denoted by it is active and progressive; and
the participle could not have been used as an adjective.

(5) τό σχεδιαζόμενο κτίριο 'the building being designed'.

Here the action is passive and progressive, and takes place at the same
time as some other action in the same utterance; it is being used as an
adjective (= πού σχεδιάζεται 'which is being planned', or πού σχεδια-
ζόταν 'which was being planned').

(6) τό σχεδιασμένο κτίριο 'the building that has been designed'
(lit. 'the designed building').

In (6) the action is passive and has been completed before some other
action in the utterance or before the time of the utterance itself; it too
is used as an adjective (= πού σχεδιάστηκε 'which was planned' or πού
ἔχει/εἶχε σχεδιαστεῖ 'which has/had been planned').

Compare an active verb which has no passive:

(7) φυτρώνοντας στό βράχο, ἕνα λουλούδι δέν εὐδοκιμεῖ 'having
planted itself on a rock, a flower doesn't thrive.'

The verb φυτρώνω, like many commonly used verbs in MG, may or
may not have an inchoative sense: i.e. it may denote the beginning of
an action or the performance of that action (in this case 'plant oneself'
or 'grow'). In view of this, and because the form φυτρωμένος exists, the
'present active participle' may have past (or inchoative) reference. In
(7), the participle is non-passive and non-adjectival, and may even be
non-progressive.

(8) βλέπω ἕνα λουλούδι φυτρωμένο στό βράχο 'I see a flower
growing on the rock.'

The 'past passive participle' in (8) is active in meaning and not necessarily past. It is adjectival, and may correspond to πού φυτρώνει 'which
is growing' (non-inchoative, present, progressive) or πού ἔχει φυτρώσει
'which has planted itself' (inchoative, past, non-progressive). Thus these

two participles may be identical in function, except that one is adjectival and the other not.

A deponent verb behaves differently again:

(9) μεταχειριζόμενος τόν ἄνθρωπο μ᾽ αὐτό τόν τρόπο θά τόν
χάσεις ἀπό φίλο '[by] treating the man in this way you'll lose
him as a friend.'

In (9) the 'present passive participle' serves the same function as the
present active participle σχεδιάζοντας in (4): its meaning is active; the
action it denotes is progressive and contemporaneous with another; and
although here the participle is adjectival in that it shows concord with
the subject, it (like most such participles with transitive meaning) cannot be used attributively.

(10) ἕνα μεταχειρισμένο αὐτοκίνητο 'a used car' (cf. 3.1.5 (c)).

In (10) the 'past passive participle' is passive in meaning (unlike (9));
the action it denotes has been completed before another action in the
utterance or before the time of the utterance itself; and it is used
adjectivally. In other words, although it belongs to the same morphological voice as (9), its function is in every respect the opposite.

The non-adjectival function of the present participle with active
meaning is shown by the Greek rendering of 'a dancing bear' as μιά
ἀρκούδα πού χορεύει/χόρευε 'a bear which is/was dancing', not *μιά
χορεύοντας ἀρκούδα (cf. also 'I saw a bear dancing' εἶδα μιά ἀρκούδα
νά χορεύει).

3.2.6 THE ASPECT OF THE IMPERATIVE

Generally speaking, the imperative often behaves with regard to aspect
in the same way as the indicative or subjunctive. Since the imperfective
imperative implies progressive or iterative action, it is often used in
ordering or forbidding action which is already in progress or which
seems to the speaker to be imminent (i.e. there is a connection between
future and present time); or else it is used for a general command
covering an unspecified number of future actions (these and other
observations have been made by Bakker, 1965).

Certain other factors, however, affect a speaker's choice of aspect in
the imperative. These are (a) specificness, (b) politeness, and (c) morphological considerations.

(a) *Specificness.* As in the indicative and subjunctive, so in the
imperative, the perfective tends to be used for actions which are viewed

as being specific rather than general. In the imperative, the perfective is often accompanied by an object, while the imperfective is less often so. Compare λέγε (imperfective) 'speak' (lit. 'say': i.e. 'go ahead and talk, I'm ready to listen to you') with πές το (perfective) 'say it' or πές μου (perfective) 'tell me'; and γράφε (imperfective) 'go ahead and write' with γράψ' το (perfective) 'write it' or γράψε μου 'write to me (on a specific occasion or a specific number of times).'

(b) *Politeness*. Since the imperfective imperative is often used to order the immediate inception or cessation of an action, it is often felt to be less polite than the perfective. This does not mean that the perfective imperative is used more often in polite commands than the imperfective, since there are several alternative ways, apart from the imperative, of issuing a polite request. But μίλα (imperfective) 'speak' sounds more peremptory than μίλησε (perfective), even though they may refer to the same reality. One consequence of this is that the plural of the imperfective imperative of many verbs is hardly used except when more than one person is addressed; in other words, it is hardly used for the polite plural; but since this form is identical to the second person plural of the indicative, it can be used, with yes/no interrogative intonation, in a polite request: μιλάτε παρακαλῶ πιό σιγά; 'would you please speak more quietly/slowly?' Here μιλάτε is not syntactically an imperative at all. On the subject of politeness, it is revealing that κοίτα 'look' and άκου 'listen' are often perceived as being truncated (and more familiar) versions of κοίταξε and άκουσε even though the former derive from the imperfective, and the latter from the perfective, of κοιτάω and ακούω respectively. With some commonly used imperatives, however, a difference in aspect may entail a substantial difference in meaning. Compare δός του (perfective) (literally, 'give to him'; and, figuratively, as a frequentative phrase) with δίνε του (imperfective) 'clear off!', and στρίψε (perfective) 'turn' with στρίβε (imperfective) (similar to δίνε του).

(c) *Morphological considerations*. Certain imperative forms are almost non-existent, while some verbs are defective in one or more types of imperative. (There are verbs which lack imperatives altogether, such as μπορῶ 'I can', είμαι 'I am', υπάρχω 'I exist', ανήκω 'I belong', ονειρεύομαι 'I dream' and πεθαίνω 'I die': by contrast, the verb ψοφῶ '(of animals) I die; (of humans) I die like an animal' does have an imperative!) Some verbs, such as μένω 'I stay, remain', have no imperfective imperative, while several verbs of motion either have no perfective imperative (e.g. πηγαίνω 'I go') or have an imperfective which is not normally used in educated speech (e.g. μπαίνω 'I go/come in' → ἔμπαωε). In all these cases, the missing aspect of the imperative may be expressed by means of a periphrasis. In some verbs of motion there is only one imperative, whose aspect cannot readily be determined (e.g. ἔρχομαι 'I come' → ἔλα, pl. ἐλᾶτε); in others there is an imperfective in -α which might be either imperfective or perfective, but is not considered polite (e.g. φεύγω 'I go away' → φεύγα (imperfective), beside φύγε (perfective); βγαίνω 'I go/come out' → ἔβγα (morphologically perfective), beside βγές (also perfective); in each case the aspectual distinction between these two forms is neutralized). In many verbs of Class 2b (see 5.2.1) the imperfective form of the imperative is more frequently found in the singular, the perfective in the plural (τραγουδάω 'I sing' → τραγούδα (imperfective), pl. τραγουδῆστε (perfective)): again the aspectual distinction is neutralized. And, finally, there is virtually no imperfective imperative of passive forms of verbs (irrespective of whether they have active or passive meaning): such forms are extremely rare. Thus morphological constraints or tendencies lead speakers either to employ a periphrasis or to use the 'wrong' aspect of the imperative. Just as the negative of the imperative is always formed periphrastically (by μή + subjunctive), the periphrasis νά + subjunctive (which it so resembles) is often found to be a convenient way of expressing positive commands. (For further information on the formation of the imperative, see 5.5.1.)

3.3   THE INTERPLAY OF ASPECT AND TENSE

Clearly, aspect, tense, and mood are inseparably interconnected, so that our attempt to examine each category separately is bound to fail to extricate each one from the meshes of the others. In particular, mood in MG affects tense considerably, in that with verbs in the subjunctive the distinctions of tense tend to be neutralized on a scale which ranges from maximum (complete) to minimum neutralization (in the latter, the differentiation is almost as great as in the indicative). Conversely, in the subjunctive, a difference of aspect may serve to differentiate time, in that the perfective may indicate an action which takes place before or after another, while one of the functions of the imperfective is to denote an action which occurs at the same time as another. In fact, as we shall see (3.3.2 and 9.2), verbs in subordinate clauses tend to indicate time in relation to the main verb rather than in relation to the speaker's present (time of utterance). Because of these complications, when talking about tense we shall concentrate on verbs in the indicative (reserving the subjunctive for the section on mood, Chapter 9: but see also 3.2.3.4 ff.), although we shall not feel inhibited from making comparisons with non-indicative uses, particularly expressions of future time.

Morphologically, the MG verb distinguishes in each of its three aspects between past and non-past, the former being differentiated from the latter in most cases by having its own endings and, sometimes, by the presence of the augment (see 5.4). It can be said that past forms are marked for pastness, while the non-past forms are not so marked. Having stated as a general principle that past forms are used to denote past actions or states, while non-past forms refer to actions or states which occur in the present, or which are timeless, or (particularly when the verb is preceded by ϑά) which occur in the future, one can proceed to note particularly the deviations from this general rule.

We shall comment on some of the forms (by which are meant here the forms of the verb as given in Table 3.1) as they are used in the indicative in a main clause, then (3.3.2) examine the differences which manifest themselves when verbs are used in the indicative in subordinate clauses.

3.3.1 USE OF THE VARIOUS VERB FORMS IN THE MAIN CLAUSE

3.3.1.1 Imperfective non-past ('present')

The normal use of this form is to refer to actions or states which are in process at the time of utterance, or to actions which occur habitually, or to states which are considered to be more or less permanent. There is also a potential meaning: e.g. μήν ἀγγίζεις τήν κατσαρόλα—καίει 'don't touch the saucepan—it's burning/very hot' (lit. 'it burns'). Many verbs possess inchoative senses by their very nature (χειμωνιάζει ' it is becoming winter'), while others may be used inchoatively (πνίγομαι! 'I'm drowning!', i.e. 'I'm beginning to drown'). Closely linked to the habitual and permanent functions is the gnomic present: e.g. ὅποιος δέν ἔχει μυαλό ἔχει πόδια 'whoever has no brain has feet' (proverb: i.e. intelligent people save themselves a lot of unnecessary physical effort).

This form is also found where English employs the present perfect continuous with words such as 'for' and 'since': δουλεύω σ' αὐτό τό γραφεῖο ἐδῶ καί τρία χρόνια, or ἀπό τό 1981 'I've been working in this office for three years', or 'since 1981'. It is also found in certain cases where English uses the present perfect simple to refer to actions which are clearly taking place in the present: e.g. πρώτη φορά βλέπω ἔκλειψη 'it's the first time I've seen an eclipse.'

More interesting, however, are those instances in which this form is used to denote actions and states which belong to the past or future.

In oral narrations, and even to some extent in literary narrative, Greek may use a historic present, in which an imperfective non-past is used instead of a perfective past (or, less often, instead of an imperfective past). It is quite usual for the imperfective non-past to co-occur with past tense forms in the same sentence, when all the verbs refer equally to the past: in such cases a perfective past tends to denote an action which is considered to be more crucial or more dramatic than the others.

There are several uses in which the imperfective non-past refers to future time. In some of these the action is considered by the speaker to be pre-planned and therefore certain of execution. Thus this form may express intention (especially in verbs of motion): φεύγω 'I'm leaving' (i.e. 'I'm about to leave'); note also that the imperfective non-past is used in MG in newspaper headlines to refer to the future (e.g. ὁ Πρωθυπουργός φεύγει αὔριο γιά τό Παρίσι 'the Prime Minister is leaving for Paris tomorrow'), while past reference must be indicated by a verb in a past tense. An imperfective non-past form is often found expressing intention after an imperative: e.g. φέρε πρῶτα τά μεζεδάκια κι ὕστερα βλέπουμε 'bring the hors d'oeuvres first, then we'll see [about the main course]'. This form may also express various kinds of assurance:

(1) ὅπου νά 'ναι ἔρχεται '(s)he's coming any moment now';
(2) ἄς το, τό κάνω ἐγώ 'leave it, I'll do it';
(3) ἄν τό θέλεις, σ' τό χαρίζω 'if you want it, I'll give it to you';
(4) μή φοβᾶσαι, δέν παθαίνω τίποτα 'don't worry, I won't get hurt' (lit. 'don't fear, I suffer nothing').

In the negative it may express a refusal, or a negative intention:

(5) δέ σ' τό δίνω 'I'm not giving it to you';
(6) ἡ Ἑλλάδα ποτέ δέν πεθαίνει 'Greece will never die.'

In addition, the imperfective non-past is very commonly used to express a polite request, normally (but not always) enunciated as a question:

(7) μοῦ ἀνοίγεις τήν πόρτα; 'would you open the door for me?';

(8) μοῦ δίνετε παρακαλῶ ἕναν Ἄσσο φίλτρο; 'would you please give me a [packet of] "Ace" [i.e. Papastratos No. 1] tipped?';

(9) ἂν δέν τά καταφέρεις, μοῦ τό λές 'if you can't manage it, let me know [lit. 'you tell it to me'].'

Similar to this function is the interrogative use of this form in the first person plural: e.g. πᾶμε; 'shall we go?'; παίζουμε κρυφτούλι; 'shall we play hide-and-seek?'

3.3.1.2 Imperfective past ('imperfect')

In most of its uses this form functions as the past equivalent of the imperfective non-past. Thus it refers to actions or states which were in progress at some (normally specified) time in the past, or to actions which occurred habitually, or to states which are considered to have been more or less permanent. Again, there is also a potential sense: e.g. ἐκεῖνο τό νερό δέν πινότανε 'that water was undrinkable'. Verbs which are by nature inchoative preserve their inchoative meaning in this form (χειμώνιαζε ὅταν φτάσαμε στό Λονδίνο 'it was becoming winter when we arrived in London'), while other verbs may combine an inchoative sense with a potential or conditional one: πνιγότανε ἡ κοπέλα, ἀλλά τή γλύτωσε ὁ Σπύρος 'the girl was drowning [i.e. 'seemed to be about to drown'], but Spyros saved her'. Here the possible insertion of θά before the first verb, which would not alter the meaning to any great extent, shows how close the above example is to a conditional (with θά, the sentence might be rendered as, 'the girl would have drowned but for the fact that Spyros saved her'); also, the imperfective past indicates clearly that the action denoted by the verb was not completed, whereas the perfective πνίγηκε would have meant that the girl did in fact drown, in which case the second clause would become meaningless.

The imperfective past is used where English employs the past perfect continuous in sentences such as the following: καθόμουνα ἐκεῖ δυό ὧρες ὅταν ἦρθες 'I'd been sitting/standing there for two hours when you came', and δούλευα ἐκεῖ ἀπό τό 1970 'I'd been working there since 1970'. It is also used in certain instances in which English uses the past perfect simple, such as, πρώτη φορά ταξίδευα μέ ἀεροπλάνο '[it was the] first time I'd travelled by plane.' This form may convey an expression of intention, assurance and refusal:

(1) δέ μοῦ τό 'δινε '(s)he wouldn't give it to me';

(2) ἂν ἤξερα ὅτι τό ἤθελες, σοῦ τό χάριζα 'If I'd known you wanted it, I'd have given it to you.'

This last example could be termed a 'conditional without ϑά' and is used when the verb in the apodosis denotes an action that did not occur, but could very easily have occurred:

(3) ἄν ἤϑελε κιόλας τό 'κανε ἀπό τώρα 'if (s)he had wanted to in fact, (s)he could [quite easily] have done it now'.

The imperfective past is used not only to denote progressive actions (cf. English past continuous) and habitual actions (cf. English 'used to'), but also to refer to actions that were performed over and over again:

(4) ἔγραφα, ἔσβηνα, δέν ἔβρισκα τά λόγια πού ταίριαξαν 'I went on writing and crossing out, but I could never find the appropriate words' (Kaz. 1965: 558).

Note how this usage functions equally well in the negative as in the positive (in (4), 'I went on not finding . . .'). Often the repeated nature of the action is reinforced by a repetition of the verb:

(5) δούλευα, δούλευα, μά δέν ἔβγαινε τίποτα 'I went on working and working, but nothing [ever] came [of it].'

Lastly, the imperfective past is used with or without ϑά (especially in ϑέλω 'I want') to formulate a polite expression of a desire:

(6) (ϑά) ἤϑελα νά μιλήσω μέ τόν κύριο Ζαίμη 'I would like to speak to Mr Zaimis.'

3.3.1.3 Perfective past ('aorist indicative')

The normal use of the perfective past is to refer to a completed action (or series of actions) which took place in the past: theoretically, the speaker should be able to specify the point(s) in time at which the action(s) occurred.

The inchoative uses of the perfective past are particularly interesting. With a number of verbs, the perfective past alone may not distinguish between present and past reference. Thus: ἄργησα 'I was late; I'm late' (the imperfective ἀργῶ tends to mean 'I become late' or 'I'm habitually late'); κουράστηκα 'I got tired; I'm tired' (κουράζομαι 'I get tired'); σ' ἀγάπησα 'I loved you (for a certain period); I've fallen in love with you' (σ' ἀγαπάω 'I love you'); κατάλαβες; 'did you understand?; do you understand?' (καταλαβαίνω 'I [begin to] understand'); κρύωσα 'I (suddenly) felt cold; I've caught cold' (κρυώνω

'I get/feel/catch cold'); ἀρρώστησε '(s)he became ill; (s)he's ill' (ἀρρωσταίνω 'I become ill'); βαρέθηκα 'I got fed up; I'm fed up' (βαριέμαι 'I'm bored; I get fed up'). In many cases, the perfective past could be rendered in English by the present perfect. (The perfective past may be replaced by the perfect past if past reference is to be emphasized.) The perfective of these verbs tends to carry an inchoative meaning more often than does the imperfective.

These aspectual differences are more obvious in certain verbs, in which another language will have to use a different word to render each of the two aspects. Compare: φόρεσε (pf.) ἕνα τόπλες μαγιώ 'she put on a topless bathing costume', and φοροῦσε (impf.) τόπλες μαγιό 'she wore/was wearing [a] topless bathing costume'; or πάτησα (pf.) τό ἅγιο χῶμα τῆς Ἑλλάδας 'I set foot on the sacred soil of Greece', and πατοῦσα (impf.) τό ἅγιο χῶμα τῆς Ἑλλάδας 'I was walking on the sacred soil of Greece'. In the examples given in the previous paragraph, the verb (some of which may be said to be inchoative by nature), when used in the perfective past, might imply a reference to the present consequences of an action which commenced in the past; in the last examples the verbs carry an exclusively inchoative meaning when used in the perfective.

As has been mentioned before, the perfective past is often used in contexts where a perfect would be equally acceptable. Thus, ἦρθα στήν Ἀθήνα γιά νά σέ δῶ could equally well be rendered as 'I came to Athens to see you' or as 'I've come to Athens to see you'; the first rendering implies that the speaker came at some time in the (near or distant) past, with no explicit link with the present, while the latter suggests that the speaker arrived recently and stresses that (s)he is still in Athens at the time of speaking. Often the choice between perfective past and perfect non-past is purely stylistic; that is, a speaker or writer might use both forms in the same utterance or piece of writing for the sake of variety. For example, in an article on the recently opened archaeological museum at Olympia (T 25 Feb. 1982, 45–9), which dealt with the changes that have taken place to the exhibits since they were moved from the old building, I counted thirty-five verbs in the perfective past and seven in the perfect non-past. Of the thirty-five perfective past forms, only ten could be said to refer to events in the past without present reference; all the others refer to alterations which have just taken place and whose consequences are visible to the visitor (in exactly the same way as the seven perfect non-past forms). There seems to be no semantic difference between the 35 perfective past and the seven perfect non-past forms, nor has the choice of one or the other been dictated by morphological constraints.

There is also a gnomic use of the perfective past, apparent in certain proverbial phrases, e.g. κύλησε ὁ τέντζερης καί βρῆκε τό καπάκι (lit. 'the cooking-pot rolled and found the lid'), used to express the speaker's lack of surprise that two people (of whom (s)he probably disapproves) have become close associates; such a phrase is not used only to comment on past events, but is perceived as having some general, timeless validity. A similar function is that in which the perfective past is used in an interrogative sentence which is equivalent to the protasis of a conditional sentence:

(1) Βρέθηκες σέ τρόλεϋ; Εἶσαι ἔρμαιο τῆς διάθεσης τοῦ ὁδηγοῦ
'Have you found yourself in a trolleybus? You're a prey to the driver's mood' (*T* 4 Oct. 1979, 71).

Another similar function of this form appears in the 'aorist of make-believe' (Ben-Mayor 1980: 38), used especially, but by no means exclusively, in children's games. Example (2) is taken from the speech of an adult:

(2) ἄς ὑποθέσουμε ὅτι ἔχουμε (non-past) ἕνα μαγικό ραβδί, καί σηκωθήκαμε (past) αὔριο τό πρωί καί εἴχαμε θαυμάσιους δασκάλους 'let's suppose we had [lit. 'have'] a magic wand, and we got up tomorrow and we had marvellous teachers.'

Having examined these more or less timeless meanings of the perfective past, it is interesting to note the frequent colloquial use of this form to refer to future time. The cases in which this occurs are expressions of promise or threat, in which the action is viewed by the speaker as being so certain that (s)he wants to avoid the rather contingent nature of a situation expressed by a 'future tense'. Thus: ἔγινε! 'done!' (i.e. 'consider your request as having already been carried out'); ἔφτασα! 'I've arrived!' (said by a waiter to reassure a customer who has summoned him; although he will most probably have to be summoned again before he comes!); ἄν σέ μάθουν, κάηκες 'if they find you out, you're done for' (lit. 'you were burned'); ψηλά τά χέρια καί σ' ἔφαγα! 'hands up or I shoot!' (lit. 'high the hands and I ate you').

3.3.1.4 'Future tenses'

Since futurity in MG is a function of the subjunctive and will therefore be dealt with under 'mood' (Chapter 9), we shall look briefly here at cases in which the same constructions that are used to express future time (θά + non-past forms) are employed with other semantic functions. Very close to the expression of simple future time is the future of intention: ἐγώ θά φύγω τώρα 'I'm going to leave now.' When used in the second and third persons, the sense of the same construction may be a polite instruction or a polite (or sometimes curt) request: θά πάρετε τήν ὁδό Πανεπιστημίου καί θά στρίψετε δεξιά 'you will take University St. and turn right' (in response to a request for directions); ὅλα τά παιδιά θά μείνουν στήν τάξη παρακαλῶ 'all the children will remain in the classroom, please'; θά σωπάσεις; 'will you be quiet?'; δέ θά τό κουνήσεις ἀπό δῶ, ἀκοῦς; 'you won't budge from here, do you hear?'

More interesting are the cases in which the future tenses are used to denote actions which do not take place in the future. The timeless consuetudinal future has already been mentioned (3.2.3.2); but there are circumstances in which the future tenses refer to past time. One of these is a *biographical future* (or *historic future*, on the analogy of *historic present*), in which a biographer makes a reference to an event which happened at a later time than the other events that (s)he has been relating: e.g.

(1) ὅταν ἦταν δώδεκα χρονῶν ἡ X. ἐπισκέφτηκε τή Νέα Ὑόρκη, ὅπου πολλά χρόνια ὕστερα θά ἐγκαινιάσει τή λαμπρή σταδιοδρομία της 'when she was twelve years old, X. visited New York, where many years later she was to [lit. 'will'] inaugurate her brilliant career.'

A similar construction is the *journalistic future*, in which a future tense is used to refer to past time simply as a stylistic variant:

(2) ὁ Σ.Ε. προσφέρει ἕνα ἀκόμα ἄγνωστο ἔργο, γιά τό ὁποῖο θά πεῖ, χθές, μέ τή δέκατη παράσταση: . . . 'S.E. is offering yet another unknown play, about which he said [lit. 'will say'] yesterday, on the occasion of the tenth performance: . . .' (*N* 3 Jan. 1980).

The 'future perfect' (i.e. θά + perfect non-past) is not very commonly used in MG, its functions normally being performed by the other future tenses. Thus while one may find a sentence such as θά 'χουμε φύγει μέχρι τήν Τρίτη 'we'll have left by Tuesday', the future construction θά φύγουμε μέχρι τήν Τρίτη may mean 'we'll leave by Tuesday', or it may have the same sense as the 'future perfect'. While on the subject of μέχρι, it is worth noting the other sense of this word: ϑά μείνουμε ἀνοιχτοί μέχρι τήν Τρίτη 'we shall remain open until Tuesday.' Whereas in the previous examples the action of the verb is dynamic and may take place at any point between the time of speaking and the time specified (the departure may occur at some time *before* Tuesday), in the last sentence the verb is stative, and there is an implication that the state will still be continuing at the time specified (the closure will occur at the end of Tuesday; the word καί inserted after μέχρι would emphasize this: 'up to and including Tuesday'). The double meaning of μέχρι according to whether it co-occurs with a dynamic or a stative verb is not peculiar to the future: but note that the future perfect may not be substituted for the future in cases where μέχρι means 'until', just as the perfect past cannot be substituted for the perfective past in the same context.

3.3.2 SEQUENCE OF TENSES IN INDICATIVE SUBORDINATE CLAUSES

We are concerned here with those kinds of subordinate clauses in which the verbs are in the indicative. Such are relative clauses, clauses which express reported speech, and temporal clauses (in the last case, only those in which no element of futurity is present). (Tense in subjunctive subordinate clauses has already been referred to: see also 9.2.)

MG does not contain an almost obligatory 'sequence of tenses' rule such as appears in certain other languages. This is most clearly shown in reported-speech clauses governed by a verb in a past tense: e.g.

(1) μοῦ εἶπες ὅτι δέ σ' ἀρέσει ὁ καφές 'you told me you didn't [lit. 'don't'] like coffee';

(2) μέ ρώτησε ἄν τελείωσα '(s)he asked me if I [had] finished.'

In cases such as these, despite the apparent subordination of the second clause to the main verb (suggested by the conjunction ὅτι), the utterance preserves in the second verb the same tense as that in which it appeared in the original direct speech (i.e. the tense is the same as if the second clause was presented as direct speech: 'δέ μ' ἀρέσει ὁ καφές'— 'τελείωσες;'). We appear to be dealing, then, with a pseudo-subordination which is really parataxis in disguise: the subordinate verb expresses time relative not to the time of utterance but to that of the action expressed in the head-verb. This means that a subordinate verb in a 'present tense' denotes an action contemporaneous with that of the main verb; one in a past tense denotes an anterior action; and one in a 'future tense' denotes a subsequent action (see also 8.3.1).

In other types of subordinate clause in which indicative verbs appear there may be a rather similar lack of sequence of tenses:

(3) αὐτός πού μπῆκε (perfective past) πρῶτος ἤτανε κι ὁ τελευταῖος πού κάθισε 'the one who had come [lit. 'came'] in first was the last to sit down' (co-ordinated equivalent: αὐτός μπῆκε πρῶτος καί κάθισε τελευταῖος).

Here, although the action of the subordinate verb took place before that of the main verb, the same tense is used in each.

Since it may not otherwise be clear, from the context of a temporal clause, which of two actions preceded the other, MG generally places the verbs according to the chronological order of occurrence of the action:

(4a) βράδιαζε ὅταν ἔφτασε στό σπίτι της 'it was becoming evening when she reached her house'; but

(4b) ὅταν ἔφτασε στό σπίτι της, ξάπλωσε καί κοιμήθηκε ἀμέσως 'when she [had] reached her house, she lay down and went to sleep immediately'.

By contrast, in narrations in which the main verb is in the historic present, a subordinate verb in a temporal clause referring to an anterior action may appear in the perfective past, since to place the subordinate verb in the imperfective non-past would, owing to the imperfectivity of this form, suggest a coincidence between the actions which would belie the fact that one action is anterior to the other. Thus:

(5) ἀφοῦ ἔφαγε, σηκώνεται 'after (s)he had eaten, (s)he stood up' (lit. 'after (s)he ate, (s)he stands up').

(See also 9.4.4.4.)

On the other hand, a change of tense in the subordinate verb may occur when the main verb is in a past tense. When this happens, non-past forms are converted into the imperfective past, and the perfective past and (rarely) the imperfective past into the perfect past. Thus, 'you said you'd go' may be rendered,

(6a) εἶπες πώς θά πᾶς ('future tense'), or

(6b) εἶπες πώς θά πήγαινες ('conditional tense');

and 'he claimed he had been working all day' may be

(7a) ἰσχυρίστηκε ὅτι δούλευε ὅλη τή μέρα (impf. past), or

(7b) ἰσχυρίστηκε ὅτι εἶχε δουλέψει ὅλη τή μέρα (perfect past).

Compare also the two possible renderings of 'I saw the girl again whom I (had) met at your house':

(8a) ξαναεῖδα πάλι τό κορίτσι πού συνάντησα (perfective past) στό σπίτι σου, or

(8b) ξαναεῖδα πάλι τό κορίτσι πού εἶχα συναντήσει (perfect past) στό σπίτι σου.

One disadvantage of following the sequence of tenses (which may in other cases make for greater clarity) is that in one output (ϑά + imperfective past) the aspectual distinction of the direct speech is neutralized: thus ϑά πήγαινα in indirect speech might correspond to the following in direct speech: ϑά πάω (perfective future), ϑά πηγαίνω (imperfective future), or ϑά πήγαινα (conditional). Since distinctions of aspect are normally more dominant in the MG verb than are those of tense, this neutralization is perhaps one of the reasons why the sequence of tenses is not commonly used. Indeed, its presence is often due to interference from some foreign language.

4

NOUN MORPHOLOGY

MG is a highly inflected language. In its morphology it makes a funda-
mental distinction between nouns (and other noun-like words) and
verbs (see Appendix I for sample inflection tables). Mirambel (1959:
71-7) has summed up the chief differences between noun and verb
morphology in MG: (a) gender is found only in the noun, not in the
verb (except in the passive-form participles); (b) the plural has different characteristics in the noun and in the verb; (c) the main stem of
nouns is always invariable, whereas some verbs alter theirs; and (d)
stress can be raised in the conjugation of verbs (i.e. it moves towards
the beginning of the word), but can only be lowered in the declension
of nouns.

4.1 THE BASIC PATTERNS OF MG NOUN DECLENSION

From the point of view of declension, MG nouns may be divided into
three chief classes.

4.1.1 CLASS 1

Class 1 nouns have two forms in each of the two numbers. Although
the plural endings are the same for all Class 1 nouns, for the singular
they have to be divided into two subclasses: masculines (1M) and
feminines (1F).

In the nominative singular, 1M nouns consist of stem + thematic
vowel (any vowel except *o*) + *-s*, while 1F nouns consist of stem +
thematic vowel (any vowel). (Examples: 1M: φύλακας 'guard', κλέφτης
'thief'; 1F: θάλασσα 'sea', τέχνη 'art'.) The singular inflection simply
entails dropping or adding final *-s* in such a way that 1M has nominative
with *-s* and vocative, accusative, and genitive without, while 1F has
nominative, vocative, and accusative without *-s* and genitive with. Thus
while the vocative and accusative are the same for both genders, the
nominative and genitive differentiate between masculine and feminine.

In the plural the endings of all Class 1 nouns are *-es* in the nominative, vocative, and accusative, and *-on* in the genitive (for those which have a genitive).

Three further factors complicate this otherwise neat pattern. First, most Class 1 nouns add the plural endings directly to the stem, while others add an epenthetic *-δ-* to the thematic vowel, and then the endings. The former are known as *parisyllabic*, the latter as *imparisyllabic*. (Examples of imparisyllabics: 1M: παπάς 'priest', καφές 'coffee', καφετζής 'café proprietor', παπούς 'grandfather'; 1F: γιαγιά 'grandmother', ἀλεπού 'fox'.) Thus, while any of these nouns whose nominative is known can safely be assigned a gender, it is impossible to predict from the dictionary entry whether it is parisyllabic or imparisyllabic. Almost all the feminines in *-a* and all feminines in *-i* are parisyllabic, while all those in *-e* and *-u* are imparisyllabic (the plural of feminines in *-o*— most of them women's names—is infrequently used and unpredictable). The situation with the masculines is more complex: while all *oxytones* (i.e., words stressed on the final syllable) in *-ás*, and all nouns in *-és* and *-ús* (which are all oxytones) are imparisyllabic, it is more difficult to predict the behaviour of nouns in *-is* and of *paroxytones* and *proparoxytones* (words stressed on the penultimate and antepenultimate syllable respectively) in *-as*, which make up the majority of nouns in Class 1M. Nevertheless, one can say that paroxytone and proparoxytone nouns in *-as* (with half a dozen exceptions) are parisyllabic, as are most paroxytone masculine nouns in *-is* (except those in *-áris*, *-jéris*, *-ákis*, and *-úlis* and about a dozen others); of the oxytones, those in *-tís* are almost all parisyllabic, while those in *-dzís*, *-tsís*, and about five others are imparisyllabic.

The second complicating factor is that of stress. In parisyllabics the stress of the nominative singular is preserved on the same vowel throughout the singular in all Class 1 nouns, and in all the plural cases except the genitive. The same is true of the imparisyllabics, with the exception of the proparoxytones, which transfer the stress to the antepenultimate vowel in the plural. It is the genitive plural of the parisyllabics which is the most problematic. While proparoxytones in *-as* lower the stress to the penultimate in this case, nouns in *-ias* and *-istas*, together with disyllabic paroxytones, lower it to the final syllable. As for the feminines, all those in *-i* which possess a genitive plural stress the final syllable in that case, while feminines in *-a* are divided between those with penultimate stress and those with final stress in the genitive plural. Most of the proparoxytones except those in *-ótita* have final stress here (those

which do not do so stress the penultimate), as do all those with stems
ending in a vowel, and all disyllables. (A large number of feminines in -a
have no genitive plural at all, especially words of foreign origin and
many words for everyday objects.)

Thirdly, there is a category of masculines in -as and -is (1Ma) and
feminines in -i (1Fa) which have different plural endings from the rest
of the nouns in Class 1. The masculines end in -éas or -ís in the nominative singular, and form their plural in -is (nominative, vocative and
accusative), and -éon and -ón respectively (genitive) (the stress is on the
syllable following the stem throughout), while the feminines, most of
which end in -si in the nominative singular, replace the -i with the same
endings as the masculines in the plural (-is and -eon), except that the
stress always falls on the final syllable of the stem. (Examples: 1Ma:
συγγραφέας 'author', συγγενής 'relative'; 1Fa: κυβέρνηση 'government'.)

4.1.2 CLASS 2

These nouns are characterized by the ending -u in the genitive singular.
They can be divided into three subclasses, of which one consists almost
entirely of masculines (the rest are feminine) and the others entirely of
neuters.

Class 2A nouns (e.g. ἄνθρωπος 'person, human being') end in -os
in the nominative singular (in conformity with the principle that all
masculine nouns and adjectives have a final -s in this case). This sub-
class is the only type of noun in MG which has four separate forms in
the singular, though it has only three in the plural. The endings are:
Singular nominative -os, vocative -e,[1] accusative -o, genitive -u; Plural
nominative and vocative -i, accusative -us, genitive -on. Note that this
declension shares the characteristic with Class 1M of dropping the
final -s in the accusative singular.

The nouns of Class 2B (e.g. δωμάτιο 'room'), like all neuters, make
no distinction between nominative, vocative, and accusative. Their
endings are: Singular nom./voc./acc. -o (compare the accusative singular of 2A), genitive -u; Plural nom./voc./acc. -a, genitive -on. All neuters
in -o decline in this way, except those in -simo (Class 3).

Class 2C nouns (e.g. ἀγόρι 'boy', παιδί 'child') end in -i in the nom./
voc./acc. singular, while in the other cases they *add* the endings to this

---

[1] Except most paroxytones referring to men—whether proper names or not
—which have -o.

-*i*, which becomes -*j*- (realized in various ways, according to the preceding sound: see 1.4.1). Thus, their genitive singular is -*jú*, plural nom./voc./acc. -*ja*, and genitive -*jón*. Those nouns which have a vowel before the -*i* of the nominative singular insert, in the orthography, an epenthetic -*γ*- before the -*ι*- of the other cases.

As far as stress is concerned, 2A and 2B behave in the same way. Oxytones and paroxytones preserve the stress of the nominative singular on the same syllable throughout. Proparoxytones, however, vary as to whether or not they lower the stress to the penultimate syllable in the genitives (and, in 2A, in the accusative plural). Most compound nouns, as well as many nouns for everyday objects, preserve the stress on the same syllable throughout, while others do not; and with some nouns there is a variation of usage among different speakers and even within the same speaker.

In Class 2C, the final syllable is always stressed in the genitives, but the stress of the nom./voc./acc. plural depends on the position of the stress in the corresponding cases of the singular: if the singular is oxytone, then so is the plural; conversely, if the singular is paroxytone, so will be the plural.

4.1.3 CLASS 3

Class 3 is a convenient category for a fairly heterogeneous group of neuter declensions which do not fit into either of the other classes. This class can be divided into 3A (imparisyllabics) and 3B (parisyllabics).

The former is by far the larger and more frequently used of the two. The basic pattern is demonstrated by neuters in -*ma* (e.g. ὄνομα 'name': with a couple of exceptions, which belong to 1F, all paroxytones and proparoxytones in -*ma* are neuter). Again, as in all neuters, the nominative, vocative, and accusative are identical. In the genitive singular and in the plural an epenthetic -*t*- is added to the nominative singular (which has a 'zero ending'), and is followed by the endings -*os* (genitive singular), -*a* (nom./voc./acc. plural), -*on* (genitive plural). A similar pattern is followed by nouns in -*simo* (all proparoxytone, e.g. πλύσιμο 'washing'), which have the allostem -*simat*- and add the same endings as above. There is also a small group of neuters in -*as* (e.g. κρέας 'meat'), and a couple in -*os*, which have allostems -*at*- and -*ot*- respectively, followed again by the same endings. Finally in 3A there is a group of nouns in -*n* (e.g. παρόν 'present'), with the allostem -*nd*- (derived from -*n*- + epenthetic -*t*-).

Class 3B (e.g. ἔδαφος 'ground, territory') is a straightforward group of neuters in *-os*, genitive singular *-us*, nom./voc./acc. plural *-i*, genitive plural *-on*.

The stress rules for 3A are that in paroxytones the stress shifts to the penultimate in the genitive plural, and in proparoxytones it not only does this but shifts to the antepenultimate in the genitive singular and nom./voc./acc. plural. In two of the three monosyllables in 3A ($\phi\tilde{\omega}\varsigma$ and $\pi\tilde{\alpha}\nu$), the stress remains on the syllable on which it falls in the nominative singular, except in the genitive singular, where it shifts to the final syllable.

In 3B the stress always falls on the final syllable in the genitive plural. In addition, proparoxytones shift the stress to the penultimate in the genitive singular and in the nom./voc./acc. plural.

The various terminations of nouns may be summarized in Table 4.1 (based on Ruge 1969). It will be noticed from the foregoing that all genitive plurals end in *-on*, while all accusative singulars (except 3B and a few in 3A) end in a vowel.

TABLE 4.1

Neuters:	SNVA	-o	-∅	-s	-os (-es)
	SG	-u	-os	-us	
	PNVA	-a	-i		
	PG	-on			

Non-neuters:	SV	-e	-o	-∅
	SN	-os	-s	-∅
	SG	-u	-∅	-s
	SA	-o	-∅	
	PNV	-i	-es	-is
	PA	-us	-es	-is
	PG	-on		

4.2 THE ADJECTIVE

Before examining the morphology of MG adjectives, it should be pointed out how similarly they behave to nouns, both morphologically and syntactically. Any adjective can readily be substantivized, not necessarily with the addition of the definite article:

ὁ χοντρός 'the fat man; the fat one (masc.)';
ἡ μικρή 'the little/young girl; the little/young one (fem.)';
τό κόκκινο 'the red one (neuter); red (concept of colour)';
οἱ νικημένοι 'the defeated (masc. pl.)'.

Similarly, a noun and an adjective may equally stand as complements:

ὁ Γιάννης εἶναι κακός 'John is bad';
ὁ Γιάννης εἶναι κλέφτης 'John is [a] thief'.

Some nouns may behave like adjectives in the sense that they may be modified by adverbs and may even have a comparative and a superlative:

ὁ Γιάννης εἶναι λίγο ἀφελής 'John is a bit naïve';
ὁ Γιάννης εἶναι λίγο κλέφτης 'John is a bit [of a] thief';
οἱ πιό κλέφτες εἶναι οἱ δικηγόροι 'the biggest [lit. 'the most'] thieves are the lawyers.'

Many concepts have two etymologically connected words, one normally classed as a 'noun' to refer to persons, the other normally classed as an 'adjective' to refer to non-humans:

ὁ Ἕλληνας πρωθυπουργός 'the Greek Prime Minister';
ὁ ἑλληνικός καφές 'Greek coffee'.

In such pairs of words, the noun often has a feminine:

ἡ Ἑλένη εἶναι λιγάκι πεσιμίστρια 'Helen's a bit of a pessimist' (cf. masculine πεσιμιστής, and adjective πεσιμιστικός to refer to non-humans).

There are two reasons why grammarians traditionally divide these pairs of words into nouns and adjectives: (a) the nouns have no neuter, unlike adjectives; and (b) the morphological masculine–feminine correspondence in the nouns is different from that which obtains in adjectives, in that the feminines of the nouns appear to be *derived from* the masculines and therefore do not stand in an hierarchically equal relationship to them.

Having stated these provisos, we shall now proceed to examine adjectives as if they constituted a separate part of speech from nouns, although we shall relate the various types of adjective declension to those of nouns.

The majority of adjectives are of the 2A–2B–1F type, and end in -os in the masculine nominative singular: the masculine declines like nouns of 2A, the feminine like 1F and the neuter like 2B. In the adjective the MG tendency towards *columnar stress* has prevailed, all forms of each adjective (with few exceptions) preserving the stress on the same syllable as in the masculine nominative singular.

While the neuter of these adjectives is formed by simply dropping the final -s of the masculine, the rules for the formation of the feminine are more complex. There are three possibilities for the feminine: -i, -a or -ja. Feminines normally end in -i when the stem ends in a consonant, or in any unstressed vowel except -i- (e.g. νόστιμος 'nice' → νόστιμη); they end in -a when the stem ends in -i- or in any stressed vowel (e.g. ἄξιος 'worthy' → ἄξια). There are, however, some paroxytones with consonant stems which take -a, not -i, in the feminine, and there appears to be no way of predicting that, for instance, the feminine of σκέτος 'neat (of drink)' is σκέτη, while that of σκοῦρος 'dark (of colour)' is σκούρα. Most of those adjectives in -os which have a feminine in -ja are oxytones whose stem ends in a velar consonant (nevertheless, the most frequently used are γλυκός 'sweet', φρέσκος 'fresh', and ἐλαφρός 'light'). But there is a certain amount of variety in usage, and most of the adjectives that form feminines in -ja are often found alternatively with -i. (Note that the genitive plural of the feminine of γλυκός is γλυκῶν, not *γλυκιῶν.) Similarly, there are some adjectives which have alternative feminine endings in -a or -i (this is the case especially with those with a stem ending in unstressed -e-: see 4.5.2.2).

There are three separate types of adjective in -is. The first (—2C–1F) is always stressed on the final syllable, forms its feminine in -já and is spelled -ύς or -ής in the masc. nominative singular (e.g. βαθύς 'deep', πορτοκαλής 'orange'). Those which have the former spelling almost all denote dimension, those which have the latter are colour adjectives. The feminine follows the inflexions of Class 1F, while the neuter (spelled -ύ or -ί) follows 2C. The masculine has some similarities with Class 2A, in that the accusative singular drops the final -s of the masculine nominative singular, and the plural has -jí and -jús in the nominative and accusative respectively. The genitives of all genders and both numbers are infrequently used; and in the masculine and neuter genitive singular there is a hesitation between the endings -*i* and -*jú*; the genitive plural of all genders ends in -*jón*.

The adverbs corresponding to these adjectives in -*is* and to those in -*os* are almost always identical to the neuter plural nominative and accusative (i.e. -*(j)a*). Exceptions include λίγος 'little' → λίγο 'a little', πολύς 'much' → πολύ 'much; very', and μόνος 'alone' → μόνο 'only'.

The second type of adjective in -*is* consists of a group of paroxytones whose masculine nominative singular ending is spelled -*ης* (1M-2B-1F: e.g. ζηλιάρης 'jealous'). The masculine behaves like the imparisyllabics of 1M; the feminine (in -*a* or -*iki*) like the parisyllabics of 1F (no genitive plural); the neuter (in -*iko*) like 2B. (The neuter ends, alternatively, in -*i*, especially when it is substantivized.) Again, there is no stress shift throughout the paradigm. The adverb (where it exists at all) is again the same as the neuter nominative plural.

Thirdly, there is a group of oxytones and paroxytones in -*is* (spelled -*ής*, e.g. ἀκριβής 'precise') in which the masculine and feminine are not distinguished and the neuter nominative singular ends in -*es* (1Ma-3B). The masculine/feminine is similar to that of the nouns in -*is* of 1Ma (which were originally adjectives), while the neuter bears some resemblance to Class 3B. (See Appendix I for endings.) The adverb is formed by adding -*os* to the stem (except εἰλικρινής 'frank, honest' → εἰλικρινά). Stress is columnar throughout, except that (a) paroxytones (except those in -*όδις*) raise the stress to the antepenultimate in the neuter nom./acc.; and (b) adjectives in -*όδις* lower the stress to the final syllable in the genitive plural and in the adverb.

In addition, there is the aberrant adjective πολύς 'much' (pl. 'many'). The feminine *polí* (πολλή) declines like 1F. (See Appendix I for endings.) The genitive singular of the masculine and neuter is infrequently used. Note that the form *polí* (though spelled in various ways) is used for the masculine accusative singular, the feminine nom./acc. singular, the neuter nom./acc. singular, and the adverb.

There is, finally, a small group of adjectives in -*on*, which can be divided into two subgroups. The first, which consists of about half a dozen adjectives (e.g. ἐνδιαφέρων 'interesting'), has a feminine in -*usa* which declines like 1F (with stress shift to final syllable in the genitive plural, though this form is generally avoided). The masculine and neuter bear a close resemblance to the nouns in -*on* of Class 3A (some of which were originally neuters of these adjectives, which in turn were ancient present participles), the oblique cases being characterized by the presence of an epenthetic -*d*- (originally -*t*-). (See Appendix I for endings.) The second subgroup consists of a similarly small number of paroxytones (e.g. μετριόφρων 'modest'), whose feminine has the same forms as the masculine and whose neuter is rare. The endings are the same as those of the masculine and neuter of the first subgroup, except that there is no epenthetic *-d-* (i.e. *-on, -ona, -onos*, etc.). In all adjectives in *-on*, stress is columnar, except that the masculine and neuter genitive plural is always stressed on the penultimate (as is the feminine in the second subgroup; the stress of the fem. gen. pl. of the first subgroup has already been mentioned). The adverb is rare, ending in *-óndos* and *-ónos* respectively.

4.2.1 COMPARISON OF ADJECTIVES

Any adjective or adverb that can be used comparatively may form a comparative by the placing of πιό (occasionally περισσότερο) 'more' in front of it (e.g. καλός 'good', πιό καλός 'better'). *Comparative superlatives*, which denote the highest degree of some quality, may be formed from the comparative of adjectives (but not of adverbs) by adding the definite article in front of the comparative (e.g. ὁ πιό καλός 'the best').

Most adjectives, however, also form a single-word comparative by adding *-τερος* to the neuter nominative singular. Many adjectives can also form an *absolute superlative*, denoting a very high degree of some quality, by adding *-τατος* to the neuter nominative singular. Neither imparisyllabic adjectives in *-is* nor adjectives in *-on* which have epenthetic *-d-* can take these endings; adjectives in *-on* without epenthetic *-d-* add *-έστερος, -έστατος* to the neuter nominative singular. The forms in *-τερος* and *-τατος* behave morphologically like adjectives in *-os*, declining in the same way and forming adverbs in *-a*. Thus: φυσικός 'natural' → φυσικότερος 'more natural' (alongside πιό φυσικός), φυσικότερα 'more naturally' (alongside πιό φυσικά), ὁ φυσικότερος 'the most natural' (alongside ὁ πιό φυσικός), φυσικότατος 'quite natural' (= 'very natural'), φυσικότατα 'quite naturally'. Some of the most commonly used adjectives form comparatives irregularly (see 4.5.2.4).

4.3 ARTICLES AND NUMERALS

The declension of the definite article shares many characteristics with Classes 2A, 1F, and 2B in its respective genders, the chief differences being that the masculine and feminine nominative singular and plural lack the initial *t-* of the other forms; there is no vocative; and the masculine nominative singular and the feminine nominative and accusative plural are aberrant.

The indefinite article (which is also the numeral 'one') shares some characteristics with 1M and 3A in the masculine and neuter, and conforms with 1F in the feminine. When used emphatically as a numeral, the stress of the feminine can be μία, and although strictly speaking only μᾶς in the genitive is considered to be correct, emphatic μίας is occasionally found.

'Three' and 'four' are both aberrant, the latter especially so in that it alters the final vowel of its stem in the genitive.

The only other declining numerals are the hundreds (from '200' to '900') and 'a thousand', which decline like the plural of ἄξιος in all genders; the noun ἐκατομμύριο 'million', which has a full declension in singular and plural, following Class 2B; and the plural noun χιλιάδες, which follows Class 1F (with no stress shift in the genitive).

4.4 PRONOUNS AND DEMONSTRATIVES

4.4.1 DEMONSTRATIVES AND NON-PERSONAL PRONOUNS

All these inflect like adjectives or numerals and almost all follow patterns which we have already encountered. The demonstratives αὐτός 'this/that', τοῦτος 'this', and ἐκεῖνος 'that' (also used as third-person pronouns) decline like νόστιμος, as do ὅσος 'as much as' (pl. 'as many as'), πόσος 'how much' (pl. 'how many'), τόσος 'so much' (pl. 'so many'), ἄλλος 'other', and ὅλος 'all'. The adverbs corresponding to ὅσος and τόσος are ὅσο and τόσο. When used pronominally and emphatically, αὐτός often has masculine singular genitive αὐτουνοῦ, feminine singular genitive αὐτηνῆς, masculine plural accusative αὐτουνούς, and masc./fem. genitive plural αὐτωνῶν. The pronouns ἴδιος 'same; self', ὁ ὁποῖος 'who; which' (relative), ποιός; 'who?; which?', κάποιος 'someone; some', ὅποιος 'whoever; whichever' decline like ἄξιος, except that when they refer to a person or persons and do not modify a noun the genitives of ποιός; are often: singular ποιανοῦ; (masculine) and ποιανῆς; (feminine) 'whose?' (either of which may be replaced by τίνος;), plural ποιανῶν; Κάποιος and ὅποιος may take the same endings. The pronouns κανένας 'no (one); any(one)' and καθένας 'each one; everyone' decline like the numeral or article ἕνας (like it, they have no plural). The pronouns τί; 'what?' and ὅ,τι 'whatever' are indeclinable, as are κάτι 'something' and τίποτα 'nothing; any' (even though they are occasionally found in environments where a genitive might be expected).

As for the reflexive ἐαυτός, this is not really a pronoun at all but a noun which declines like Class 2A.

4.4.2 PERSONAL PRONOUNS

These are divided into *emphatic* (disjunctive) and *non-emphatic* (clitic) forms. The emphatic forms are typically disyllabic or trisyllabic and are stressed on the second syllable; the clitics are unstressed monosyllables.

Only the first and second persons have separate emphatic forms (the third person using the pronoun αὐτός or another demonstrative). The emphatic forms are shown in Table 4.2.

TABLE 4.2

		Singular	*Plural*
1st person			
	Nominative	ἐγώ	ἐμεῖς
	Acc./Gen.	ἐμένα	ἐμᾶς
2nd person			
	Nominative	ἐσύ	ἐσεῖς
	Acc./Gen.	ἐσένα	ἐσᾶς

The clitic forms are shown in Table 4.3.

TABLE 4.3

		Singular	*Plural*
1st person			
	Accusative	μέ	μᾶς
	Genitive	μοῦ	
2nd person			
	Accusative	σέ	σᾶς
	Genitive	σοῦ	

The third person of the clitic pronoun (which indicates gender as well as case and number) is identical in form to the definite article, except that it has a masculine nominative singular τος and nominative plural τοι (both used only in the phrases νά τος/τοι! 'there he is/they are!' and ποῦν' τος/τοι; 'where is he/are they?', where the accusative is used in the feminine and neuter), and a genitive plural τούς for all genders. There is also an alternative feminine accusative plural τες, used after νά and πούν', and (sometimes) after the present participle.

When used as *proclitics* (i.e. before verbs), these clitic pronouns are written with an accent, as they appear in Table 4.3; when they are *enclitics* (i.e. when they follow verbs, nouns, etc.) they are written with no accent. In neither case, however, are these clitic pronouns actually pronounced with stress; they form a single phonological word with the word which they precede or follow.

Enclitics (which may be used after nouns, verbs, adjectives, adverbs, numerals, and pronouns), since they are perceived as forming part of the preceding word, may affect the stress of that word if otherwise the 'three-syllable rule' would be contravened. Thus a word which on its own is proparoxytone receives a stress on its final syllable when followed by an enclitic; although in the orthography the main word is written with two accents (μίλησέ μου 'speak to me', ἡ οἰκογένειά μου 'my family'), in practice the second accented syllable is stressed more than the first (the first may even not be stressed at all). Where two clitics follow a paroxytone, the stress will fall on the first of the clitics (φέρε μού το 'bring it to me', with little or no stress on the first -e-).

4.5   DIVERGENCE FROM THE BASIC PATTERNS

Having dealt with the basic structures of MG nominal declension in the previous pages, giving chiefly those forms which belong to the traditional demotic pattern and which appear in the prescriptive grammars, we shall now examine at length the two factors which complicate this pattern. These are (a) exceptions and other irregularities within the system; and (b) alternative forms of learned origin which are found in SMG. These two factors will be examined separately in connection with substantives, but both together with regard to adjectives and pronouns.

4.5.1   NOUNS

4.5.1.1 Exceptions and other irregularities

1M. Here it is necessary to mention only a few phenomena. Νούς 'mind' has no plural. A few proparoxytone nouns in -ας form paroxytone plurals in -οι (e.g. μάστορας 'skilled workman', pl. μαστόροι), while a few paroxytones in -ας have plurals in -ηδες (this latter type consists of two groups of colloquial nouns referring to male persons:

(i) nouns in -άκιας from diminutives in -άκι(α), such as γυαλάκιας 'four-eyes' (pl. γυαλάκηδες), from γυαλάκια, diminutive of γυαλιά 'glasses (= spectacles)'; and (ii) nouns in -ας from feminines in -α, e.g. σαχλαμάρας 'drip', from σαχλαμάρα 'nonsense'). There are also two common words with alternative forms which are used in different circumstances. Μήνας 'month' has genitive singular μήνα or μηνός, the latter used when giving the date (e.g. στίς δεκαπέντε τοῦ μηνός 'on the fifteenth of the month'), and the former elsewhere. The noun δεσπό-της 'despot; bishop' has the parisyllabic plural δεσπότες in the first meaning, the imparisyllabic δεσποτάδες in the second.

1F. Of those feminine nouns ending in -α it would be desirable for dictionaries to mark which lower the stress to the final syllable in the genitive plural and which do not, since from the rules given above (4.1.1) it is not always possible to predict the behaviour of a particular noun. (Those which shift the stress to the final syllable belonged to the first declension in AG, while many of the others are derivatives of ancient third-declension feminines.)

One anomalous noun in this category is μέρα 'day', which has genitive plural ἡμερῶν: the initial ἡ-, which was present in AG, can optionally be added to the other cases too, except the nom./voc., but the genitive plural has only this form, partly because this case is felt to have a learned flavour, and partly to avoid confusion with τῶν μερῶν 'of the parts/places'.

The imparisyllabic feminines in -α and -η are few, and are also diffi-cult to distinguish from the parisyllabics. They are all oxytone and include γιαγιά 'grandmother', νταντά 'nanny', ὀκά 'oke' (this measure is officially obsolete) and κυρά 'missus' (but not usually its compound νοικοκυρά 'housewife'); as for those in -η, the epenthetic -δ- appears only in the genitive plural, e.g. τῶν ἀδερφάδων 'of the sisters', to dis-tinguish this from τῶν ἀδερφῶν 'of the brothers'.

Regarding feminines in -ο, apart from female pet-names (all spelled -ω, with varying plurals: e.g. ἡ Μάρω 'Molly', pl. οἱ Μάρες, but ἡ Μαριγώ 'Polly', pl. οἱ Μαριγούδες), one occasionally finds place-names (mostly Greek islands) and certain other nouns in -ο from feminines in -ος (e.g. ἡ Μύκονο, alongside ἡ Μύκονος 'Mykonos', ἡ μέθοδο, alongside ἡ μέθοδος), but these are not generally accepted as part of the standard language.

For predicting whether a noun in -η has a plural in -ες or in -εις (the latter being a remnant of the ancient third declension), the basic rule is that all and only those nouns in -si (spelled -ση, -ξη, -ψη) form plurals in -εις. The exceptions are that δύναμη 'strength, power' and πόλη 'town, city' follow nouns in -si, whereas βρύση 'spring; tap' and a few others have their plural in -ες.

2A and 2B. The only problem with these nouns is whether in a proparoxytone the stress moves to the penultimate in certain cases. There is some variety in usage in certain words (e.g. τοῦ δασκάλου or τοῦ δάσκαλου 'of the teacher', and τούς πονοκεφάλους or τούς πονοκέφαλους 'the headaches' (acc.), the more common of each pair being the second of the former and the first of the latter word). Stress-shift occurs in many of the most basic nouns of these classes (e.g. ἄνθρωπος 'man, human being', θάνατος 'death', πόλεμος 'war'). The place-name Γιάννινα or Γιάννενα (neuter pl.) has genitive Ἰωαννίνων. A few neuters (notably ποσόν 'sum, amount') are usually found with final -ν in the nom./voc./acc. singular.

2C. The noun πρωί 'morning' is defective, being complemented by πρωινό in the genitive singular and throughout the plural. Certain of the neuters in -ι lack genitives, e.g. diminutives in -άκι and -ούλι, although nouns with these endings which are not perceived as diminutives decline regularly: thus, παιδάκι 'little child' has no genitive *παιδακιοῦ, so that τοῦ μικροῦ παιδιοῦ 'of the little child' has to be used instead; whereas σακάκι 'jacket' (despite being etymologically a diminutive) forms its genitive regularly, τοῦ σακακιοῦ. Certain place-names in -ι have genitives which appear to derive from forms in -ιο, such as Παγκράτι → τοῦ Παγκρατίου, Κολωνάκι → ἡ πλατεία Κολωνακίου 'Kolonaki Square'.

3C. There are a few neuters which have not been accounted for in the above rules (4.1.1 and 4.1.2). These include γάλα 'milk' and μέλι 'honey': the former has plural γάλατα and a rare genitive singular γάλακτος (used almost exclusively in culinary expressions such as ἀρνάκι γάλακτος 'sucking lamb'); the latter has no plural, and its genitive singular is used almost exclusively in the phrase ὁ μήνας τοῦ μέλιτος 'honeymoon'. Μηδέν 'zero' shares a similarity with the numeral ἕνας (with which it is cognate): its genitive is μηδενός, and it has no plural. Finally, the noun ὀξύ 'acid' (originally the neuter of the adjective ὀξύς 'sharp') has genitive singular ὀξέος, plural nom./acc. ὀξέα, genitive ὀξέων; and ὕδωρ 'water' (only used in certain scientific or official phrases) has genitive singular ὕδατος, plural nom./acc. ὕδατα, genitive ὑδάτων.

4.5.1.2 Alternatives of learned origin

There are several alternative noun endings of learned origin which are found in the spoken and written styles of SMG. Most of these concern feminine nouns, others involve masculines. Some speakers almost invariably use the demotic forms: many of these speakers seem to have made a deliberate decision to do so. Others almost invariably use the non-demotic alternatives: most of these are older speakers to whom the demotic forms sound unfamiliar. Yet others (and it is perhaps these whose usage reflects the natural, unforced speech of educated Greeks) use both sets of forms, each in different linguistic contexts.

Of 1F nouns in -a which historically belonged to the AG third declension, some are sometimes found with their ancient inflection in the singular, e.g. δεσποινίς (demotic δεσποινίδα) 'miss; young lady' (nom./voc.), accusative δεσποινίδα, genitive δεσποινίδος: such usage is felt by many speakers to be more polite than the out-and-out demotic pattern. Again, the word for 'Greece' is often found in its ancient form, ἡ Ἑλλάς, τῆς Ἑλλάδος, alongside its demotic equivalents ἡ Ἑλλάδα, τῆς Ἑλλάδας. Genitives in -ος are in fact more often found than nominatives in -ς: thus the declension ἡ ταυτότητα (katharevousa ταυτότης) 'identity', τῆς ταυτότητος is quite common, the latter form being found especially in the phrase δελτίο ταυτότητος 'identity card', although the same speaker who says this is quite likely to use the demotic form of the genitive in other contexts. It appears that the use of the genitive of any noun, which is not nearly as commonly used as the nominative and the accusative, is often likely to entail the use of a non-demotic form; and it is also noteworthy that the demotic form is likely to be found when an article is used, while a non-demotic form is often not preceded by the article. In traditional demotic, a noun in the genitive which was not preceded by an article was rare, and genitives without articles in SMG are usually found in collocations which have entered the language (often as translations of French phrases in which the article is absent) through *katharevousa* (see also 6.1.2). But there is no rigid adherence to the principle: article + genitive → demotic ending, no article + genitive → *katharevousa* ending; one finds mixed constructions such as the official title of the Communist Party of Greece, Κομμουνιστικό Κόμμα Ἑλλάδας (i.e. neither the strictly demotic τῆς Ἑλλάδας nor the strictly *katharevousa* Ἑλλάδος), and although some speakers find such constructions—which are basically literal translations from *katharevousa* to demotic by a change of endings—alien to their ears, they seem to be gaining ground.

Some of those feminine nouns in -a which historically belonged to the first declension are sometimes found with archaic genitive singular

forms. These involve a shift of stress on proparoxytones to the penultimate, and the ending -ης for -ας on those nouns whose stems end in
a consonant other than -ρ-. Thus one finds ἡ χορήγηση ἀδείας 'the
granting of a licence' (alongside τῆς ἄδειας), τά μέλη τῆς οἰκογενείας
μου 'the members of my family' (also τῆς οἰκογένειάς μου). There are
numerous more or less fixed collocations such as ὁ ὑπουργός Ἐθνικῆς
Ἀμύνης 'the Minister of National Defence' (cf. τῆς ἄμυνας) and especially names of streets, which are almost all given in their *katharevousa*
forms (ὁδός Κονίτσης 'Konitsa St.'; cf. also Σταθμός Λαρίσης 'Larisa
Station [in Athens]', alongside τῆς Λάρισας 'of Larisa', and λεωφόρος
Κηφισίας 'Kiphisia Avenue', retaining its ancient stressed -ί-, alongside
στήν περιοχή τῆς Κηφισιᾶς 'in the Kiphisia area', with its demotic
change of stress and weakening of /i/ to ʝ). Names of places are especially
prone to *katharevousa* genitive forms, many of which are quite normal
even in colloquial speech, such as, πέρασε [sc. τό λεωφορεῖο] τῆς
Κονίτσης; 'has the Konitsa bus come by?', or αὐτά τά φιστίκια εἶναι
Αἰγίνης 'these are Aegina pistachios', from the phrase φιστίκια Αἰγίνης
(cf. demotic τῆς Αἴγινας), itself based on a French model such as
pistaches d'Égine.

Lastly, although the standard word for 'Athens' is ἡ Ἀθήνα (genitive
τῆς Ἀθήνας), the (plural) genitive Ἀθηνῶν is found in certain fixed
phrases: e.g. Πανεπιστήμιο Ἀθηνῶν 'University of Athens'.

Feminines in -(s)i with plurals in -(s)is (1Fa) have alternative nominative and genitive singular forms in -ις and -εως respectively (in the
latter, the stress of proparoxytones shifts to the following syllable:
ἡ κυβέρνησις 'government', τῆς κυβερνήσεως). Many speakers (including
those who do not use the nominative in -ις) prefer the genitive in -εως,
arguing that the plural of these nouns is already different from others
in -η (such as τέχνη 'art'). There are analogical arguments for using any
one of these alternatives: those who use the -ις ending for the nominative
singular of disyllables do not distinguish between nominative singular
and plural (ἡ πόλις 'town, city', pl. οἱ πόλεις, both pronounced *ipólis*);
those who use the -ης ending for the genitive singular of disyllables do
not distinguish between this case and the accusative plural (τῆς θέσης
'position' (gen. sing.), τίς θέσεις (acc. pl.), both pronounced *tisthésis*).
Thus those who use ἡ θέση, τῆς θέσεως (which is a normal combination) achieve maximum differentiation among the various cases.

Of the masculines, the group that displays the largest variety is that
consisting of oxytones in -τής, which have an alternative genitive
singular in -τοῦ, a nominative plural in -ταί and an accusative plural in

-τάς. Most speakers are fairly consistent in using either always the demotic endings (Class 1M) or always the learned endings given here. It is by no means necessarily the more educated who use the more learned endings of this and other types of noun: on the contrary, educated speakers will often make an effort to use demotic more consistently; while the less educated often use the -αι and -ας endings even on purely demotic words (e.g. οἱ τραγουδισταί 'singers') and on paroxytones (e.g. οἱ συνταγματάρχαι 'colonels'), even those of foreign origin (e.g. οἱ τουρίσται 'tourists'). In addition, certain nouns in -ης denoting professions have a separate polite form of the vocative singular in -α, usually preceded by κύριε 'Mr' (e.g. κύριε καθηγητά 'professor; (high-school) teacher', κύριε δικαστά 'your honour' (addressed to a judge), κύριε συνταγματάρχα 'Colonel'). Such polite forms do not exist for most nouns in -ης, however (thus κλέφτη! 'thief!').

As in the feminine, so in the masculine and neuter, forms of learned origin tend to be used in certain fixed phrases, such as names of streets. Thus, 'Mr Papadiamandopoulos' is ὁ κύριος Παπαδιαμαντόπουλος (genitive τοῦ κυρίου Παπαδιαμαντόπουλου); his wife and unmarried daughter, however, are ἡ κυρία and ἡ δεσποινίς Παπαδιαμαντοπούλου respectively, and the street named after one of his forebears is ἡ ὁδός Παπαδιαμαντοπούλου: whereas in the normal genitive of his name there is no stress shift, there is when the genitive is used as a feminine name or as the name of a street. (Feminine forms of surnames, which are always indeclinable, are frequently of learned origin: thus many masculine surnames in -ης also have feminines in -ου.) Side by side with τά παιδιά τοῦ Πειραιᾶ 'the lads of Piraeus' there is the learned genitive in ὁ δήμαρχος Πειραιῶς 'the mayor of Piraeus'. But it is not only in place-names that such learned influence is evident: alongside μαῦρα γυαλιά 'dark glasses' there is the more technical γυαλιά ἡλίου 'sunglasses' (from the *katharevousa ílios* rather than the demotic *íljos*, both spelled the same). The fact that γυαλιά ἡλίου is felt to be the equivalent of a single word (i.e. it is a fixed phrase) is shown by the possibility of an utterance such as Ποῦν' τά γυαλιά ἡλίου μου; 'Where are my sun-glasses?', in which the possessive μου is attached to the whole phrase rather than to the word denoting what the speaker actually possesses.

4.5.1.3 Irregular plurals

There is a small number of commonly used nouns whose plural is of a different gender from the singular (and therefore belongs to a different morphological class), or which possess two separate plural forms denoting two different referents. Such nouns are: ὁ βράχος 'rock', pl. τά βράχια (less usually οἱ βράχοι); ὁ πλοῦτος 'riches', pl. τά πλούτη 'great riches'; ὁ δεσμός 'bond', pl. οἱ δεσμοί 'bonds' and τά δεσμά 'fetters'; ὁ καπνός 'smoke; tobacco', pl. οἱ καπνοί 'plenty of smoke' and τά καπνά 'tobaccos'; ὁ λόγος 'word; speech; reason', pl. οἱ λόγοι 'reasons; speeches' and τά λόγια (no genitive) 'words'; ὁ σταθμός 'station', pl. οἱ σταθμοί 'stations' and τά σταθμά 'weights'; ὁ χρόνος 'year; time; tense', pl. οἱ χρόνοι (all meanings) and τά χρόνια (genitive χρονῶ(ν)) 'years'; τό στεφάνι 'wreath, garland', pl. τά στεφάνια 'wreaths, garlands' and τά στέφανα 'marriage wreaths'.

4.5.2 ADJECTIVES

4.5.2.1 Various learned forms

There is an infrequently used paradigm that has not been mentioned: the learned declension of adjectives in -ύς. The cases in which they differ from the pattern given for βαρύς in Appendix I are the masculine and neuter genitive singular (-έος), the masculine nom./acc. plural (-εῖς), the neuter nom./acc. plural (-έα) and the feminine (-εία etc.), like Class 1F, with lowering of stress in genitive plural). The adverb ends in -έως. Not many of these adjectives are used in all cases; rather, they are found sporadically in certain collocations, such as βαρέα πυροβολικά 'heavy artillery', ταχεία ἐξυπηρέτηση 'quick service', and ὀξεία σκωλη-κοειδίτιδα 'acute appendicitis'.

A few neuters of the 2A–2B–1F type of adjective take a final -ν in the nom./acc. singular in certain circumstances: δυνατόν 'possible' (cf. δυνατό 'strong'), ἀδύνατον 'impossible' (cf. ἀδύνατο 'weak; thin') and πιθανόν 'probable'.

4.5.2.2 Feminine formations

As has already been observed, there is some variety in the formation of the feminines of certain adjectives in -ος, particularly those whose stems end in vowels. Thus, from βέβαιος 'sure', βέβαιη is found beside βεβαία (the latter displaying a stress shift characteristic of *katharevousa*). In certain other adjectives with stems in unstressed -e-, while the grammars prescribe -η, everyday usage often has -a (e.g. παμπάλαια 'age-old' for παμπάλαιη, στέρεα 'solid' for στέρεη). There are other adjectives in -ος, of learned origin, whose feminine was identical to their masculine in *katharevousa*. Here one finds that the oxytones retain their -ός ending (e.g. ἡ ἐνεργός ἀνάμειξη 'active intervention'), while paroxytones waver between -ος and -α, the former belonging to more formal styles, the latter to more colloquial usage or to the style of the conscientious demoticist. There is variation among words and even within certain words: thus ἡ πτυχιοῦχος '(female) graduate' generally forms the plural οἱ πτυχιοῦχες (partly because otherwise the hearer would not know whether the speaker was talking about males or females).

Colour adjectives in -ής regularly form a feminine singular in -ί, despite prescriptive grammars (e.g. μιά βυσσωί Τζάγκουαρ 'a cherry-red Jaguar', but pl. βυσσωιές Τζάγκουαρ).

Since the declensions of adjectives in -ων and of those in -ης which have neuters in -ες are felt to belong to *katharevousa*, there is often a conscious or unconscious attempt to bring them into line with demotic morphology. One sometimes encounters a feminine μετριό-φρονη 'modest' (for μετριόφρων), or an adverb ἀτέρμονα 'interminably' (for ?ἀτερμόνως), but grammarians and others counsel the avoidance of both these forms. A masculine genitive singular in -η is sometimes found for -ους in 1Ma-3B adjectives in -ης (the feminine and neuter of this case seem to be avoided completely by those who do not like to use the -ους ending). Grammarians countenance the use of the genitive in -η only in adjectives which have actually become nouns, such as ὁ εὐγενής 'nobleman' and ὁ συγγενής 'relative' (the latter even has a feminine noun derivative συγγένισσα); but in practice there is some wavering, for instance, in τοῦ ἀσθενῆ/ἀσθενοῦς 'of the patient; sick/weak (gen. sing.)', which is perhaps a noun in its first meaning and an adjective in its second, but most speakers will hardly make such a fine distinction. It is noticeable that speakers will often use absolute superlatives in preference to primary forms of certain problematic adjectives: e.g εἶναι ἀναιδέστατη 'she is most impudent' (for ἀναιδής), τόν ἐπιτίμησαν δριμύτατα 'they reprimanded him very severely' (for δριμέως).

4.5.2.3 Stress

The rules laid down in the grammars for stress state that all forms of a given adjective preserve the stress of the masculine nominative singular, whereas many nouns of Classes 1 and 2 shift their stress according to the principles outlined above (4.1.1, 4.1.2). This means that there is a distinction between, for instance, the genitive plurals of the adjective κύριος 'main; chief' and of the two nouns which derive from it, ὁ κύριος 'Mr; gentleman; sir; Lord' and ἡ κυρία 'Mrs; lady; madam', thus: τῶν κύριων στόχων μας 'of our chief aims', but τῶν κυρίων 'of the gentlemen' and τῶν κυριῶν 'of the ladies'. In practice, whereas the last of these is invariable, the other two forms sometimes become confused, and each can stand for the other. Similarly, grammarians give the example τοῦ ἄρρωστου λοχία 'of the sick sergeant' (without stress shift: adjective), and τοῦ ἀρρώστου 'of the patient/sick man' (with stress shift: noun); here the tendency is towards levelling the stress in the second example, and the frequent occurrence on radio and television of such avoidance of stress shift in substantivized adjectives no doubt not only reflects an actual tendency, but reinforces it. Nevertheless, there are certain adjectives which resist such levelling in the usage of many speakers, a notable example being διάφοροι 'various' (e.g. ἔργα δια-φόρων συνθετῶν 'works by various composers'); and a phenomenon can be observed of attraction by a following noun: e.g. τούς δημοσίους ὑπαλλήλους 'civil servants (acc.)' (the noun, which undergoes stress shift, attracts the adjective to do the same).

4.5.2.4 Formation of adverbs

There is also some variety in the formation of adverbs from adjectives in -ος: alongside adverbs in -α, forms in -ως are also found. There are some cases in which a clear difference in meaning is involved: e.g. ἁπλός 'simple' → ἁπλά 'in simple terms' and ἁπλῶς 'simply (= only, just)'; ἄμεσος 'immediate' → ἄμεσα 'directly, without intermediary' and ἀμέσως 'immediately'; τέλειος 'perfect' → τέλεια 'to perfection' and τελείως 'completely'; εὐχάριστος 'pleasant' → εὐχάριστα 'pleasantly' and εὐχαρίστως 'with pleasure'. With other adjectives there may be slight nuances of meaning, which may not be distinguished by many speakers, the -α form being used as an adverb of manner and the -ως form with some other meaning: αὐτός ζεῖ πολύ οἰκονομικά 'he lives very economically', but οἰκονομικῶς δέν πᾶμε καλά 'we're not doing very well, financially speaking': one of these adverbs here is *adjunctive*, the other *disjunctive*. Certain adjectives take only the -ως form: e.g. προηγούμενος 'previous' → προηγουμένως 'previously'; κύριος 'chief, main' → κυρίως 'chiefly, mainly'; ἔγκαιρος 'timely' → ἐγκαίρως 'in time'; ταχυδρομικός 'postal' → ταχυδρομικῶς 'by mail'; κακός 'bad' → κακῶς 'wrongly' (although increasingly frequently forms in -α are met in utterances of those who deliberately attempt to be more demotic than the standard language normally permits). Finally there are certain syntactical structures (particularly where an adverb modifies an adjective or another adverb) in which the -ως is preferred by many speakers: e.g. τό ἔκανε ἀπείρως καλύτερα ἀπό τούς ἄλλους '(s)he did it infinitely better than the others', or τά αἰτήματά τους εἶναι ἀπολύτως λογικά 'their demands are absolutely reasonable'; in the latter example the ambiguity which might have been caused by using ἀπόλυτα (either neuter plural adjective agreeing with αἰτήματα, or adverb) has been avoided.

4.5.2.5 Comparison of adjectives and adverbs

The chief irregular formations of the comparative and the absolute superlative are as follows: ἀπλός 'simple' → ἀπλούστερος, -τατος; κακός 'bad' → χειρότερος, κάκιστος/χείριστος; καλός 'good' → καλύτερος, κάλλιστος/ἄριστος; κοντός 'short' → κοντότερος 'shorter in height', but κοντύτερος 'shorter in length'; λίγος 'little (pl. few)' → λιγότερος, ἐλάχιστος; μεγάλος 'large' → μεγαλύτερος, μέγιστος; μικρός 'small' → μικρότερος, ἐλάχιστος; πολύς 'much (pl. many)' → περισσότερος. There are also some comparatives or pseudo-comparatives from other parts of speech than adjectives and adverbs of manner, such as ἀρχή 'beginning' → ἀρχήτερα (only in the phrase μιά ὥρα ἀρχήτερα 'as soon as possible'); ἰδίως 'especially' → ἰδιαίτερα 'more especially'; νωρίς 'early' → νωρίτερα, -τατα; προτιμῶ 'I prefer' → προτιμότερος 'preferable'; πρῶτα 'first' → πρωτύτερα 'previously'; συμφέρον 'advantage; interest' → συμφερότερος 'more profitable/advantageous'. While the adverb from all other comparatives and superlatives of adjectives ends in -α, λιγότερος and περισσότερος have adverbs λιγότερο 'less' and περισσότερο 'more'.

A kind of comparative of many adverbs of place and time may be formed with πιό: e.g. ἐδῶ 'here', πιό ἐδῶ 'in this direction'; κάτω 'down', πιό κάτω 'further down'; ἀργά 'late', πιό ἀργά 'later', etc.

Greek speakers are not averse to emphasizing comparatives and superlatives in a way which grammarians do not recommend: e.g. πιό καλύτερος (literally, 'more better'), or πολύ ἐλάχιστα (lit. 'very hardly any', i.e. 'very few'). It should be noted, however, that there is no comparative superlative form of adverbs: for 'he ran fastest' one has to say ἔτρεξε πιό γρήγορα ἀπό ὅλους [τούς ἄλλους] (lit. 'he ran faster than all [the rest]'). Nevertheless, the comparative of an adverb is sometimes used as a comparative superlative: e.g. εἶναι οἱ περιοχές πού δεινοπάθησαν περισσότερο κατά τήν Κατοχή 'they are the areas which suffered most [lit. 'more'] during the [Axis] Occupation.'

In fact, there is not such a rigid distinction in MG between comparative and superlative as exists in English, and one often encounters sentences in which the superlative form of the adjective is actually being used as a comparative:

(1) οἱ πελάτες τοῦ ξενοδοχείου θεωροῦνταν οἱ καλύτεροι ἀπό ὅλους τούς ἄλλους ξένους ἐπισκέπτες (lit. 'the hotel's guests were considered to be the best of all the other foreign visitors') (*T* 25 June 1981, 18).

Here either the definite article *οἱ* (which converts the comparative into the superlative) or the word ἄλλους ('other') is superfluous.

Under the influence of *katharevousa*, there are phrases consisting of definite article + comparative adjective in the neuter singular with the meaning 'as . . . as possible' (e.g. *τό ταχύτερο* 'as quickly as possible'; also *τό συντομότερο δυνατόν* 'as soon as possible'), standing for the demotic (but admittedly less concise) ὅσο γίνεται πιό γρήγορα (lit. 'as much as it happens more quickly') or ὅσο τό δυνατόν πιό γρήγορα (lit. 'as much as possible more quickly'). A similar construction to this *katharevousa* type may be used adjectivally (e.g. πιάνεις τό λιγότερο δυνατό χῶρο 'you take up the least possible space'). Also, again under learned influence, and almost exclusively in writing, certain absolute superlative forms are sometimes used as comparative superlatives. Thus, alongside the absolute ἔχει μέγιστη σημασία 'it has the utmost importance' (note the absence of article), there are phrases such as ὁ μέγιστος κοινός διαιρέτης 'the highest common factor' (mathematical style is notoriously archaic in MG); and even,

(2) *τό μεγαλύτερο, τό μέγιστο τμῆμα τοῦ λαοῦ* 'the greatest, by far the largest section of the people' (And. 1976: 340)

(in which *τό μέγιστο* seems to be seen as more emphatic than *τό μεγαλύτερο*); and the same word used as a noun in the neuter:

(3) *τό μέγιστο τοῦ ἑλληνικοῦ λαοῦ* 'the majority of the Greek people' (And. 1976: 343)

(a stylistic alternative for ἡ πλειοψηφία or ἡ πλειονότητα 'the majority').

4.5.3 PRONOUNS AND ARTICLES

Concerning pronouns and articles it will be necessary to examine briefly certain details of alternative forms, and to explain the use of the reflexive *τόν ἑαυτό (μου)*.

4.5.3.1 Alternative forms

The most noticeable variation that occurs in these classes of words is the addition or deletion of the final -ν in the masculine and feminine accusative singular. The prescriptive rule for the definite article states that the -ν is deleted when the following word begins with any consonant except a stop (the same applies to the negatives δέ(ν) and μή(ν): cf. 1.4.2.4). The same rule is valid for the feminine accusative singular of the clitic pronoun, whereas the masculine always retains its -ν. In those pronouns which decline like adjectives (and certain adjectives, such as πολύς and λίγος, and the article and numeral ένας) the addition of the -ν in the feminine accusative singular before vowels and stops is optional, while its retention in the masculine is obligatory when the pronoun is not used attributively (e.g. σ᾽ αὐτό(ν) τόν ἄνθρωπο 'to this/that man', but σ᾽ αὐτόν 'to him'). The rationale behind this is that the masculine in -ον should be distinguished from the neuter in -ο in order to avoid ambiguity (although this does not occur in most adjectives, and it is therefore difficult to see why the distinction should be made only in certain words and not in others). In practice, however, the final -ν is added by some speakers to the article τόν (and the negatives δέν and μήν) even when it is not strictly necessary, while conversely it is often omitted from pronouns which decline like adjectives. Many speakers, on the other hand, retain the -ν in the accusative singular of certain pronouns but place an additional vowel after it (this is considered to be a mark of less educated speech, but it is often used by educated speakers when speaking casually). One finds τονε and τηνε used as proclitics and enclitics (in the latter case, τονα and τηνα are found in Salonica) and αὐτόνε, αὐτήνε (αὐτόνα, αὐτήνα in Salonica). Especially common is the accusative singular of the first and second person singular emphatic pronouns ἐμέναvε and ἐσέναvε.

Very occasionally, when speakers want to use a true genitive of a first or second person pronoun rather than the pseudo-genitives ἐμένα, etc., they may use the learned ἐμοῦ (1st sing.) and, very rarely, ἡμῶν and ὑμῶν (which are homophones: 1st and 2nd plural respectively): e.g. μεταξύ ἐμοῦ καί τοῦ κοινοῦ 'between myself and the public'.

As an alternative to ὁ ἴδιος 'the same', there is the learned ὁ αὐτος, found especially in the phrase ἕνας καί ὁ αὐτός 'one and the same' (which declines fully): e.g. ἔχουμε μιά καί τήν αὐτή λέξη γιά τίς δυό ἔννοιες 'we have one and the same word for the two concepts.'

4.5.3.2 Τόν ἐαυτό (μου)

Although grammars normally talk of the 'reflexive pronoun' in MG, it is clear that ἐαυτός is strictly speaking a masculine noun which declines like Class 2A. It is always preceded by the definite article and accompanied by a possessive enclitic. It even has a diminutive ἐαυτούλης (αὐτός ὅλο σκέφτεται τόν ἐαυτούλη του 'he's always thinking about his little self'). Ἐαυτός is invariable for gender; although it is most commonly found in the accusative as an object of a verb or a preposition, it occurs in the genitive, and even in the nominative (although this last use is literary); it is usually invariable for number, but it may optionally be used in the plural if it refers to more than one person (it is not used for inanimate referents):

(1) ἡ Καίτη ἔπιασε τόν ἐαυτό της νά κρυφακούει τούς γείτονές της
'Katy caught herself eavesdropping on her neighbours';
(2) οἱ Φίξ θεωροῦν τούς ἐαυτούς τους Ἕλληνες 'the Fix [family] consider themselves Greeks.'

The plural is used in (2) because the singular would be awkward with the plural Ἕλληνες in apposition to it.

4.6 DERIVATIVES OF NOUNS

MG is exceptionally rich in derivational suffixes, which are so numerous and varied that there is not enough space to deal with more than a fraction here (for fuller details, see Sotiropoulos 1972, but also 10.3.1). Nouns may be converted with ease into adjectives (usually with the addition of -ικός or -ινός to the stem) or verbs (by adding -ίζω, -εύω, -ώνω, etc.). They can also be made into other nouns, and it is two morphological aspects of this last process which will be examined here: (a) diminutives and augmentatives, and (b) feminines from masculines.

4.6.1 DIMINUTIVES AND AUGMENTATIVES

Diminutives are frequently used in MG, especially in speech, to express not only smallness but familiarity and endearment, and on occasion disparagement. Augmentatives, which tend to be restricted to more familiar styles of speech, are used to express not only largeness but also admiration. The most frequent diminutive suffix is -άκι (neuter: mostly added to neuters but also to nouns of other genders), followed by -ούλα and -ίτσα (both feminine: added to feminines). The diminutive and augmentative endings are added directly to the stem of the noun, or to the allostem with the epenthetic consonant in those nouns which have one, or after a special epenthetic syllable which varies from word to word.[1]

Examples of morphology: παιδ-ί 'child' → παιδ-άκι 'little child'; τσάι 'tea' (allostem τσαγ-) → τσαγ-άκι '(little) cup of tea'; πρά(γ)μα 'thing' (allostem πρα(γ)ματ-) → πραματ-άκι 'little thing'; καφές 'coffee' (allostem καφεδ-) → καφεδ-άκι '(little) cup of coffee'; αὐγ-ό 'egg' → αὐγ-ουλ-άκι 'little egg', αὐγ-ουλ-άρα 'whopping great egg'; σύκ-ο 'fig' → συκ-αλ-άκι 'little fig'; βάρκ-α 'boat' → βαρκ-ούλα 'little boat'; ὥρ-α 'hour' → μιά ὡρίτσα 'just one little hour'. There are not so many diminutives with masculine endings: δρόμ-ος 'road, street' → δρομ-άκος 'little street'; πατέρ-ας 'father' → πατερ-ούλης 'daddy'. (There is also the learned diminutive in -ίσκος: ἀπατεών-ας 'swindler' → ἀπατεων-ίσκος 'petty swindler'.) Diminutive endings can even be added to indeclinable nouns of foreign origin, thus making it possible for them to show a morphological distinction between singular and plural: (τό) σλίπ 'underpants' → σλιπ-άκι (same meaning); (τό) φάουλ 'foul (in football)' → φαουλ-άκι 'little foul'; (τό) ραντεβού 'appointment, date' → ραντεβου-δ-άκι (same meaning). There is also an ending -άκιας (< -άκι) which is applied disparagingly to a man who possesses a certain physical or moral quality: (τά) γυαλιά 'glasses' → ὁ γυαλ-άκιας 'four-eyes'; (τό) κόρτε 'flirting' → ὁ κορτάκιας 'flirt'. Some adjectives may receive diminutive endings in the same way, when they are not used attributively but are thought of as nouns: μικρ-ός 'small' → ὁ μικρ-ούλης 'little boy'; μελαχριν-ή 'dark-haired' (fem.) → μελαχριν-ούλα 'brunette'; κίτριν-ο 'yellow' → θά φορέσω τό κιτρινάκι μου 'I'll wear my yellow [dress]'; τυχερ-ός 'lucky' → ὁ τυχερ-άκιας 'lucky beggar'. (One might also add the diminutive adjective τοσοδούλικος 'teeny-weeny', from the phrase τόσος δά 'tiny'.) There are also adjectival diminutive endings -ούτσικος (καλός 'good' → καλούτσικος 'goodish') and -ωπός (used with names of colours: πράσινος 'green' → πρασινωπός 'greenish').

Examples of change of meaning: καζάνι 'cauldron; boiler' → καζανάκι '(lavatory) cistern'; ζευγάρι 'pair, couple' → ζευγαράκι 'courting couple'; (ὁ) λάκκος 'pit' → λακκάκι 'dimple'; παράθυρο 'window' → παραθυράκι

---

[1] The epenthetic consonant or syllable is usually present in other derivatives too: ρολόι 'watch, clock' (allostem ρολογ-) → ρολογ-άς 'watchmaker'; πράγμα (allostem πραγματ-) → πραγματικός 'real'; ψωμάς 'baker' (allostem ψωμαδ-) → ψωμάδ-ικο 'baker's shop'; αὐγό (allostem αὐγουλ-) → αὐγουλ-ιέρα 'egg-cup', αὐγουλ-άς 'egg-seller'.

'loophole (in law or regulation)'; ποδόσφαιρο 'football' → ποδοσφαιράκι 'bar-football'; ξυράφι 'razor' → ξυραφάκι 'razor-blade'; (ἡ) πλάκα 'slab, paving-stone' → πλακάκι 'tile'; πρόβατο 'sheep' → προβατάκια 'little sheep; "white horses" (in sea)'.

The chief augmentative endings are -άρα and -α (fem.), and -αρος and -αράς (masc.). The last (which corresponds rather to the diminutive -άκιας) sometimes denotes the male possessor of a quality (there is an occasional feminine -αρού), while the other three (which frequently entail a change of gender) are straightforward augmentatives.

Examples: κοιλιά 'stomach, belly' → κοιλάρα 'paunch'; (ὁ) κῶλος 'arse' → κωλάρα 'fat arse'; (ὁ) φιλόλογος 'literature teacher' → φιλολογάρα 'fantastic literature teacher'; (τό) γκόλ 'goal (football)' → γκολάρα 'great goal'; (τό) μπουκάλι 'bottle' → μπουκάλα 'big bottle'; (τό) ντουλάπι 'cupboard' → ντουλάπα 'wardrobe'; ψεύτης 'liar' → ψεύταρος 'big liar'; (τό) κορίτσι 'girl' → κορίτσαρος 'beautiful (and perhaps buxom) girl'; κοιλάρα 'paunch' → κοιλαράς 'paunchy man'; τραγουδιστής 'singer' → τραγουδισταράς 'marvellous singer'. There are other augmentative endings with more restricted use: e.g. (τό) αὐτί 'ear' → αὐτούκλα 'huge ear'; (τό) σπίτι 'house' → σπιταρόνα 'fantastic (large) house'; (ἡ) μύτη 'nose' → (ὁ) μύτος 'conk'; (τά) ἑλληνικά 'Greek (language)' → (ἡ) ἑλληνικούρα 'piece of highfalutin Greek'; ἄντρας 'man' → ἄντρακλας 'great hunk of a man'; φωνή 'voice' → φωνάκλα 'loud voice' → φωνακλάς 'loud-mouth'.

4.6.2 FEMININES OF MASCULINE NOUNS REFERRING TO PERSONS

As has been mentioned (4.2), the distinction between substantives and adjectives in MG is not always clear, since any adjective can be substantivized. Nominals (i.e. nouns and adjectives) referring to persons can perhaps be divided into three categories from this point of view: (a) those for which all genders exist and are morphologically predictable, such as ζηλιάρης—ζηλιάρα—ζηλιάρικο 'jealous' (these can be forthwith classed as adjectives and be ignored for the purposes of this section); (b) those for which there is a feminine version that is not predictable from the masculine; and (c) those for which only a masculine exists, this form being used for females as well as for males (cf. 2.1.1).

The endings for deriving feminines from masculine nouns are various, and each feminine has to be learned with its masculine counterpart. Examples: βασιλιάς 'king' → βασίλισσα 'queen'; μαθητής 'schoolboy' → μαθήτρια 'schoolgirl' (the -τρια ending is a highly productive one from

masculines in -της); νοσοκόμος 'male nurse' → νοσοκόμα 'nurse'; πρό-
σκοπος 'boy scout' → προσκοπίνα 'girl guide'; λουλουδάς 'flower-seller'
→ λουλουδού (same (fem.)); ψεύτης 'liar' → ψεύτρα (same (fem.)). With
certain words the situation is quite confused: e.g., corresponding to ὁ
συνεργάτης 'assistant, contributor', one finds ἡ συνεργάτης, ἡ συνερ-
γάτις (gen. συνεργάτιδος), ἡ συνεργάτιδα, ἡ συνεργάτρια, and perhaps
even ἡ συνεργάτισσα. It is noteworthy that a satisfactory feminine of
ὁ βουλευτής 'member of parliament' has not yet been found: the
frequently used βουλευτίνα is felt to be too familiar for official use,
which prefers ἡ βουλευτής: the form *βουλεύτρια, which from a linguistic point of view would seem the obvious solution, does not exist
(despite the numerous parallel formations, including ἑρμηνευτής →
ἑρμηνεύτρια 'interpreter (of song etc.)'). There are also a few examples
of the converse process, i.e. the formation of a masculine noun from
a feminine: e.g. γεροντοκόρη 'spinster, old maid' → γεροντοκόρος 'old
woman (of man)'.

There is a large number of nouns denoting professions which have
common gender but only masculine-type declension, despite the
marked tendency in traditional demotic to use separate forms for each
sex. Examples include: ὑπάλληλος 'employee', ψυχολόγος 'psychologist'
(together with all profession nouns in -λόγος), θυρωρός 'concierge',
ἐπαγγελματίας 'professional', γραμματέας 'secretary', μάρτυρας 'witness'. Some common-gender nouns do not refer to professions as such:
e.g. σύζυγος 'spouse'. There is nothing in the morphology of these
nouns which prevents them from forming separate feminines. On the
other hand, many speakers feel uneasy about using the masculine endings with feminine articles, and tend to avoid using the demotic genitive
singular of some of them, preferring the learned version if they use the
genitive at all: thus one finds τῆς συγγραφέως 'of the author' for τῆς
συγγραφέα, in which the presence of a final -ς in the article and its
absence in the noun strikes some speakers (and hearers) as strange.

4.7   INDECLINABLE NOUNS AND ADJECTIVES

There is now in MG a large number of indeclinable nouns and adjectives (from French and English), which fail to comply with the morphological patterns of the language. The tendency today is for the majority
of new loanwords to be treated as indeclinable. One unfortunate
phenomenon is that many speakers place a final -s on the plural of
certain loanwords from English, thus introducing a completely new

paradigm into the language (e.g. τό κομπιοῦτερ 'computer', pl. τά κομπιοῦτερς). This English final -s has even spread to words which are not derived from English (e.g. οἱ Βίκιγκς 'the Vikings'); but confusion on such matters leads to the final -s being used also in some singulars (e.g. τό τάνκς '(mil.) tank'), leaving the words in question indeclinable.

4.8 CONCLUSION

To sum up, the noun morphology of MG presents a variety of alternative forms. Educationalists, who are painfully aware of the difficulties of teaching and learning the complete range of MG declensions, constantly call for a greater standardization through the elimination of all terminations which do not conform to the basic demotic pattern. It must be admitted that for anyone who has not mastered the intricacies of MG noun morphology the areas that lie outside the basic system represent a *terra incognita* into which (s)he will fear to venture: the result is that, since a thorough familiarity with this rough ground is a prerequisite for any discourse in the more abstract or profound realms of thought, all but the most highly educated tend to be cut off from such discourse. (Similar—if not more acute—problems arise with verb morphology.) For this reason alone it would be highly desirable for as many of the anomalies as possible to be removed. On the other hand, there are those who relish the subtleties of MG πολυτυπία (the existence of several alternative realizations of the same underlying form) and who delight in manipulating the various possibilities in order to produce a pleasing, 'natural' style (and not only, it should be stressed, to show off their superior linguistic education).

5

VERB MORPHOLOGY

5.1 GENERAL

The inflectional behaviour of any given verb in MG is highly unpredictable. Ideally one should know six pieces of data about each verb, viz.:
(i) the imperfective stem; (ii) the imperfective non-past ('present tense')
active conjugation type; (iii) the perfective active stem; (iv) the imperfective non-past passive conjugation type; (v) the perfective passive
stem; and (vi) the past passive participle. With some verbs it is also useful to know the imperfective past active conjugation type.

There appear to be, apart from the various imperfective stems:
(a) two chief types of imperfective non-past conjugation, the first
having penultimate stress in the second person singular (Class 1), the
second having final stress (Class 2: this is divided into two sub-groups
according to whether the second person singular ends in *-ís* or *-ás*);
(b) three types of perfective active stem, depending on whether it ends
in *-s-* or not (if not, it ends in *-n-*, *-l-* or *-r-*), and, if not, whether the
radical vowel of this stem is the same as or different from that of the
imperfective stem; (c) five chief types of imperfective non-past passive
conjugation; (d) two types of perfective passive stem, according to
whether it ends in *-ϑ-* or in a voiceless fricative + *-t-*; and (e) five types
of past passive participle stem, depending on whether the *-ménos* ending is preceded by *-z-*, *-γ-*, *-v-*, or another consonant, or zero. In addition, there are three types of imperfective past active conjugation.

The two factors which complicate even further this already complex
pattern are (1) the lack of correlation among these five sets of data
((a)–(e)), and (2) the lack of consistency among speakers (and even
within idiolects) in the use of this material. This means that, given one,
two, three, four, or even five of the essential parts of a particular verb,
it is not always possible to predict the other part(s); and this is true
even in cases where speakers are in agreement as to which form is used
for each part.

While conjugation tables of sample verbs are given in Appendix I, an

attempt will be made here both to generalize on the MG verb formations and to place them in categories. Since there is not always a correlation between the various stems and the various endings, it will be
necessary to examine stems and endings separately.

5.2 THE STEMS

5.2.1 THE IMPERFECTIVE

Class 1 verbs are those whose stress falls on the penultimate syllable in
the second person singular of the imperfective non-past active (e.g.
δen- 'tie' → second singular δénis). The imperfective stem is used in the
imperfective past and non-past of the active and (sometimes with modi-
fications) of the passive: once the stem is known, these four forms are
normally predictable.

Class 1 verbs may have imperfective stems ending in any of the
following sounds or combinations of sounds:

Vowels (e, i, u);
Labials (v, p, pt, f, ft);
Velars (γ, ng, k, x, xn);
Dentals (δ, ϑ, t);
Voiced sibilant (z);
Voiceless sibilant (s);
Nasals (n, m); or
Liquids (l, r, ln, rn).

For the purposes of forming the other stems, the epenthetic -n- which
appears as the second member of some of the above combinations is
omitted. Most verbs with imperfective stems ending in labials or velars
may be considered as having an unspecified underlying consonant with
the same point of articulation as that of the final consonant of the
imperfective stem but which varies in manner of articulation according
to the nature of the following sound in stems other than the imperfective.

Class 2 verbs are those which are stressed on the final syllable in the
second person singular of the imperfective non-past active. The imperfective stem of these verbs may be considered to end in a consonant followed by a stress, which is thrown on to the following vowel

in the imperfective non-past active (e.g. *aγap-* 'love' → second singular *aγapás*).

5.2.2 THE PERFECTIVE ACTIVE

The perfective active stem is used to form (a) the perfective active and (b) the singular of the perfective passive imperative. The perfective active stem of most Class 1 verbs, except those with imperfective stem ending in a liquid, and some ending in a nasal, ends in *-s-*. There are, in other words, verbs that have *sigmatic perfectives* and others that have *asigmatic perfectives*. Verbs that have asigmatic perfectives (sometimes known as *strong verbs*) have a perfective active stem identical to the imperfective, except (in some verbs) for an alteration in the radical vowel (see 5.2.5). Sigmatic perfectives may be considered as being formed by the addition of *-s-* to the stem-vowel or underlying stem-consonant of the imperfective. Vowel-stems simply add *-s-* (e.g. *iδri-* 'found' → *iδris-*); labials and velars are realized as voiceless stops (*p* and *k* respectively) before the *-s-* (as is normal in MG phonology: e.g. *klev-* 'steal' → *kleps-*, *rixn-* 'throw' → *riks-*); and dentals are deleted (e.g. *plaϑ-* 'mould' → *plas-*). Most voiceless sibilant stems have an underlying velar (e.g. *apalas-* 'rid' → *apalaks-*), while voiced sibilant stems are divisible into those that have an underlying sibilant, which is (as always in MG phonology) deleted before the *-s-* (e.g. *xoriz-* 'separate' → *xoris-*), and those that have an underlying velar (e.g. *alaz-* 'change' → *alaks-*). Those stems in *-n-* that have a sigmatic aorist delete the nasal before the *-s-* (e.g. *δen-* 'tie' → *δes-*).

The two chief exceptions to these rules are (a) those verbs of *katharevousa* origin in *-εύω*, many of which have their perfective stem in *-ευσ-*, and (b) verbs of Romance origin in *-άρω*, whose perfective non-past is identical to their imperfective non-past, but whose perfective past ends in *-άρα* or *-άρισα*.

All Class 2 verbs have sigmatic perfectives; most insert *-i-* before the *-s-* (e.g. *aγap-* → *aγap-i-s-*). Many verbs of this class, however, in which the final consonant of the imperfective stem is a liquid, and some others, insert *-a-* or *-e-* instead of *-i-* (e.g. *jel-* 'laugh' → *jel-a-s-*, *bor-* 'be able' → *bor-e-s-*): this is also the case with Class 2 verbs which have an epenthetic *-n-* in the imperfective alone (e.g. *ksexn-* 'forget' → *ksex-a-s-*). A few Class 2 verbs have an underlying velar (preceded by *-a-* or *-i-*) which surfaces in all stems except the imperfective (e.g. *vast-* 'hold' → *vast-ak-s-*, *trav-* 'pull' → *trav-ik-s-*).

Class 1 and Class 2 differ only in the inflections of the imperfective tenses and in the formation of the perfective active stem. They can thus be treated together as far as the formation of the perfective passive and the past passive participle stems is concerned.

5.2.3 THE PERFECTIVE PASSIVE

Perfective passive stems are divisible into two chief types: (i) those of verbs whose underlying stem ends in a labial, velar, or sibilant, in which case this consonant is realized as a voiceless fricative followed by *-t-* (according to the normal rules of MG phonology: e.g. *kleP-* → *klef-t-*, *arpaK-* 'snatch' → *arpax-t-*, *plaS-* → *plas-t-*); and (ii) those of verbs whose underlying stem ends in a vowel or a liquid, in which this sound is followed by *-ϑ-* (e.g. *δe-* → *δe-ϑ-*, *psal-* 'chant' → *psal-ϑ-*). These include many verbs of Class 2, whose underlying stem ends in a vowel (e.g. *aγapi-* → *aγapi-ϑ-*). Some nasal stems preserve the nasal as *-n-* before the *-ϑ-*, others delete it (e.g. *δiefϑin-* 'direct' → *δiefϑin-ϑ-*, but *krin-* 'judge' → *kri-ϑ-*).

It is not always possible to predict the perfective passive stem from either the imperfective or the perfective active stem. For instance, while almost all vowel-stem verbs of Class 1 and all Class 2 verbs have a perfective active in *-s-*, some appear to have an underlying *-s-* and others do not: thus ἐλκύω 'I attract', perfective active *elki-s-*, perfective passive *elki-s-t-*, but ἰδρύω 'I found', perfective active *iδri-s-*, perfective passive *iδri-ϑ-*; κυλῶ 'I roll', perfective active *kil-i-s-*, perfective passive *kil-i-s-t-*, but ρωτῶ 'I ask', perfective active *rot-i-s-*, perfective passive *rot-i-ϑ-*. Similarly, some imperfective stems in *-n-* have underlying *-s-*, others no underlying consonant: thus ψήνω 'I roast', perfective active *psi-s-*, perfective passive *psi-s-t-*; κρίνω 'I judge', perfective active *krin-* (identical to the imperfective stem), perfective passive *kri-ϑ-*; δένω 'I tie', perfective active *δe-s-*, perfective passive *δe-ϑ-*.

5.2.4 THE PAST PASSIVE PARTICIPLE

All past participles end in *-ménos* and are fully inflected for gender, number, and case. Verb stems in underlying vowel or liquid simply add *-ménos* to that sound; while underlying sibilants, labials, and velars are realized as voiced fricatives before the *-m-* (although some verbs delete their labial, and a few their velar, before the *-m-*). Some verbs with underlying *-n-* delete the *-n-*, others replace it with *-z-*. Thus: *aγapi-* 'love' → *aγapi-ménos*; *psal-* → *psal-ménos*; *luS-* 'bathe' → *luz-ménos*; *δimosieP-* 'publish' → *δimosiev-ménos*, but *kriP-* 'hide' →

kri-ménos; *petaK-* 'throw; fly' → *petaɣ-ménos* or *peta-ménos*; *apoϑarin-* 'discourage' → *apoϑari-ménos*, but *apomakrin-* 'remove' → *apomakriz-ménos*.

It is normally, but not always, possible to predict the past participle from the perfective passive stem: most verbs with *-ϑ-* in the perfective passive simply delete this before *-ménos*, while those with voiceless fricative + *-t-* voice the fricative before *-ménos*. It is, as usual, verbs with underlying *-n-* which cause most problems.

5.2.5 IRREGULARITIES IN THE FORMATION OF VERBAL STEMS

There is a large number of irregular verbs in MG. The irregularities appear not in the endings but in the formation of the stems. These verbs vary in their degree of irregularity, in that while a few have four different underlying stems, others have three, and others only two. This means that in the last category, only one of the stems may be aberrant, the others being predictable from each other on the basis of the rules given in the preceding sub-sections.

Irregularities include (a) change of radical vowel; (b) change of stem-final consonant; (c) deletion or addition of a sound or sounds; (d) metathesis of sounds; (e) *suppletion* of one root by another; and (f) lack of dental in the perfective passive stem. Up to three of these irregularities may coexist within the paradigm of a single verb.

Instances of the deletion of the final *-n-* of the imperfective stem have already been noted. There are certain verbs in *-en-* in which in other stems the *-en-* becomes *-an-* or *-in-* (change of radical vowel: e.g. *trelen-* 'madden' → *trelan-*; *paxen-* 'fatten' → *paxin-*), *-a-* or *-i-* (change of radical vowel + deletion of stem-final consonant: e.g. *proften-* 'have time (to)' → *profta-*; *anasten-* 'resurrect' → *anasti-*), or *-aK-* (change of radical vowel + change of stem-final consonant: e.g. *vizen-* 'suckle' → *vizaK-*), or is deleted (e.g. *maϑen-* 'learn' → *maϑ-*).

With verbs which change the radical vowel (i.e. the vowel of the final syllable of the imperfective stem), there may be either two or three different vowels in the imperfective, perfective active and perfective passive stems. Verbs with *-a-*, *-o-*, or *-u-* as radical vowel in the imperfective do not undergo such changes. Examples of these changes are given in Table 5.1 (the past passive participle has been omitted because it generally has the same vowel as the perfective passive).

TABLE 5.1

Examples		*Perfective active*	*Perfective passive*
φθείρω	'I spoil'	fθir-	fθar-
ἀφήνω	'I leave'	afi-s-	afe-ϑ-
κλέβω	'I steal'	klep-s-	klap-
σέρνω	'I pull'	sir-	sir-ϑ-
ψέλνω	'I chant'	psal-	psal-(ϑ)-
στέλνω	'I send'	stil-	stal-(ϑ)-
ἀγγέλλω	'I announce'	angil-	angel-ϑ-

In two very common verbs the perfective active stem in the past is different from that in the non-past: παίρνω 'I take', perfective active non-past πάρω, perfective active past πῆρα, perfective passive par-ϑ-; πάω or πηγαίνω 'I go', perfective active non-past πάω, perfective active past πῆγα (no passive). The characteristic -i- of the perfective past of these two verbs (a remnant of the ancient vocalic augment) is also found as a prefix in the past of certain perfectives; e.g. pj- 'drink', non-past πιῶ, past ἤπια; rϑ- 'come' (optionally for erϑ-), non-past 'ρϑω, past ἦρϑα (for other examples, see below).

In some common verbs the perfective active is formed by deletion of a syllable and then behaves like the perfective passive of most other verbs, except for the position of the stress in the past tense: thus μπαίνω 'I go/come in', perfective active b- (non-past μπῶ, past μπῆκα); βρίσκω 'I find', perfective active vr- (non-past βρῶ, past βρῆκα; cf. perfective passive vreϑ- (non-past βρεϑῶ, past βρέϑηκα)).

Examples of the addition of sounds in stems other than the imperfective are: ke- 'burn', perfective active kap-s- (with radical vowel change), perfective passive ka-; pne- 'blow', perfective active exceptionally pnefs-, not *pneps-, as a result of the verb being of learned origin; ϑel- 'want', perfective active ϑeli-s-; efx- 'wish', perfective passive efxi-ϑ- (no active). Examples of the change of stem-final consonant are βάζω 'I put' and βγάζω 'I take out/off' (in which the -z- changes to -l- in all other stems). Examples of metathesis are -val- and -kal-, whose perfective passive stems are -vli-ϑ- and -kli-ϑ- respectively.

Suppletion is found in many common verbs, in which the root supplying the imperfective stem is completely different from that of the other stems. Examples are: le(γ)- 'say', perfective p- (i-p- in past and passive); vlep- 'see', perfective δ- (i-δ- in past and passive); and tro(γ)- 'eat', perfective fa(γ)-.

Some deponent verbs with active meaning have their perfective in active form: γίνομαι 'I become' → γίνω (past ἔγινα); κάθομαι 'I sit' → καθίσω (past κάθισα); ἔρχομαι 'I come' → ἔρθω or 'ρθω (past ἦρθα).

A number of verbs lack the characteristic dental at the end of the perfective passive stem. A large proportion of these verbs also undergo radical vowel change, although there is synchronically no absolute correlation between the two phenomena. Thus: *xer-* 'be joyful' → *xar-*; *kov-* 'cut' → *kop-*; *(kata)plis-* (underlying *-pliK-*) 'amaze' → *-plaγ-*; *pniγ-* 'drown' → *pniγ-*, etc. Some verbs have alternative perfective passives with or without the dental (e.g. γράφω 'I write' → γraf-t- or γraf-), the former being felt to be more colloquial or more literary, the latter more formal. There is also a tendency with some such verbs, however, for the dental to be preferred in the past but not in the non-past (e.g. ἀπαλλάσσω 'I rid' → perfective past ἀπαλλάχτηκα, but non-past ἀπαλλαγῶ).

A most chaotic situation is presented by the remnants of AG verbs in -μι, which warrant a couple of paragraphs to themselves here. The chief verbs of this type (Classes 3a and 3b) in use in MG (where in their ancient form they were used only in the passive and almost exlusively in prepositional compounds) are ἵστημι 'I stand' and τίθημι 'I place'. The former has seven different imperfective avatars in MG, the inflections of which interpenetrate in a most confusing manner. These may be exemplified by the following verbs: (1) παρα-σταίνω 'I represent' and ἀνα-σταίνω 'I resurrect'; (2) στήνω 'I set up'; (3) παρ-ιστάνω 'I represent'; (4) καθ-ιστῶ 'I render' and συν-ιστῶ 'I recommend'; (5) στέκω 'I stand', and the deponents (6) στέκομαι 'I stand' and (7) παρ-ίσταμαι 'I am present'. Leaving aside past tenses, the intricacies of whose internal augments we shall examine later (5.4.3), we notice that some of those non-deponents which have passives have a separate imperfective stem for each of the two voices, but that in some verbs the distinction between voices is not clear. Table 5.2 gives the non-past tense forms of these verbs. The forms -σταίνω, στήνω, and στέκω/στέκομαι are of popular origin, and are more frequently used than the other, less colloquial, verbs. It is clear that παρασταίνω and παριστάνω, for example, are essentially the same verb, the former being less, the latter more, formal; but both forms are found in SMG.

The AG τίθημι has only one manifestation in MG: θέτω, used on its own ('I place') or in prepositional compounds. The imperfective passive is -τίθεμαι (although a regularized -θέτομαι is sometimes found among demoticists, and in speech one may detect some hesitation: e.g.

TABLE 5.2

	Imperfective passive	Perfective active	Perfective pass.
παρα-σταίνω	-σταίνομαι		-σταϑῶ
ἀνα-σταίνω			(-)στηϑῶ
στήνω	στήνομαι	(-)στήσω	
παρ-ιστάνω	-ιστάνομαι		-σταϑῶ
καϑ-ιστῶ	-ίσταμαι		
συν-ιστῶ			-στηϑῶ
στέκω ⌐			
— └→	στέκομαι	—	σταϑῶ
—	παρ-ίσταμαι	—	-στῶ

προδιαϑ- . . . προδιατίϑεμαι 'I am predisposed'); the perfective active is regular (-ϑέσω), and the perfective passive is -τεϑῶ. The past participle passive is also irregular (-τεϑειμένος), although a somewhat regularized -ϑεμένος is also found.

5.2.6 PERFECT TENSES

As has been stated before, the perfect tenses are formed by the non-past or past of ἔχω 'I have' followed by the *perfect formant*, which is identical to the third person singular of the perfective non-past active or passive. The only difficulties in the formation of the perfect formant occur in two types of verb: (a) those in -άρω, and (b) compounds of the AG verb ἄγω. While the perfective active stem of verbs in -άρω may end in -αρ- or in -αρισ-, the perfect formant active is normally formed only from the first of these (e.g. σοκάρω 'I shock' → ἔχω σοκάρει). The perfective active stem of verbs in -άγω (except φυλάγω) is properly -αγαγ-; nevertheless, many speakers confuse the two stems, and the perfect formant varies in usage (e.g. εἰσάγω 'I export' → ἔχω εἰσαγάγει beside the more popular verb παράγω 'I produce' → ἔχω παράγει). (See also 3.2.4.1.)

5.2.7 THE PHONOLOGY OF DEVERBAL DERIVATION

Without embarking here on the vast subject of derivation, it is worth noting that deverbal derivatives (and other words cognate with verbs) are formed by using the various phonetic realizations of the verb stems. Thus deverbal nouns in -si and -simo are usually formed in the same way as perfective actives (e.g. ἱδρύω 'I found', perfective active *iδris-*, noun ἴδρυση '(act of) foundation'; πλάθω 'I mould, knead', perfective active *plas-*, noun πλάση 'creation'; κόβω 'I cut', perfective active *kops-*, noun κόψιμο 'cutting'; πνίγω 'I drown', perfective active *pniks-*, noun πνίξιμο 'drowning', etc.): this means that with some words at least there is homonymy between the second person singular of the perfective non-past active of the verb and the nom./acc. plural of the noun (e.g. κυβερνήσεις 'you govern; governments'). Note however that asigmatic perfective active stems either add *-s-* or substitute *-s-* for *-n-* in the noun: e.g. διευθύνω 'I direct', perfective active same, noun διεύθυνση 'address'; κρίνω 'I judge', perfective active same, noun κρίση 'judgement; crisis'.

Deverbal adjectives in *-tos*, *-tikós* and *-téos* and nouns in *-tis*, *-tíras* and *-tíri* are often formed in the same way as the perfective passive: e.g. κλείνω 'I close', perfective passive *klis-t-*, adjective κλειστός 'closed'; απογοητεύω 'I disappoint', perfective passive *apoγoitef-t-*, adjective απογοητευτικός 'disappointing'; διατηρῶ 'I preserve', perfective passive *δiatiri-ϑ-*, adjective διατηρητέος 'to be preserved'; ράβω 'sew', perfective passive *raf-t-*, noun ράφτης 'tailor'; συνδέω 'connect', perfective passive *sinδe-ϑ-*, noun συνδετήρας 'paper-clip'; ποτίζω 'I water', perfective passive *potis-t-*, noun ποτιστήρι 'watering-can'.

Most deverbal nouns in *-ma* and *-mós* are formed in the same way as the past passive participle: e.g. βασιλεύω 'I set (of sun)', past participle (with active meaning) βασιλεμένος 'having set', noun ηλιοβασίλεμα 'sunset'; τάζω 'I promise', past participle ταμένος, noun τάμα 'vow'; σπαράζω 'I rend; I distress', past participle σπαραγμένος, noun σπαραγμός 'rending; distress'; δέρνω 'I beat', δαρμένος, noun ξυλοδαρμός 'thrashing' (lit. 'wood-beating').

Many verbs which change their radical vowel have cognate nouns containing either one of the verb's alternative vowels or a completely different one. In most cases, in fact, the noun's radical vowel is *-o-*: e.g. βρέχω 'I wet; I rain', perfective passive *vrax-*, noun βροχή 'rain'; σπέρνω 'I sow', perfective passive *spar-ϑ-*, nouns σπορά 'sowing' and σπόρος 'seed', beside σπέρμα (also 'seed'); πνέω 'I blow', perfective active *pnef-s-*, noun πνοή 'breath'; but χαίρομαι 'I enjoy', perfective *xar-*, noun χαρά 'joy'.

5.3 THE ENDINGS

Despite differences among dialects, idiolects, and registers, the endings of MG verbs present a greater regularity than does the formation of their various stems. For most forms, once the relevant stem is known, all persons of both numbers can be predicted.

5.3.1 ACTIVE-TYPE ENDINGS

The five chief sets of endings of the active type can be divided into four non-past and one past. The *non-past* endings of the imperfective active are those which present the greatest variety from verb to verb and from speaker to speaker.

	I	S	P
1		-o	-ume/-ome
2		-is	-ete
3		-i	-un(e)

The endings are used (a) for the non-past imperfective active of Class 1 verbs, and (b) for the non-past perfective active of all verbs except those which have final stress in this form (see below). In the former, the endings are attached to the imperfective stem (e.g. δέν-ω), in the latter to the perfective active stem (e.g. δέσ-ω). The following remarks should be made about variants: (i) 1st person plural: although some (mainly older) speakers and writers use -ome, which is historically by far the older ending, -ume has become more common, and is even counselled by grammarians (e.g. Andriotis 1976: 25-7) as differentiating this person from the first person singular of the imperfective non-past passive in -ome; (b) all forms of the MG verb except the imperfective non-past passive have alternative third person plural endings with or without -e: the latter is more formal, and is usually prescribed by grammarians, while the former is more common than the other in colloquial speech and in some literary writing, especially when the following word begins with a consonant.

	II	S	P
1		-ó	-úme
2		-ís	-íte
3		-í	-ún(e)

These endings are used (a) for the non-past imperfective active of Class 2a verbs (which, apart from μπορῶ 'I am able' and ζῶ 'I live', are mostly of learned origin); (b) for the non-past perfective *passive* of all

verbs; and (c) for the non-past perfective active of those verbs in which
the stress falls on the final syllable in this tense (e.g. μπαίνω 'I enter'
→ μπῶ, βλέπω 'I see' → δῶ, λέω 'I say' → πῶ, ἔρχομαι 'I come' →
'ρθῶ). In (a) the endings are added to the imperfective stem (e.g.
θεωρ-ῶ 'I consider'); in (b), to the perfective passive stem (e.g. δε-θ-ῶ).
It will be noticed that, with the exception of the second person plural,
the only difference between II and I is the position of the stress (as long
as the first plural -úme is used in (I)).

	III	S	P
	1	-áo	-áme
	2	-ás	-áte
	3	-ái	-án(e)

These endings are used for the non-past of the verbs κοιτάω 'I look at',
σπάω 'I break', σκάω 'I burst', φυλάω 'I keep, guard' (all imperfective),
πάω 'I go' (imperfective and perfective) and φάω 'I eat' (perfective).
They may also be used for the non-past imperfective active of the most
frequently used verbs in Class 2b. A version of these endings, with
a different thematic vowel instead of -á-, is used for the non-past imperfective active of ἀκούω 'I hear' (-ú-), καίω 'I burn', κλαίω 'I cry (weep)',
λέω 'I say', φταίω 'I am to blame' (all -é-), and τρώω 'I eat' (-ó-).

	IV	S	P
	1	-ó	-úme
	2	-ás	-áte
	3	-á	-ún(e)

These endings are those preferred for the more formal use of the imperfective non-past of verbs in Class 2b: indeed, some of the more
learned verbs of that class (such as διασπῶ 'I split') can only have these
endings. In view of what has already been said about the third-person-
plural endings, it is obvious that the alternative -e ending is less commonly used with this kind of verb. Note that the first singular and first
and third plural of IV are the same as for II, while the second person of
both numbers is the same as for III.

In practice, in the imperfective non-past of a large number of
verbs there is much wavering between II, III, and IV endings, and
in some verbs between I and the rest. There is a number of verbs from

katharevousa, for instance, which originally took II endings, and still do so in formal use, but have taken on III endings (which are by far the most frequently found of II–IV) in colloquial speech: e.g. formal τηλεφωνεῖ '(s)he telephones', colloquial τηλεφωνάει. The difference between III and IV is again chiefly one of register, σ' ἀγαπῶ 'I love you' sounding far less familiar than σ' ἀγαπάω. On the other hand, anyone who used the -άω/-άει endings for verbs with more technical meanings (e.g. τό νερό διαθλάει τό φῶς 'water refracts light', for διαθλᾱ̃) is likely to be accused of 'hyperdemoticization'. Nevertheless, the popular trend is undoubtedly towards making all verbs of Class 2 take the endings in III. Lastly, there are some verbs whose endings display a variation between -ίζω and -άω among speakers, and can therefore take either I or II endings (e.g. ξεφτίζει or ξεφτάει 'it's becoming frayed', the latter being felt to be more informal; cf. also κοιτάω/κοιτάζω 'I look at', σπάω/σπάζω 'I break' and σκάω/σκάζω 'I burst': see Ebbesen 1979).

Each of these sets of non-past endings (I–IV) exhibits *columnar stress*, i.e. within each set of endings the stress falls on the same syllable throughout: on the final vowel of the stem in I and on the first vowel of the ending in II–IV.

	V	S	P
1	´-a	´-ame
2	´-es	´-ate
3	´-e	´-an/´-an(e)

In V *past* endings are shown: they are used for (a) the imperfective active past (see below for the exceptions to the stress-patterns given in the table); (b) the perfective active past; and (c) the perfective passive past. In (b) they are added to the perfective stem (e.g. ἀγάπησ-a); for the formation of (c), the infix -ik- is added to the perfective *passive* stem and then followed by these endings (e.g. δέ-θ-ηκ-a). In certain verbs of learned origin there is a different set of endings for the perfective past passive (S1 -in, S2 -is, S3 -i, P3 -isan); the first and second persons plural are hardly used. Thus, from συλλαμβάνω 'I arrest; I conceive':

	S	P
1	συν-ε-λήφ-θ-ην	
2	συν-ε-λήφ-θ-ης	
3	συν-ε-λήφ-θ-η	συν-ε-λήφ-θ-ησαν

The formation of the imperfective past active varies between verb classes: those of Class 1 add the endings directly to the imperfective stem (e.g. σπούδαζ-α 'I used to study/was studying'), while Class 2 verbs require an infix to be inserted before the endings. The infix -ús- (always stressed) may be inserted in all Class 2 verbs (e.g. μπορ-ούσ-α 'I was able'), except σκάω, σπάω, φυλάω, and πάω (the last of which forms this tense from the alternative imperfective stem: πήγαινα). But although the -ús- infix is that which is prescribed by most grammarians, and is found most commonly in the written word, whether literary or non-literary, colloquial usage prefers the infix -αγ- in most of the commonly used Class 2 verbs (i.e. in Class 2b(i): e.g. κράτ-αγ-α 'I was holding/used to hold'), and it is always found with σκάω, σπάω, and φυλάω. There tends to be a correlation between the use of II endings in the non-past and -ús- in the past of the imperfective active (e.g. μπορεῖ '(s)he is able', past μπορούσε; and especially more formal verbs such as ϑεωρεῖ '(s)he considers', past ϑεωροῦσε). (Note that the -ús- infix is preferred for all Class 2 verbs in the Salonica variety of SMG. The tendency to preserve -ús- throughout the paradigm is historically a characteristic of northern dialects: its adoption by the standard language may be due in part to the influence of Greeks from Istanbul (Newton 1974–5: 309).)

The verbs specified under III above insert an intervocalic -γ- between their thematic vowel and the V endings; this formation is thus similar to the -αγ- formation: cf. ἀγαπ-άω → ἀγάπ-αγ-α with φ-άω → ἔ-ϑε-αγ-α, ἀκ-ούω → ἄκ-ουγ-α, κ-αίω → ἔ-κ-αιγ-α, κλ-αίω → ἔ-κλ-αιγ-α, λ-έω → ἔ-λ-εγ-α, φτ-αίω → ἔ-φτ-αιγ-α, and τρ-ώω → ἔ-τρ-ωγ-α. For the *augment* prefix *e-*, see below, 5. 4 ff.

In the past tenses the stress falls on the third syllable from the end. The only exceptions to this are (a) those forms which include the -ús-infix (where columnar stress is preserved), and (b) certain alternative forms ending in -n (in V, the third person plural). As far as the latter is concerned, it is the -́an version (e.g. ἀγάπησαν) which is normally prescribed in the grammars (and is historically by far the oldest). The -́an(e) forms (e.g. ἀγαπήσαν or ἀγαπήσανε) clearly arose by analogy with the other plural forms: with or without the final -e, they preserve the stress on the same syllable as in the first and second persons (giving, at least in the plural, the kind of columnar stress which is noticeable in the non-past tenses); and the version with the -e preserves the same number of syllables as the other two persons of the plural.

The interplay of the stems and endings examined so far is shown in Table 5.3.

TABLE 5.3

	Imperfective active		Perfective active		Perfective passive	
	Non-past	Past	Non-past	Past	Non-past	Past
Stem	Impf.	Impf.	Pf. act.	Pf. act.	Pf. pass.	Pf. pass.
Endings	I, II, III, IV	(-ús-) $\Big\}$V (-aγ-)	I, II	V	II	-ik- + V

It is clear that, despite differences in detail, all the active endings can be reduced to the following common characteristics (V = Vowel, V_1 = -o or -a, V_2 = -i, -a, or -e):

$$\begin{array}{ccc} & \mathbf{S} & \mathbf{P} \\ 1 & \text{-}V_1 & \text{-me} \\ 2 & \text{-s} & \text{-te} \\ 3 & \text{-}V_2 & \text{-n(e)} \end{array}$$

It might be said that $(V_1 + \emptyset)$, -s, $(V_2 + \emptyset)$, m, t, and n are *person markers* (with the second singular and the first plural, compare the characteristic s and m of the second- and first-person pronouns respectively: σέ/σᾶς and μέ/μᾶς), while 'person marker + $\emptyset$' and 'person marker + e' are the markers for singular and plural respectively (this provides further motivation for the use of the optional -e of the third plural). Matthews (1974: 151–2) suggests that the third singular of the MG verb is the maximally unmarked form, an argument supported by the fact that (a) the third singular is used for impersonal verbs, and (b) the third singular of the perfective non-past also acts as the perfect formant, which is essentially non-personal. Similarly, tense is marked by the opposition -a vs. -o in the first singular, -e- vs. other vowels before the final -s in the second singular, -e vs. other vowels in the third singular, and -a- vs. other vowels throughout the plural (cf. Newton 1973a: 196). That such a *tense marker* is sufficient even in the absence of other conventional markers (such as position of stress, or the absence/presence of the augment) may be seen in the pairs *tóxis* 'you have it' (for τό ἔχεις) and *tóxes* 'you had it' (for τό εἶχες), in which there is no possibility of confusion for the hearer/reader.

5.3.2 PASSIVE-TYPE ENDINGS

These endings fall into two basic paradigms, used for the imperfective passive non-past and past respectively. The multiplicity of dialectal, idiolectal, and stylistic variants of these two basic sets of tense-endings presents a bewildering picture to the foreign learner (and is not without difficulties for native speakers too). The past tense endings in particular have led linguists to describe them as a 'jungle' (Ruge 1973: 142) and 'the generativist's nightmare' (Newton 1973b: 336).

For convenience, we shall adopt a slightly different approach here from that taken when considering the active-type endings, preferring to examine the thematic vowel after giving each paradigm.

The *imperfective non-past* endings are:

VI	S	P
1	-me	-maste
2	-se	-ste/-saste
3	-te	-nde

(Note that the first singular and third singular endings are identical in some classes of verb with the first and second plural of the imperfective non-past active; since in the former the final -*e* is spelled -*αι* and in the latter -*ε*, this is a source of confusion for writers of Greek—and for readers of badly spelled texts!)

These endings are straightforward enough: but in order to specify the thematic vowel (i.e. the vowel immediately preceding each of the above endings), it is necessary not only to use the class-labels that have already been employed, but to invent additional ones.

Class 1 verbs (those stressed on the stem-final vowel in the imperfective non-past active) have the following thematic vowels:

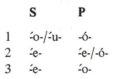

	S	P
1	´o-/´u-	-ó-
2	´e-	´e-/-ó-
3	´e-	´o-

The less common -*úme* of the first singular is also more colloquial than the -*óme*, which is prescribed in most grammars; the -*ósaste* of the second plural has a similar relationship to the -*éste*. The stress is not columnar, but falls always on the third syllable from the end.

The more learned verbs of *Class 2a* (those which end in stressed -*ís* in the second singular of the imperfective non-past active) have the following thematic vowels, which correspond in their distribution to the predominant pattern of Class 1, the mid vowels of Class 1 becoming high vowels in Class 2a:

	S	P
1	-ú-	-ú-
2	-í-	-í-
3	-í-	-ú-

Here there are no colloquial alternatives: on the contrary, even more formal alternatives *-úmeϑa* (P1) and *-isϑe* (P2) are occasionally found. Stress is columnar, on the thematic vowel throughout.

Verbs of *Class 2b(i)* (those which may end in *-ái* in the third singular of the imperfective non-past active), and some colloquially used verbs of Class 2a, have the following thematic vowels, always preceded by *-j-*:

	S	P
1	-jé-	-jó-
2	-jé-	-jé-/-jó-
3	-jé-	-jú-

The same holds for the alternative forms of the second plural (*-jéste* and *-jósaste*) as for those mentioned under Class 1. Stress is on the thematic vowel throughout.

The (learned) verbs of *Class 2b(ii)*, which have the third singular of the imperfective non-past active in *-á* only, form passives in a different way again. Once more, the stress is on the thematic vowel throughout:

	S	P
1	-ó-	-ó- (-ómeϑa)
2	-á-	-á- (-ásϑe)
3	-á-	-ó-/-ú-

In practice (like the passives of Class 2a), these verbs are found more often in the third singular and plural than in any other person, while the first and second person of both numbers are rare; the more formal versions (given in brackets) are preferred by many writers and speakers to the alternative, more demotic, forms. In the third plural, the *-únde* ending is sometimes found (wrongly, according to the grammarians) by analogy with the paradigm of Class 2c, whose conjugation this learned passive paradigm of Class 2b(ii) so resembles.

Class 2c consists of deponent verbs (θυμᾶμαι 'I remember', κοιμᾶμαι 'I am asleep; I sleep', λυπᾶμαι 'I am sorry' and φοβᾶμαι 'I am afraid, I fear'), which have the following thematic vowels, always stressed:

	S	P
1	-á-	-ó-
2	-á-	-á-/-ó-
3	-á-	-ú-

Again, there are alternative forms *-áste* and *-ósaste* in the second plural. The distribution of the thematic vowels is similar to that in 2b(i).

Finally there are the remnants of AG verbs in *-μι*. This conjugation, which we shall call *Class 3*, preserves the same thematic vowel throughout, and the stress pattern is similar to that of Class 1. Compounds of *-ίσταμαι* (Class 3a) present the following pattern:

	S	P
1	´-a-	-á-meθa
2	´-a-	´-a-sθe
3	´-a-	´-a-

The verb τίθεμαι and its compounds (Class 3b) follow the same pattern, except that the thematic vowel is *-e-* throughout.

The *imperfective past* endings of the passive are the following:

VII	S	P
1	´-mun(a)	´-maste/´-mastan
2	´-sun(a)	´-saste/´-sastan
3	´-tan(e)/´-ndan	´-ndusan/´-ndan(e)/´-ndan

The stress is normally columnar, falling on the thematic vowel. It is clear that even before we examine the thematic vowel there are more observations to be made about possible variant forms in VII than in VI. It might be worth giving first the forms which tend to appear in prescriptive grammars (e.g. Triandaphyllidis 1949: 155), and then commenting on the variants:

	S	P
1	-́mun	-́maste
2	-́sun	-́saste
3	-́tan	-́-ndan

These are also the forms which are the most frequently found in writing. The forms with the final -a or -e in the singular are more colloquial than those without. The choice of other variants is normally dictated by a speaker's/writer's regional provenance. Northern varieties of Greek (e.g. that spoken in Salonica) favour the -an endings in the first and second persons plural, which admittedly make a useful distinction between past and non-past which is otherwise neutralized. The -ndusan of the third plural is characteristic of Athens and the Peloponnese: in the capital it is by far the most frequently found form of this person, while the prescribed ending (without -e) is actually the least common in everyday speech. In Salonica, however, the reverse order of frequency could be said to operate, the -ndusan ending being decried by Salonicans as vigorously as the -aγ- infix of the imperfective active past of Class 2; on the other hand, northerners tend to use the same form for the third singular as they do for the third plural (viz. -́-ndan). This particular ending, with its stress on the vowel which precedes the thematic vowel, represents an anomaly in the stress system.

Having dealt with these endings from the point of view of region and register, we shall now approach them according to type of verb.

Class 1 verbs are simple in this respect, preserving the thematic vowel -o- throughout the paradigm. The verbs that have -jé- in VI, and those of Class 2c, similarly preserve the same thematic vowel throughout, namely -jó- and -ó- respectively (always stressed).

The other classes are not however so straightforward. The learned verbs of Class 2a (those in -úme in the imperfective non-past passive) have the stressed thematic vowel -ú- throughout, but the third singular has the 'northern' ending -ndan, like the third plural. This, at least, is the demoticist theory, which is followed in much literary and journalistic writing today; but the fact is that the imperfective past passive of this kind of verb is rare in speech, and is thought by many speakers to be susceptible of katharevousa endings. The first and second persons of this type of verb are hardly ever used in this tense, but the third persons are often found in the form *-íto* (sing.) and *-úndo* (pl.), with or without the augment (e.g. (ἐ)ϑεωρεῖτο, (ἐ)ϑεωροῦντο). The augment is obligatory in *katharevousa*: thus these forms without the augment belong strictly neither to demotic nor to *katharevousa*, but are used by certain speakers and writers who seem to find the *-úndan* ending too vulgar for such elegant verbs!

Class 3 verbs are likewise hardly used in the imperfective past passive except in the third person. The thematic vowels are as for the non-past, and the endings like the learned alternatives in 2a.

As in the active, there is much shifting of verbs from one class to another, and in Class 2 verbs (except those in 2c), the 2b(i) endings tend to attract verbs from other paradigms. Thus, for instance, although εὐχαριστῶ 'I thank; I please' belongs to 2a in the active, the passive εὐχαριστιέμαι 'I am pleased' belongs to 2b(i); although the stereotyped form ἐξαρτᾶται 'it depends' is frequently found in speech as well as in writing (from ἐξαρτῶμαι, 2b(ii)), the imperfective past is often found following 2b(i) (e.g. ἐξαρτιόταν(ε) 'it depended'); and, similarly, many speakers avoid using either ϑεωροῦνταν or (ἐ)ϑεωρεῖτο '(s)he/it was considered' in the singular, preferring ϑεωριότανε (2b(ii)) or even ϑεωρόταν (1 or 2c?). Nevertheless, such a shift of class is not always possible: note the pair καταργεῖται (*katarjíte*) 'it is abolished' (2a) and καταριέται (*katarjéte*) '(s)he curses' (2b(ii)).

Despite all these complications, the fact remains that εἶμαι 'I am' is the only truly irregular verb in MG as far as its endings are concerned. It does, however, show many of the characteristics of the passive-type endings in its two tenses (it lacks the perfective and the perfect). The thematic vowel is *í-* (stressed) throughout, spelled ει- in the present and (usually) η- in the past; the endings are shown in VIa (*non-past*) and VIIa (*past*).

VIa	S	P
1	-me	-maste
2	-se	-ste/-saste
3	-ne	-ne

Note that the third person singular and plural are not distinguished, and that the other endings are the same as in paradigm VI: the same observations hold for the alternatives of the P2 as in VI. The first plural has a more formal alternative *ímeϑa* which is sometimes heard in the speech of older people.

	VIIa	S	P
1		-́mun(a)	-́maste/-́mastan
2		-́sun(a)	-́saste/-́sastan
3		-́tan(e)	-́tan(e)/-́san(e)

Again, the endings are for the most apart those of VII, and similar observations apply. Most speakers do not distinguish between the singular and plural in the third person, although the *-san(e)* of the plural is also found. Again, some speakers use *imeθa* in the first plural, which has the same disadvantage of neutralizing the tense distinction as has *imaste*.

With the exception of *eĩµai* and the rather aberrant endings of some of the other verbs mentioned above, the two chief passive-type paradigms can be reduced to the following common characteristics:

	S	P
1	-m-	-mast-
2	-s-	-(sa)st-
3	-t-	-nd-

These sounds may be designated person markers, and there is indeed a remarkable similarity (except in the third plural) between them and the accusative of the clitic personal pronouns:

	S	P
1	me	mas
2	se	sas
3	to(n)/ti(n)	[ta]

It is not easy to specify any particular number marker, as one can in the active-type endings. Again, since in many speakers the tense distinctions are not made in certain persons of the plural, it is obvious that there is no unambiguous tense marker in that number; although the *-e/-n-* opposition in the singular does distinguish between tenses.

5.4 THE AUGMENT

In Classical Greek almost all verb stems underwent an alteration of their initial sound(s) in all past tenses: this involved either prefixing *è-* if the first sound of the verb stem was a consonant, or *augmenting* (lengthening) the initial vowel if the stem began with a vowel. The first type of change is traditionally called *syllabic augment*, the latter *vocalic augment*. Today, syllabic augment is still obligatory in certain circumstances, while vocalic augment too is sometimes found. There is a general principle, however, that augment does not occur in SMG unless the vowel produced by augmentation is stressed (this will be explained below). A further complication is that in Classical Greek the augment took place in the verb *stem*: in compound verbs consisting of prepositional prefix + verb stem, the augment took place *after* the prefix. This phenomenon, known as *internal augment*, could be either syllabic or vocalic. Many traces of internal augment are found in SMG today. *Katharevousa* applied the Classical rules for augment fairly rigorously (but not completely): although non-internal syllabic augment was obligatory in certain situations in demotic, most instances of vocalic augment and of internal augment are part of the legacy of *katharevousa* to SMG. (In certain dialects, however, non-internal vocalic augment was the norm.)

5.4.1 SYLLABIC AUGMENT

Syllabic augment is obligatory in SMG only when all the following conditions are fulfilled: that the verb (a) is in a past tense; (b) has a stem beginning with a consonant; and (c) would, but for the augment, consist of only two syllables. These conditions are closely connected with the fact that in most past-tense forms the stress falls on the third syllable from the end. In the past tenses, there is a 'floating' antepenultimate stress which falls on whatever vowel is available, whether this be part of the stem (ἀγάπησα), an augment (ἔδεσα) or the final syllable of a preceding clitic (τό 'δεσα) (Kaisse 1976: 169). It follows that the syllabic augment is obligatory only when it constitutes the stressed syllable. It also follows that it is obligatory only in the past tenses of the active (perfective and imperfective), and then only in the singular and (unless the optional *-e* is added) in the third person plural. This explains the behaviour of the augment in the imperfective past active of δένω (see Appendix I).

The following verbs do not obligatorily take the syllabic augment in the perfective active: βγῆκα 'I went/came out', βρῆκα 'I found', μπῆκα 'I went/came in', πῆρα 'I took' and πῆγα 'I went'. Note that these verbs are stressed on the first syllable throughout this paradigm (i.e. they have columnar stress).

Conversely, since the augment was normally compulsory in *katharevousa* and in certain dialects, some speakers and writers use it (albeit usually without any great consistency, and often for purely euphonic reasons) even where it is not obligatory: this occurs more frequently in verbs which are felt to be more learned, and it always occurs when a *katharevousa* perfective passive past is used (e.g. certain forms found in journalism, such as ἐλέχϑη (= εἰπώϑηκε) 'it was said' and ἐστάλη (= στάλϑηκε) '(s)he/it was sent').

5.4.2 VOCALIC AUGMENT

The only example of Classical Greek lengthening of an initial vowel of a verb-stem in past tenses which was realized phonetically in *katharevousa* was that *e*- and *a*- were 'augmented' to *i*- (spelled η-). This phenomenon still occurs in SMG in a restricted number of verbs, and then only when the initial vowel of the stem is stressed; it is never really obligatory, even though some speakers find the unaugmented vowel 'unnatural'. These verbs include ἐλπίζω 'I hope', ἐλέγχω 'I check, control' and αἴρω 'I lift (ban, etc.)'.

Thus a typical idiolect might have the following paradigm of the imperfective past active of ἐλπίζω:

	S	P
1	ἤλπιζα	ἐλπίζαμε
2	ἤλπιζες	ἐλπίζατε
3	ἤλπιζε	ἤλπιζαν/(ἐλπίζανε)

(The last alternative is questionable for such an idiolect, since a speaker who uses the vocalic augment in one person is unlikely to use such a colloquial variant in another: the vocalic augment tends to be used— outside newspapers and rather official styles—by older people whose idiolect contains a substantial dose of 'learnedisms'.)

In addition, there are traces of vocalic augment in one of the most basic verbs in the language, namely ἔχω 'I have' (→ *ixa*, spelled εἶχα), while other basic verbs have a *double augment*, in which an initial consonant is prefixed by *i*- rather than by *e*-: πιῶ 'I drink' (perfective) → ἤπια; πῶ 'I say' (perfective) → εἶπα; δῶ 'I see' (perfective) → εἶδα; ϑέλω 'I want' (imperfective) → ἤϑελα.

5.4.3 INTERNAL AUGMENT

In SMG there are about eighteen *prepositional prefixes* (i.e. prefixes which were used in AG as prepositions), and two or more of these may be used in the same word (these are dealt with at length by Warburton, 1970b: 49–67). *Katharevousa* brought with it a huge number of verbs with these prefixes, and with them a number of complications in phonology and morphology, (a) because of internal augment, and (b) because the final sound of most of these prefixes is affected according to what sound immediately follows it (or, to be more precise, what sound immediately followed in AG).

Internal augment may be either syllabic or vocalic, according as the verb-stem begins with a consonant or a vowel (the augment follows immediately after the last prepositional prefix if there is more than one). The rules concerning the presence or absence of the augment, and the form it takes if present, are the same as those given in 5.4.1 and 5.4.2. Thus, again, the augment is usually present only if it constitutes the stressed syllable.

The complicated nature of the internal syllabic augment can be seen from the following paradigm of the perfective active past of συλλαμβάνω 'I arrest; I conceive', in which the prefix {sin} loses its -*n*- before -*l*- but regains it before a vowel:

	S	P
1	συνέλαβα	συλλάβαμε
2	συνέλαβες	συλλάβατε
3	συνέλαβε	συνέλαβαν/συλλάβανε

It is little wonder that in colloquial speech the form τόν πιάσανε 'they caught him' is preferred to τόν συνέλαβαν 'they arrested him' (and especially to συνελήφθη 'he was arrested'). Even in the weekly press nowadays there is a tendency to avoid the internal augment in the third person plural of such compound verbs by resorting to forms such as συλλάβαν.

Most prepositional prefixes which end in a vowel delete the final vowel before another vowel. A further complication arises when the initial vowel of the verb-stem was aspirated (i.e. preceded by an *h*-sound, noted in the orthography by a rough breathing) in AG. The aspirate had the effect of aspirating the final consonant of the prepositional prefix (that is, the consonant which immediately precedes the verb stem after the final vowel has been elided) if this is -*p*- or -*t*- (synchronically, these sounds become the fricatives -*f*- and -*ϑ*- respectively). The interplay of these tendencies is especially apparent in certain remnants of the AG verbs in -*μι*, in which the prefix has a stop in certain tenses and a fricative in others: e.g. ἐγκαϑ-ίσταμαι 'I settle', perfective past ἐγκατα-στάϑηκα, or ὑφ-ίσταται '(s)he/it undergoes', perfective past ὑπ-έστη (cf. Table 5.2).

Vocalic augment is far more frequently found in internal than in external position. It is used in such common verbs as ὑπ-άρχω 'I exist' (obligatorily, → ὑπ-ῆρχα) and παρ-αγγέλλω 'I order' (optionally, → παρ-ήγγελλα). Conversely, it is sometimes possible in *katharevousa* to place an augment before the prepositional prefix, and in SMG the past of πρό-κειται 'it is a question of; be about to' is ἐπρόκειτο (instead of the form which would have been correct in AG, namely προῦκειτο).

The problem of the internal augments is an acute one for most speakers of Greek, and it is not surprising that several strategies are employed to avoid a decision whether to use it or not (e.g. the use of a perfect instead of a perfective past, or the use of a synonymous verb or paraphrase). It should not however be thought that the avoidance of the internal augment is necessarily natural for educated speakers. Conscientious demoticists who deliberately shun the internal augment (writing, e.g., μετάφρασα for μετέφρασα 'I translated') are often criticized for using forms which are not simply 'wrong' but 'unnatural'.

The extent to which the internal augment of some verbs comes naturally to educated (and even many uneducated) spakers is witnessed by its extension to the imperative, in which its presence is historically incorrect (the imperative not possessing tense and therefore 'pastness'). Thus utterances such as,

(1) ἐπέστρεψε τά μπουκάλια παρακαλῶ 'return the bottles please' (for ἐπίστρεψε), or

(2) προσέϑεσε καί τίς δέκα δραχμές πού σοῦ χρωστάω 'add the ten drachmas I owe you' (for πρόσϑεσε),

may be even more common in casual speech than those in which the unaugmented forms are used. Even the poet Cavafy was not averse to using such a form: the imperfective imperative ἐπέστρεφε 'return' stands as the title of one of his poems, and is used again in the poem itself (Kav. 1963: I. 56). One may even hear,

(3) παρήγγειλε δυό πορτοκαλάδες 'order two orangeades',

which displays internal vocalic augment. This phenomenon is motivated by the fact that in most verbs of more than two syllables the active imperative singular is identical to the third singular of the past (e.g. κοίταξε, γύρισε, πήγαινε, etc.); that the augment has spread from a past tense to a tenseless form is evidence of how deeply ingrained the augment is in the consciousness of educated speakers.

Despite this, normative grammarians have decried the augmented imperative and have counselled the avoidance of vocalic and internal augment altogether; and it must be admitted that MG verb morphology would be neater without these encumbrances (e.g. there would not be a potentially disorientating change in stem between the noun μετάθεση 'transfer' and the verb μετέθεσε '(s)he transferred').

In traditional demotic verbs, internal syllabic augment is often found as an optional alternative (e.g. ξαναέκανα or ξανάκανα 'I re-did'). In some verbs, however, there is a difference in meaning according to whether the augment is present or not (e.g. the idiomatic τά παράκανε '(s)he overdid it', but παραέκανε κρύο 'it was too cold').

5.5 NON-FINITE FORMS

The only non-finite forms of the MG verb are the imperative and the participles. There is no infinitive. The imperative varies for number, is invariable for person (always second), and is never past. There is one active-form participle, which is invariable. The passive-form participles decline like adjectives for number, gender and case, and indicate tense.

5.5.1 THE IMPERATIVE

The most frequently used forms of the imperative in SMG are the imperfective and perfective active and the perfective passive. The perfect aspect has no imperative.

The imperfective active imperative of Class 1 verbs is formed by adding -e (sing.) or -ete (plural) to the imperfective stem: the stress falls as far forward as possible (i.e. on the penultimate syllable in disyllabic forms and on the antepenultimate in longer forms). For Class 2a, -i (= -ει) (sing.) and -ite (plural) are added to the imperfective stem (the singular is rare); for Class 2b, -a (sing.) and -áte (plural) are added. The stress for all Class 2 verbs is on the penultimate syllable in both numbers. The plural of the imperfective active imperative of all verbs is the same as the second person plural of the imperfective active non-past.

The perfective active imperative is formed by adding -e (sing.) and -te (plural) to the perfective active stem. The stress of the singular is the same as that in the imperfective of Class 1; the plural is stressed on the penultimate syllable. In many frequently used verbs the final -e of the singular (especially of disyllabic forms) commonly drops before t: e.g.

κόψ' το (= κόψε το) 'cut it'. In some verbs (and sometimes, in more formal style, in others too) the plural ending is -ete: these are verbs whose perfective stem ends in a nasal, a dental, a velar or a labial (nevertheless, κάντε (kánte) 'do' is more common than κάνετε), and here the stress falls on the antepenultimate syllable. It is clear that the plural of the imperative is a reduced form of (or identical to) the plural of the perfective non-past, and in practice there is a certain amount of interchangeability between them. In many common labial- and velar-stem verbs, the -ps- or -ks- of the perfective active imperative may optionally be reduced to -f- and -x- respectively before t to form a more colloquial variant: e.g. κοιτάχτε 'look' (= κοιτάξτε), ρίχ' το 'throw it' (= ρίξ' το).

The perfective passive imperative is normally formed by adding -u to the perfective *active* stem (sing.) and -íte to the perfective passive stem (plural). Stress always falls on the penultimate syllable. (The singular is not as commonly found as the plural, and is not formed from many verbs with asigmatic perfective active stems.)

There is also an imperfective passive imperative which is hardly used. This exists in SMG only for Class 1 verbs, and is formed by adding -u (sing.) and -este (plural) to the imperfective stem. Stress falls on the penultimate syllable in the singular and on the antepenultimate in the plural. Again, as in the perfective passive, the plural form is identical to the second person plural of the corresponding non-past tense.

Certain common verbs have irregular imperative forms, particularly in the singular. Some of these are abbreviated: e.g. ἀκούω → ἄκου 'listen' (for *ἄκουγε); σωπαίνω → σώπα (besides σώπαινε) 'be quiet'; σηκώνομαι → σήκω (for *σηκώσου) 'get up'; ἀνεβαίνω → ἀνέβα (besides ἀνέβαινε) 'go up; get on'; κατεβαίνω → κατέβα (besides κατέβαινε) 'go down; get off'. Others have monosyllabic perfective imperatives in -s in the singular: βγαίνω → βγές (also less polite ἔβγα) 'get out'; μπαίνω → μπές (also ἔμπα) 'go in'; βλέπω → δές (besides imperfective βλέπε) 'see, look'; βρίσκω → βρές 'find'; λέω → πές (besides imperfective λέγε) 'say, tell'; πίνω → πιές (besides imperfective πίνε) 'drink'. The plurals of these may end in -éste or -íte. There are some alternative (less polite) forms in -a: τρέχω → τρέχα, pl. τρεχᾶτε (more polite τρέξε, τρέξτε) 'run'; φεύγω → φεύγα, pl. φευγᾶτε (more polite φύγε, φύγετε) 'go away'. The verb ἔρχομαι has ἔλα, pl. ἐλᾶτε 'come', while ἀφήνω has ἄσε (shortened to ἄσ' before t), pl. ἄστε (besides ἄφησε, ἀφῆστε) 'leave; let'; and τρώω has φάγε (shortened to φᾶ' before t) 'eat', beside τρῶγε. (For further information on the aspect of the imperative, see 3.2.6.)

5.5.2 THE PARTICIPLES

Traditional demotic possessed two participles, one with active form, the other with passive form; *katharevousa* has bequeathed to SMG an additional present participle passive.

The active participle (sometimes called the gerundive) is formed by adding *-ondas* to the imperfective stem (*-όντας* in Class 1, *-ώντας* in Class 2). It can be formed in SMG only from verbs which possess an active voice. The sole participle of εἶμαι, however, is the active-form ὄντας 'being', which is not frequently used.

The formation of the (past) passive participle has already been dealt with (5.2.4).

The present participle passive, being a legacy from *katharevousa*, tends to be formed only in verbs which could be used in *katharevousa*. It is formed by adding *-μενος* to the thematic vowel of the first person singular of the imperfective non-past passive. Verbs with *-jé-* (2b(i)) and *-á-* (2c) as their thematic vowel do not form this participle. Of verbs in *-ων-* in the imperfective, those that derive from ancient *-όω* normally have *-ούμενος* in the present passive participle.

In a few demotic verbs there is a form which superficially resembles the present passive participle: thus τρέχω → τρεχούμενος 'running (water); current (account)'; τρέμω → τρεμάμενος 'trembling'; χαίρομαι → χαρούμενος 'joyful'.

A perfect participle is occasionally found in either voice, formed by the participle of ἔχω (ἔχοντας) + the perfect formant (see also 3.2.5).

Katharevousa attempted to resurrect all the AG participles (present, aorist, future, and perfect in active, middle, and passive). There are traces of some of these in SMG, especially in journalistic writing, while, as we have seen, the present passive participle has become an integral part of the language of educated people. The additional learned participles which are sometimes found today are the present and aorist active and the aorist and perfect passive.

Those who use the *katharevousa* present participle, which is formed by adding *-ων* (Class 1) or *-ῶν* (Class 2) to the imperfective stem, and declines in all numbers, genders, and cases like the adjective ἐνδιαφέρων (see 4.2), see it as having an advantage over the demotic active participle in that it can be used as an adjective or a noun and is therefore useful for translating French or English present participles with the minimum of effort. Thus one finds: ἡ ἐπικρατοῦσα ἰδεολογία 'the prevailing ideology' (= ἡ ἰδεολογία πού ἐπικρατεῖ 'the ideology that prevails'), μιά φθίνουσα μειονότητα 'a dwindling minority' (adjectives in both examples), οἱ συμπαθοῦντες τῆς Νέας Δημοκρατίας 'the sympathizers of the New Democracy [Party]' (cf. F *les sympathisants*, noun); and occasionally such a participle is even used with an object: e.g. οἱ περιοικοῦντες τό Ὑπουργεῖο Συντονισμοῦ 'those who have contacts in the Ministry of Co-ordination' (*T* 18 Aug. 1979, 8) (lit. 'the neighbouring (plural) the Ministry . . .'). The present participle is also used humorously to indicate one who plays at being something: e.g. ὁ τροτσκίζων (fem. ἡ τροτσκίζουσα) 'one who plays the Trotskyite'.

The aorist participle is also fully declinable, and is formed by adding -ας (masc.), -ασα (fem.), -αν (neuter) to the perfective active stem (the masc. acc. sing. is -αντα, and the rest declines like ἐνδιαφέρων, except for the -a- instead of -o- before the -n-; but it is very rare outside the nominative and accusative of the masculine and neuter). Like the present participle, the aorist is used as an adjective or noun, but with past reference. It is hardly used except with a slightly comic colouring: e.g.

(1) οἱ λίγοι ἐναπομείναντες ὑπερασπιστές τῆς σεξουαλικῆς ἠθικῆς 'the few remaining [lit. 'having remained'] champions of sexual morality'; or

(2) οἱ ὀλίγον χουντίσαντες 'those who collaborated slightly with the junta [of 1967–74]' (*T* 17 Dec. 1981, 16) (lit. 'the a-little (*kath.*) having-juntaized', using a coined verb χουντίζω).

The aorist passive participle is similarly declinable; it is formed by adding -είς to the perfective passive stem (fem. -εῖσα, neuter -έν). The masc. acc. sing. is -έντα, and the participle from then on declines like ἐνδιαφέρων (again, it is hardly used except in the masculine and neuter nominative and accusative). It too is used as an adjective or a noun, with past reference. The difference in meaning between this and the past passive participle is minimal (or non-existent), the aorist being sometimes preferred simply because the formation of the past participle of the particular verb is problematic. Examples: οἱ συλληφθέντες ἀξιωματικοί 'the having-been-arrested officers', οἱ συγκεντρωθέντες ἐκπρόσωποι 'the having-gathered representatives' (both adjectives), οἱ θιγέντες ἀπό τά ἔργα 'those who have been disturbed by the [engineering] works', οἱ δικηγόροι τῶν ἀπολυθέντων 'the lawyers of those who have been dismissed' (both substantivized).

Lastly, the learned perfect participle passive is formed in the same way as the demotic past passive participle (see 5.2.4), except that the first sound of the verb-stem undergoes *reduplication*: this is a similar phenomenon to augmentation, and may be internal (cf. 5.4.3). Reduplication is achieved in the case of stems beginning with a consonant (except voiceless fricatives) by adding the same consonant + -*e*- at the beginning (e.g. τρίβω → τετριμμένος), unless the initial consonant is followed immediately by another consonant (except -*r*-), in which case the initial consonant is prefixed by *e*-; an initial *z*-, *ks*- or *ps*- is prefixed by *e*- alone; a voiceless fricative is prefixed by a voiceless stop with the same place of articulation + -*e*-; an initial vowel is reduplicated by means of augmentation, as in vocalic augment (5.4.2).

Most learned perfect passive participles are now fossilized forms, and many speakers think of them as being adjectives (or nouns) in their own right, without close connection with any verb. Thus ὁ ἐπιτετραμμένος 'chargé d'affaires' is not always connected in a speaker's mind with ἐπιτρέπω 'I permit', while συγκεκριμένος 'specific' could hardly be connected with συγκρίνω 'I compare'. On the other hand, ἐκτεταμένος 'extensive' (← ἐκτείνω 'I extend') and ἐνδεδειγμένος 'indicated, called for' (← ἐνδεικνύω 'I indicate') seem to be more motivated or transparent, in that they show their origin more clearly.

There is much wavering between the use of the learned perfect and demotic past passive participles (i.e. between reduplicated and unreduplicated forms), according to linguistic attitude of the speaker/writer: thus one may say either κατεστραμμένος or καταστραμμένος 'destroyed' (← καταστρέφω), ὑπογεγραμμένος or ὑπογραμμένος 'signed' (← ὑπογράφω). On the other hand, many such participles cannot lose their reduplication (παρατεταμένος 'extended' ← παρατείνω), while others have a different meaning according as they show reduplication or not: cf. μεμονωμένος 'isolated' with μονωμένος 'insulated' (← μονώνω 'I isolate; I insulate'), or τετριμμένος 'trite' with τριμμένος 'rubbed; worn (down)' (← τρίβω 'I rub; I wear (down)'); cf. also τεταμένος 'tense' (← τείνω 'I tend') with ταμένος 'vowed' (← τάξω 'I vow').

Many verbs, in addition to participles, possess a verbal adjective in -*τος* which has a similar meaning to that of the past passive participle (the difference in meaning is sometimes comparable to that which exists in English between two forms of the passive participle: e.g. ψημένος 'roasted', but ψητός 'roast'; ἀνοιγμένος 'opened', but ἀνοιχτός 'open'). Sometimes, however, the verbal adjective implies susceptibility to a certain action: e.g. ἕνα φουσκωτό στρῶμα 'an inflatable mattress' (cf. φουσκωμένο in this context, 'inflated'). In this positive form the final syllable is stressed. Some verbs have a negative verbal adjective, stressed on the third syllable from the end, which may be used as the negative of the past passive participle or of the positive verbal adjective, and which may denote either subjection or susceptibility to the action of the verb: e.g. παρμένος 'taken, captured' → άπαρτος 'not captured; impregnable'; ἐξερευνημένος 'explored' → ἀνεξερεύνητος 'unexplored; unfathomable'. Sometimes, however, only one of the meanings is possible: e.g. ἐξαρτημένος 'dependent' → ἀνεξάρτητος 'independent', not '*independable'. There are also compounds with forms resembling verbal adjectives as their base, e.g. εὐκολομάϑητος 'easily learned'; δυσκίνητος 'slow-moving, sluggish'.

6

THE NOUN PHRASE, PREPOSITIONS, AND PRONOUNS

6.1 THE NOUN PHRASE

6.1.1 ORDER OF CONSTITUENTS

Word order is rather flexible in MG, as we shall see when dealing with the order of constituents within the clause (7.1.1). There is also a certain amount of flexibility within the noun phrase itself. To provide full details concerning the possible combinations of elements in the noun phrase and the order in which they may appear would be an almost endless task. Here we shall confine ourselves to the basic principles.

A noun in MG is normally preceded by its modifiers (always by the article, usually by demonstratives, adjectives, and numerals). Apart from the definite article itself, modifiers of the noun may be divided into those which are normally placed between the article and the noun (when the article is present), and those which normally fall outside the scope of the phrase beginning with the article and ending with the noun. The second category consists of the demonstratives αὐτός, τοῦτος, and ἐκεῖνος, and the quantifiers ὅλος 'all' and ὁλόκληρος 'whole'. When they modify a noun, these are used in conjunction with the definite article (except ὁλόκληρος, which may be accompanied by the definite or the indefinite article, or by neither, and ὅλος, which may modify a noun without an article). The regular position of these modifiers is before the definite article (the quantifiers preceding the demonstratives), but they may alternatively follow the noun, in which case they usually receive special emphasis.

(1) αὐτός ὁ ἄνθρωπος (or ὁ ἄνθρωπος αὐτός) 'this person';
(2) ἐκείνη ἡ κοπέλα (or ἡ κοπέλα ἐκείνη) 'that girl';
(3) ὅλος ὁ κόσμος 'all the world; everyone';
(4) ὁλόκληρο τό διπλωματικό σῶμα 'the whole diplomatic corps'.

When ὅλος means 'whole' it may follow the article (under *katharevousa* influence):

(5) ἡ ὅλη κατάσταση 'the whole situation'.

Other quantifiers and restrictive modifiers tend to come immediately after the definite article (or at the beginning of the noun phrase when the definite article is absent). Those which may be used with the definite article include numerals, κάθε 'each', μόνος 'only', τόσος 'so much', λίγος 'little', and πολύς 'much'. Those which are not used with an article (nor with demonstratives) include μερικοί 'a few', ὁρισμένοι 'certain', κάμποσοι 'quite a few', and κανένας 'no; any'.

The interrogative pronoun ποιός 'who; which' comes first in the noun phrase. The modifiers κάποιος 'some (or other)' and ὅποιος (or ὁποιοσδήποτε) 'whichever; any at all' come early in the phrase, but may be preceded by ἕνας 'a; one'.

Following these appear ἄλλος 'other' and τέτοιος 'such' (preceded optionally by the definite or indefinite article), and ἴδιος 'same' (almost always used with the definite article). Next comes the possessive δικός (μου) '(my) own', then other adjectives, and finally the noun. There are of course constraints on the number of modifiers that may appear in any one phrase, as also on which modifiers may co-occur with which others.

(6) ἔρχονταν κάθε μέρα αὐτά τά ἴδια τρία παιδιά 'these same three children used to come each day';

(7) θά πεθάνουν τόσοι ἄλλοι δικοί μου ἄνθρωποι 'so many others of my nearest and dearest will die' (lit. 'so-many other my-own people');

(8) βρῆκα πολλές τέτοιες πράσινες χάντρες 'I found many such green beads';

(9) κανένας ἄλλος μεγάλος ἥρωας 'no/any other great hero';

(10) κάποιες ἄλλες ψάθινες καρέκλες 'some [= 'certain'] other straw chairs'.

Before proceeding, two oddities concerning the position of ἄλλος must be pointed out. While τόσος ἄλλος means 'so much other', ἄλλος τόσος means 'as much again'; ἕνας ἄλλος 'another (a different)', but ἄλλος ἕνας 'another (one more)'.

As for adjectives proper, these may follow the noun if they need to receive special emphasis; but if they follow a noun which is accompanied by a definite article, the definite article must be repeated before each of the postposed adjectives:

(11) τά παλιά παλικάρια or τά παλικάρια τά παλιά 'the old-fashioned heroes'.

Note that when a Christian name and a surname are said together in colloquial Greek, the article is usually placed before each of the names (the colloquial word for 'surname', ἐπίθετο, is the same as the word for 'adjective'):

(12) ὁ Γιῶργος Παπαδόπουλος or ὁ Γιῶργος ὁ Παπαδόπουλος 'George Papadopoulos'.

When an adjective is used in apposition to a noun (and therefore belongs to a separate phrase), it stands outside the noun phrase:

(13a) εἶδα τή γυναίκα γυμνή 'I saw the woman naked'; cf.

(13b) εἶδα τή γυμνή γυναίκα or εἶδα τή γυναίκα τή γυμνή 'I saw the naked woman'.

When more than one adjective modifies a noun, there is a certain flexibility in their order of appearance. There does not appear to be any set of rules according to which, for instance, an adjective denoting some inherent quality precedes or follows one which conveys a subjective attitude. There follow some examples of phrases in which the order is different from in English:

(14) θρησκευτικές ἀκατανόητες φράσεις 'incomprehensible religious phrases' (Sef. 1977: 70);

(15) γύψινες ἀποκρουστικές Καρυάτιδες 'repulsive plaster Caryatids' (Tsi. 1973: 28);

(16) λαϊκές τεράστιες ἀφίσες 'huge popular posters' (*T* 11 Oct. 1979, 22);

(17) εἰσαγόμενα ἀνάλογα ἀγαθά 'analogous imported goods' (*R* 25 July 1980).

In each case, the order of the adjectives could be reversed; or, alternatively, any one of the two could be placed after the noun.

A peculiarity of the combination of adjective and demonstrative is that where one or more adjectives precede the noun, the demonstrative may be placed after the adjective (or before the last adjective if there is more than one). Thus:

(18) αὐτοί οἱ μεγάλοι ποιητές or οἱ μεγάλοι αὐτοί ποιητές 'those great poets';

(19) οἱ ὅμορφες αὐτές καλοκαιρινές βραδιές 'those beautiful summer evenings/nights'.

Where an adverb modifies an adjective, the former normally precedes the latter:

(20) μιά καθαρά προσωπική γνώμη 'a purely personal opinion';
(21) τή σχεδόν πλήρη ἄρνηση 'the almost complete refusal'.

There is a number of adverbs and other words which may act as adjectives, i.e. they may directly modify nouns. These adverbs include adverbs of place and time, but not of manner:

(22) κατά τήν ἐδῶ παραμονή του 'during his stay here';
(23) ἡ πάνω πόλη 'the upper town';
(24) ἡ τότε κυβέρνηση 'the government of the time';
(25) ἡ κυρίως Ἑλλάδα 'Greece proper';
(26) ἡ περαιτέρω ἐλάττωση 'the further decrease';
(27) θά λάβει ὑπόψη της τά τυχόν νόμιμα συμφέροντα ἄλλων χωρῶν 'it will take into account the possible legal interests of other countries' (T 11 Oct. 1979, 10).

The MG noun phrase is a flexible series of units whose order may be altered, as we have seen; it is also receptive of interpolations in the form of adverbs or even conjunctions. It is possible to observe how a construction such as (28) or (29), in which the adverb has been placed after the adjective (or other word) which it modifies, can become one (31) in which the adverb bears a looser relationship (or none at all) to the adjective etc.

(28) ἡ ἐργαζόμενη ἐπαγγελματικά γυναίκα 'the woman who works professionally';
(29) οἱ 'ἀντικειμενικοί' τάχα μελετητές τῶν γλωσσικῶν μας πραγμάτων 'the supposedly "objective" students of our linguistic affairs' (Kri. 1979: 34) (cf. οἱ τάχα ἀντικειμενικοί μελετητές (ibid.: 35));
(30) δέκα περίπου περιπολικά σκάφη 'about ten patrol vessels';
(31) ἀναγράφονται μέ τήν κυριότερη συνήθως σημασία τους '[the words] are recorded usually in their principal meaning'.

The conjunctions that may interrupt a noun phrase are those which may not stand as the first word of a clause (e.g. μέν 'on the one hand', δέ 'on the other hand; but; now'), or those which may optionally appear after the beginning of the clause (e.g. ὅμως 'but; however'; λοιπόν 'so, then'):

(32) ὁ δέ Πέτρος . . . 'but/now Peter (on the other hand) . . .';
(33) ἕνα λοιπόν πλέγμα ἀπ᾽ αὐτούς τούς τέσσερις παράγοντες
. . . 'so an aggregate of these four factors . . .'

An extreme example of the discontinuous nature of the MG noun phrase, characteristic of certain styles of Greek (journalism and scholarly writing in particular), is the *hyperbaton*, in which the article is separated from the noun by one or more phrases (usually adverbial). Although this type of construction, which has come into SMG by way of *katharevousa*, may owe something to AG, it is probably rather a sign of German influence on the language. In fact, the interpolated phrase usually appears between an adjective and a noun, and normally modifies the former:

(34) ὁρισμένα διαφημιζόμενα ὡς δημοκρατικά σχολεῖα 'certain schools which are promoted as [being] democratic' (*P* 29.7);
(35) οἱ ἀρχαιολογικοί θησαυροί βρῆκαν τήν ἀντάξια στέγη τους, στό σχεδιασμένο γι᾽ αὐτούς, ἀπό τό Γερμανό ἀρχιτέκτονα Ντόρπφλωτ [*sic*], μουσεῖο 'the archaeological treasures found a fitting home in the museum designed for them by the German architect Dörpfeld' (*T* 25 Feb. 1982, 45);
(36) τό δεύτερο σέ μέγεθος (μετά τήν ΕΣΣΟ ΠΑΠΑΣ στή Θεσσαλονίκη) διϋλιστήριο τῆς χώρας 'the second largest [lit. 'the second in size'] refinery in the country, after ESSO Papas in Salonica' (*T* 4 Oct. 1979, 16).

Occasionally the adverbial phrase may even contain a verb:

(37) μιά διαμορφωμένη ὅπως ἁρμόζει νέα ἑλληνική γραπτή γλῶσσα 'a modern Greek written language which has been suitably [lit. 'as is-fitting'] formed' (Kri. 1979: 94);
(38) στόν ἀνήμπορο νά ἀντιδράσει Γκίκα 'to Gikas, who is incapable of reacting' (from oral football commentary).

Sometimes the phrase qualifies a deverbal noun rather than an adjective:

(39) τήν ὁριστική σέ ὅλα τά πεδία ἐπικράτηση τῆς δημοτικῆς 'the definitive prevalence of the demotic at all levels' (Kri. 1979: 96).

Hyperbaton may sometimes be avoided by means of discontinuous modification:

(40) ἀποκλεισμένα χωριά ἀπό τά χιόνια 'villages cut off by the snow' (*K* 23 Dec. 1980).

6.1.2 THE USE OF THE ARTICLES

MG has a definite and an indefinite article. While the former is used in a similar way to the French definite article (with some additional uses), the latter (which is the same as the numeral 'one') is used rather less than in French.

The definite article is used to refer to a specific referent which has already been mentioned or is in some way readily identifiable by the hearer/reader:

> (1a) μιλοῦσα σέ μιά κυρία 'I was talking to a lady' (indefinite);
> (1b) μιλοῦσα στήν κυρία πού ἦρθε χθές 'I was talking to the lady who came yesterday' (definite).

Specific referents are taken to include the following (except when used indefinitely with the indefinite article): (a) all proper names, whether of people, places, heavenly bodies, days, months, seasons, festivals, etc.; (b) nouns used with possessive pronouns or demonstratives; and (c) other instances where the existence of the referent is presupposed but not previously mentioned:

> (a) (2a) ἦρθε ὁ Γεράσιμος/ὁ κύριος Πονηρίδης 'Gerasimos/Mr Poniridis has come';
>   (2b) ἦρθε ἕνας (or κάποιος) Γεράσιμος/κύριος Πονηρίδης 'a certain Gerasimos/Mr Poniridis has come';
>   (3) ἡ Ἀθήνα εἶναι πρωτεύουσα τῆς Ἑλλάδας 'Athens is [the] capital of Greece';
> (b) (4a) ὁ φίλος μου 'my friend';
>   (4b) ἕνας φίλος μου 'a friend of mine';
>   (5) αὐτό τό ψυγεῖο 'this refrigerator';
> (c) (6) τό εἴδαμε στήν τηλεόραση 'we saw it on (the) television';
>   (7) ἤρθαμε μέ τό τραῖνο 'we came by (the) train.'

The indefinite article may be used figuratively with a proper name to indicate 'someone like X' or 'a work of art by X':

> (8) ἡ Ἑλλάδα χρειάζεται ἕνα Σαίκσπηρ 'Greece needs a Shakespeare';
> (9) πέντε Βασιλείου εἰδικά ζωγραφισμένοι 'five specially painted Vasilious'.

The definite article is also used in expressing times and dates (στίς τρεῖς 'at three o'clock; on the third'), in expressing fractions (τά τρία τέταρτα τῶν ʽΕλλήνων 'three-quarters of the Greeks'), and in phrases such as 'one and the other' (τό ἕνα καί τό ἄλλο).

In order to express 'both', 'all three', etc., the definite article is used, preceded by καί:

(10) κι οἱ τρεῖς ὑπουργοί παραιτήθηκαν 'all three ministers resigned.'

The definite article is also used for generic specification in singular or plural; in such cases no distinction is made between specific and generic reference:

(11) τό ἄλογο εἶναι ὡραῖο ζῶο 'the horse is a lovely animal';
(12) τά ἄλογα εἶναι ὡραῖα ζῶα 'horses [or 'the horses'] are lovely animals';
(13) τραγουδάει σάν τό ἀηδόνι '(s)he sings like a/the nightingale.'

Nevertheless, a correlation between the generic or specific meaning of the definite article and the aspect of the verb has been noted (3.2.3.4.3).

Names of substances and of abstract concepts are also specified with the definite article, especially when they stand as the subject of a sentence. Again, no distinction is made between specific and generic reference, except where (a) the meaning is partitive (no article), or (b) the indefinite article (or equivalent) is used. In these respects, plurals in general often behave in a similar way to names of substances and of abstract concepts:

(14a) τό μελάνι εἶναι μαῦρο 'ink [or 'the ink'] is black'; cf.
(14b) χρειάζομαι μελάνι 'I want [some] ink';
(15) φοβᾶμαι τό θάνατο 'I'm afraid of (the) death';
(16a) ζεῖ μέ τήν ἐλπίδα '(s)he lives in [lit. 'with the'] hope'; cf.
(16b) δέν ἔχω καμιά ἐλπίδα 'I have no hope.'

The definite article is used in a distributive sense with a noun in the accusative:

(17) παίρνει ἑκατό χιλιάδες τό μήνα '(s)he earns a hundred thousand a month.'

Finally, the neuter of the definite article is used to substantivize other parts of speech (and even whole phrases and clauses) in a variety of ways:

(18) ἡ δράση τοῦ φίλμ τοποθετεῖται στό σήμερα 'the action of the film is set (in the) today';

(19) ἔλα λίγο πρός τά ἐδῶ 'come a little in this direction' (lit. 'towards the (plural) here');

(20) φύγανε στά κρυφά 'they left secretly' (κρυφά is either an adverb or a substantivized adjective in the neuter plural);

(21) μή ρωτᾶς τό γιατί 'don't ask (the) why';

(22) τό μόνο πού τόν ἐνδιαφέρει εἶναι τό πόσα θά εἰσπράξει 'the only [thing] that interests him is (the) how much [money] he will collect.'

In addition, any word or phrase, when talked about as a word or phrase (i.e. when one is talking about language) may be preceded by the neuter of the definite article, as may the title of a book, song, etc. (cf. 2.1.2):

(23) δέ μοῦ ἀρέσει τό ὑποβαθμίζω 'I don't like the [word] ὑποβαθμίζω';

(24) ψάλαμε τό Χριστός Ἀνέστη 'we sang the [hymn] "Christ is risen".'

Since the indefinite article ἕνας is identical to the numeral 'one', it is not always possible to decide in which function the word is being used. It is nevertheless true to say that the meaning 'one' is often present even when the word is used as an article; and where the notion of singularity is not being emphasized the article is often omitted.

Apart from its meaning of 'one', ἕνας is used to mean 'some (one)', 'a certain' (even with abstract nouns), i.e. in a similar sense to κάποιος (cf. (2b)):

(25) ἦρθε ἕνας καί σέ ζητοῦσε 'someone came (and was) asking for you';

(26) τό ποίημα ἔχει μιά θαυμαστή ἑνότητα 'the poem has an admirable unity.'

The indefinite article is often used to emphasize the particularly good or bad qualities of the referent:

(27) ἔχω μιά πείνα 'I've got a [great] hunger';

(28) μιά ὁλόκληρη Ἰταλία δέν μπόρεσε νά μᾶς νικήσει 'even Italy itself [lit. 'a whole Italy'] wasn't able to defeat us';

(29) ἔριχνε μιά βροχή 'it was pouring down' (lit. 'it-was-throwing a rain').

Having examined the uses of the articles, we shall now look at the circumstances in which they are not used. These are chiefly instances in which the noun is used as a complement, in apposition, or in a partitive sense.

The indefinite article is not normally used before a complement (referring either to the subject or to the object); the complement may however be made more specific by the use of the definite article:

(30) ἔγινε ναύτης 'he became [a] sailor';
(31) τόν διόρισαν καθηγητή 'they appointed him professor';
(32) μέ λένε Μάρκο 'I'm called Mark';
(33) ἡ ἀπαίτηση εἶναι ἀπαίτηση 'a demand is [a] demand';
(34) ἡ ἑρμηνεία πού δίνεις δέν εἶναι ἡ σωστή 'the interpretation you're giving isn't the right [one]' (σωστή without the article would simply mean 'right').

When nouns are used in a partitive sense (whether they are plurals or refer to substances or to abstract concepts), they are used without an article. In such cases, the nouns refer neither to specific instances of their referents, nor to all their referents in general:

(35) μ' ἀρέσει νά τρώω ψάρια 'I like eating fish' (i.e. neither particular fish, nor all fish, but simply the fish I eat);
(36) γράφει βιβλία '(s)he writes books' (cf. ἀγαπάει τά βιβλία '(s)he loves (the) books': in the second case, books as a whole are referred to);
(37) θέλω ψωμί 'I want [some] bread' (neither particular bread, nor all bread in general);
(38) μυρίζεις κολόνια 'you smell of cologne';
(39) αὐτό τό φίλμ θυμίζει ντοκυμανταίρ 'this film is reminiscent of [a] documentary' (i.e. no particular documentary, nor documentaries as a class).

A large number of demotic collocations (especially with κάνω or ἔχω + object) contain no article: e.g. κάνω μπάνιο 'I have a bath; I have a swim'; κάνω ἐμετό 'I vomit'; κάνει ζέστη 'it's hot'; ἔχω πονοκέφαλο 'I've got a headache'; ἔχω δίκιο 'I'm right.'

The absence of an indefinite article in AG led to its being used less frequently in *katharevousa* than in demotic. In the present situation, the indefinite article is found less often in writing of an abstract or official kind than in either the spoken language or in literature. A large number of collocations of learned origin consist of verb + noun, preposition + noun, or noun + noun, with no article before the subordinated noun (which is usually abstract): e.g. δέν ἔχει σημασία 'it has no significance, it's not important', δηλώνω συμμετοχή 'I register my entry [for a competition]', έδωσαν διαταγή 'they issued [an] order', σπουδάζω μουσική 'I study music', μοῦ ἔκανε ἐντύπωση '[it] made [an] impression on me'; σέ τελευταία ἀνάλυση 'in the last analysis' (based on F en dernière analyse), ἀπό ἐπιστημονική ἄποψη 'from [a] scientific point of view', σέ κοινωνικό ἐπίπεδο 'on [a] social level', μέ προθυμία 'willingly, readily', κάτα προσέγγιση 'approximately', μέσω Ἀθηνῶν 'via Athens'; λόγος ὑπάρξεως 'raison d'être', ἄδεια ὁδηγήσεως 'driving licence', δελτίο ταυτότητος 'identity card'. In most cases the noun again refers neither to a specific instance nor to the whole concept viewed in general terms. There is no article in many official phrases which include proper names: e.g. ὁδός Εὐριπίδου 'Euripides Street' (cf. οἱ τραγωδίες τοῦ Εὐριπίδη 'Euripides' tragedies'), Πανεπιστήμιο Θεσσαλονίκης 'University of Salonica' (cf. στούς δρόμους τῆς Θεσσαλονίκης 'in the streets of Salonica'), Δῆμος Καισαριανῆς 'Kaisariani Borough Council' (cf. στό κέντρο τῆς Καισαριανῆς 'in the centre of Kaisariani'), Κομμουνιστικό Κόμμα Ἑλλάδας 'Communist Party of Greece' (cf. σ' ὅλα τά μέρη τῆς Ἑλλάδας 'in all parts of Greece' (see also 4.5.1.2)).

In journalistic and official writing an effort is often made, under the influence of *katharevousa*, to omit the indefinite article in contexts in which it would appear in ordinary speech:

(40) ὁ ὑπουργός, σέ συνέντευξη σέ ἑβδομαδιαῖο περιοδικό ... 'the minister, in [an] interview with [a] weekly magazine ...';

(41) ἄγνωστος μπῆκε μέ ἀντικλείδι στό σπίτι τοῦ κ. Χ. '[an] unknown [person] entered the house of Mr X with a skeleton key' (from broadcast news bulletin).

Colloquially, the definite article is sometimes omitted with names of places in certain uses (it is noticeable that the preposition is often omitted at the same time):

(42) ἄν μένετε Ψυχικό, ... 'if you live Psychiko way ...';

(43) θά πᾶς Ἀθήνα; 'are you going Athens way?';

(44) δέν πιάνουν Ἀθήνα στίς συσκευές τῆς τηελόρασής τους 'they can't get Athens [TV station] on their television sets.'

In collocations such as πάω περίπατο 'I go [for a] walk', πῆγε φυλακή '(s)he went [to] prison', εἴμαστε σπίτι 'we're [at] home', the noun is best regarded as being used adverbially (cf. 2.2.3).

When two nouns stand as co-subjects or co-objects linked by καί, the article is repeated if the two nouns refer to non-abstract referents,

but may be omitted before the second noun if the referents are abstract
or if both nouns have the same referent:

(45) ἔφερε τά βιβλία καί τά περιοδικά '(s)he brought the books and
      (the) magazines';
(46) ἡ ἔρευνα καί ἀνακάλυψη τῶν τάφων ἔχει ὁλοκληρωϑεῖ 'the
      search [for] and discovery of the tombs has been completed';
(47) ὁ γιός της καί ἀνηψιός τους 'her son [who is] their nephew'.

Note the singular verb in (46): the two subjects are being considered as
part of a single process (cf. 2.3).

6.2 SIMPLE AND COMPLEX PREPOSITIONS

The simple (one-word) prepositions which SMG has inherited from
traditional demotic are few: ἀπό, γιά, μέ, σάν, σέ, χωρίς (or δίχως)
and ὡς. All these govern the accusative and may be called *primary
prepositions*. (Of these, σέ, ἀπό, μέ, and γιά are by far the most frequently used prepositions, σέ being used more often than all the other
prepositions combined: Householder *et al.* 1964: 34.) To these may be
added prepositions from *katharevousa* which have entered SMG, where
they too take the accusative: ἀντί, κατά, μετά, μέχρι, παρά, and πρός.
(For the use of the nominative and genitive after prepositions which
normally govern the accusative, see 2.2.1 and 2.2.4.7 respectively.)
Those prepositions that govern other cases, and those that are still
thought of as belonging to *katharevousa*, will be examined later. In
addition to these simple prepositions, there is a number of adverbs
of time and place which combine with one of the primary prepositions
to form complex prepositions (and many more which are followed
directly by a clitic pronoun in the genitive).

One syntactical characteristic common to all the simple prepositions
is that they may not govern clitic pronouns; and only the primary
prepositions are normally found governing an emphatic pronoun.
A semantic characteristic of some of the simple prepositions is that
they may refer equally to time or place. Thus σέ may denote 'position
at' or 'motion to', but also 'point in time' (although this is often
rendered with a simple accusative); ἀπό may indicate 'motion from' or
'position away from', but also 'time since' (in addition to 'agent');
ὡς and μέχρι 'until' may also mean 'as far as' (ϑά σέ πάω μέχρι τό
Χίλτον 'I'll take you as far as the Hilton'); πρίν (ἀπό), in addition to its
temporal meaning 'before', may be used of place (ϑά σταματήσεις λίγο

πρίν ἀπό τήν 'Ομόνοια 'you'll stop just before Omonia [Square]'); and μετά 'after' may similarly be used of time or place (μένουμε μετά τίς γραμμές 'we live just past the [railway] lines').

Just as the ancient dative was replaced by the genitive or by εἰς (> σέ) + accusative, so there is a tendency today to use a preposition (usually ἀπό or γιά) + accusative instead of the genitive in circumstances where there is no sense of possession (cf. 2.2.4.2). Thus one often finds constructions such as the following in the writing of those who want to make a show of avoiding katharevousa:

(1) ἕνα ποσό ἀπό σαράντα ἐκατομμύρια δολλάρια 'a sum of forty million dollars' (usually ἕνα ποσόν σαράντα ἐκατομμυρίων δολλαρίων) (T 4 Oct. 1979, 16);

(2) τεχνίτες ἀπ' ὅλες τίς εἰδικότητες 'skilled workmen of all specialities' (usually τεχνίτες ὅλων τῶν εἰδικοτήτων) (T 23 Aug. 1979);

(3) ὁ Ὑπουργός γιά τή Δημόσια Τάξη 'the Minister of Public Order' (normally the katharevousa formula ὁ Ὑπουργός Δημοσίας Τάξεως is used).

Such constructions are not usually approved by demoticist grammarians, who consider them as vain attempts to translate katharevousa constructions literally into demotic. (In (1), for example, the phrase ἕνα ποσό ἀπό is redundant; while perhaps a more acceptable version of (3) might be ὁ Ὑπουργός τῆς Δημόσιας Τάξης.) There seems to be no evidence, however, of a breakdown of the case system in Greek, as occurred in the Romance languages, and there is still no alternative to the genitive of possession.

Many of the prepositions (simple and complex) have a wider range of meanings today than they had in traditional demotic. The previously restricted uses have been augmented by a number of different functions based on Western European languages, particularly French. Thus, while σέ generally meant 'to; at; in; on', of time and place (as well as being used with the indirect object), there is now a large number of collocations in which this preposition is used with an abstract noun (e.g. εἶμαι σέ δύσκολη θέση 'I'm in [a] difficult position', σέ σημαντικό βαθμό 'to [a] significant degree', σέ μηνιαία βάση 'on [a] monthly basis', σέ εἶδος 'in kind', etc.). Again, ἀπό, apart from its functions of denoting the agent of a verb or of substituting for a genitive, acted chiefly as a preposition of time and place; nowadays, there are collocations in which ἀπό has taken on other functions (e.g. ἀπό οἰκονομική ἄποψη 'from [the] economic point of view').

Simple prepositions may govern not only nouns and emphatic pronouns, but (in certain cases) question words: e.g. ἀπό τί 'from what' (e.g. is something made), γιατί 'why' (written as one word), σέ τί 'in what [respect]', μέ ποιόν 'with whom', ἀπό ποῦ 'from where, where from', ὡς/μέχρι πότε 'till when, how long'. Ἀπό, γιά, and ὡς/μέχρι may also govern adverbs of time and place: e.g. ἀπό κεῖ 'from there', γιά πάντα 'for ever', ὡς τότε 'up to then', γιά σήμερα 'for today', ἀπό μακριά 'from a distance'. Finally, ἀπό may govern the relative ὅπου: ἀπ' ὅπου 'from where'.

The adverbs that may combine with prepositions before a noun or emphatic pronoun (in the accusative) and which may directly govern a clitic pronoun (in the genitive: cf. 2.2.4.4) are the following (in brackets is the preposition that must follow if the governed word is a noun or emphatic pronoun; as will be seen below, even those normally followed by σέ may also be followed by ἀπό): ἀνάμεσα (σέ) 'between; among', ἀπεναντι (σέ) 'opposite', γύρω (σέ/ἀπό) 'around', δίπλα (σέ) 'next to', ἐμπρός (σέ/ἀπό) 'in front of', κάτω (ἀπό) 'under', κοντά (σέ) 'near', μαζί (μέ) '(together) with', μακριά (ἀπό) 'far from; away from', μπροστά (σέ/ἀπό) 'in front of; compared with', μέσα (σέ) 'in(side)', μέσα (ἀπό) 'through; from inside', πάνω (σέ) 'on; during, in the middle of', πάνω (ἀπό) 'over', πίσω (ἀπό) 'behind'; and πλάι (σέ) 'beside'.

Other complex prepositions (in which however the adverb may not govern a clitic pronoun) include ἐκτός ἀπό 'except for', ἔξω ἀπό 'outside', πέρα ἀπό 'beyond', πρίν ἀπό 'before' (also found as a preposition without ἀπό) and ὕστερα ἀπό 'after'. Generally, πρίν ἀπό is used to mean 'before', πρίν alone to mean 'ago, previously' (e.g. πρίν ἀπό τόν πόλεμο 'before the war', but πρίν δυό μέρες 'two days ago; two days previously'; the latter type of phrase is probably originally a translation from katharevousa πρό δύο ἡμερῶν, and is consequently condemned by certain demoticists, despite its frequent use). There are also of course many adverbs of manner which may be followed by one of the primary prepositions.

Like the simple prepositions, the complex prepositions have also taken on figurative, abstract functions: e.g. πάνω στό θέμα αὐτό 'on this subject', γύρω στό Σολωμό 'about [= concerning] Solomos', ἀπέναντι στίς ὑποχρεώσεις της 'vis-à-vis her obligations', πέρα ἀπό τίς φυλετικές διακρίσεις 'beyond racial discrimination(s)'.

Some uses of the most important primary prepositions σέ, ἀπό, γιά, and μέ will now be examined in turn, after which some comments will be made about other prepositions.

6.2.1 ΣΕ

Σέ loses its vowel before the definite article, and (optionally) before a word beginning with a vowel (particularly *a*, *o*, or *e*). In the first case it is written as one word with the article (στό(ν), στή(ν), etc.); in the second it is written as a separate word with an apostrophe (σ' ἕνα μήνα 'in a/one month').

The prime uses of σέ are to express (a) the indirect object; (b) position in place or time; and (c) progress towards a point in place or time.

When the indirect object is a clitic pronoun, the genitive is used (see 2.2.4.1); when it is a noun or emphatic pronoun, σέ + accusative is normally used, although even here the genitive is sometimes found instead of σέ + accusative:

(1) τό 'δωσα στήν κόρη μου/σ' αὐτήν 'I gave it to my daughter/to her' (also τῆς κόρης μου).

An indirect-object construction is of course also found after nouns and adjectives with meanings connected with verbs which take indirect objects: e.g.

(2) ἕνα κληροδότημα στήν ἐκκλησία 'a bequest to the church'.

The semantic connection between the indirect object and 'motion to' is clear to see, since with verbs of giving etc., there is usually some movement of the direct object to the indirect object.

MG generally makes little or no distinction, except in verbs, between position at a point and movement to a point. This is clear in cases where σέ cannot be used, such as with adverbs of place (or time); compare (3(a–f)), in which no preposition is used, with (4(a–c)), which use ἀπό:

(3a) εἶμαι ἐδῶ 'I'm here';
(3b) πῆγα ἐκεῖ 'I went there';
(3c) ποῦ εἶσαι; 'where are you?';
(3d) ποῦ πῆγες; 'where did you go?';
(3e) κάθομαι κοντά της 'I sit/live near her';
(3f) ἦρθα κοντά της 'I came near her (= to her side)';
(4a) εἶμαι ἀπό δῶ 'I'm from here';

(4b) ἔφυγα ἀπό κεῖ 'I left (from) there';
(4c) ἔφυγα ἀπό κοντά της 'I left her side' (lit. 'I-left from near her').

Thus the distinction that is made is between (a) position or motion to and (b) position or motion away from. This binary distinction is comparable to that between the two tenses in MG: non-past (including present ('at') and future ('to')) and past ('from'). So too, σέ of place may be locative or directional, the nature of the verb indicating which interpretation should be attached to it:

(5a) εἴμαστε στό γραφεῖο 'we're at the office';
(5b) πήγαμε στό γραφεῖο 'we went to the office'

(cf. also elliptical constructions such as εἶναι σπίτι '(s)he's [at] home' and πῆγε σπίτι '(s)he went home (= to home)').

When σέ is used of position, it denotes a range of spatial relationships between the referents concerned (corresponding to English 'at', 'in', 'on', etc.); precisely which of the possible relationships is meant may usually (but not always) be inferred from the context: e.g. στό τραπέζι 'on the table', στό ταβάνι 'on the ceiling' (i.e. on its nether side), but στό πανεπιστήμιο 'at [or 'at the'] university; in [or 'in the'] university'. Thus the adverbs μέσα 'in' or πάνω 'on' may be prefixed to the prepositional phrase to avoid ambiguity:

(6a) μέσα στό αὐτοκίνητο 'in(side) the car';
(6b) πάνω στό αὐτοκίνητο 'on (top of) the car'.

In the absence of such an adverb, a relationship of contiguity which is neither necessarily 'inside' nor 'on top of' is generally assumed, according to the context.

Just as, of position, σέ may mean 'at', 'on', or 'in', so of motion it may denote 'to', 'towards', 'on to', or 'into'. Again, μέσα may be added to make clear that the last meaning is intended:

(7a) πῆγα [μέσα] στό σπίτι 'I went [in]to the house';
(7b) πέρασα μέσα στό σπίτι 'I proceeded into the house.'

Adverbs such as μέσα and πάνω are thought to be sufficiently separate from the prepositional phrase to be placed, alternatively, after it:

(6c) στό αὐτοκίνητο μέσα ⎫
(6d) στό αὐτοκίνητο πάνω ⎬ (meanings as in (6a) and (6b))

Thus, as in (6c) and (6d), the speaker may state the general spatial relationship first (i.e. 'not "away from" ') before specifying the relationship more precisely. This placing of the adverb after the prepositional phrase may occur with other adverbs too, and not only with those which are commonly constructed with σέ (see (8d)):

(8a) στό σπίτι μπροστά (= μπροστά στό σπίτι) 'in front of the house';

(8b) στό σπίτι κοντά (= κοντά στό σπίτι) 'near the house';

(8c) στόν τοῖχο καβάλα (= καβάλα στόν τοῖχο) 'astride the wall';

(8d) στό σπίτι ἀπ᾽ ἔξω (= ἀπ᾽ ἔξω ἀπό τό σπίτι) 'outside the house'.

But for the fact that some of these adverbs may directly govern a clitic pronoun, one might conclude that the preposition (σέ or ἀπό) does not actually depend on the adverb, but that the prepositional phrase and the adverb are simply two adverbial phrases of place in apposition to each other. This latter phenomenon does actually occur, especially in cases where the adverb in question cannot govern the particular preposition:

(9a) κάτω στό σπίτι (or στό σπίτι κάτω) 'down at the house'; cf.

(9b) κάτω ἀπό τό σπίτι (or στό σπίτι ἀπό κάτω) 'under the house'.

Since κάτω cannot be constructed with any preposition but ἀπό it is clear that in (9a) the adverb κάτω and the prepositional phrase στό σπίτι are not syntactically interdependent.

Apart from place, σέ is used (though with more restricted uses) for time; again, one can observe that in some cases σέ denotes a point at which something takes place, while in others it indicates progress (over a period of time):

(10)   στίς τέσσερις ἡ ὥρα 'at four o'clock';

(11)   σέ δυό ὧρες θά 'χουμε τελειώσει 'we'll have finished in two hours';

(12)   τήν κάναμε τή δουλειά [μέσα] σέ δυό μέρες 'we did the job [with]in two days.'

Other meanings of σέ, apart from indirect object, time, and place, are too numerous to be covered extensively here. In these figurative uses, the prepositional phrase may be governed (a) by a verb or phrase, (b) by a noun, (c) by an adjective or adverb, or (d) by a numeral.

(a) Verb or phrase:

(13) ἦρθαν στά χέρια 'they came to blows [lit. 'to the hands']';

(14) [πίνω] στήν ὑγεία σου '[I drink] to your health';

(15) θ' ἀντισταθοῦμε στή βία 'we shall resist violence';

(16) δέν μπορεῖς ν' ἀλλάξεις τό σίδερο σέ χρυσό 'you can't change iron into gold';

(17) δέν ἔφταιγε σέ τίποτα '(s)he wasn't to blame in any way [lit. 'in anything']';

(18) τόν μαύρισαν στό ξύλο 'they gave him a good beating-up' (lit. 'they blackened him in-the wood').

(b) Noun (usually deverbal):

(19) ἡ ὄξυνση στίς σχέσεις μέ τήν Τουρκία 'the exacerbation of relations with Turkey' (the genitive could be used here instead of σέ + accusative);

(20) ἡ περιεκτικότητα τῶν τροφίμων σέ λίπος 'the fat content of foodstuffs' (lit. 'the content of-the foodstuffs in fat').

(c) Adjective (usually deverbal):

(21) ἦταν ντυμένη στά μαῦρα 'she was dressed in black';

(22) ἡ Ἀθήνα εἶναι πνιγμένη στό τσιμέντο 'Athens is drowned in cement';

(23) δέν εἶμαι δυνατός στά μαθηματικά 'I'm not good [lit. 'strong'] at mathematics';

(24) εἶμαι πτῶμα στήν κούραση 'I'm dead tired' (lit. 'I-am corpse in-the tiredness': the noun is used as an adjective).

(d) Numeral:

(25) ὁ ἕνας στούς τρεῖς κερδίζει 'one in [every] three [people] wins.'

6.2.2 ΑΠΟ

In spoken Greek, ἀπό is not stressed; it is often shortened to ἀπ' in front of the definite article or before a word beginning with *a* or *o*. In more elevated styles, it generally preserves its final vowel in front of the article.

Its prime meanings are 'from' (of place or time), 'out of' (of place), and 'since' (of time), but its other important spacial sense is 'through' or 'past'. In addition, it is used to specify the agent of a verb (not only of a passive verb) or to denote cause or reason, and as an alternative to the genitive (especially of content: see also 6.2, example (1)). It may also mean 'than' after comparatives, and it has a distributive meaning.

Like σέ, it is also used after various adverbs, to produce complex prepositions.

In its spatial meaning of 'position or motion from', ἀπό acts as the opposite of σέ. Thus, while σέ indicates direction to or location at a point which is inside, on top of, or at least very close to the referent of the noun or pronoun it governs, so ἀπό indicates location or direction away from (or provenance from) such a point: e.g.

(1) ἡ Θεσσαλονίκη βρίσκεται σέ ἀπόσταση 540 χιλιομέτρων ἀπό τήν Ἀθήνα 'Salonica is situated at a distance of 540 km. from Athens' (location away from);

(2) ἔβγαλε τό καναρίνι ἀπό τό παλιό κλουβί καί τό 'βαλε στό καινούριο '(s)he took the canary out of the old cage and put it in the new [one]' (direction out of);

(3) ἀπό τήν Ἀθήνα πήγαμε στούς Δελφούς 'from Athens we went to Delphi' (direction away from);

(4) μάζεψε τά παιχνίδια ἀπ' τό τραπέζι καί βάλ' τα στό πάτωμα 'pick up the toys off the table and put them on the floor' (direction from on top of).

It is also the converse of σέ in the latter's indirect object use:

(5) τό πῆρα ἀπ' τό Στέφανο καί τό 'δωσα στόν Πάνο 'I got/took it from Stephen and gave it to Panos.'

Like σέ, ἀπό may be used in conjunction with a number of adverbs which specify the precise spatial relationship between the referents. In some cases (but not all), there is a correspondence between constructions with ἀπό and those with σέ:

(6) τά μυρμήγκια ἔβγαιναν μέσα ἀπό τόν κορμό τοῦ δέντρου 'the ants were emerging from inside the tree-trunk' (cf. μέσα στόν κορμό 'inside/into the trunk');

(7) αὐτοί οἱ τύποι εἶναι πάντοτε πρώην ἐπίθετα δίπλα ἀπό τά ὁποῖα παραλείφθηκε κάποιο οὐσιαστικό 'these forms are always former adjectives from beside which some noun has been omitted' (Lyp. 1977: 100) (cf. δίπλα στά ὁποῖα 'beside which');

(8) τό νέφος δέ λέει νά ξεκολλήσει πάνω ἀπό τά κεφάλια μας 'the cloud [of smog] refuses to go away [lit. 'unstick'] from over our heads' (T 27 May 1982, 131) (cf. πάνω σέ 'above and in contact with' with πάνω ἀπό 'above and not in contact with');

(9) βγῆκε κάτω ἀπ' τό τραπέζι '(s)he/it came out from under the table' (here κάτω ἀπό would also have to be used for 'motion to' or 'position at', since κάτω σέ is impossible).

In (8) and (9), if the speaker feared the possibility of ambiguity, an additional ἀπό could be inserted before πάνω or κάτω. (The order adverb + prepositional phrase is not normally reversible when the sense of 'movement away from' is present.) When the noun or emphatic pronoun after adverb + ἀπό is transformed into a clitic pronoun, ἀπό is removed from after the adverb and placed before it:

(6a) τά μυρμήγκια ἔβγαιναν ἀπό μέσα του 'the ants were emerging from inside it.'

In phrases of time, ἀπό is again largely the converse of σέ, since it indicates time that elapses from a certain point. Nevertheless, it may correspond rather to ὡς or μέχρι 'until', or to an absence of a preposition:

(10) σέ περίμενα ἀπό τίς ἔξη 'I was/had been waiting for you since six' (cf. στίς ἔξη 'at six', but μέχρι τίς ἔξη 'till six').

The other chief spatial function of ἀπό, that of 'passage', does not correspond to any use of σέ, nor does it possess any analogy in time. This use of ἀπό is so frequent in MG that it is worth examining in detail, especially since the construction is different from those which are found in certain other European languages (e.g. English and French). This function is regularly associated with the verb περνάω 'I pass' (transitive or intransitive), but is also found with other verbs of motion. Like most other verbs of motion in MG, περνάω in itself gives no indication of the manner in which the motion takes place (including the means of transport).

The use of ἀπό for 'passage' may have one of two meanings: 'through' (i.e. passing inside the perimeter of the referent of the word it governs), or 'past' (i.e. passing outside the perimeter of the referent). When ἀπό in the sense of 'passage' is not preceded by an adverb, it usually (but not always) means 'through':

(11) θά περάσω ἀπ' τό σπίτι σου 'I'll drop in at your house' (lit. 'I'll pass from your house');

(12) πέρασε τή σφαίρα ἀπ' τό δαχτυλίδι '(s)he shot the bullet through the ring';

(13) μπήκανε στό σπίτι ἀπό τήν πίσω πόρτα 'they entered the house by the back door';

(14) θά πᾶμε στήν 'Ομόνοια ἀπό τό Σύνταγμα 'we'll go to Omonia [Square] by [way of] Syndagma [Square].'

The sense of 'through' may be made more explicit by means of μέσα:

(15) ὁ σιδηρόδρομος περνάει μέσα ἀπό τό σπίτι 'the railroad runs through [the middle of] the house.'

When the passage is not actually through but past (including over and under), an adverb is usually necessary before ἀπό:

(16) δυό αὐτοκίνητα πέρασαν μπροστά ἀπό τό σπίτι 'two cars drove by (in front of) the house';

(17) ἔνα κοπάδι πουλιά πέρασε πάνω ἀπό τό λιμάνι 'a flock of birds flew over the harbour';

(18) τό ποτάμι περνάει κάτω ἀπό μιά γέφυρα 'the river flows under a bridge';

(19) τό πλοῖο μας θά περάσει κοντά ἀπό τή Νάξο 'our boat will sail right by Naxos.'

Note that MG often fails to distinguish between 'across' and 'along': motion across and along is normally expressed equally by περνάω. Position across and along is not easily expressible: an expression such as ἀπό τή μιά ἄκρη στήν ἄλλη (lit. 'from the one side/end to the other') is usually resorted to.

'Από is used to designate the agent or quasi-agent of a verb (see 3.1.2.1 and 3.1.4.4). In fact, this sense of ἀπό is wider than simply the designation of agent or quasi-agent, and includes cause and reason:

(20) 'Απ' τό πολύ φῶς ἔβλεπα τόν κόσμο μαῦρο 'the light was so bright that the world looked black to me' (lit. 'from the much light I-was-seeing the world black') (Pre. n.d.: 9).

The use of ἀπό to designate agent or cause also appears after deverbal nouns and adjectives:

(21) ὁ ἐνθουσιασμός ἀπό τήν ἀνακάλυψη τῆς ἀξίας ἔργων ὅπως τοῦ Μακρυγιάννη 'the enthusiasm [caused] by the discovery of the value of works such as [those] of Makriyannis' (A 15 Nov. 1979);

(22) ἡ φρεγάτα ''Ελλη' εἶναι ἀπλησίαστη ἀπό ἐχθρικές ἐπιθέσεις,

ἀκόμα ἀπό πυρηνική 'the frigate *Elli* is unapproachable by foreign attack(s), even by [a] nuclear [one]' (*T* 17 Dec. 1981, 55).

Certain other uses of ἀπό (e.g. of content or material or part) might be semantically connected with its senses of provenance or cause:

(23) ἕνα πλῆθος ἀπό προβλήματα 'a host of problems' (= genitive of content in more formal styles);

(24) τό ἐργοστάσιο καλύπτει τό μεγαλύτερο μέρος ἀπό τίς ἀνάγκες τῶν Ἐνόπλων Δυνάμεων 'the factory covers most [lit. 'the greater part'] of the needs of the Armed Forces' (= genitive);

(25) τό γραφεῖο εἶναι ἀπό μαόνι 'the desk is [made] of mahogany';

(26) ἕνα κουτί ἀπό μπισκοτα 'a biscuit tin' (i.e., a tin that has contained biscuits: cf. ἕνα κουτί μπισκότα 'a tin of biscuits');

(27) ἕνας ἀπό τούς φαντάρους 'one of the soldiers';

(28) πάρε κι ἀπ' αὐτά 'take [some] of these too.'

Ἀπό is used, as we have already seen, after comparatives and superlatives and after ἄλλος 'other', διαφορετικός 'different', etc.: here ἀπό implies difference, otherness (comparable to its meanings of distance in time and place):

(29a) ἡ Λένα εἶναι πιό ὄμορφη ἀπ' ὅλες τίς ἄλλες 'Lena is more beautiful than all the others';

(29b) ἡ Λένα εἶναι ἡ πιό ὄμορφη ἀπ' ὅλες 'Lena is the most beautiful of all [of them]';

(30) ἡ εἰκόνα τῶν ἀνωτάτων σπουδῶν μας, ἡ ὁποία δέν ἦταν τίποτε ἄλλο ἀπό παραλλαγές τῆς βίας καί τῆς ὑποβαθμίσεως 'the picture [presented by] our higher education, which was nothing other than variations of violence and degradation' (*K* 23 Dec. 1980).

In its distributive use, ἀπό followed by a cardinal numeral has the sense of 'each':

(31) θά φᾶμε ἀπό δυό αὐγά 'we'll eat two eggs each' (lit. 'we'll eat from two eggs').

In its other, more figurative meanings, some sense cf 'movement from', cause, etc., is usually present. The following examples will serve to indicate the range of its uses:

(32) εἶναι ἄρρωστη ἀπό γρίπη 'she's ill with 'flu';

(33) τό τοπίο ἦταν ἔρημο ἀπό ἀνθρώπους 'the landscape was deserted [lit. 'desolate of people']';

(34) χθές κονόμησα 300 δραχμές ἀπό καύσιμα 'I saved 300 drachmas on fuel yesterday' (*T* 13 Dec. 1979, 15);

(35) μείναμε ἀπό βενζίνη 'we've run out of petrol' (lit. 'we-remained from petrol');

(36) γνώρισα τόν "Αλκη ἀπό τήν Τζένη 'I met Alkis through Jenny';

(37) δέν ξέρω ἀπό μουσική 'I don't know anything about music';

(38) ἀπό φαΐ τί ἔχεις; 'what have you got in the way of food?';

(39) ἀπό τή μιά μεριά . . . ἀπό τήν ἄλλη 'on the one hand [lit. 'side'] . . . on the other';

(40) τόν ἄρπαξε ἀπό τό χέρι '(s)he grabbed him by the arm/hand';

(41) δύο ἀπό πέντε τρία 'two from five [makes] three';

(42) τό πέταξα ἀπό φόβο μήπως δέ σοῦ ἄρεσε 'I threw it away for fear that you might not have liked it.'

6.2.3 ΓΙΑ

The chief meanings of γιά are 'for' (benefit, time, purpose, destination, price) and 'about' (= 'concerning'):

(1) τά 'φερα γιά σένα 'I brought them for *you*';

(2) κάθισα ἐκεῖ γιά δυό ὧρες 'I sat/waited there for two hours';

(3) πῆγε στή βρύση γιά νερό 'she went to the spring for water';

(4) αὔριο φεύγω γιά τήν Ἰσπανία 'I'm leaving for Spain tomorrow';

(5) τό ἀγόρασα γιά ἔνα κομμάτι ψωμί 'I bought it for a song [lit. 'for a piece of bread']';

(6) μιλούσαμε γιά τό Χρῆστο 'we were talking about Christos'.

Γιά is also used to express cause:

(7) γι' αὐτό δέν εἶπες τίποτα; 'is what why [lit. 'for that'] you said nothing?';

(8) ἡ ἔκπληξή μου γιά τήν ξαφνική ἀλλαγή 'my surprise at the sudden change'.

Γιά may designate subject or object complements in certain types of construction:

(9) περνάει γιά ὠραία 'she passes for [being] beautiful';

(10) γιά τόσο κορόιδο μ' ἔχεις; 'do you think me such a sucker?' (lit. 'for so-much sucker me you-have?');

(11) πρότεινε τόν ἐαυτό του γιά ὑποψήφιο δήμαρχο 'he proposed himself as prospective mayor.'

In (11), γιά could be replaced by the conjunction ὡς 'as'.

Most other meanings of γιά can be readily connected with the foregoing. Examples:

(12) ἡ συνάντηση αὐτή θεωρεῖται καθοριστική γιά τό μέλλον 'this meeting is considered [to be] decisive for the future' (i.e. it will determine the future) (T 20 Sept. 1979);

(13) οἱ ἐργασίες κατεδαφίσεως τοῦ κτιρίου Κατράντζου ἀνεστάλησαν γιά αὔριο τό βράδι 'the demolition work(s) on the Katrantzos building has been suspended until tomorrow evening' (K 23 Dec. 1980);

(14) τό Παλάτι παραμέριξε τό Στεφανόπουλο γιά τόν Καραμανλή 'the Palace was pushing aside Stephanopoulos in favour of Karamanlis' (T 30 Aug. 1979, 8);

(15) ἐσύ τρῶς γιά δύο! 'you eat [enough] for two!'

When there might be doubt whether γιά means 'for' or 'about', the former interpretation is more likely:

(16) ἕνα βιβλίο γιά παιδιά 'a book for children' (cf. ἕνα βιβλίο μέ θέμα τά παιδιά 'a book about children [lit. 'with subject the children']').

6.2.4 ME

The chief uses of μέ correspond broadly with English 'with' (accompaniment or instrument). In its sense of accompaniment, μέ may be preceded by μαζί 'together'; and when μαζί is used with a clitic pronoun it may stand for either μαζί μέ or plain μέ + noun or emphatic pronoun:

(1) πήγαμε ἐκεῖ μέ τόν πατέρα μου 'we/I went there with my father';

(2) — Πόσοι εἴσαστε; — Τέσσερις μαζί μέ τόν ὁδηγό ' "How many of you are there?" "Four including [lit. 'together with'] the driver" ';

(3) τόν σκοτώσανε μέ περίστροφο 'they killed him/he was killed with [a] revolver.'

In addition, μέ also indicates means of transport (μέ τά πόδια 'on foot' [lit. 'with the feet'], μέ αὐτοκίνητο 'by car'), and may express certain other types of means or manner:

(4) τό 'γραψα μέ μελάνι 'I wrote it in ink';

(5) διαβάζαμε μέ τό φῶς τοῦ φεγγαριοῦ 'we were reading/used to read by moonlight';

(6) τά πορτοκάλια πουλιοῦνται μέ τό κιλό κι ὄχι μέ τό κομμάτι '(the) oranges are sold by the kilo, (and) not singly [lit. 'by the piece'].'

Other uses of μέ include the following: carrying or wearing (7-8); characteristic or possession (9); weather or time of day (10-11); contents (12); cause or pseudo-agent (13); opposition ('against': 14-15); contrariety ('despite'), always followed by the relevant form of ὅλος 'all' (16); identity or similarity (after ὁ ἴδιος 'same' and μοιάζω 'resemble': 17-18); with numerals (two different senses of 'by': 19-20); with an abstract noun, instead of an adverb of manner (21); in expressions of time (two different meanings: 22-3); 'concerning' or 'in relation to' (24); and exchange or replacement (25):

(7) φάνηκε μέ τήν τραγιάσκα στό χέρι 'he appeared with the/his cloth-cap in his hand';

(8) τό κορίτσι μέ τά μαῦρα 'the girl in black';

(9) ἡ δασκάλα μέ τά χρυσά μάτια 'the schoolmistress with the golden eyes';

(10) δέν ταξιδεύω μέ τέτοια βροχή 'I'm not travelling in rain like this';

(11) ξυπνοῦσα μέ τήν αὐγή 'I used to wake up at dawn' (implying 'as soon as dawn came');

(12) ἕνα βάζο μέ μέλι 'a jar containing honey';

(13) γελάσανε μέ τήν ἀμηχανία του 'they laughed at his embarrassment';

(14) πολεμήσαμε μέ τούς Ἰταλούς 'we fought against the Italians' (this could be alternatively interpreted as 'together with', in which case μέ is usually preceded by μαζί);

(15) μήν τά βάζεις μέ τή Βάσω 'don't take it out on Vaso' (lit. 'don't put them with Vaso');

(16) μ' ὅλα τά ἐλαττώματά του εἶναι τό καλύτερο λεξικό πού ἔχουμε 'for all its faults it's the best dictionary we have';

(17) τό αὐτοκίνητό σου εἶναι ἡ ἴδια μάρκα μέ τό δικό μου 'your car is the same make as mine';

(18) ὁ Βαγγέλης μοιάζει μέ τόν πατέρα του 'Vangelis is like his father';

(19) τό 32 δέ διαιρεῖται μέ το 3 '32 is not divisible [lit. 'divided'] by 3';

(20) ἡ Λίβερπουλ νίκησε μέ 2-0 [δύο-μηδέν] τήν Ἄρσεναλ 'Liverpool beat Arsenal 2-0';

(21) μέ βοήθησε μέ προθυμία (= πρόθυμα) '(s)he helped me willingly';

(22) δέκα μέ ἔντεκα ἔχουμε μάθημα 'we've got a lesson from ten to eleven';

(23) ἔλα στίς δυόμιση μέ τρεῖς 'come about 2.30 to three';

(24) ἔχει μανία μέ τό κυνήγι 'he's mad about hunting' (lit. 'he-has madness with the hunting');

(25) οἱ ἔμποροι ἄλλαξαν τίς χάντρες μέ χρυσό 'the merchants used to [ex]change (the) beads for gold.'

There are other frequently used constructions with μέ, including those in which it is followed by an abstract noun and a noun phrase in apposition: e.g.

(26) μέ βάση τά ἐπίσημα στοιχεῖα 'on the basis of the official figures' (lit. 'with basis the official figures').

Other such phrases are μέ ἀποτέλεσμα 'with the result', μέ σκοπό 'with the purpose', μέ στόχο 'with the aim'. Some of these phrases may be followed by a νά-clause instead of a noun phrase:

(27) ἔκανε τίς ἀποκαλύψεις μέ σκοπό νά δυσφημήσει τούς ἀντιπάλους του 'he made the revelations with the aim of discrediting his opponents.'

Finally, a frequently used phrase in colloquial Greek is μέ τίποτα (lit. 'with nothing'), indicating impossibility:

(28) δέν τό βάξει κάτω μέ τίποτα 'nothing will make him/her give in' (lit. '(s)he doesn't put it down with anything').

6.2.5 OTHER COMMON PREPOSITIONS

It is necessary to comment here only on certain semantic and syntactical aspects of the prepositions σάν, παρά, κατά, μετά, ἀντί, and πρός.

Σάν. This word acts sometimes as a conjunction, sometimes as a preposition. As a conjunction it may introduce a subordinate temporal clause ('when, as'); or it may introduce a phrase of comparison, in which the noun or other word after it is syntactically in apposition to another noun or pronoun in the clause (1-2). As a preposition, σάν takes the accusative (3). Normally, the noun after the conjunction σάν is non-specific, and therefore has no article; after the preposition σάν, the noun is accompanied by the definite article:

(1) τρώει σάν βασιλιάς 'he eats like a king';
(2) στέκονταν σάν μουδιασμένοι 'they were standing dazed [lit. 'as/ like numb']';
(3) τρώει σάν τό βασιλιά 'he eats like the king.'

Παρά. This too may act as a conjunction or as a preposition; it may also act as an adverb. As a conjunction it may introduce a 'than'-clause (e.g. περισσότερο έβλαψε παρά ωφέλησε 'it did more harm than good'); or it may be an adversative after a negative (e.g. στόν έρημο δρόμο δέν ακουγόταν τίποτα άλλο παρά ὁ χτύπος ἀπό τά καινούρια παπούτσια της 'nothing could be heard in the deserted street but the sound of her new shoes'). As an adverb, πάρα (stressed on the first syllable) may modify only the adjective πολύς (πάρα πολλοί 'very many; too many') or certain adverbs (mostly of place): here πάρα, which often combines with the adverb into one word, may be replaced by πιό 'more' (e.g. παρακάτω 'further down, further on'; παραπέρα 'further on, further away'). Finally, παρα- is a colloquial verbal prefix denoting excess (παραείναι πικρό 'it's too bitter', παραέφαγα 'I've overeaten').

As a preposition, παρά has three distinct meanings: 'against' or 'despite' (1); 'less' (with numerals), or by a certain margin (2–4); and temporal alternation (5):

(1) παρά τή θέλησή μου 'against my will';
(2) στίς δώδεκα παρά πέντε 'at five to twelve';
(3) έχασες τό Πρό-Πό παρά ένα νούμερο 'you've lost the football pools by one digit';
(4) παρά λίγο νά σκοτωθούμε 'we were nearly killed' (lit. 'by a-little to we-be-killed');
(5) μέρα παρά μέρα 'every other day'.

Κατά. This is not stressed when followed by the accusative; it has several quite separate meanings. Its traditional demotic meaning of 'towards' has largely been superseded in its spatial sense by πρός, but still remains in relation to time (= 'about': κατά τίς δέκα 'about 10 o'clock'). In SMG κατά has also preserved the meanings that it took on in katharevousa: 'according to' (often equivalent to σύμφωνα μέ, which is sometimes preferred by demoticists: (1)–(2)); 'during' (3); measure of difference (also (3)); and 'in respect of' (4):

(1) κατά τή γνώμη μου 'in my opinion';
(2) κατά τούς ἐμπειρογνώμονες 'according to the experts' (= σύμφωνα μέ);
(3) αὔξηση κατά 40% σημειώθηκε κατά τό πρῶτο τρίμηνο 'an increase of 40 per cent occurred [lit. 'was noted'] during the first three months' (κατά could be omitted each time);
(4) κατά τά ἄλλα περάσαμε καλά 'in other respects we had a good time [lit. 'we-passed well']'.

Κατά is also used with the genitive (see 6.2.6).

Μετά. Although demoticists often urge the use of the complex prepositions ὕστερα ἀπό or ἔπειτα ἀπό for 'after', μετά is the most frequent way of expressing this (it is also an adverb: 'afterwards', as in μετά τρεῖς μέρες or τρεῖς μέρες μετά 'three days later'). Syntactically, μετά is normally followed by ἀπό when it governs anything but a noun preceded by the definite article (μετά τόν πόλεμο 'after the war'; but μετά ἀπό ἔνα πόλεμο 'after a war'). Nevertheless, this general rule is not always followed, and many speakers always place ἀπό after μετά.

'Αντί. This too may be used with or without an additional preposition (in this case, γιά). Here the choice is a matter of style, ἀντί τό Γιάννη 'instead of John' being considered more elegant than ἀντί γιά τό Γιάννη. 'Αντί is never used as an adverb.

Πρός. In addition to its primary spatial meaning ('towards'), πρός has several other functions, especially 'towards' (of time: (1)); 'in respect of' (after nouns and adjectives: (2)–(3)); and purpose (4):

(1) πρός τό βράδι 'towards evening';
(2) ἡ ὑποστήριξη τῆς Σοβιετικῆς Ἑνωσης πρός τούς Κούρδους 'the support of the Soviet Union for the Kurds';
(3) ἡ γλώσσα στάθηκε μισαλλόδοξη πρός κάθε δάνειο 'the language remained intolerant towards all loanwords' (Kri. 1979: 34);
(4) ἀρνητική ἀπεδείχθη ἡ αὐτοψία πού ἔγινε χθές, ἀπό εἰδικούς ἀξιωματικούς τῶν Σωμάτων 'Ασφαλείας, πρός ἐντοπισμό στοιχείων γιά τούς δράστες τῶν ἐμπρησμῶν 'the on-the-spot investigation which was carried out yesterday by special officers of the Security Police with the aim of locating evidence concerning the culprits of the acts of arson proved negative' (K 23 Dec. 1980).

The expression ὡς πρός is used to mean 'in respect of, with respect to'.

6.2.6 OTHER PREPOSITIONS INHERITED FROM KATHAREVOUSA

There are numerous other prepositions which SMG has inherited from *katharevousa*. Some of these are in active use, some have a more restricted range, while others are mostly confined to fixed collocations.

Those prepositions in active use include:

ἐπί + acc. 'for the duration of': ἐπί τρεῖς συνεχεῖς μέρες 'for three days on end'; + gen. 'in the time of; under the rule of': ἐπί Νέας Δημοκρατίας 'under [the government of the] New Democracy [Party]'; or 'at the expense of': μιά νίκη ἐπί τῆς ΑΕΚ 'a victory over AEK [football team]';

κατά + gen. (stressed) 'against': κατά τῆς δικτατορίας 'against the dictatorship' (cf. κατά τή δικτατορία 'during the dictatorship');

μεταξύ + gen. 'among; between': μεταξύ φίλων 'among/between friends', μεταξύ μας 'between ourselves' (F *entre nous*); also used with reciprocal verb or equivalent: δέν πρόκειται νά ξαναπαντρευτοῦν μεταξύ τους 'there's no question of their marrying each other again', τά ὑφάσματα πρέπει νά ἔχουν τό ἴδιο πάχος μεταξύ τους 'the materials must have the same thickness (as each other)';

ὑπέρ + gen. 'for, on behalf of': εἶμαι ὑπέρ τῆς δημοκρατίας 'I'm in favour of democracy', τά ὑπέρ καί τά κατά 'the pros and cons'.

Μεταξύ is syntactically unusual among prepositions from *katharevousa* in being capable of governing clitic pronouns. Two other words of learned origin used as prepositions which may govern clitics are ἐναντίον 'against' and ἐξαιτίας 'because of', both always followed by the genitive.

Other, less active, prepositions include:

διά + gen. 'through the agency of': διά τῆς βίας 'by force';

ἐκτός + gen. 'outside': ἐκτός Ἀθηνῶν 'outside Athens', μία νίκη ἐκτός ἕδρας 'an away victory' (in football: lit. 'a victory outside seat');

περί + acc. 'about (approximately)': περί τά δύο ἐκατομμύρια 'about two million(s)'; + gen. 'about (concerning)': περί τίνος πρόκειται 'what it's all about';

πρό + gen. 'before; ago': πρό Χριστοῦ 'before Christ', πρό δέκα ἐτῶν 'ten years ago';

ὑπό + acc. 'under (fig.)': ἔπαιξε ἡ ὀρχήστρα τῆς Ρωμανικῆς Ἑλβετίας ὑπό τή διεύθυνση τοῦ Ἐρνέστ Ἀνσερμέ '[it] was played by the Suisse Romande Orchestra conducted by [lit. 'under the direction of'] Ernest Ansermet.'

To these should be added the prepositions used in mathematics:
σύν 'plus', also used colloquially and figuratively with either acc. or nom.;

ἐπί 'multiplied by', especially in phrases of measurement: ἔνα κελλί τρία ἐπί τέσσερα 'a three by four [metre] cell';

διά 'divided by';

μεῖον or πλήν 'minus'.

Finally there are prepositions which are used only in fixed expressions:

ἄνευ + gen. 'without': ἐργασία ἄνευ ἀποδοχῶν 'unpaid work' (lit. 'work without emoluments');

εἰς + acc. 'in, at, etc.': εἰς βάρος 'at the expense (of)', εἰς ὑγείαν 'to [your] health', εἰς εἶδος 'in kind';

ἐκ + gen. 'from': ἐκ τῶν προτέρων 'in advance';

ἐν + dative (a case which exists in *katharevousa* but not in demotic) 'in': ἐντάξει 'O.K.' (lit. 'in order'), ἐν ἀνάγκη 'if need be' (lit. 'in need').

Despite the large number of examples that have been provided in the previous sections, there is an even larger number of special uses of the various prepositions which have not been included. The aim of these sections on prepositions has been simply to divide them into valid categories and to examine the general tendencies within each category.

6.3 THE USES OF THE PRONOUNS

6.3.1 PERSONAL PRONOUNS

MG has two types of personal pronoun: *clitic* (unemphatic) and *emphatic* (disjunctive).

6.3.1.1 *Clitic pronouns*

These may be either *proclitic* (i.e. placed immediately before a verb) or *enclitic* (i.e. immediately following the word which governs them). Except in a limited number of circumstances, clitic pronouns have no nominative, since the subject of a verb (if it is not a noun, adjective or clause) is not stated unless it is to be emphasized.

Clitic pronouns are used with the following classes of word, with which they form a single phonological word:

(i) Verbs: in the accusative or genitive (cf. 2.2.4.1), as direct and indirect objects respectively; the pronouns precede finite forms of the verb, but follow the imperative and the present participle (e.g. σοῦ τό ἔστειλα 'I sent it to you', δός μου το 'give it to me', βλέποντάς τες 'seeing them (fem.)');

(ii) Nouns: in the genitive, as possessive pronouns (e.g. ὁ πατέρας μου 'my father') (cf. 2.2.4.2);

(iii) Adjectives: occasionally, in the genitive, after comparatives (e.g. μεγαλύτερή σου 'larger/older (fem.) than you') (cf. 2.2.4.3);

(iv) Pronouns: in the genitive, in order to specify person (κανένας μας 'any/none of us', ὁ καθένας σας 'each of you', ὅλες τους 'all (fem.) of them' (cf. 2.2.4.3);

(v) Numerals: in the genitive, to specify person (ὁ ἕνας τους 'one of them', οἱ δυό τους 'the two of them; both of them') (cf. 2.2.4.3);

(vi) Adverbs of place and time: in the genitive (e.g. μαζί μας 'with us) (cf. 2.2.4.4);

(vii) Exclamatory words (usually in wishes or curses): in the genitive (e.g. μπράβο της 'good for her', ἀλίμονό σου 'woe betide you', περαστικά του 'may he get well soon') (cf. 2.2.4.6);

(viii) Καλῶς: in the accusative (καλῶς τον 'welcome') (cf. 2.2.3);

(ix) Ποὖν' and νά: (third person) in the nominative or (first and second persons, only after νά) in the accusative (e.g. ποὖν' τος; 'where is he?', νά τος! 'there he is!', νά με πάλι! 'here I am again!' (cf. 4.4.2).

With nouns taking clitic pronouns should be included the reflexive τόν ἐαυτό (μου) '(my) self' (cf. 4.5.3.2). The possessive pronoun may also follow an adjective or other premodifier either when the premodifier functions as a noun (ἕνας γνωστός μας ἀξιωματικός 'an acquaintance of ours who is an officer' [lit. 'a known of-us officer']), or when the pronoun really qualifies the noun modified by the premodifier (τό παλιό μας αὐτοκίνητο 'our old car': = (a) 'our car, which happens to be old', or (b) 'our previous car'): this last phenomenon appears to take place often for purely euphonic reasons, in order to avoid the placing of a second stress on a proparoxytone (i.e. τό παλιό αὐτοκίνητό μας, which is equally normal, but only in meaning (b)). The possessive is often absent when parts of the body or personal belongings are referred to:

(1) στεκότανε στήν πόρτα μέ τό καπέλο στό χέρι 'he stood at the door with [his] hat in [his] hand.'

Verbs may be found with up to two clitic pronouns; but if there are two together, the first must be in the genitive and the second both accusative and third-person. This means that (a) first- and second-person clitic pronouns do not co-occur; (b) a first- or second-person pronoun precedes a third-person; and (c) a genitive precedes an accusative.

The neuter singular τό (sometimes the plural τά) is often used to refer to a whole clause:

(2)   — Τά 'μαϑες; Πέϑανε ὁ Μπρέζνιεφ. — Ναί, τό ξέρω. ' "Have you heard (it)? Brezhnev's died." "Yes, I know (it)" ';

(3)   τό 'κανα χωρίς νά τό ϑέλω 'I did it without wanting [to do] it.'

In (2), τά perhaps refers to τά νέα 'the news', while τό before ξέρω is optional. In (3), the τό before ϑέλω stands for νά τό κάνω.

There are many idiomatic expressions in which a proclitic pronoun used with a verb does not appear to refer to any particular referent: some of these will be examined in 11.2.

An important function of the clitic pronoun is its *proleptic* and *resumptive* uses. When used proleptically, the clitic pronoun anticipates the object proper (a noun, emphatic pronoun, etc.) (4); when used resumptively it recalls an object which has already been stated (5):

(4)   τήν ξέρεις τή Λούλα; 'do you know (her) Loula?';

(5)   τή Λούλα τήν ξέρω 'I know (her) Loula.'

A clitic pronoun is always used when ὅλα ('all') is the direct object (τά ξέρεις ὅλα 'you know everything').

Whether or not a proleptic or resumptive pronoun is used depends largely on which part (if any) of the clause is being emphasized by the speaker/writer, that is (in most cases) which part of the clause contains new information (the *focus* or *rheme*) as opposed to the already known topic (or *theme*) of the discourse. Nevertheless, the proleptic and resumptive uses must be examined to some extent separately.

When a clitic pronoun is used proleptically, the object proper of the verb must be a noun (or some other word) preceded by a definite article, or an emphatic pronoun (which includes a demonstrative used pronominally), or a clause. When the object proper is anything but a clause, the presence of the proleptic pronoun is normal in ordinary speech if the emphasis is on any part of the clause *except* the object (i.e. the object is the topic of the clause) (6a and 6b); the absence of a proleptic pronoun may make the expression neutral (with no particular emphasis on any element) or may serve to place an emphasis on the object (which then becomes the focus) (7a and 7b). In speech, of course, a heavy stress is placed on that part of the utterance which is to be emphasized.

(6a) τό θέλω αὐτό τό βιβλίο 'I *want* this book' (the book has already been mentioned);

(6b) θέλω αὐτό τό βιβλίο 'I want this *book*' or '*this* book' (perhaps in answer to the question τί θέλεις; 'what do you want?' or ποιό βιβλίο θέλεις; 'which book do you want?');

(7a) ὁ Γιάννης τήν ἀγαπάει τή Μαρία '*John* loves Mary' or 'John *loves* Mary';

(7b) ὁ Γιάννης ἀγαπάει τή Μαρία 'John loves Mary' (either neutral, or with emphasis on *Mary*, depending on stress).

In more elevated styles, however, perhaps under the influence of *katharevousa*, the proleptic pronoun may be absent even when the emphasis is on the verb or subject. When the object of the verb is a noun clause (especially one introduced by ὅτι or πώς or by an interrogative), a proleptic pronoun is used in colloquial speech when the verb is the focus:

(8a) τό φαντάζόμουνα πώς δέ θυμᾶσαι 'I *imagined* you wouldn't remember' (the speaker's collocutor has already given indications that (s)he does not remember);

(8b) φαντάζόμουνα πώς δέ θυμᾶσαι 'I imagined you wouldn't *remember*' (here the indications are that the collocutor *does* remember);

(9) σέ ξέρω τί ψεύτης εἶσαι 'I *know* what a liar you are.'

Again, in more elevated styles, the proleptic pronoun may be absent even when the verb is the focus of the clause.

The resumptive uses of the pronoun are similar to these except that (a) the exclusion of nouns without definite articles does not apply (10); (b) more types of noun clause are used with resumptive than with proleptic pronouns (e.g. clauses introduced by ὅ,τι, ὅσος, etc.) (11); and (c) resumptive pronouns are used to recall the relative pronouns πού and (occasionally) ὁ ὁποῖος. Once again, the resumptive pronoun is often absent in less colloquial styles.

(6c) αὐτό τό βιβλίο τό θέλω 'I *want* this book';

(6d) αὐτό τό βιβλίο θέλω 'I want *this* book' or 'this *book*' (depending on intonation);

(7c) τή Μαρία τήν ἀγαπάει ὁ Γιάννης '*John* loves Mary' or 'John *loves* Mary';

(7d) τή Μαρία ἀγαπάει ὁ Γιάννης 'John loves *Mary*';

(10) φροῦτα τά τρώει καμιά φορά '(s)he *eats* fruit from time to

time' (i.e. 'as for fruit, (s)he does eat it . . .': this is connected with τρώει φρούτα, not τρώει τά φρούτα);

(11) ὅ,τι εἶχα νά πῶ, τό εἶπα 'what I had to say I've said (it)'.

For the correlation between word order and focus, see 7.1.

With the relative pronoun the resumptive clitic has various different functions. One of these is (a) to distinguish a defining from a non-defining clause: in the former (12a), unlike in the latter (12b), the clitic pronoun is not normally used for the direct object when it has the same referent as the relative:

(12a) ἡ γυναίκα πού εἶδε ὁ Γιάννης ἦταν ἡ μητέρα τῆς κοπέλας 'the woman John saw was the girl's mother';

(12b) ἡ Μαρία, πού τήν εἶδε ὁ Γιάννης, ἦταν ἡ μητέρα τῆς κοπέλας 'Mary, whom John saw, was the girl's mother.'

Another function of the resumptive clitic is (b) to distinguish a relative clause in which the antecedent of the relative pronoun acts as the subject of the verb from one in which it acts as the object: the clitic cannot of course be used in the former (13a), whereas it may in the latter (13b):

(13a) ὁ ἄντρας πού σκότωσε τό παιδί 'the man who killed the child';

(13b) ὁ ἄντρας πού τόν σκότωσε τό παιδί 'the man whom the child killed', or 'the man who was killed by the child'.

It appears that the function which distinguishes (13a) from (13b) (i.e. subject from object) is more powerful than the one that distinguishes (12a) from (12b) (i.e. defining from non-defining clause), in that function (b) may override function (a), especially when (as in (13a) and (13b)) it is not clear from the morphological form of a noun phrase in the relative clause (in this case τό παιδί) whether it is the subject or object of the verb. A clitic pronoun may also be used in other instances where the clause would otherwise be ambiguous; and it regularly stands as the indirect object in the relative clause (see 8.1.1).

6.3.1.2 Emphatic pronouns

These are used only when their referents are to be given special emphasis. The first- and second-person emphatic pronouns have a nominative and an accusative form (the latter acting additionally as a genitive); the third-person pronouns are broadly identical to demonstratives: see 4.4.1.

Despite being emphatic, these pronouns do not always constitute the focus of a clause: thus they may or may not co-occur with clitic pronouns:

(14a) ἐμένα τό εἶπε '(s)he told *me* (it)' (i.e. not you or anyone else: ἐμένα is the focus);

(14b) ἐμένα μοῦ εἶπε τό ἀντίθετο '(s)he told *me* the *opposite*' (i.e. 'of what (s)he told you': here the direct object is the focus: i.e. 'as for me, (s)he told me the opposite').

When the emphatic pronoun represents a genitive of possession, it generally co-occurs with a clitic possessive pronoun:

(15) ἐσένα ἡ μάνα σου εἶναι ἄσκημη '*your* mother's *ugly*.'

Finally, emphatic pronouns are used in elliptical sentences:

(16) — Ποιός ἔσπασε τό τζάμι; — 'Εγώ. ' "Who broke the window?" "I [did]." '

6.3.2 DEMONSTRATIVES

The demonstratives αὐτός, ἐκεῖνος, and τοῦτος may be used adjectivally (with a noun) or pronominally (as emphatic third-person pronouns). What Tzartzanos (1946: 138–9) says about the difference in meaning between these three words may once have been true: namely, that τοῦτος was used for referents close to the speaker, αὐτός for those close to the hearer, and ἐκεῖνος for those removed from either (cf. the three adverbs of place 'here' and 'there': ἐδῶ, αὐτοῦ, ἐκεῖ). But today this three-term system appears to have broken down, with τοῦτος being largely absent from more elevated styles (unless, paradoxically, the writer/speaker is imitating *katharevousa* οὗτος), it being considered to sound rather vulgar, at least when it is used about a person; the same is true of αὐτοῦ, which traditionally corresponded not to τοῦτος but to αὐτός. A two-term system now prevails, αὐτός being the unmarked form, indicating referents close to either speaker or hearer, while ἐκεῖνος is the marked form, for referents distant from both.

When the demonstratives are used to indicate a referent which is present not in reality but in the discourse, αὐτός may stand in opposition to ἐκεῖνος, αὐτός meaning 'the latter', ἐκεῖνος 'the former'. 'Εκεῖνος is often used to indicate a change of grammatical subject:

(1) παρακάλεσε τήν κόρη της νά γυρίσει πίσω, ἀλλά ἐκείνη δέν τήν ἄκουσε 'she begged her daughter to return, but she [i.e. the daughter] did not listen (to her).'

Αὐτός however is commonly used to refer to an indefinite subject modified by a relative clause:

(2) αὐτοί πού λένε τέτοια πράγματα . . . 'those who say such things . . .'

The neuter αὐτό is used to refer to the content of a whole phrase, whether preceding or following:

(3) Ποιός τόν σκότωσε; Αὐτό νά μοῦ πεῖς. 'Who killed him? That's what you should tell me.'

An important function of αὐτός in speech is as a substitute for a noun which the speaker cannot bring to mind: it is normally preceded by the definite article, and is often followed characteristically by πῶς (τό) λένε; 'what's (it) called?'. It may even be used in the vocative:

(4) δός μου τό αὐτό [, πῶς τό λένε;] 'give me the thingummy [, what's it called?'];

(5) δέν ἦρθε ἀκόμα ἡ αὐτή; 'hasn't whatsername come yet?';

(6) ἔλα δῶ αὐτέ [, πῶς σέ λένε;] 'come here you [, what's your name?]'

This use of αὐτός has also given rise to a verb, αὐτώνω 'I whatsit', when the speaker cannot recall (or, in its vulgar use, does not want to utter) the relevant verb:

(7) θά 'ρθουν σήμερα τά μηχανήματα ν' αὐτώσουνε [here = στρώσουν] τό δρόμο 'the machines are coming today to whatsit [= resurface] the road.'

The above use of αὐτός should not be confused with another meaning of ὁ αὐτός, namely 'the same' (see 4.5.3.1).

The other MG demonstratives are τέτοιος 'such [a]; that sort of' and τόσος 'so much/many'.

6.3.3 REFLEXIVE AND RECIPROCAL EXPRESSIONS

With many verbs, reflexive and reciprocal meanings can be achieved with the use of the passive; the construction ὁ ἕνας τόν ἄλλον (only used with verbs in active sense) may also convey reciprocal action (see 3.1.2.2 and 3.1.2.3).

With these alternatives available for the expression of reflexive meaning, the reflexive ὁ ἑαυτός (μου) is not used as frequently as the reflexive pronoun is in French or English. In fact, ὁ ἑαυτός (μου) tends to be used mostly when it does not function as the direct object of a verb, except when the reflexive has a relationship with some other word(s) in the same sentence:

(1) δέν μπόρεσε νά τό ὁμολογήσει στόν ἑαυτό της 'she was unable to admit it to herself';

(2) καμιά φορά πιάνουμε τόν ἑαυτό μας νά λέει πράγματα πού δέ θέλουμε νά ποῦμε 'sometimes we catch ourselves saying things we don't want to say.'

As in English, so in MG, a personal pronoun, not a reflexive, is used after prepositional phrases expressing spatial relationship:

(3) κοίταξε γύρω της 'she looked around her';

(4) ἔχεις λεφτά πάνω σου; 'have you [any] money on you?'

6.3.4 INTENSIVE PRONOUNS

The pronoun ὁ ἴδιος has two different functions. When followed immediately by a noun, it means 'the same'; when followed by a definite article modifying a noun, or when preceded by a pronoun or by a noun with a definite article, it means '(my)self' not in a reflexive but in an emphatic sense. In each sense, ὁ ἴδιος may also be used (as in (4) and (5)) without modifying a stated pronoun or noun:

(1) εἶδαν τήν ἴδια ταινία τρεῖς φορές 'they saw the same film three times';

(2) ἐσύ ὁ ἴδιος τό εἶπες 'you yourself said it';

(3) θέλω νά μιλήσω στόν ἴδιο τόν Ἀλέξη 'I want to speak to Alexis himself';

(4) τό ἴδιο ἔγινε καί σέ μᾶς 'the same thing happened to us';

(5) θά τό κάνει ὁ ἴδιος 'he'll do it himself.'

Ὁ ἴδιος may be used by a speaker on the telephone to inform the caller that (s)he is the person sought:

(5) — Τήν κυρία Παυλοπούλου παρακαλῶ. — Ἡ ἴδια. ' "Mrs Pavlo-poulos, please." "Speaking." '

Ὁ ἴδιος may be used with a possessive personal pronoun when the emphasis is not on the possessor but on what is possessed (contrast δικός (μου)), and even with the reflexive τόν ἑαυτό (μου):

(7) τό εἶδα μέ τά ἴδια μου τά μάτια 'I saw it with my own eyes';

(8) τέτοια πράγματα δέν τά λέμε ἀκόμα καί στόν ἴδιο μας τόν ἐαυτό 'we don't say such things even to our own selves.'

The intensive pronoun μόνος (μου) 'by myself' may be used, like its English rendering, to mean 'in solitude' or 'without assistance' (see 2.2.4.3). It may also be used in a reflexive sense: see 3.1.2.2.

6.3.5 INTERROGATIVE, INDEFINITE, AND PARTITIVE PRONOUNS

The interrogative pronouns τί 'what' and ποιός 'who; which' (like the interrogative adverbs) are used in both direct and indirect questions; each may be used with or without a noun. When a person is referred to, but a noun is absent, ποιός is used. When τί or ποιός is used with a noun (whether the referent is a person or not), the difference in meaning is broadly similar to that between 'what' and 'which' in English: i.e. ποιός is used to refer to one or more of a specified group of referents, while τί is more universal (often with the implication 'what sort of'):

(1) βλέπουμε σέ τί κατασκευάσματα ὁδηγοῦνται ὁρισμένοι ῥήτορές μας 'we see what [linguistic] concoctions certain of our public speakers are led to' (Kri. 1979: 34);

(2) ποιό εἶναι τώρα τό συμπέρασμα ὅπου πρέπει νά καταλήξουμε; 'which is the conclusion we should now reach [lit. 'where we must finish']?' (ibid.: 38).

Τί is often used to express disbelief or contradiction when it precedes a word or phrase repeated from the interlocutor's speech:

(3) — Δουλεύω σκληρά. — Τί σκληρά βρέ, πού βλέπεις ὅλη μέρα τηλεόραση; ' "I work hard." "What [do you mean,] hard, when you watch television all day?" '

Τί may often be substituted for γιατί (cf. English 'what for') when the meaning is clear from the context:

(4) τί μέ κοιτᾶς ἔτσι; 'what are you looking at me like that for?'

Τί is also used as an exclamatory word, especially with an adjective or adverb:

(5) τί ὡραία πού εἶσαι! 'how beautiful you are!'

Finally, it may be used to indicate that the difference between the referents of two nouns is minimal:

(6) τί Λωζάννη, τί Κοζάνη; 'Kozani is every bit as civilized as Lausanne' (lit. 'what Lausanne, what Kozani?').

The equivalents of the interrogative pronouns in declarative sentences are κάτι 'something', τό κάθε τί 'every single thing', κάποιος 'someone', and (ὁ) καθένας 'each one'. While τό κάθε τί may not be used with a noun, κάτι may modify an animate or inanimate noun in the plural (i.e. it may appear as a partitive determiner, in which case it is never obligatory: (7)); καθένας is not normally used with a noun (contrast κάθε 'each, every') and may refer only to a person (no plural); and κάποιος may refer only to a person when it is used without a noun, but with a noun it may have an animate or inanimate referent (8):

(7) ἥρθανε κάτι φαντάροι 'some soldiers came/have come' (κάτι could be omitted or replaced by κάποιοι);
(8) τό πρόσωπό της φανέρωνε κάποια στενοχώρια 'her face displayed a certain worry.'

The negative equivalents are τίποτα 'nothing' and κανένας 'no one; no' (which in these meanings always co-occur with a verbal negative except when used elliptically in a verbless sentence). These may also be used non-negatively in 'yes/no' questions ('anything', 'anyone; any') and in sentences expressing possibility, that is, especially with verbs in the subjunctive or imperative ('something or other', 'some[one] or other'). When τίποτα is used with a noun (animate or inanimate), the latter must be plural; κανένας refers to a person when used without a noun, but may refer equally to an animate or an inanimate referent when used with a noun:

(9a) δέ θέλω τίποτα 'I don't want anything';
(9b) — Τί θέλεις; — Τίποτα. ' 'What do you want?" "Nothing." ';
(10a) δέ βρήκαμε κανέναν 'we didn't find anyone';
(10b) — Ποιόν βρήκατε; — Κανέναν. ' "Whom did you find?" "No one." ';
(11) ψώνισες τίποτα φροῦτα; 'did you buy any fruit(s) at all?';
(12) μπορεῖ νά κολλήσω καμιά ἀρρώστεια ἐκεῖ μέσα 'I may catch some disease or other in there';

(13) φέρε μας καί καμιά πατάτα τηγανητή 'bring us some chips [lit. 'some fried potato or other'] too.'

Κανένας, especially in its non-adjectival personal use, has an alternative form κανείς in the masculine nominative singular. When used after a verb without a negative, κανείς means 'one' (French *on*); in this meaning, κανείς is uninflected for gender and may only be the subject of the verb.

There are some assertive uses of κανένας. These include the phrase καμιά φορά 'from time to time, occasionally', and constructions with a group of nouns denoting approximate number (e.g. καμιά δεκαριά 'about ten').

In speech, the genitive of κάποιος and κανένας, when used as an indirect object referring to a person, is often replaced by κάπου (lit. 'somewhere') and πουθενά ('nowhere') respectively. A similar phenomenon occurs with αλλού 'elsewhere', which is often used to mean 'to someone else'; and sometimes with πού ('where') for 'to whom':

(14) μήν τό πετάς—δός το κάπου 'don't throw it away—give it to someone';

(15) αλλού νά τά λές αυτά! 'don't give me that nonsense!' (lit. 'elsewhere to them you-say these');

(16) πού έμοιασες; 'whom do you take after?' (lit. 'where you-resembled?').

There are no partitive pronouns for use with singular nouns:

(17a) ήπιαμε κάτι 'we drank something';
(17b) ήπιαμε κρασί 'we drank wine/some wine';
(18a) ήπιατε τίποτα; 'did you drink anything?';
(18b) ήπιατε κρασί; 'did you drink wine/any wine?';
(19a) δέν ήπιαμε τίποτα 'we didn't drink anything';
(19b) δέν ήπιαμε κρασί 'we didn't drink wine/any wine.'

Nothing need be said about the quantifiers πολύς 'much; many' and λίγος '(a) little; (a) few', except that the latter is more often used in a negative (= 'not much/many') than in a positive sense. The positive quantifiers include μερικοί 'some, a few' (always plural) and κάμποσος 'quite a lot of'.

TABLE 6.1. Correspondence table of proforms

	Pronoun†		Adverb		
	Animate	*Inanimate*	*Place*	*Time*	*Manner*
Contrastive	ἄλλος 'other'	ἄλλο 'other'	ἀλλοῦ 'elsewhere'	ἄλλοτε 'at another time'	ἀλλιῶς 'otherwise'
Indefinite (assertive)	κάποιος 'someone' ἕνας 'one' μερικοί 'some'	κάτι 'something'	κάπου 'somewhere'	κάποτε 'once'	κάπως 'somehow; somewhat'
Indefinite (non-assertive)	κανένας 'no one; anyone'	τίποτα 'nothing, anything'	πουθενά 'nowhere; anywhere'	ποτέ 'never; ever'	καθόλου 'not at all; at all'
Interrogative (and exclamatory*)	ποιός 'who' πόσοι 'how many'	τί* 'what' πόσο* 'how much'	ποῦ 'where'	πότε 'when'	πῶς 'how' (γιατί 'why')
Demonstrative	αὐτό, ἐκεῖνος 'this, that' τέτοιος 'such a one' τόσοι 'so many'	αὐτό, ἐκεῖνο 'this, that' τέτοιο 'such a one' τόσο 'so much'	ἐδῶ 'here' ἐκεῖ 'there'	τώρα 'now' τότε 'then'	ἔτσι 'thus'

Relative and correlative	ποὖ, ὁ ὁποῖος 'who' ὅποιος 'whoever' ὅσοι 'as many as'	ὅ,τι 'that which' ὅσο 'as much as'	ὅπου 'where'	ὅταν 'when' ὅποτε 'whenever'	ὅπως, καθώς 'as'
Universal	κάθε 'each' καθένας 'each one' ὅλοι 'everyone' ὁποιοσδήποτε 'anyone'	τό κάθε τί 'each thing' ὅλα 'everything' ὁτιδήποτε 'anything'	παντοῦ 'everywhere' ὁπουδήποτε 'anywhere'	(σέ κάθε στιγμή 'at every moment') πάντα 'always' ὁποτεδήποτε 'at any time'	(μέ κάθε τρόπο 'in every way') (πάντως 'in any case') ὁπωσδήποτε 'in any case'

† Most of these can also be used adjectivally, in which case πόσος, τόσος, ὅσος, and ὅλος are fully declinable.

7

THE CLAUSE: WORD ORDER; CO-ORDINATION; NEGATION

7.1 WORD ORDER IN THE CLAUSE

7.1.1 THE ORDER OF SUBJECT, VERB, AND DIRECT OBJECT

As has been said before, MG presents a high degree of flexibility in its word order. Since MG is a highly inflected language, it is normally clear from the morphological forms which word or phrase is the subject of the verb and which is the object. (In this section, 'object' refers to a noun phrase (not a clitic pronoun) used as the direct object of a verb.) Thus word order in MG does not serve a *syntactical* function, as it does in English, where the order SVO (Subject–Verb–Object) is almost always obligatory in a declarative clause. This does not however mean that any order of subject, verb, and object in MG has precisely the same sense as any other; word order in MG is used (together with clitic pronouns, and with intonation in speech) to indicate which part of the clause contains the new information which is being conveyed (the *focus*).

What is certain is that the order SVO in MG is not the only neutral one (i.e. that in which no part of the clause bears more emphasis than any other, because each element conveys equally new information). Warburton (1982) has shown that the order SVO may be the result of the thematization of the subject, that is, the process whereby the *theme* (the already known topic of the sentence) is placed early in the clause as the subject of the verb: the *focus*, if any, tends to be placed at the end. MG tends to have *end-weight*: i.e. the main emphasis of a sentence regularly falls at the end, unless some other part of the sentence is heavily stressed in speech. (A distinction should be made here between stress, which is phonetic, and emphasis, which is semantic.) If one examines sentences which have no theme or topic (e.g. ones that begin a new subject of conversation and do not presuppose that the hearer knows any of the information contained in them), one notices that a large number of them have the order VSO. Thus the order VSO must be considered as being one of the neutral orders:

(1) Τά 'μαθες τά νέα; Ὁ Ἐλύτης πῆρε τό Νόμπελ, or Πῆρε ὁ Ἐλύτης τό Νόμπελ. 'Have you heard the news? Elytis has won the Nobel [Prize].'

Here the speaker is not trying to emphasize that it is Elytis (and not another writer) who has won the prize, nor that Elytis has won the Nobel Prize rather than any other prize; (s)he is simply stating a bare fact. Nevertheless, in normal speech, the strongest stress (and emphasis) in an unmarked sentence will fall on the last phonological word.

When a neutral clause has no object or complement, the order VS is far more likely than SV: indeed, SV is normally impossible if the verb denotes existence or occurrence (this last seems to be a tendency in English too):

(2) μιά φορά κι ἔναν καιρό ἦταν ἔνας βασιλιάς 'once upon a time there was a king';

(3) Τά 'μαθες; Ἔγινε σεισμός στή Θεσσαλονίκη. 'Have you heard? There's been an earthquake in Salonica.'

Horrocks (1980) has formulated some convincing rules about MG word order. According to his analysis, SVO and VSO are the neutral orders in declarative main clauses and in subordinate clauses introduced by ὅτι/πώς. One could also add causal clauses introduced by γιατί, ἐπειδή and ἀφοῦ, or, roughly, most of those types of clause (except relative clauses) which are not introduced by a subjunctive marker. The word order in yes/no interrogative sentences is normally no different. Horrocks gives the following examples (which I have slightly amplified):

(4a) ὁ πατέρας μου διαβάξει Καζαντξάκη (SVO);
(4b) Καζαντξάκη διαβάξει ὁ πατέρας μου (OVS);
(4c) διαβάξει ὁ πατέρας μου Καζαντξάκη (VSO);
(4d) διαβάξει Καζαντξάκη ὁ πατέρας μου (VOS) 'my father is reading/reads Kazantzakis.'

The following alternative interpretations may be made of each of (4a)–(4d):

(4a) (i) No particular emphasis (neutral); in speech, main stress fall on last word;

(ii) Heavy stress on subject: 'it's my *father* (not anyone else) who . . .';

(iii) Heavy stress on verb: 'my father *is* reading [or '*does* read'] Kazantzakis' (contradicting previous speaker);

(iv) Heavy stress on object: 'it's *Kazantzakis* (not any other author) that . . .'.

(4b) (i) Heavy stress on object: as (4a) (iv);

(ii) Heavy stress on verb: rather like (4a) (iii), but more tentative; the meaning of the verb is likely to be habitual rather than progressive, and the clause is likely to be followed by some qualification (e.g. 'my father *does* read K., but not often');

(iii) Heavy stress on subject: as (4a) (ii).

(4c) (i) No particular emphasis (as (4a) (i));

(ii) Heavy stress on verb: as (4a) (iii).

(4d) (i) Heavy stress on verb: as (4a) (iii);

(ii) Heavy stress on object: as (4a) (iv).

The most frequently found orders for each type of emphasis are the following:

(i) No particular emphasis: SVO or VSO;

(ii) Heavy emphasis on subject: OVS;

(iii) Heavy emphasis on verb: VOS;

(iv) Heavy emphasis on object: OVS.

It should be pointed out that not all the possible interpretations have been included in the above list, and that it is not impossible for the verb to appear at the end of the clause. In addition, as we have seen, when the object is a noun preceded by the definite article, special emphasis can be indicated by the presence or absence of a proleptic or resumptive pronoun (6.3.1.1).

In direct and indirect question clauses introduced by interrogative adverbs (or by interrogative pronouns governed by prepositions), SVO, VSO, and VOS are all possible neutral orders (Horrocks 1980). Nevertheless, the verb more usually comes first (i.e. immediately after the interrogative word):

(5a) πότε ἔγραψε ὁ Γιάννης τό γράμμα; } 'when did John write

(5b) πότε ἔγραψε τό γράμμα ὁ Γιάννης; } the letter?'

In direct and indirect question clauses introduced by interrogative pronouns, in which the interrogative word is the subject or direct object of the verb, the verb must stand immediately after the interrogative pronoun:

(6) τί θέλει ὁ κύριος; 'what does the gentleman want?';
(7) δέν ξέρω ποιός θά βρεῖ τή λύση 'I don't know who will find the solution.'

(In sentences such as τί δικαιολογία ἔχεις; 'what excuse have you?', the noun phrase τί δικαιολογία cannot be split, the τί acting not as a pronoun proper but as a determiner.) When the interrogative pronoun is in the genitive, the verb may precede or follow the other constituents of the clause:

(8) δέν ἤξερα ποιανοῦ ἦταν τό σπίτι πού βρισκόμουνα 'I didn't know whose house I was in';
(9) τίνος παιδί εἶσαι; 'whose child are you?'

In other subordinate clauses the most common neutral order is for the verb immediately to follow the conjunction. Nevertheless, in written styles (but never in νά- or ἄς-clauses), the subject is often placed before the verb. It is possible that in writing, Greek speakers have been influenced by *katharevousa*, which tries to approximate to the SVO order of French, and that this influence extends even to those kinds of subordinate clause in which this order was not frequently found in natural speech. Moreover, today the written order seems to have influenced the spoken, especially when the subject is emphasized:

(10) ἐσύ θά κάνεις πίσω μέ τό πρῶτο σημάδι καί θά τῆς ξαναδίνεις ὅταν ἡ ἴδια θά σοῦ ζητήσει τό φαγητό 'you will draw back at the first sign and you will give [it] to her again when she herself asks for the food.'

Again, if the verb denotes existence or occurrence, the order is always VS. The relative pronoun πού always comes at the beginning of the clause, whether it is the subject or direct object, or neither; and it is almost always followed immediately by the verb. When the genitive of the relative pronoun ὁ ὁποῖος is used, the subject or object frequently comes immediately after it:

(11) τά δέκα περιπολικά σκάφη, τῶν ὁποίων τή ναυπήγηση ἀνέθεσε τό Πολεμικό μας Ναυτικό στά Ναυπηγεῖα Σκαραμαγκᾶ . . .

'the ten patrol vessels, whose construction our (Military) Navy has entrusted to the Skaramanga Shipyards . . .' (*T* 2 July 1981, 26).

In *νά*-clauses, the verb must immediately follow *νά*. But the topic of the *νά*-clause (subject or object) may be placed before *νά* so that the emphasis may fall on the focus at the end of the clause:

(12a) θέλω ἡ Ρούλα νά παντρευτεῖ τό Μίμη 'I want Roula (nom.) to marry *Mimis*';

(12b) θέλω τό Μίμη νά τόν παντρευτεῖ ἡ Ρούλα 'I want *Roula* to marry Mimis';

(13a) πέρασε τό λεωφορεῖο χωρίς ὁ Πέτρος νά τό προσέξει 'the bus went by without Peter (nom.) *noticing* it';

(13b) πέρασε τό λεωφορεῖο χωρίς νά τό προσέξει ὁ Πέτρος 'the bus went by without *Peter* (nom.) noticing it.'

Nevertheless, as has been mentioned before, thematization of a direct object may be achieved by the use of a clitic pronoun, irrespective of word order. Thus (12c) has the same emphasis as (12b) (i.e. on the subject of the subordinate verb):

(12c) θέλω νά τόν παντρευτεῖ ἡ Ρούλα τό Μίμη.

When the main stress of a clause falls at the end, any part of the clause from the end forward may convey new information (14); but when the heavy stress falls further forward, nothing *after* the stress is new information ((15)–(17)). The latter phenomenon is shown especially in answers which partially echo their questions:

(14) — Τί κάνετε τώρα; — Πᾶμε στήν Ἀθήνα. ' "What are you doing now?" "We're going to Athens" ';

(15) — Ποῦ πᾶτε τώρα; — Στήν Ἀθήνα πᾶμε. ' "Where are you going now?" "We're going to *Athens*" ';

(16) — Πῆγες χθές; — Ὄχι, σήμερα πάω. ' "Did you go yesterday?" "No, I'm going *today*" ';

(17) — Πέτυχε ὁ Σάκης; — Ὄχι, τόν κόψανε τόν καημένο. ' "Did Sakis pass?" "No, they *failed* the poor fellow." '

In (15) and (16) the information after the emphasized words is repeated from the question (thus it constitutes the topic); and in (17) the last two words add no new *information* to what has already been said.

In some styles, however, especially in journalism and broadcasting, the focus is often placed at the very beginning of a long sentence:

(18) καιρό καλό μέ λίγες τοπικές νεφώσεις στά ἠπειρωτικά προ-
βλέπει γιά σήμερα ἡ Ἐθνική Μετεωρολογική Ὑπηρεσία
'the National Meteorological Service forecasts good weather
with local cloud in mainland [Greece] (for) today';

(19) ξυπόλυτος μπῆκε σέ κατάστημα τῆς περιοχῆς Νέας Ἐλβετίας
νεαρός, καί ἔφυγε . . . παπουτσωμένος '[a] youth entered [a]
shop in the Nea Elvetia district barefoot, and left wearing
shoes!' (the emphasis in the first clause is on the fact that he
was barefoot) (T 4 Nov. 1982, 64).

A similar front-focusing occurs in elliptical press headlines:

(20) μάγειρας ὁ δολοφόνος 'the murderer [is/was a] cook.'

7.1.2 THE POSITION OF ADVERBIALS

Just as there is a large measure of flexibility in the order of subject,
verb, and direct object in MG, so adverbs and adverbial phrases may be
placed in various positions in the clause. It is difficult to generalize on
this matter; but a characteristic position of an adverbial of time, as also
that of a sentential adverb, is at the beginning of a clause, while an
adverbial of manner usually immediately follows the verb (it hardly
ever immediately precedes the verb unless it is to receive special emphasis); when an adverbial of time and an adverbial of place immediately follow one another, the former usually precedes the latter. Again,
there are some constraints (optional or obligatory) operating according
to the type of clause concerned. When the direct object is the topic of
the clause, adverbials are normally placed late in the clause (τόν Παῦλο
τόν εἶδα σήμερα 'I saw Paul today', or 'I saw Paul today'). In a subordinate clause, an adverbial does not usually stand before the verb
(indeed, in a νά-clause it cannot). Nevertheless, exceptions can be
found:

(1) ἄν μιά φορά δέν πλυθεῖ, θά πλυθεῖ τήν ἄλλη 'if (s)he doesn't
wash once [= on a certain occasion], (s)he'll wash next time';

(2) πρίν καλά-καλά καταλάβω τί γίνεται . . . 'before I realized
properly what was happening . . .'.

Finally, it is characteristic of MG that the chief constituents of
a sentence are often found far removed from one another. In the
following example, taken from an oral source, note how far removed

the *νά* of the subordinate clause is from the adjective *ἐνδεχόμενο* which governs it:

(3) εἶναι πολύ ἐνδεχόμενο κατά τή μεταφορά τους τά σύκα ἀπό τά ἀπεντομωτήρια εἰς τούς χώρους ἐπεξεργασίας, καί κατά τή διάρκεια ἀκόμα τῆς ἐπεξεργασίας, νά ὑποστοῦν μόλυνση ἀπό τά ἔντομα αὐτά 'it is quite possible [for] the figs, during their transportation from the insecticide chambers to the processing areas, and even during the processing, to undergo infection from these insects.'

7.2 CO-ORDINATION; *KAI* AS CO-ORDINATING CONJUNCTION AND FOCUSING PARTICLE

The chief co-ordinating conjunctions in MG are: *καί* 'and', *ἤ* 'or', *ἤ* . . . *ἤ* or *εἴτε* . . . *εἴτε* 'either . . . or' (the latter may also subordinate: 'whether . . . or'), *ἀλλά* and *μά* 'but', *ὅμως* and *ὡστόσο* 'however' (the former often standing after the first word in the clause), *ἐνῶ* 'whereas' (also a subordinating temporal conjunction: 'while') and *ὄχι μόνο* . . . *ἀλλά καί* 'not only . . . but also'. Of these, *καί* and *ἤ* may co-ordinate anything from single words to whole clauses, while the rest are normally used only to co-ordinate clauses. One should also add *δέ* 'but', which never stands first in a clause; although it is of *katharevousa* origin, it is frequent in speech, but not in creative literature.

The conjunction *καί* is by far the most frequently used of all these: its functions are wide-ranging. When doubled (*καί* . . . *καί*), it means 'both . . . and'. In this sense it acts as a focusing particle, placing emphasis on the word or phrase which immediately follows (as a focusing particle, it is often stressed in speech):

(1) καί ὑπάρχει παθητική φωνή καί εἶναι διαφορετική ἀπό τήν ἐνεργητική 'the passive voice both exists and is different from the active' (i.e. 'not only does it exist but it is different').

Even without being doubled, *καί* is very frequently used as a focusing particle, with the sense of 'also' or 'even', although often it is not possible to render it precisely in English. In this function, *καί* may be placed before nouns, adjectives, adverbs, pronouns, and prepositions, but not often before verbs.

(2a) καί σήμερα ὁ Παῦλος τηλεφώνησε στήν Ἀγγέλα 'Paul phoned Angela today too';

(2b) σήμερα κι ὁ Παῦλος τηλεφώνησε στήν ᾽Αγγέλα 'Paul too phoned Angela today';

(2c) σήμερα ὁ Παῦλος τηλεφώνησε καί στήν ᾽Αγγέλα 'Paul phoned Angela too today';

(3) δέν τῆς ἔκανα καί τίποτα 'I didn't really do anything to her';

(4) ὅπως εἶπα καί προηγουμένως . . . 'as I (also) said previously';

(5) καλή 'σαι κι ἔτσι, Μαρίνα μου, ἀλλά . . . 'you're fine as you are, Marina dear, but . . .' (the implication is that she could improve!);

(6) κάτσε κι ἐσύ 'you too sit down' (imperative).

As is exemplified by (2c), καί is not placed between any of certain prepositions (ἀπό, γιά, μέ, σέ) and its noun phrase. Καί may be followed by a third-person pronoun even when the noun it refers to is specified in the sentence:

(2d) σήμερα ὁ Παῦλος τηλεφώνησε κι αὐτός στήν ᾽Αγγέλα (same meaning as (2b)).

Since καί is not often used to focus a verb, the phrase καί λίγο (lit. 'a little also') is frequently used instead in colloquial speech:

(7) ἀνησυχῶ καί λίγο 'I'm also worried.'

Καί may also be used before certain conjunctions in order to focus the whole of the following clause (e.g. κι ἄς 'even though', κι ἄν or καί νά 'even if': but cf. ἄν καί 'although'); but καί may also be used as a focusing particle with ἄς or νά outside these set expressions:

(8) δέν πρέπει καί νά ἔληξε 'it can't have finished' (i.e. 'it might have done all sorts of things, but it can't have finished');

(9) ἔ, ὄχι καί νά μοῦ πάρεις τήν καρέκλα 'now don't take my chair as well' (i.e. 'haven't you done enough already, without taking . . . ?').

Spoken Greek uses parataxis (as opposed to subordination of clauses) far more than certain Western European languages. As well as meaning simply 'and' (and often 'but'), καί may also introduce a clause which substitutes for one of the following: a participle or a temporal clause (10); a νά-clause ((11–15)); a relative clause (16); or a clause expressing result (17–20) or reason ((21) and (22)). A καί-clause may also stand as the apodosis in the equivalent of a conditional sentence ((23) and (24)), including a negative condition ((25) and (26)):

(10) βρισκόταν στόν πρῶτο ὄροφο τοῦ σπιτιοῦ του κι ἔβλεπε

τηλεόραση 'he was on the first floor of his house (and he was) watching television' (= βλέποντας/ἐνῶ ἔβλεπε);

(11) ἀρχίζω καί πεινάω 'I'm beginning to get hungry' (= νά πεινάω);

(12) βλέπω καί χαμογελᾶς 'I see you're smiling' (cf. σέ βλέπω νά/ πού χαμογελᾶς 'I can see you smiling');

(13) τόν ἄκουσα καί φώναξε 'I heard him shouting' (= νά φωνάξει/ πού φώναξε);

(14) μποροῦσε καί τό 'κανε '(s)he was able to do it and (s)he did it' (νά τό κάνει would not make it clear whether or not (s)he succeeded);

(15) μ' ἔκανες καί σέ πίστεψα 'you made me believe you' (= νά σέ πιστέψω);

(16) μιά φορά ἦταν ἕνας βασιλιάς κι εἶχε δυό κόρες 'once there was a king who had two daughters' (= πού εἶχε);

(17) τί ἔπαθες καί δέ μιλᾶς; 'What's the matter with you? Why don't you speak?' (lit. 'what you-suffered and not you-speak?');

(18) μπορεῖ νά μή βρίσκει ἐργάτες καί δέν ἔρχεται 'it may be he can't find workmen and [that's why] he's not coming' (the last verb is not governed by μπορεῖ νά);

(19) τί μπορεῖ νά τούς ἔφταιξε ἡ Ἰφιγένεια, καί θέλουν τώρα τό θάνατό της; 'what harm can Iphigenia have done them for them now to desire her death?' (Hadz. 1976: 74);

(20) καλά ἔκανες κι ἦρθες 'you've done well to come' (in the future the second clause must be subordinated: καλά θά κάνεις νά ἔρθεις);

(21) ποῦ εἶναι ὁ Σταῦρος καί τόν θέλω; 'Where's Stavros? I want him';

(22) φάε κι εἶναι ὡραῖο τό φαΐ 'eat [up], the food's lovely';

(23) λύσε με καί σ' τό δείχνω 'untie me and I['ll] show you (it)';

(24) τό παραμικρό καί φύγαμε '[if you do] the slightest thing, we're leaving';

(25) ἄνοιξε τό παράθυρο καί θά σκάσουμε 'open the window or we'll suffocate';

(26) ψηλά τά χέρια καί σ' ἔφαγα! 'hands up or I shoot!' (lit. 'high the hands and you I-ate').

It cannot be overemphasized how common such uses of καί are, especially with the sense of result (e.g. (17)–(20)).

After verbs of perception καί, like πού and νά, may clearly indicate a change of grammatical subject even when both verbs are in the third person:

(27) βρῆκε τὴν κόρη κι ἔκλαιγε 'he found the girl weeping' (= νά κλαίει/ποὺ ἔκλαιγε) (Seiler 1952: 117).

Here the imperfective of the second verb indicates temporal coincidence. One of the two characters was weeping at the same time as the man found the girl, and in such a context the present participle κλαί-γοντας could have been used if the man were the subject. The perfective ἔκλαψε would also refer to the man: he began weeping after finding the girl.

7.3 NEGATION

MG is unusual among European languages in possessing two different negative particles for the verb. Μή(ν) is used after νά and ἄς, and to negate a participle (the morphological imperative is used only for positive commands: see 9.4.4.1), while δέ(ν) is used to negate any other form of the verb. It is certainly not true to say (as does Tzartzanos 1946: 280 n.) that δέν is used with the indicative and μήν with the subjunctive (if 'subjunctive' is defined according to morphological criteria), since each negative particle can be used with either mood: ἄν δέν ἔρθουν (not *ἄν μήν ἔρθουν) 'if they don't come' (ἔρθουν is traditionally known as the 'aorist subjunctive'); μπορεῖ νά μήν ἦρθαν (not *μπορεῖ νά δέν ἦρθαν) 'they may not have come' (ἦρθαν is traditionally called the 'aorist indicative'). The fact is that if one considers 'subjunctive' to be a morphological category, as do traditional grammarians, there is no precise correlation between negative and mood: while νά and ἄς *always* take μήν, other particles and conjunctions *never* do so. The use of μήν rather than δέν (apart from the participle) is conditioned purely by whether or not the verb is in a νά- or ἄς-clause: compare the two clauses κι ἄν δέν ἔρθουν and κι ἄς μήν ἔρθουν, both meaning 'even if they don't come'. Although for this reason some linguists now reserve the term 'subjunctive' solely for νά- and ἄς-clauses, calling verbs in all other finite forms 'indicative', the scheme adopted in this book has been to term 'subjunctive' all verbs in clauses introduced by subjunctive markers, with verbs in νά- and ἄς-clauses being treated as belonging to a special category of subjunctives: see further, 9.3.

As well as δέν and μήν, there are the negatives ὄχι and οὔτε (μήτε).

We shall now examine the ways in which different types of words and phrases are negated.

As a substitute for a word or phrase, ὄχι or μή (not μήν) is used. Ὄχι means 'no' in response to a question or statement:

(1) — Θά πᾶς; — Ὄχι. ' "Will you go?" "No" ' (ὄχι here stands for δέ θά πάω 'I won't go').

Similarly it means 'not' when substituting for a word or phrase in the same sentence:

(2) θά πᾶς ἤ ὄχι; 'will you go or not?';
(3) ὁ ἄνθρωπος, μαρξιστής ἤ ὄχι, . . . 'a man, [whether a] Marxist or not . . .'.

To negate a noun or adjective, producing in effect its antonym ('non-'), μή (not μήν) may be placed before it (e.g. ὁ μή φασίστας 'the non-fascist', οἱ μή διανοούμενοι 'non-intellectuals'). Sometimes, under the influence of *katharevousa*, μή (not μήν) is used instead of ὄχι in similar circumstances to (3):

(4) οἱ αἰθουσάρχες ὀφείλουν νά ἐλέγχουν οἱ ἴδιοι τόν βαθμό σεμνό-τητας ἤ μή τῶν ταινιῶν πού προβάλλουν 'cinema managers must themselves check/control the degree of seemliness or otherwise of the films they show' (μή here seems to stand for a non-existent noun derivative of ἄσεμνος 'unseemly, obscene') (*T* 25 Feb. 1982, 82);

(5) τά παρκαρισμένα καί μή IX 'those private cars that are parked and those that are not' (for 'IX' see 10.3.5).

Similarly, ὄχι can be used before most parts of speech in a verbless sentence:

(6) ὄχι ἐδῶ, ἐκεῖ 'not here, there';
(7) ὄχι ἡ Πόπη, ἡ Ρένα 'not Poppy, [but] Rena'.

Μή (not μήν) may also be used on its own as a universal negative imperative ('don't!'), or, again, elliptically, before most parts of speech when a verb form which would normally be negated by μή(ν) is understood:

(8) μή χειρότερα! (an elliptical expression of disapproval, suggesting, 'may I never live to see worse than this');

(9) μή τά χέρια σου ἔξω 'don't [put] your hands out' (e.g. 'of the window').

A noun after μή used in this way is normally in the accusative.

Ὄχι is often used as a phrase negator: that is, it may negate most parts of speech that are present in the clause: noun (10), adjective (11), numeral (12), adverb (13), or clause ((14)–(15)):

(10) μοῦ δήλωσε πῶς ὄχι ζήτημα γάμου, ἀλλά οὔτε μόνιμου συν-δέσμου μπορεῖ νά ὑπάρξει μεταξύ μας 'he declared to me that not [only] could there be no question of marriage between us, but not even of a permanent liaison' (Kar. n.d.: II 72–3);

(11) μιά ἁπλή, ὄχι σημαντική προσαρμογή 'a simple, not significant adjustment' (= ἀσήμαντη 'insignificant');

(12) ὄχι ἕνα, μά δέκα Νόμπελ θά πάρεις 'you'll get not one, but ten Nobel [prizes]' (Kar. n.d.: I 62);

(13) μιά ὄχι καί τόσο ἐπικίνδυνη σέντρα 'a not so dangerous centre [in football]' (i.e. 'not very dangerous');

(14) ἔπρεπε ὄχι νά εἰδοποιήσω, ἀλλά σχεδόν νά πάρω τήν ἄδειά του 'I was obliged not [simply] to inform [him], but almost to obtain his permission' (Kar. n.d.: I 62);

(15) ὄχι τή θαυμάζω, τή λατρεύω 'I don't admire her, I adore her' (here the negative covers the whole clause, not just the verb).

After ἄν, the negative in such cases is normally ὄχι (16), but under the influence of *katharevousa* μή is occasionally found (17):

(16) τά ἴδια, ἄν ὄχι χειρότερα 'the same, if not worse';

(17) εἶναι δύσκολο—ἄν μή ἀδύνατον 'it is difficult—if not impossible.'

The set phrase ἄν μή τι ἄλλο 'if nothing else' is frequently used, although it is sometimes found in demotic translation (ἄν ὄχι τίποτε ἄλλο).

Although in a negative sentence non-assertive proforms are characteristically used, assertive proforms are not excluded:

(18) ρίχνει τόσο φῶς σ' ὅλη τήν ὑπόθεση, ὥστε νά μή μείνουν περιθώρια νά πῶ ὀτιδήποτε 'he throws so much light on the whole affair that there remains no room for me to say anything' (A 9 May 1982) (cf. τίποτα 'nothing').

The negative particle οὔτε (sometimes μήτε) may substitute for or co-occur with δέν or μήν in an indicative or subjunctive clause with the meaning 'neither', 'nor', or 'not even'. It may also stand for μήν in front of a participle; and οὔτε νά may substitute for μήν in a negative command. When οὔτε precedes the verb, a second negative particle (δέν or μήν) is not normally added, but is not excluded; when it follows the verb, however, another negative is obligatory:

(19) οὔτε ἐσύ [δέ] μ' ἄκουσες, or δέ μ' ἄκουσες οὔτε ἐσύ 'not even *you* listened to me', or 'nor did *you* listen to me either';

(20) ὄχι μόνο δέν ὑποδαύλιζε τή συζήτηση, μά οὔτε τήν παρα-κολουθοῦσε 'not only was he not encouraging the discussion, but he was not even following it', or '. . . but he was not fol-lowing it either' (Kar. n.d.: I 133);

(21) δέ θά σέ ξεχάσω οὔτε μιά στιγμή 'I shan't forget you even for a/one moment';

(22) τό ἐμπόριο τό παραμέλησε, οὔτε φαινόταν κάν στό κατάστημα 'he neglected [his] business, and he did not even appear at the shop' (here οὔτε is equivalent to καί δέν 'and not'; κάν 'even' adds further emphasis);

(23) δέ θέλω οὔτε τό ἕνα οὔτε τό ἄλλο 'I don't want either of them' (lit. 'I want neither the one nor the other').

In (19), (21), and (23), it is either possible or obligatory for two negatives to appear in the same clause. Within the clause two negatives do not cancel each other out but reinforce each other. Nevertheless, two negatives usually retain their separate force when they appear in different clauses, whether these clauses are co-ordinated, or whether one of them is subjunctive and subordinated to the other (as in (24) and (25)):

(24) δέν μπορῶ νά μήν πάω 'I can't not go', or 'I can't avoid going';

(25) δέν ἄντεξα νά μήν τό κάνω 'I couldn't resist doing it' (lit. 'I didn't resist not to do it').

The negative of a main verb may carry its force into an indicative sub-ordinate clause:

(26) δέ νομίζει ὅτι καμιά ἀπό τίς δουλειές πού ἔκανε, [δέν] ταίριαζε στόν χαρακτήρα της 'she doesn't think that any of the jobs she has done suited her character' (*T* 18 Oct. 1979, 80) (the δέν, which did not appear in the actual sentence quoted, could be optionally inserted, but then the sentence might mean, 'she doesn't think that none of the jobs . . .').

Sometimes, however, especially in colloquial speech, a negative may be used redundantly in a subordinate clause after a verb which is negative in meaning:

(27) ἀρνήθηκε ὅτι δέν τό πῆρε 'he denied he had taken it' (lit. 'he denied he didn't take it').

Here the speaker was clearly influenced by the (actual or hypothetical) words of the person he is quoting (δέν τό πῆρα 'I didn't take it'). Such a construction is consistent with what has been said (3.3.2) about the indirect speech clause preserving the structure of the direct speech in MG. In some constructions, however, the negative cannot cover the subordinate verb as well as the main verb:

(28) δέ λυπᾶμαι πού πέθανε 'I'm not sorry (s)he died' (the fact that (s)he died is not disputed: contrast (26)).

Further examples of double negatives in which each preserves its force (e.g. πρόσεχε νά μήν κοιμηθεῖς καί δέν ἀκούσεις τό κουδούνι 'be careful not to go to sleep and miss hearing the bell') are given later (9.4.4.1).

Lastly, there are some idiomatic uses of δέν when placed between reduplicated instances of the same verb:

(29) ἦταν δέν ἦταν δέκα χρονῶν '(s)he was only just ten years old';
(30) θέλεις δέ θέλεις, πρέπει νά πᾶς 'whether you want to or not, you've got to go.'

8

SUBORDINATING CONJUNCTIONS INTRODUCING INDICATIVE CLAUSES

8.1 THE USES OF ΠΟΥ

Πού (not to be confused with the interrogative adverb ποῦ 'where') has a multiplicity of uses. It is almost always a subordinating conjunction, and is not normally a subjunctive marker in itself (but see below, 8.1.3.5). Its three chief functions are to act (i) as a relative pronoun, (ii) as a *semi-relative* whose antecedent is not a noun or pronoun, and (iii) as an introductive of a clause governed by a verb or by a whole clause. In its first use, it introduces adjectival clauses, while in the others the clauses it introduces normally have an adverbial or nominal function.

8.1.1 ΠΟΥ AS A RELATIVE PRONOUN

This is the most important function of πού, and πού-clauses are by far the most common relative clauses. (Despite the fact that strictly it might be correct to talk about πού always as a conjunction rather than as a pronoun, the traditional approach will be adopted here for convenience.) In this function πού has a (stated or unstated) noun or pronoun as the antecedent whose semantic role πού then plays in the relative clause. Since πού is indeclinable and therefore unmarked for gender, number and case, and since MG does not clearly indicate the subject and object of a verb by means of word order, there are instances where there may be some ambiguity about the syntactical function of πού in the relative clause. In some cases, the alternative relative pronoun ὁ ὁποῖος, which is fully inflected, may serve to remove the ambiguity. Ὁ ὁποῖος, whose avoidance is often counselled by demoticist grammarians as being clumsy and alien to the true demotic style, is found fairly frequently in speech and in non-literary writing even in circumstances in which πού would be quite unambiguous.

But πού is not restricted to standing for the subject or direct object of the verb in its clause. It may act as the indirect object or it may be the equivalent of a prepositional phrase. When πού acts as indirect object, a clitic pronoun in the genitive is normally placed before the verb in order to indicate that πού serves this function, just as a clitic pronoun in the accusative often precedes the verb when πού acts as a direct object (see 6.3.1.1). When πού stands for a prepositional phrase, there may be no indication of its function other than its semantic context; but in cases of possible ambiguity the appropriate preposition followed by a pronoun is normally placed within the relative clause. The declinable ὁ ὁποῖος is especially useful in such circumstances.

(a) πού as subject: (1) ὁ ἄνθρωπος πού ἦρθε εἶναι ὁ θεῖος μου 'the man who came is my uncle' (= ὁ ὁποῖος);

(b) πού as direct object: (2) ὁ ἄνθρωπος πού εἶδες εἶναι ὁ θεῖος μου 'the man you saw is my uncle' (= τόν ὁποῖο);

(c) πού as indirect object: (3) ὁ ἄνθρωπος πού τοῦ δάνεισα τά λεφτά εἶναι ὁ θεῖος μου 'the man I lent the money to is my uncle' (= στόν ὁποῖο δάνεισα);

(d) πού standing for various prepositional phrases: (4) οἱ δράστες χρειάστηκε νά κόψουν τίς ἀλυσίδες πού ἦσαν δεμένα τά κιβώτια 'the culprits had to cut the chains [with] which the crates were tied' (= μέ τίς ὁποῖες) (T 29 Mar. 1979, 14);

(5) γιά ἐκεῖνες πού ὑπῆρξε θαυμάσιος ἐραστής, θά ἦταν ὁπωσδήποτε ἀπαίσιος σύζυγος 'for those women [for] whom he was a marvellous lover he would certainly have been an awful husband' (= γιά τίς ὁποῖες: the fact that γιά has already been used would have rendered any alternative construction cumbersome) (Kar. n.d.: I 180);

(6) ἐκεῖ εἶναι ἡ πόρτα πού μπῆκε ὁ κλέφτης 'there's the door [through] which the thief entered' (= ἀπό τήν ὁποία);

(7) φτάσαμε στό σπίτι πού καθόταν ὁ ποιητής 'we reached the house [in] which the poet lived' (= στό ὁποῖο or ὅπου 'where');

(8) δέ ζοῦμε πιά στήν ἐποχή πού δέν μπορούσες νά κάνεις μπάνιο γυμνός 'we no longer live in the age [in] which [i.e. 'when'] one couldn't go swimming in the nude' (= στήν ὁποία);

(e) as (d), but with prepositional phrase present: (9) τό σχολεῖο ποὺ κοντά του ἦταν ἕνας πλάτανος 'the school near which [lit. 'which near it'] there was a plane-tree' (= κοντά στό ὁποῖο) (without κοντά του, the sentence would mean, 'the school where . . .').

According to the context, a given relative clause may have two quite different meanings:

(10) ποῦ μένει ὁ γέρος ποὺ παίρνει τό κρασί; 'where does the old man who takes/buys the wine live?' or 'where does the old man (s)he buys the wine from live?'

In addition to the above, the antecedent of ποὺ may appear as a possessive genitive in the relative clause:

(11) ὁ κύριος ποὺ γνωρίσαμε τή γυναίκα του εἶναι γιατρός 'the gentleman whose wife we met [lit. 'who we met his wife'] is a doctor' (= τοῦ ὁποίου);
(12) τά παιδιά ποὺ οἱ γονεῖς τους τά ἔχουν παρατήσει 'children whose parents have abandoned them'.

Since ποὺ is not tied to any one syntactical relationship with the verb, it may be found in more than one different function in the same sentence (13) (and it could be said to perform two functions within the same clause in (12)):

(13) θά σᾶς ἀπατᾶ βέβαια, μέ γυναῖκες ποὺ θά τόν ἀγαποῦν καί δέν θ' ἀγαπάει 'he's most probably being unfaithful to you, with women who love him and [whom] he doesn't love' (Kar. n.d.: I 180) (ποὺ may optionally be repeated after καί).

It will be noticed in (7) and (8) above that ποὺ may be used as a relative adverbial of place or time ('where' or 'when'). There is sometimes a free alternation between ποὺ and ὅπου, the latter also being sometimes used for time rather than for place (e.g. στίς περιπτώσεις ποὺ/ὅπου . . . 'in the cases where . . .', σέ μιά ἐποχή ποὺ/ὅπου 'in an age when . . .'), but ποὺ tends to be found more frequently in such circumstances than ὅπου in colloquial speech, and in any case when the relative clause is *restrictive* or *defining* (ὅπου may normally be used only with an inanimate antecedent). Also, contrast 'from which' with 'to which' in (15a) and (15b):

(14) τό ἐπόμενο βῆμα ποὺ κάνει ὁ ποιητής εἶναι τό Πρῶτο Σχεδίασμα, ὅπου καί στρεφόμαστε 'the next step which the poet takes is

the First Draft, to which we [now] turn' (here the relative
clause introduced by ὅπου is non-defining) (*P* 22.31);

(15a) ἡ γλώσσα ἀπ' ὅπου μεταφράζεις 'the language you translate
from' (lit. 'from where');

(15b) ἡ γλώσσα στὴν ὁποία μεταφράζεις 'the language you translate into' (lit. 'in/to which').

Greek speakers are so accustomed to πού standing in a rather vague
relation to its antecedent that it is sometimes used elliptically, as in
(16). Example (17) shows the writer attempting to be more specific
about the relationship of πού to its antecedent:

(16) τὴν ἐπομένη πού 'διωξες τὴν Κατερίνα 'the day after you
dismissed Catherine' (lit. 'the next-day which you-dismissed')
(Kar. n.d.: II 71);

(17) ἡ συνομιλία του μέ τόν Πρωθυπουργό ἔγινε τὴν ἐπομένη
μέρα ἀπό ἐκείνη πού ζήτησε ραντεβού ὁ βουλευτής 'his conversation with the Prime Minister took place the day after the
Member of Parliament sought a meeting' (lit. '. . . the following day from that which he sought meeting') (*T* 9 Sept.
1982, 6).

Let us now examine some instances of possible ambiguity with πού.
One is where both subject and direct object of the verb in relative
clause are either neuter singular or neuter plural, and therefore do not
indicate whether they are to be taken as nominative or accusative:

(18a) ἔρχεται τό κορίτσι πού χτύπησε τό ἀγόρι,

(18b) ἔρχεται τό κορίτσι πού τό χτύπησε τό ἀγόρι 'here comes the
girl who hit the boy', or '. . . whom the boy hit.'

In (18a), τό ἀγόρι would be more likely to be taken as the object; in
(18b) the reverse is true. But neither sentence precludes the opposite
interpretation, and the use of τό ὁποῖο would not make the meaning
any clearer. In practice, of course, the ambiguity is normally neutralized by the linguistic or situational context, and especially by intonation. (On the presence or absence of the clitic object pronoun, see
6.3.1.1.)

Again, it is sometimes not clear whether πού acts as the subject or
indirect object of the verb:

(19) ὁ ὑπουργός, πού τοῦ ἔδωσε πλαστά στοιχεῖα γιά νά ἀπαντήσει
σέ σχετική ἐρώτηση στή Βουλή . . . 'the minister, to whom he

gave false figures so that he [= the minister] could answer a question on the subject in Parliament...' (*T* 2 July 1981).

The context of this example made it more likely that the rendering given here is correct; but the phrase could equally mean that it was the minister who provided the other man with the false figures. The use of στόν ὁποῖο instead of πού τοῦ would have removed the ambiguity.

Another possible source of ambiguity is a more complex sentence in which the πού-clause contains an embedded subordinate clause:

(20)   ἡ βασιλοπούλα πού ἤθελε νά τή φάει τό θεριό (a) 'the princess whom the monster wanted to eat'; or (b) 'the princess who wanted the monster to eat her' (if the clitic τή is removed, the example could reasonably be interpreted as (c) 'the princess who wanted to eat the monster'!).

Since in this case the object pronoun can be placed only before the sub-ordinate verb, there is no way, using πού, of specifying which is the subject of the main πού-clause verb. Thus a sentence of type (20) can be interpreted as in (a) or (b): only the context can elucidate the matter.

It is perhaps a consciousness of the inherent possibilities of ambiguity provided by πού that has led speakers to produce sentences which, from a strictly syntactical point of view, are examples of anacolouthon. Such constructions, in which the antecedent, instead of the relative pronoun, indicates government by the verb of the *relative* clause or by a preposition which equally belongs to the relative clause, are frequently found in speech, although they are usually avoided in serious writing:

(21)   τούς μόνους (acc.) πού ἄκουσε ὁ δικαστής ἤταν οἱ ἀστυνομικοί 'the only people the judge listened to were the policemen' (strictly, οἱ μόνοι (nom.));
(22)   σ' αὐτό πού ὅλοι συμφωνοῦν εἶναι ... 'what everyone agrees on is ...' (strictly, but awkwardly, αὐτό πού ὅλοι συμφωνοῦν σ' αὐτό εἶναι ...).

In (21) the case in which πού would stand were it inflected (the accusative) is transferred to the antecedent, which is nevertheless the subject or complement of the main verb; likewise, in (22), the preposition which would have governed the relative had the relative been susceptible of being so governed is transferred to the antecedent (a better alternative for (22) might have been αὐτό στό ὁποῖο, or simply ἐκεῖ πού).

Thus, while on a colloquial level the versatility of the relative pronoun ποὺ makes it possible for the speaker to express a range of relationships with great ease, in the written language, where a greater syntactical complexity is often desired and where ambiguity should be avoided, there are difficulties involved with ποὺ which can sometimes be eased by using ὁ ὁποῖος. When a sentential relative is required (i.e. one whose antecedent is a whole clause), ὁ ὁποῖος (often πρᾶγμα τό ὁποῖο '[a] thing which') must be used:

(23) ἄν ἔρϑει, πρᾶγμα τό ὁποῖο μοῦ φαίνεται ἀδύνατον . . . 'if (s)he comes, which seems to me impossible . . .'.

There is also the stylistic problem that (at least according to some writers, especially those brought up in the *katharevousa* tradition) the frequent use of ποὺ is felt to be inelegant (see, for example, Babiniotis 1979b: 60, for an attack on 'που-που-ισμός').

There is certainly a case for occasionally using ὁ ὁποῖος either to avoid ambiguity or as a stylistic variant; but ποὺ remains the MG relative pronoun *par excellence*.

8.1.2 ΠΟΥ AS A PSEUDO-RELATIVE

Closely connected with the use of ποὺ as a relative pronoun is its function with an antecedent which is not a noun or pronoun, but an adverb of place or time (ἐκεῖ 'there', ἐδῶ 'here', τότε 'then', τώρα 'now'). Here ποὺ is a relative adverbial, and the clause it introduces is also adverbial rather than adjectival. Ἐκεῖ ποὺ has the sense 'at/to the place where', ἀπό κεῖ ποὺ 'from where'. Similarly, τότε ποὺ means 'at the time when' and ἀπό τότε ποὺ 'since'. Clearly such constructions are not far removed from true relative uses such as στό μέρος ποὺ 'at/to the place where', or ἀπό τήν ἐποχή ποὺ 'since the time when'.

(1) ἐκεῖ ποὺ βρισκόταν ἡ παλιά ταβέρνα τώρα ὑψώνεται μιά ϑεόρατη πολυκατοικία 'where the old tavern used to be, there now rises a huge block of flats';

(2) πέρασαν εἴκοσι χρόνια ἀπό τότε ποὺ πρωτοπῆγα στήν Ἑλλάδα 'twenty years have passed since I first went to Greece';

(3) τώρα ποὺ τελείωσες τή διατριβή σου, τί ϑά κάνεις; 'now that you've finished your thesis, what are you going to do?'

As in its use as a relative pronoun, so as a pseudo-relative ποὺ may enter into a rather loose relationship with its apparent antecedent and the subordinate verb:

(4) ἐκεῖ ποὺ τά πράγματα σκάλωσαν ὅμως, ἦταν στά ϑέματα τῆς

ὕφεσης 'where there was a hitch, however, was on matters of *détente* [or, 'the recession']' (*T* 1 Nov. 1979, 10);

(5) ἔφυγαν ἀπό κεῖ πού ἦρθαν 'they returned from whence they came' (lit. 'they-left from there that they-came').

In (4), ἐκεῖ is a proform for στά θέματα 'on matters', while the verb ἦταν would strictly require (τά) θέματα 'matters' as subject or complement ('the matters on which there was a hitch were matters of *détente*'): the preposition σ(έ), which belongs syntactically to the relative clause, has been transferred to the main clause. In (5), ἀπό belongs semantically with ἦρθαν, not with ἔφυγαν.

There are also some idiomatic uses of ἐκεῖ πού (temporal: 'while'; adversative: 'whereas') and ἐδῶ πού (ἐδῶ πού τά λέμε 'by the way').

8.1.3   ΠΟΥ AS A NON-RELATIVE CONJUNCTION

Πού is frequently used to introduce a clause acting as object or subject of a verb, or linking some other word, or a phrase, or a whole clause, to the clause which it introduces.

Its chief uses as a non-relative conjunction are to introduce (a) clauses governed by verbs of perception and expressions of emotion; (b) other clauses expressing cause or reason; (c) clauses expressing result or consequence; (d) contrary clauses; and (e) clauses governed by various other words.

As an introductive of a nominal clause, πού is used where the truth of what is stated in the subordinate clause is presupposed. With those verbs which may be followed by either πού or ὅτι/πώς, the main verb expresses an attitude to the *fact* stated in a πού-clause, but an attitude to the *truth* of the assertion contained in an ὅτι/πώς-clause (Christidis 1982).

While grammarians class these uses of πού as different from its relative functions, there is often a noun or pronoun in the main clause which might be construed as an antecedent: indeed, it may be that most speakers would consider πού to be no different from a relative pronoun in such circumstances.

8.1.3.1   *Πού after verbs of perception and expressions of emotion*

Verbs of perception (and certain other verbs, such as θυμᾶμαι 'I remember', ξεχνάω 'I forget') often govern a πού-clause:

(1) εἶδες πού δέν ἦταν τίποτα; 'you see, it was nothing' (i.e. 'I *told* you there was nothing to worry about');

(2) θυμᾶσαι πού τό 'χαμε πεῖ τήν περασμένη φορά; 'do you remember our having said it last time?' (θυμᾶμαι πού suggests
immediate recall, θυμᾶμαι ὅτι suggests remembering as a result
of effort).

Πού-clauses may be governed by words or phrases (including exclamations), such as λυπᾶμαι 'I'm sorry', στενοχωριέμαι 'I'm upset',
μετανοιώνω 'I regret', (μοῦ) ἀρέσει '(I) like'; the adverbs εὐτυχῶς 'fortunately', δυστυχῶς 'unfortunately', καλά 'it's a good thing'; the noun
κρίμα 'it's a pity'; and the adjectives (preceded by εἶναι 'it's') συγκινη-
τικό 'touching', παρήγορο 'consoling', etc.:

(3) λυπᾶμαι πού δέ σέ εἶδα 'I'm sorry I didn't see you';
(4) μέ συγχωρεῖτε πού ἄργησα 'excuse me for being late';
(5) μοῦ λειπει πού δέν ἀκούω τή γλώσσα μου 'I miss hearing my
language' (lit. of-me it-lacks that not I-hear . . .');
(6) εἶμαι περήφανος πού ἔλαβα μέρος στήν ἐπιχείρηση 'I'm proud
to have taken part in the operation';
(7) μ' ἀρέσει πού μ' ἀγαπᾶς 'I like your loving me' (cf. μ' ἀρέσει
νά μ' ἀγαπᾶς 'I like you to love me');
(8) καλά πού τό θυμήθηκες! 'it's a good thing you remembered it!'

Note that in each of the examples (3)-(6) there is a first person in the
main clause which might be considered as the antecedent of the πού.

8.1.3.2 Πού *introducing cause or reason clauses*

Πού may also introduce a cause or reason clause, even when it is not
governed by an expression of emotion. Here the precise syntactical and
semantic relationship between πού and the main clause is not always
easily discernible:

(9) σοῦ κάνω χάρη πού σέ μεταφέρω 'I'm doing you a favour by
transporting you';
(10) ἔλα δῶ πού σέ θέλω 'come here, I want you';
(11) ἤδη φαίνεται " ι τῆς ἔχεις πάρει τήν πρωτοβουλία — φαίνεται
αὐτό, πού δέ θέλει νά πάρει τό κουτάλι καθόλου 'it's already
apparent that you've taken away her initiative—that's apparent [from the fact] that she doesn't want to pick up the
spoon.'

Such loose uses of πού as in (11) (which was recorded from conversation) are frequently used, despite the fact that grammarians might

not approve of them. On the other hand, one can find loose uses in written Greek too, such as *τόσο μάλλον πού* or *πολύ περισσότερο πού* 'all the more so because' (which are probably influenced by F *d'autant plus que*).

8.1.3.3 *Πού introducing result clauses*

Πού is the most frequently used introductive of result clauses, when a word such as *τέτοιος* 'such [a]', *τόσο(ς)* 'so much', or *ἔτσι* 'in such a way' is found in the main clause:

(12) ὁ Στέφανος κέρδισε τόσα λεφτά στό Πρό-Πό πού δέ χρειάζεται πιά νά δουλεύει 'Stephen won so much money on the football pools that he doesn't need to work any more.'

(Result and final clauses introduced by *πού νά* are discussed in 9.4.2.2.6; for the alternative result-clause introductive *ὥστε* see 8.4.)

Clauses loosely expressing result may be introduced by *πού* even when there is no such preceding adjective, pronoun, or adverb as those mentioned above:

(13) δέ φταίω ἐγώ πού χάλασε τό αὐτοκίνητο 'it's not my fault the car broke down';

(14) ἔνιωσα μιά λαχτάρα πού κόντεψα νά πεθάνω 'I got such a fright that I almost died' (*μιά* here stands for *τέτοια* 'such a').

8.1.3.4 *Πού introducing contrary clauses*

In contrary clauses, *πού* has the meaning of 'whereas'. In most such cases, the syntactical relation of *πού* to the main clause is rather loose, except that often an antecedent may be found:

(15) ἀπόψε κοιμήθηκε πολύ, πού ἄλλες βραδιές ξυπνάει συνέχεια 'last night (s)he slept a lot, whereas other nights (s)he's continually waking up.'

8.1.3.5 *Other uses of πού*

The other uses of *πού* are many and varied. In some sentences the clause introduced by *πού* acts as a noun clause (i.e. it may be replaced by a noun phrase), but in others the *πού*-clause cannot be viewed separately from the word or phrase which governs it. Since there is no space for a full discussion of the matter, some examples must suffice. First, some instances of the *πού*-clause standing for a noun phrase:

(16) ὁ Μάκης, ἐκτός πού εἶναι ἄσχημος, εἶναι καί πολύ κουτός 'Makis, quite apart from being ugly, is also very stupid' (cf. ἐκτός ἀπό + noun);

(17) τό σπίτι δέν ἔχει τζάμια, λόγω πού τά σπάσανε τά παιδιά 'the house has no window-panes, owing to the fact that the kids have broken them' (cf. λόγω + noun in genitive);

(18) κάθε πού πηγαίνω στήν Ἀγγλία, ἀρρωσταίνω 'every time I go to England, I get ill' (cf. κάθε + noun);

(19) παρ' ὅλο πού δουλέψαμε σκληρά, δέν κατορθώσαμε τίποτα 'despite the fact that we worked hard, we achieved nothing' (cf. παρ' ὅλες τίς προσπάθειές μας 'despite our efforts');

(20) μέ τό πού πέρασα τήν κεντρική πόρτα, εἶδα τήν Ἕλενα 'no sooner had I gone through the main door than I saw Elena' (very colloquial);

(21) νά πού τό ξέχασες κιόλας! 'there, you've forgotten it already!' (cf. deictic particle νά + noun).

Then some examples of various other constructions:

(22) μιά πού [or μιά καί] ἦρθες, κάτσε καί θά σοῦ φτιάξω ἕνα καφεδάκι 'since/now you've come, sit down and I'll make you a cup of coffee';

(23) ἔχετε ὥρα πού ἤρθατε; 'have you been here long?' (lit. 'you-have hour/time that you-came');

(24) θέλω νά πάω, μόνο πού φοβᾶμαι λίγο 'I want to go, [it's] only (that) I'm a bit frightened';

(25) ἔτσι πού πᾶνε τά πράγματα, δέ θά τελειώσουμε πρίν ἀπ' τά Χριστούγεννα 'the way things are going, we shan't finish before Christmas';

(26) ἔλεγα πώς δέ θά γυρίσει, μά ἔλα πού ἦρθε 'I reckoned (s)he wouldn't return, but nevertheless [lit. 'come that'] (s)he came';

(27) ὁ Φίλιππας μόλις πού κρατιότανε στά πόδια του 'Philip could hardly stand on his feet' (πού, which is not obligatory here, may serve to distinguish μόλις as adverb 'hardly' from its use as conjunction 'as soon as');

(28) δέν τό 'σπασα ἐγώ, οὔτε πού τό ἄγγιξα 'I didn't break it: I didn't even touch it' (again, πού may optionally be used to distinguish the meaning of οὔτε 'not even' from 'neither' or 'nor');

(29) φαίνεται περισσότερο νέος παρά πού εἶναι στήν πραγματικότητα 'he looks/seems younger than he really is' (usually ἀπ'
ὅ,τι is used instead of παρά πού).

Finally, there are some functions of πού which do not seem to fit
into any of the categories already mentioned. One is the phrase πού λές,
used colloquially (like λοιπόν) to mean 'so, well' to link an utterance
with a previous one, or even to embark on a new subject of conversation; syntactically similar is πού λένε 'as they say', placed after a proverbial expression or some other expression that the speaker uses while
disclaiming it as his/her own. There is also an idiomatic use of πού
between two identical verb forms, corresponding to the English 'anyway' in the following:

(30) θά 'ρθω πού θά 'ρθω στό συνέδριο· γιατί δέ μ' ἀφήνεις νά
μιλήσω; '[since] I'm coming to the conference anyway, why
don't you let me speak?'

Thus πού is an extremely useful linking word whose versatility is
positively Protean. Together with the equally ubiquitous νά, πού links
phrases and clauses without some of the problems of subordination
which exist in other languages; thus it enables the Greek speaker to
form complex sentences with the minimum of effort, and contributes
greatly to the special genius of the MG language.

Before leaving πού, however, it must be pointed out that there are
instances in which πού acts as a subjunctive marker. This phenomenon
occurs in a limited number of contexts (i.e. after a limited number of
governing words), usually where the clause has some future or universal
reference. In some cases, therefore, πού is equivalent to one of the
universal relatives (see 8.2):

(31) κάθε τι πού δῶ μοῦ φέρνει ἕνα θέμα, μιά τραγικότητα νά
ἐκφράσω 'each thing I see brings me a subject, a tragic situation to express' (cf. ὅ,τι δῶ 'whatever I see') (Tsa. 1973: 93);

(32) θά ἐξαρτηθεῖ ἀπό τό βαθμό πού ὑπάρξει συνεννόηση μεταξύ
τους 'it will depend on the degree [to] which there [will] be
[an] understanding between them' (alternatively, θά ὑπάρξει)
(Τ 16 Aug. 1979, 8).

8.2 OTHER RELATIVE WORDS

The other relative pronouns are the universal relatives ὅποιος 'anyone
who; whoever; whichever', ὅ,τι 'that which; whatever' and ὅσο(ς) 'as

much/many as; those who/which'. In addition, the adverbial conjunctions ὅπου 'wherever' (also 'where': 8.1.1), ὅποτε 'whenever', and ὅπως 'however' (also 'as') behave in many respects similarly to the universal relatives. All these words are distinguished in use from πού and ὁ ὁποῖος in that (a) they never have an antecedent, and (b) semantically they form part of two clauses simultaneously. Their chief uses are (i) to introduce noun clauses which act as subjects or objects (this does not apply to the adverbial conjunctions); (ii) to introduce adverbial clauses; and (iii), in certain circumstances, to act solely as pronouns or adverbs, without introducing a clause. In many of these functions, the universal relatives may be used either pronominally (i.e. without a noun) or attributively (i.e. adjectivally). Used pronominally, ὅ,τι functions as the neuter singular (and occasionally plural) of ὅποιος in any grammatical case; adjectivally, it may replace any form of ὅποιος. Ὅσος is not used in the singular to refer to persons; in the plural it may act as the plural of ὅποιος or ὅ,τι. Its neuter singular ὅσο may also act as an adverb.

After first examining the three uses mentioned above, we shall look at some other functions of the versatile ὅσο(ς).

8.2.1 NOMINAL RELATIVE CLAUSES

Nominal relative clauses may function as the subject of a verb, as the object of a verb or preposition, or instead of a genitive noun governed by a noun or verb. As in adverbial clauses introduced by these relatives, they may be subjunctive markers if their sense is not actual but potential (see 3.2.3.4.1 (12)–(17) and 9.4.4.5); to make their scope even more general, they may be followed by κι ἄν (or καί νά) and/or by the suffix -δήποτε. Thus 'whoever' may be rendered (in ascending order of universality) as ὅποιος, ὅποιος κι ἄν, ὁποιοσδήποτε, and ὁποιοσδήποτε κι ἄν. In nominal relative clauses ὅποιος and ὅσος link two clauses, in each of which they may stand in a different relation to the rest of the clause; in such circumstances, if the subordinate clause precedes the main clause, the relative stands in the case suitable to the subordinate clause; if the main clause precedes, then the relative appears in the case suitable to its function in that clause.

(1) ὅποιος θέλει, ἄς ἔρθει 'whoever wants [to], let him come' (subject);

(2) πάρε ὅσο νερό θέλεις (or νερό ὅσο θέλεις) 'take as much water as you want' (object of verb);

(3) μπορεῖς νά δανειστεῖς ότιδήποτε χρήματα σοῦ χρειάζονται 'you may borrow as much money as you need' (object of verb);

(4) ἀπάντησε σέ ὅσους τοῦ ἔκαναν ἐρωτήσεις 'he answered those who asked him questions' (object of σέ);

(5) ὅποιος πῆγε μέ τούς ἀντάρτες, πιάσανε τόν πατέρα του 'they arrested the father of anyone who joined the partisans' (lit. 'whoever went with the partisans, they arrested his father') (instead of genitive governed by πατέρας);

(6) σάν συνέχεια τῶν ὅσων εἴπαμε, . . . 'as a continuation of what we said . . .'

On the other hand, a clause introduced by one of these relatives may be not strictly nominal but adjectival:

(7) ὁ ἄνθρωπος, ὅποιος κι ἄν εἶναι, δέν μπορεῖ νά ζήσει χωρίς ψωμί 'a man, whoever he might be, cannot live without bread.'

Two observations should be made about nominal relative clauses. First, the definite article is sometimes used before the relative. With ὅσος, the article may optionally be used when the relative is neuter plural only, as in (6). When ὅποιος is used attributively, it too may be preceded by the article:

(8) θίγονται τά ὅποια προβλήματα δημιουργεῖ ὁ νέος νόμος 'whatever problems the new law creates are touched on' (alternatively, ὅσα προβλήματα).

Secondly, as with πού, so with other relative pronouns, the anacolouthon construction is frequently found, in which the relative (like the antecedent in πού-constructions) is attracted into a case which does not appear to be syntactically suitable:

(9) σέ ὅσους τό 'χω πεῖ τό ἀνέκδοτο ἔχουν σκάσει στά γέλια 'those to whom I've told the joke have burst out laughing' (cf. σ' αὐτούς πού τό 'χω πεῖ . . .);

(10) κανένας ἀπ' ὅσους ἔστειλα γράμματα γιά τό περιοδικό δέν ἀπάντησε 'none of those to whom I wrote about the magazine has replied' (cf. κανένας ἀπ' αὐτούς πού τούς ἔστειλα . . .) (Kaz. 1958: 124).

In (9) the case of the relative is determined by its function in the subordinate clause ('I've told the joke *to them*'), while its other syntactical function is as the subject of the main verb; in (10) it is the function of the relative in the subordinate clause that is neglected (i.e. the fact that the speaker sent letters *to* them is not expressed explicitly). Clearly, when the relative has two conflicting syntactical functions in the same sentence, one has to be expressed at the expense of the other. Which of the two will be preferred will depend on the likely ambiguity or otherwise of the alternative constructions.

An added complication arises when ὅλοι 'all' is added to the relative ὅσοι (when ὅλοι is followed by a relative, this is almost always ὅσοι: ὅλοι πού is rare). Grammarians usually urge that ὅλοι should be in the case appropriate to its function in the main clause, while the relative should be in that appropriate to its role in the subordinate clause. Some even go so far as to insist that ὅλοι should be inserted (even when it is semantically redundant) so that the two cases can be indicated:

(11) νά τό συμπέρασμα ὅλων (gen.) ὅσα (acc.) εἴπαμε πιό πάνω 'that's the conclusion of what we said above' (Dorbarakis (11–12 Nov. 1979) actually claims that ὅσων instead of ὅλων ὅσα is grammatically incorrect).

In practice, however, most speakers and writers make little attempt to put the two words into different cases, and are quite content with utterances such as (12):

(12) χάρισε τά βιβλία σέ ὅλους (acc.) ὅσους (acc.) τά ἤθελαν '(s)he gave away the books to all those who wanted them.'

8.2.2 ADVERBIAL RELATIVE CLAUSES

The same relatives that are used to introduce nominal clauses may also introduce adverbial clauses (which may in addition be introduced by adverbial conjunctions). The adverbial clauses themselves are constructed in exactly the same way as the nominal clauses, the difference lying rather in their relationship with the main clause: that is, the adverbial relative clause does not act like a noun in relation to any element in the main clause. When used with κι ἄν or καί νά, the relatives often have more of a concessive sense than when they introduce nominal clauses (see example (1)).

(1) ὅποιον καί νά καλέσεις, δέ θά 'ρθω στό πάρτυ σου 'whoever [= 'no matter who'] you ask, I'm not coming to your party';

(2) ὄσες φορές σοῦ εἶπα νά καθίσεις νά μιλήσουμε, ἐσύ ἔκανες λογαριασμούς 'every time I told you to sit down so we could talk, you were doing calculations' (cf. κάθε φορά πού) (Fra. 1962: 243);

(3) κατόρθωσα νά μείνω πιστός καί συγκινημένος θαυμαστής αὐτῆς τῆς ἀνθρώπινης νίκης, ὅπου τήν εἶδα, ὅπου τήν βρῆκα 'I managed to remain a faithful and responsive admirer of this human victory, wherever I saw it, wherever I found it' (Hadz. 1976: 40–1);

(4) ἀπό ὁπουδήποτε βρεθῶ, θά ἐξακολουθήσω νά κατευθύνω τόν EOT 'from wherever I find myself, I shall continue to control EOT [= the National Tourist Organization]' (T 24 Jan. 1980, 6);

(5) νά μοῦ τηλεφωνήσεις ὅποτε χρειαστεῖς τίποτα 'phone me whenever you need anything.'

Such adverbial relative clauses are subject to anacolouthon constructions in a similar way to other relative clauses:

(6) κοιτάζουμε ἀπ' ὅπου φύγαμε 'we look [back to] where we left from' (Kaz. 1965: 524);

(7) τό μικρό θά πρέπει νά κοιμηθεῖ ἀπ' ὅπου δέ θά περνᾶμε 'the baby will have to sleep [somewhere] where we won't keep passing by [and disturbing it].'

In both (6) and (7), the ἀπό which appears to govern the relative is itself actually governed by the verb in the subordinate clause, not, as it appears superficially, by the main verb. Both sentences become syntactically clearer if an antecedent which could govern ἀπό is inserted: in (6), τό μέρος '[at] the place', and, in (7), σ' ἕνα μέρος 'in a place'. For this reason, it may be more correct to say that these particular sentences are instances of ellipsis rather than of anacolouthon.

8.2.3 UNIVERSAL RELATIVES IN NON-CONJUNCTION USES

These relatives (usually either reduplicated or with the suffix -δήποτε) may act purely as pronouns, adjectives, or adverbs without introducing clauses. There is great variety in usage, but certain relatives are used only in a limited number of contexts.

Examples of reduplicated uses:

(1) δέν τό δίνει σέ ὅποιον ὅποιον '(s)he doesn't give it to just anyone';

(2) τώρα πρέπει νά βγεῖ τό ψωμί ὅπως ὅπως 'the bread must

come out [of the oven] now somehow or other' (Tzartzanos 1963: 215);

(3) τό πούλησα ὅσα ὅσα 'I sold it for peanuts.'

Sometimes these relatives are used unreduplicated in elliptical constructions:

(4) γιά νά παρακάμψουν τίς ὅποιες πιθανότητες νά κολλήσει κάπου ἡ υἱοθεσία . . . 'in order to evade whatever possibilities [there might be] that the adoption might get bogged down somewhere . . .'

In (4), τίς could have been omitted and πιθανότητες have been followed by ὑπάρχουν to produce a full clause; in fact, ὅποιες is here equivalent to ἐνδεχόμενες or the indeclinable τυχόν 'possible, contingent'.

The relative ὅ,τι is used eliptically in two chief types of construction: followed by an adjective (where an existential verb such as ὑπάρχει 'there is; (it) exists' is understood: (5)–(6)); or preceded by a preposition such as ἀπό or παρά 'than' (after a comparative: (7)), or παρά 'despite' (8):

(5) Ὅ,τι Νέο 'Whatever['s] New' (name of shop in Athens);

(6) ἡ 'Αὐτοκίνηση' εἶναι ὅ,τι πιό 'ἴν' στήν ἀθηναϊκή νύχτα 'Aftokinisi [name of a discotheque] is the most "in" thing in Athens night[-life]' (Τ 25 June 1981, 33);

(7) ἡ φαντασία μου δουλεύει τήν ἡμέρα πολύ περισσότερο ἀπό ὅ,τι ὅταν ὀνειρεύομαι 'my imagination works far more in the daytime than when I'm dreaming' (after ὅ,τι, a potentially repetitious δουλεύει has been deleted);

(8) παρ' ὅ,τι στεριανός ἀπό καταγωγῆς, ὁ Κυριάκος ὑπηρέτησε στό ναυτικό 'although [he is a] landsman by origin/descent, Kyriakos served in the Navy.'

The relatives in -δήποτε may also serve as non-conjunctions, although in such circumstances they could be considered to be conjunctions introducing elliptical clauses in which, e.g. the verb 'to want' has been deleted:

(9) ὁποιοσδήποτε θά μποροῦσε νά τό γράψει 'anyone could write/ have written it';

(10) προσπαθοῦν τήν ὁποιαδήποτε σχολική ἐπίδοση νά τή χαρακτηρίσουν σάν μαθητικό βῆμα τοῦ μαθητῆ 'they try to characterize

just any performance at school as a learning step by the pupil';

(11) πάρε ὁτιδήποτε 'take anything [= 'whatever you like']';

(12) — Ποῦ νά καθίσω; — Ὁπουδήποτε. ' "Where should I sit?" "Wherever [you like]" ' (or, 'It doesn't matter where');

(13) θά 'ρθοῦμε ὁπωσδήποτε 'we'll definitely come.'

Because of the dual role of the relatives in -δήποτε, it is quite common (especially in spoken Greek) to find the relative followed by a redundant πού, suggesting that the speaker does not see it as a conjunction:

(14) δέν πρόκειται νά ἐπηρεάσει ὁποιαδήποτε ἀπό τίς ἀποφάσεις πού ἔχουν ληφθεῖ ἤδη ἀπό τήν Πρεσβεία 'it is not going to influence any of the decisions that have already been taken by the Embassy.'

8.2.4 OTHER USES OF ΟΣΟΣ

Ὅσος is an extremely versatile relative, whose various functions can be divided into more than twenty different categories. For our purposes, however, it is convenient to observe its functions under four heads, according to whether or not it is used together with its correlative τόσος, and whether or not it is used only in its adverbial form ὅσο (although one should bear in mind that some of its adverbial uses are little different from its adjectival and pronominal ones).

8.2.4.1 Adjectival/pronominal ὅσος without τόσος

The prime use of ὅσος as a straightforward relative introducing a nominal or adverbial clause has already been dealt with (8.2.1, 8.2.2). The concessive function of ὅσος κι ἄν (or καί νά) has also been mentioned (see also 9.4.2.2.6 (4)). Two chief uses remain to be looked at: its use after comparatives, and its use in phrases meaning 'as . . . as possible'.

The use of ὅσος after comparatives is similar to that of ὅ,τι (see 8.2.3 (7)). In the simplest kind of comparative sentence ἀπό 'than' may directly govern a noun phrase (e.g. ὁ Γιάννης εἶναι μεγαλύτερος ἀπό τό Γιῶργο 'John is older/bigger than George'); but when the second term of the comparison is not a noun phrase, ἀπό (or sometimes παρά) is followed by ὅσο (or ὅ,τι). Even when the second term is a noun phrase, but it is the subjects and not the objects of the verb(s) that are being compared, ἀπ' ὅσο (or ἀπ' ὅ,τι) is often used:

(1) αὐτή ἀγαπάει πιό πολύ τό γείτονα ἀπ' ὄσο ἡ γειτόνισσα 'she loves the neighbour more than the neighbour's wife [does]' (ἀπό τή γειτόνισσα would not make it clear whether the sentence is to be given the above interpretation or 'more than she loves the neighbour's wife').

Certainly ἀπ' ὄσο is preferable to simple ἀπό in more complex sentences, in which otherwise it would not be at all clear what was being compared:

(2) οἱ λίγες εὔθυμες νότες πού προηγήθηκαν συνιστοῦν ἴσως γιά μερικούς ἀκροατές μας ἔνα κάπως πιό εὐοίωνο προμήνυμα ἀπ' ὄσο τήν προηγούμενη φορά οἱ βαθυστόχαστες ρομαντικοδαι-μονικές μελωδίες τοῦ Γκούσταβ Μάλερ 'the few cheerful notes which preceded [this programme] perhaps constitute for some of our listeners a somewhat more auspicious portent than [did] the Romantic and demonic melodies of Gustav Mahler last time.'

Normally, however, ἀπ' ὄσο is used before clauses, before adverbial phrases, or before noun phrases in the genitive (already governed by some word in the main clause). Ὅσος may be inflected to agree with some clearly stated noun or pronoun in the main clause (as in (3)); in the absence (or sometimes, especially in speech, in the presence) of such a word, the indeclinable (adverbial) ὄσο is used (as in (1), (2), and (4)).

(3) πήραμε περισσότερες ἐπιστολές ἀπ' ὄσες περιμέναμε 'we received more letters than (those which) we expected';

(4) τό κυβερνεῖο σείστηκε περισσότερο ἀπό τήν ὀργή τοῦ πρωθυ-πουργοῦ ἀπ' ὄσο μέ τό σεισμό 'Government House was shaken more by the Prime Minister's anger than by the earthquake' (E 30 June 1978).

Another use of ὄσος also involves comparatives; here the comparative is not in the main clause but in the ὄσος-clause. There are several variants of this construction, which corresponds to English 'as . . . as possible'. The ὄσος-clause may contain the verb μπορῶ 'I am able' (in the requisite person), or γίνεται 'it is done; it is possible', or the (indeclinable) τό δυνατό(ν) '(the) possible'. The construction with γίνεται is sometimes criticized as being too colloquial for serious written use.

(5) ἔκανα τή δουλειά ὄσο πιό καλά μποροῦσα (or ὄσο μποροῦσα πιό καλά) 'I did the job as best I could';

(6) προσπαθῶ νά δείξω ὅσες γίνεται περισσότερες ὄψεις τῆς ζωῆς
'I'm trying to show as many aspects of life as possible' (*K*
6 Sept. 1979) (since the adjective περισσότερες already displays
agreement with the noun, the adverbial ὅσο could have been
used instead of ὅσες);

(7) νά καλύψουμε ὅσο τό δυνατόν εὐρύτερο φάσμα ἐπιχειρήσεών
μας . . . 'to cover as broad a spectrum of our businesses as
possible . . .' (*K* 23 Dec. 1980).

8.2.4.2 Adverbial ὅσο without τόσο

There are two temporal constructions with ὅσο, in the first of which it
means 'while, as long as, during the time that' (= ὅσην ὥρα, ὅσον καιρό),
in the second (followed by πού or νά) 'until' (= ὥσπου (νά): see
9.4.2.2.6 (3)):

(1) ὅσο ἔμεινα ἐκεῖ ἤμουν εὐχαριστημένος 'while I was there [or
'during my stay there'] I was content';

(2) ἔκλαιγα στά γιομάτα, ὅσο πού μ' ἔπιασε λόξιγκας 'I went on crying my eyes out, until I got hiccups' (Tzartzanos 1963: 217).

The indeclinable ὅσο is used with γιά or (in the form ὅσον) with the
verb ἀφορᾶ '(it) concerns' to mean 'as for' or 'as far as . . . is concerned':

(3) ὅσο γιά μένα, προτιμῶ νά μήν ἔρθω μαζί σας 'as for me, I prefer
not to come with you';

(4) ὅσον ἀφορᾶ τήν Κοινή Ἀγορά, δέν ξέρω ἄν ἡ κυβέρνηση θά
κατορθώσει ὥστε νά βγοῦμε 'as far as the Common Market is
concerned, I don't know whether the government will manage
[it] so that we leave [it].'

The adverbial ὅσο is used especially to introduce a clause with a positive sense in contrast to a main clause containing a negative verb (or the
equivalent of a negative, such as λίγος 'little; few', σπάνια 'rarely'):

(5) δέ βοήθησε ὅσο ἔπρεπε '(s)he didn't help as much as (s)he
should';

(6) δέν ἐπιζητοῦμε νά διασκεδάσουμε, ὅσο νά ἐνημερώσουμε 'we do
not aim to amuse as much as to inform.'

Ὅσο may be used as a correlative of adverbs other than τόσο, such as
ἐξίσου or τό ἴδιο 'equally':

(7) τό παιχνίδι εἶναι ἐξίσου σημαντικό ὄσο τά μαθήματα 'playing is just as important as learning [lit. 'lessons'].'

Finally, ὄσο followed by καί acts as a coordinating conjunction, usually between adjectives or adverbs ('as well as'):

(8) εἶναι ἔνα ἐντυπωσιακό, ὄσο καί χαρακτηριστικό δεῖγμα τῶν προϊόντων τῆς ἑταιρείας μας 'it is an impressive, as well as characteristic, sample of our company's products.'

8.2.4.3 Adjectival/pronominal ὄσος with τόσος

An important use of the correlatives τόσος . . . ὄσος 'as much/many . . . as' is to link two clauses in which the nouns they modify are different:

(1) ἡ νέα ποίηση ἐπιτρέπει τόσες ἀναγνώσεις ὄσοι εἶναι καί οἱ ἀναγνῶστες της 'the new poetry permits as many readings as there are (its) read⌐ ⌐' (Arg. 1979: 86);

(2) ἡ βασίλισσα μπορεῖ νά γεννήσει τόσα αὐγά, ὄσο βάρος ζυγίζει τό σῶμα της δυόμιση φορές 'the queen [bee] is capable of laying eggs to a total of two and a half times her body weight' (lit. 'so-many eggs, as weight weighs the body of-her two-and-a-half times').

The main clause may contain a negative, or an equivalent; in such cases the correlatives need not modify more than a single noun:

(3) λίγα πράγματα περίμενα μέ τόση ἀνυπομονησία ὄλ᾽ αὐτά τά χρόνια πού μεσολάβησαν ἀπό τό θάνατό του, ὄσο τήν ἔκδοση τῶν ''Ἀπάντων' του 'in all the years that have elapsed since his death, I have awaited few things with as much impatience as the publication of his Complete Works' (Mal. 1938: 19).

Alternatively, the subordinate clause may contain a negative:

(4) δέχτηκα τόσες ἐπιθέσεις ὄσες δέν ἔχω πάρει ποτέ 'I was attacked more than ever before' (lit. 'I-received so-many attacks as not I-have taken ever') (cf. without τόσος: ὁ Μιχάλης μᾶς βοήθησε ὄσο κανένας 'Michael helped us more than anyone').

Finally, ὄσος precedes τόσος in expressions where ὄσος could be used on its own, but where the amount specified is in some way restricted:

(5) ὄσα δίνεις, τόσα παίρνεις 'you take no more than you give' (cf. παίρνεις ὄσα δίνεις 'you take as much/many as you give').

8.2.4.4 Adverbial ὅσο with τόσο

There are several different uses of the indeclinable versions of the correlatives. In some constructions, τόσο precedes ὅσο, while in others it follows.

There are two chief constructions in which τόσο precedes. In the first, the correlatives have the sense of καί . . . καί 'both . . . and':

(1) ἐναντίον τόσο τῆς Ἑλλάδας ὅσο καί τῆς Τουρκίας 'against both Greece and Turkey'.

In the second, the main clause is negative (or equivalent), and the correlatives have the sense 'so (much) . . . as'; τόσο may be followed either by a noun phrase or by an adjective:

(2) δέν τούς ἀνησύχησε τόσο τό τραγούδι, ὅσο τά πονηρά βλέμματα τῶν ἀντίθετων 'they were worried not so much by the singing [lit. 'song'] as by the cunning glances of the[ir] opponents' (Tzartzanos 1963: 216) (cf. 8.2.4.2 (6) and 8.2.4.3 (3));

(3) τά πράγματα δέν εἶναι τόσο ἁπλά ὅσο φαίνονται 'things aren't as simple as they seem.'

The uses of these correlatives with ὅσο preceding can be divided into three categories, which are closely interconnected. One of their functions is to correlate two comparatives in clauses of proportion:

(4) ὅσο περισσότερο ἐργάζονται οἱ ὑπουργοί, τόσο περισσότερα λάθη κάνουν 'the harder ministers work, the more mistakes they make.'

On the other hand, τόσο may be used (often followed by a comparative) as a correlative of the temporal conjunction ὅσο (cf. 8.2.4.2 (1)):

(5) ὅσο περνοῦσαν οἱ ὧρες, τόσο τό μαρτύριο γινόταν φοβερότερο 'as the hours passed, the torment became more awful' (Tzartzanos 1963: 216).

Finally, there is the idiomatic ὅσο . . . ἄλλο τόσο:

(6) ὅσο ἐγώ λογαριάζω τό Μίλτο γιά γιό μου, ἄλλο τόσο ἐκεῖνος μέ λογαριάζει γιά πατέρα του 'Miltos looks upon me as his father just as much—if not more—as I look upon him as my son' ('as I look upon Miltos . . . he looks upon me as much again . . .').

8.3 INDIRECT SPEECH

In MG, direct speech is transformed into indirect speech, after the relevant verb or equivalent phrase, in the following ways: statements are introduced by ὅτι or πώς; 'yes/no' questions by ἄν (if however the direct-speech clause begins with an interrogative pronoun or adverb, this is preserved in the indirect speech); and commands by νά. Clauses formed in this way may be nominal or adjectival (or appositional). Such noun clauses may stand as the object or subject of a verb, as the object of a preposition, or in place of a genitive noun. The adjectival/appositional clauses are used after the nouns which it is their function to elucidate.

First such clauses will be examined syntactically, then semantically.

8.3.1 INDIRECT-SPEECH CLAUSES AS OBJECTS OF VERBS

Such clauses involve the most common functions of ὅτι and πώς, which are used after verbs (or equivalent phrases) of saying, showing, perceiving, knowing, believing, etc. There is no difference in meaning between ὅτι and πώς, but the fact that the former is of more learned origin while the latter is genuinely demotic means that ὅτι is used more in formal styles, πώς in less formal. The use of πώς is generally more restricted than that of ὅτι, the former being found most often with simple verbs such as λέω 'I say, tell', ξέρω 'I know', νομίζω 'I think', μαθαίνω 'I learn, find out', and κάνω 'I pretend'.

Ἄν 'whether' is, naturally, used after verbs such as ρωτάω 'I ask', ἀναρωτιέμαι or διερωτῶμαι 'I wonder' (the latter more formal than the former), and ξέρω 'I know' (in interrogative and negative uses); ἄν is sometimes replaced by μήπως, especially if the latter appeared in the direct speech. Νά is used after verbs such as λέω 'I tell' and διατάξω 'I order'.

As has been mentioned elsewhere (3.3.2), the tense of the verb in the indirect-speech clause is normally that in which it would have been if the clause had recorded the direct speech; that is, the tense of the indirect speech verb is relative not to the time of utterance of the whole sentence, but to the time indicated by the sense of the main verb (i.e. the time of the main verb becomes the present of the subordinate clause).

The following examples illustrate various types of indirect speech:

(1) πάντα μοῦ ἔλεγε πώς θά 'ρθει '(s)he always used to tell me (s)he would come';

(2) *νόμιζα πώς πῆγες* 'I thought you had gone';

(3) *θά κάνει πώς δέ θά καθίσει* '(s)he'll pretend not to be staying';

(4) *εἶσαι σίγουρος ὅτι δέν τέλειωσαν*; 'are you sure they haven't finished?';

(5) *μέ ρώτησαν μήπως εἶμαι κατάσκοπος* 'they asked me whether I was a spy';

(6) *ξέρετε ἄν ἄρχισε ἡ παράσταση*; 'do you know if the performance has begun?';

(7) *τή ρώτησα τί θέλει* 'I asked her what she wanted';

(8) *τόν διατάξανε νά κόψει τά δέντρα* 'they ordered him [or 'he was ordered'] to cut [down] the trees.'

In addition to its use after a verb of questioning, the indirect-question *ἄν*-clause is used elliptically either as an echo question when the speaker is not sure whether (s)he has heard the question or, as an exclamation, when (s)he thinks the answer should be obvious:

(9) — *Πῆγες στή συγκέντρωση*; — *Ἄν πῆγα;/*! ' "Did you go to the meeting?" [lit.] "If I did?/!" ' (the answer means either (a) '[did you ask] if I went?', or (b) 'of course I went!').

8.3.2 INDIRECT-SPEECH CLAUSES IN OTHER NOMINAL USES

Clauses introduced by *ὅτι/πώς* may act as the subject of impersonal verbs (including *εἶναι* with a neuter adverb); they may also act as verbal or adjectival complements:

(1) *φαίνεται πώς δέν τοῦ ἀρέσει* 'he doesn't seem to like it/him/her' (lit. 'it seems that he doesn't . . .');

(2) *ὑποτίθεται ὅτι τά μαγαζιά εἶναι κλειστά σήμερα* 'the shops are supposed to be closed today' (lit. 'it-is-supposed that . . .');

(3) *τό συμπέρασμά μου εἶναι ὅτι . . .* 'my conclusion is that . . .';

(4) *εἶμαι βέβαιος ὅτι . . .* 'I'm sure that . . .'

In other nominal uses, *ὅτι* and *ἄν* are preceded by the definite article (*πώς* is not used in such a way). Such is the case when a clause introduced by *ὅτι* or *ἄν* precedes the main clause, or when the clause is governed by a preposition, or by a noun which usually governs a genitive noun:

(5) *τό ὅτι ἀνταποκρίνονται στό αἴτημά μας εἶναι παρήγορο* '[the fact] that they are responding to our demand is heartening';

(6) τό ἄν ἡ Ἑλλάδα πρέπει νά βγεῖ ἀπό τό ΝΑΤΟ εἶναι ἄλλο ζήτημα 'whether Greece should leave NATO is another matter';

(7) ὅσο γιά τό ἄν θά πετύχει ἤ ὄχι, δέν μπορῶ νά κάνω καμιά πρόγνωση 'as to whether it will succeed or not, I cannot make any prediction';

(8) κριτήριο τοῦ ἄν μιά λέξη ξένης καταγωγῆς ἀνήκει ἤ ὄχι στό σῶμα τῆς γλώσσας μας θεωρεῖται τό ἄν ἀφομοιώθηκε ἀπό τήν ἑλληνική γραμματική '[the] criterion as to whether a word of foreign origin belongs to the body of our language or not is considered to be whether it has been assimilated by Greek grammar' (And. 1967: xiii).

8.3.3 INDIRECT-SPEECH CLAUSES IN ADJECTIVAL OR APPOSITIONAL USES

Clauses introduced by ὅτι, ἄν, or νά may be used to elucidate the meaning of a noun. Often the noun can be seen as corresponding to a verb; and the following examples are not very different from the example of verbal complement given in 8.3.2 (3):

(1) ἔχουμε πληροφορίες ὅτι ὁ ἔνοχος βρίσκεται τώρα ἔξω ἀπό τήν Ἑλλάδα 'we have information that the culprit is now outside Greece' (cf. πληροφορούμαστε ὅτι... 'we are informed that ...');

(2) τό γεγονός ὅτι ἐπανῆλθε ἡ δημοκρατία στή Βολιβία θά ἔπρεπε νά τούς ἐνθαρρύνει 'the fact that democracy has returned to Bolivia should encourage them';

(3) δέν ξέρω τί νά ἀπαντοῦσα στό ἐρώτημα ἄν θά κερδίσουμε 'I don't know what I would reply to the question whether we shall win.'

The use of νά governed by a noun is examined later (9.4.2.2.4).

8.4 OTHER SUBORDINATE INDICATIVE CLAUSES

There is little need to dwell on causal clauses introduced by γιατί 'because', ἀφοῦ and ἐπειδή 'since' (contrast the temporal ἀφοῦ, 9.4.4.4), and clauses of time, reason, or manner introduced by καθώς or ὅπως 'as' (contrast the universal function of ὅπως, 8.2.), since they are straightforward and present little interest.

Γιατί and ἐπειδή may often be interchangeable, although a clause introduced by the former does not normally precede the main clause.

Also there are cases in which the scope of a negative or of some other particle is different according to whether γιατί or ἐπειδή is used, the scope being wider with the latter than with the former:

(1) θά τήν εἶχε κλέψει ἀπό κάποιον ἄλλον, γιατί δέ γνώριζε τήν Ἑλένη Φωκᾶ προσωπικά 'he must have stolen [the photograph] from someone else, because he didn't know Helen Foka personally' (The. 1940: 81).

In (1), γιατί introduces the speaker's reason for making his assumption; ἐπειδή would have given the subject's reason for stealing the photograph. These observations lead to the conclusion that γιατί is not a true subordinator, as ἐπειδή is, but stands somewhere between a subordinating and coordinating conjunction.

One idiomatic use of ἀφοῦ is worth mentioning: this is the function of an ἀφοῦ-clause as an indignant exclamation:

(2) — Γιατί δέν ἔπλυνες τά πουκάμισα; — Ἀφοῦ τά 'πλυνα! ' "Why didn't you wash the shirts?" "But I *did* wash them!" '

Among temporal conjunctions, ἐνῶ 'while' (which is also used in the adversative sense of 'whereas'), καθώς 'as', and ἀφότου '(ever) since' are never subjunctive markers. The consecutive conjunction ὥστε '(so) that' is not in itself a subjunctive marker (though it often combines with νά when it is the logical consequence rather than the actual result that is being expressed: see also 9.4.2.2.5 (6)):

(3) τόση ἦταν ἡ συμπόνια μου γιά τά δυό παιδιά ὥστε θά μπορούσα νά κάνω καί αὐτή τή θυσία 'such was my compassion for the two children that I could make this sacrifice too' (Hesse 1980: 105).

When the main clause is negative, the clause introduced by ὥστε without νά has a positive meaning (unless of course it contains a negative); the presence of νά in such circumstances would give the subordinate clause a negative meaning:

(4) ἡ ἱστορική μνήμη δέν εἶναι ἀπό τίς ἀρετές τῆς φυλῆς μας [. . .], ὥστε εἶναι κέρδος πάντα νά τήν τονίσουμε 'a historical memory is not one of the virtues of our race [. . .], so that it is always profitable to stress it' (Pol. n.d.: 198).

In (4), νά after ὥστε would alter the meaning to: 'so that it is not always profitable' (i.e. the scope of the negative would extend to the subordinate clause). In addition to being a subordinating conjunction, ὥστε may introduce main clauses and elliptical sentences indicating inference:

(5) ὥστε φεύγεις 'so you're leaving';
(6) ὥστε ἔτσι, ἔ; 'so that's how it is, is it?'

Finally, certain concessive conjunctions are not subjunctive markers, nor can they combine with νά. These are mostly compound conjunctions: ἄν καί, μόλο πού, μολονότι 'although'.

9

MOOD:
SUBJUNCTIVE CLAUSES

9.1 GENERAL

As has been stated before (3.2.2), the term 'subjunctive' is used in this book not as a morphological but as a semantic and syntactical category. The only morphological difference between the indicative and the subjunctive uses of verbs in MG is that the perfective non-past may appear only in subjunctive uses; conversely, the perfective past is not normally found in subjunctive clauses, except in epistemic (inferential), comparative and concessive clauses (since these express an actual, not a theoretical, possibility). The term 'subjunctive' is employed here for want of anything better: it is not really satisfactory, since it suggests that the clause in which a subjunctive appears is subjoined (i.e. subordinated) to another, whereas the MG subjunctive, like the indicative, may appear equally in main clauses or in subordinate clauses.

Semantically, the indicative normally expresses a *reality*, an action or state which has occurred or prevailed in the past, or is occurring or prevailing in the present: in other words, it makes some statement whose truth is potentially *verifiable*; the indicative is strictly 'non-modal' (Lyons 1968: 307). The subjunctive, on the other hand, may make a statement about future time (which is not verifiable, at least at the time of speaking); it may express a supposition, a wish, a command, a desire, or it may appear in some utterance which is not actually a *statement*. Thus 'subjunctive' is used here as a blanket term to cover various moods traditionally known as subjunctive, optative, volitive, epistemic, deontic, and others, even imperative (when not realized morphologically as an imperative) and future. (The negative and interrogative are viewed here merely as varieties of either the indicative or the subjunctive; they generally do not in themselves alter the mood—or lack of mood—of the declarative clause.)

Syntactically, the subjunctive verb is preceded by one or more *subjunctive markers* (also known as 'mood formants' or 'syntactic converters': Barri 1981): *θά, νά, ἄς, πρίν*; temporal conjunctions expressing anteriority and universal relatives, when reference is not to the past; and a few other conjunctions. There are a very few, mostly stereotyped, constructions, in which the perfective non-past (which may appear only in subjunctive clauses) is found without one of these markers: e.g. *ἔρθει δέν ἔρθει, θά πᾶμε ἐκδρομή αὔριο* 'whether (s)he comes or not, we shall go [on an] excursion tomorrow.' Thus our definition of 'subjunctive' is a rather circular one: it is the mood of the verb when that verb is preceded by a subjunctive marker; and a subjunctive marker is a particle or conjunction which may condition a perfective non-past verb form.

Perhaps the most interesting facet of modality in MG is that declarations (or questions) concerning future time are equated with non-affirming statements, which express hypotheses or inferences about the past, present, or future, by virtue of the fact that they are all expressed by the use of *θά* before the verb. Consider the following examples of verbs preceded by *θά*:

(1) Imperfective non-past:
    θά τῆς μιλάει 'he will talk to her (habitually)' (future; iterative);
    'he will be talking to her' (future; progressive);
    'he must talk/be talking to her' (present; inferential; progressive or iterative);

(2) Imperfective past:
    θά τῆς μιλοῦσε 'he would talk/be talking to her' (present; conditional; progressive, iterative, or non-progressive);
    'he would have talked/been talking to her' (past; conditional; progressive, iterative, or non-progressive);
    'he was about to talk to her' (future-in-past);
    'he must have talked/been talking to her' (past; inferential; progressive or iterative);

(3) Perfective non-past:
    θά τῆς μιλήσει 'he will talk to her' (future; non-iterative and non-progressive);

(4) Perfective past:
    θά τῆς μίλησε 'he must have talked to her' (past; inferential; non-iterative and non-progressive).

In most cases, the same utterances (with different intonation or, ortho-graphically, with a question mark) could be interpreted as questions; and any of these utterances may appear in a main or a subordinate clause (subject to certain restrictions). The common factor in all these examples is that, irrespective of what (s)he believes, the speaker does not positively know that what (s)he says is a true fact, since either the event has not happened and is not happening, or, even if it has or is, (s)he cannot be absolutely certain that this is the case.

9.2 THE SUBJUNCTIVE MARKERS AND TENSE

The subjunctive markers are a syntactically heterogeneous group of words: ϑά may precede a main or subordinate verb but is not in itself a subordinator; νά, ἄς, and certain other markers may be found with a main verb, but may act as subordinating conjunctions; while most of the other subjunctive markers may act only as subordinating conjunc-tions. They are also semantically heterogeneous; for example, ϑά generally indicates future time or condition, while νά acts purely as a modal particle with no semantic function. They all however share the common characteristic that in the verbs which they govern tense dis-tinctions tend to be neutralized, since in the most frequently used sub-junctive constructions only non-past forms are possible: this is especially true in subordinate clauses (and it is also true in the morphological imperative). There is in fact a scale of neutralization, the degree depend-ing on the syntactical and semantic function of the clause.

Maximum neutralization can be observed in verbs governed by πρίν and προτοῦ 'before', in which only the perfective non-past is normally possible (irrespective of temporal reference), since (a) the perfective is a mandatory component of a subjunctive clause in the expression of a non-progressive and non-iterative action which failed to coincide with another, and (b) a past tense is precluded (as it is in expressions of future time), since the verb governed by the conjunction denotes an action which takes place in the future *in relation to the other verb*. Thus:

(1) πρίν κοιμηϑῶ, διάβασα ἕνα ποίημα 'before going to sleep, I read (past) a poem' (probably referring to a single occasion);

(2) πρίν κοιμηϑῶ, διάβαζα ἕνα ποίημα 'before going to sleep, I used to read a poem';

(3) πρίν κοιμηϑῶ, διαβάζω ἕνα ποίημα 'before going to sleep, I read (pres.) a poem' (habitual; or historic present);

(4) πρὶν κοιμηθῶ, θά διαβάσω ἕνα ποίημα 'before going to sleep, I'll read a poem' (either about one occasion, or consuetudinal: see 3.2.3.2);

(5) πρὶν κοιμηθῶ, θά διαβάζω ἕνα ποίημα 'before going to sleep, I'll read/be reading a poem' (habitual, progressive, or inferential).

In all these examples, the verb governed by πρίν is invariable.

Minimum neutralization may be observed in epistemic, comparative, and concessive constructions. Thus (epistemic/inferential):

(6) μπορεῖ νά ἦρθε '(s)he may have come' (non-iterative);

(7) μπορεῖ νά ἐρχόταν '(s)he may have been coming'; '(s)he may have come (habitually)';

(8) μπορεῖ νά ἔρχεται '(s)he may be coming'; '(s)he may come (habitually)';

(9) μπορεῖ νά ἔρθει '(s)he may come' (non-iterative).

Here, the verb governed by νά is free to alter according to the temporal reference. Between these two extremes is the most usual situation, in which the subjunctive verb indicates aspect but not time:

(10) ἤθελα νά φεύγω/φύγω 'I wanted to leave (habitually/non-habitually');

(11) θέλω νά φεύγω/φύγω 'I want to leave (habitually/non-habitually)';

(12) θά θέλω νά φεύγω/φύγω 'I shall want to leave (habitually/non-habitually)';

(13) θά ἤθελα νά φεύγω/φύγω 'I would like to leave (habitually/non-habitually.'

Only in the last case (when the main verb is in the 'conditional') is any variation possible: θά ἤθελα νά ἔφευγα (using the imperfective past in the subordinate verb) expresses the same meaning in a more wistful manner, but the aspectual distinction is thereby sacrificed. Outside epistemic, concessive, and comparative clauses, the construction subjunctive marker + imperfective past is a *modal past*, which expresses an action that has not taken and is not taking place. On the other hand, past reference relative to the main verb may be expressed by using a perfect form:

(14) ἤθελα νά εἶχα φύγει 'I wanted to have left' (if the utterance were preceded by θά, it would be rendered, 'I would like to have left').

Such potential neutralization sometimes leads speakers and writers to use alternatives which will give a clearer indication of time. Thus verbs of perception with a direct object and a verb expressing what this object is perceived as doing may be expressed by means of *νά*, after which only an imperfective non-past is possible in the subordinated verb (cf. 9.4.2.2.1 (c)):

(15)
κοιτάζω		
κοίταξα		
κοίταξα	} τό ποτάμι νά κυλάει	
θά κοιτάξω		

	watch/am watching	
'I	was watching/used to watch	} the river flowing [by].
	watched	
	shall watch	

But, alternatively, *πού* and the indicative (or subjunctive if *θά* is used) may indicate temporal reference:

(16)   κοιτάζω τό ποτάμι πού κυλάει
κοίταξα τό ποτάμι πού κυλοῦσε
κοίταξα τό ποτάμι πού κυλοῦσε/κύλησε
θά κοιτάξω τό ποτάμι πού θά κυλάει/κυλήσει.

In (16) the form of the subordinate verb may vary according to the temporal reference and the nature of the action. (In fact, the four sentences in (16) are not completely synonymous with those in (15): while in the former the focus of attention is on the action of the river's flow, in the latter it is on the river itself.)

Another method of avoiding the neutralization of tense which may occur in a subordinate verb is *parataxis* (with *καί* 'and'), which is commonly found in colloquial speech. This most often occurs when there is temporal coincidence between the actions denoted by the two verbs (i.e. if in more formal Greek the subordinated verb would appear in the imperfective non-past): this is also true of the *νά/πού* alternation mentioned above. In such circumstances, the clause introduced by *καί* is normally a statement (see 7.2).

Sometimes, however, the verb in the *καί*-clause is actually in the perfective non-past (i.e. it is a subjunctive), when the action denoted is not real:

(17)   μή μέ κάνεις κι ἀρχίσω πάλι 'don't make me start again' (= ν' ἀρχίσω).

9.3 SYNTACTICAL HETEROGENEITY OF SUBJUNCTIVE MARKERS

Subjunctive markers differ among themselves with regard both to negatives and to word order. While νά and ἄς are always negated by μή(ν), the others use the same negative as is used with the indicative, namely δέ(ν); on the other hand, οὔτε 'neither . . . nor; not even' may be used whether or not the verb is governed by νά or ἄς. But although it is convenient for the purposes of distinguishing the negative particles to separate νά- and ἄς-clauses from others, for other purposes such clauses may be viewed simply as a subcategory of subjunctive clauses. (Μή(ν) is a subjunctive marker in itself only when it is used without another subjunctive marker, as for example in negative commands.) Again, whereas ϑά is preceded by the negative, all other subjunctive markers are followed by the negative, which in turn immediately precedes the proclitic-+-verb phrase. And whereas νά and ἄς (with or without the negative) and μή(ν) (when used in negative commands) are immediately followed by the proclitic-+-verb phrase, this order is not obligatory after those subjunctive markers which are true conjunctions; nevertheless, the conjunction is not usually separated from the verb in ordinary speech, and the only words that may appear between them are adverbials or subject noun phrases (see also 7.1.1 (10) and 7.1.2 (1)-(2)). There are certain co-occurrence restrictions on subjunctive markers: ἄς and μή(ν) (as a subjunctive marker) cannot co-occur with any other; and νά may not co-occur with ϑά or with certain conjunctions (e.g. ἄμα, μόλις, ὅταν, ἀφοῦ, ἄν).

9.4 USES OF THE VARIOUS SUBJUNCTIVE MARKERS

It would make little sense to divide the uses of the subjunctive according to whether it appears in a main or a subordinate clause, since there is often little difference in usage. For example, the sentence,

(1a) νά περάσει μέσα ὁ κύριος ᾿Αμπατζόγλου 'let Mr Abadzoglou go/come [lit. 'pass'] in',

in which νά governs a main verb, differs structurally only in the addition of one word from the sentence,

(1b) ϑέλω νά περάσει μέσα ὁ κύριος ᾿Αμπατζόγλου 'I want Mr Abadzoglou to go/come in',

in which it governs a subordinate verb. Similarly,

(2a) μή φύγει ὁ Τάκης 'don't let Takis leave',

is not very different in structure from,

(2b) φοβᾶμαι μή φύγει ὁ Τάκης 'I'm afraid (lest) Takis [might] leave.'

It might even be said that underlying each of (1b) and (2b) there are two separate sentences which have become linked only by the removal of a full stop ('I want. Let him come in'; 'I'm afraid. Don't let him leave'). It has also been decided not to deal with mood according to the various semantic mood categories (future, volitive, conditional, jussive, etc.), since this would entail a high degree of repetition. Instead, the chief subjunctive markers will be examined in turn.

9.4.1 ΘΑ

The particle ϑά may be used with any form of the verb. As well as being used to refer to future time, it may also endow the verb with a conditional (potential) or epistemic (inferential) sense (cf. 9.1).

In future reference proper (i.e. future in relation to the time of utterance), ϑά is used with the perfective or imperfective non-past:

(1a) ϑά σοῦ γράψω αὔριο 'I'll write to you tomorrow';
(1b) ϑά σοῦ γράφω ταχτικά 'I'll write to you regularly.'

To refer to an action which takes place before another action in the future, ϑά may be used with the perfect non-past:

(2) ὅταν ἔρθετε ϑά ἔχουμε φύγει 'when you come we'll have left.'

Note also the construction ϑά πεῖ 'means' (with inanimate subject: τί ϑά πεῖ Δημοκρατία; 'what does "Democracy" mean?'—contrast, with animate subject, ϑέλω νά πῶ 'I mean': τί ϑέλεις νά πεῖς; 'what do you mean?').

In conditional sentences, ϑά is followed by the imperfective or perfect past: the former may have present, past, or future reference, but the latter may be used only if the speaker/writer wishes to make it clear that the verb refers to the past:

(3) ἄν πήγαινες ϑά τόν ἔβλεπες 'if you went, you would see him' (present/future); 'if you'd gone you'd have seen him' (past);
(4) χωρίς τόν Ἄλκη ϑά εἶχα σκοτωθεῖ 'but for [lit. 'without'] Alkis, I would have been killed' (past only).

A notable feature of the 'conditional' is that it is 'the one pattern in the [MG] temporal system which is relative only and not aspectual' (Kahane and Kahane 1958: 470): that is to say, not only does the conditional not necessarily indicate tense, but it always fails to show aspect too. Neither of the above sentences (3) and (4) indicates whether the potential actions are viewed as occurring habitually/progressively or non-habitually/non-progressively. Thus, whereas normally mood is not a powerful category in MG, in ϑά + past it takes precedence over both aspect and tense. It was not always thus: until at least the late nineteenth century, at least in some dialects, it was possible to distinguish between aspects in the conditional, with forms such as ἤϑελα δένει (impf.) 'I would be tying' and ἤϑελα δέσει (pf.) 'I would tie'. A construction that looks much like a conditional is the iterative (the past equivalent of the consuetudinal future: see 3.2.3.2):

(5) κάϑε μέρα ϑά καϑόταν στό ἴδιο καφενεῖο 'every day he would/ used to sit at the same café' (more normal without ϑά).

While the future is expressed only with non-past forms, and the conditional only with past forms (and never with the perfective), epistemic (inferential) constructions may use any verb form; though it is characteristic that only ϑά + perfective past is unambiguously epistemic (since this combination is not found for the other functions of ϑά), and some forms are more commonly found in epistemic uses than are others (see examples (1)–(4) in 9.1, to which could be added further examples of ϑά with the perfect past and non-past tenses in epistemic uses). With the perfective non-past, it is impossible (and unnecessary) to distinguish the future from the epistemic meanings, since in either case the speaker is making a prediction, which by its very nature is a statement that cannot be verified at the time of speaking. It will be noticed that, apart from (3), the examples given in 9.1 could have been uttered (with a greater sense of certainty) without ϑά. (Inferential epistemic utterances are often alternatively expressed by means of πρέπει νά.)

The imperfective past is used after ϑά in certain future-in-the-past uses, in which the verb phrase acts as a past version of one referring to the future. Such is the case when the future of direct speech is (optionally) altered, according to the sequence of tenses, after a main verb in a past tense: e.g.

(6a) 'Τί ϑά κάνει;' ' "What will (s)he do?" ';
(6b) περίμενα νά δῶ τί ϑά ἔκανε 'I waited to see what (s)he would do.'

The presence of a past-tense main verb is not however necessary. Consider the following scenario:

(7a) (Present reference) 'Θά βγῶ τώρα.' — Ντρίν-ντρίν! ' "I shall go out now."—Brr-brr!';

(7b) (Past reference) Θά ἔβγαινα ὅταν χτύπησε τό τηλέφωνο 'I was about to go out/just going out when the phone rang.'

The imperfective past is used here in the same way as in the 'potential' example given in 3.3.1.2. In narrative it is usual to use θά + imperfective past of actions which were to take place at a time posterior to the past of the main action.

Finally, θά + imperfective past may be used to formulate a polite and tentative expression of request, intention or wish (whether fulfilled or not):

(8)   θά ἤθελα νά πάω στήν 'Αμερική 'I'd like to go to America';
(9)   θά ἤθελες νά μᾶς πεῖς . . .; 'would you like to tell us . . .?';
(10) θά ἤθελαν νά μήν εἶχαν πάει 'they wished they hadn't gone';
(11) συμπερασματικά, θά ἔλεγα τά ἐξῆς . . . 'in conclusion, I would [like to] say the following . . .';
(12) θά ἔπρεπε νά φύγουμε 'we should leave' (cf. πρέπει . . . 'we must . . .').

9.4.2 NA

The use of νά is so frequent and so varied that a systematic and comprehensive survey of its uses would be beyond the range of this book. As has already been mentioned, it may govern a main verb as a subjunctive marker pure and simple, or it may serve to subordinate a clause: such a clause may act as the subject of a verb, or it may be subordinated to a verb, a noun, an adjective, a preposition, a conjunction, a definite article, or another clause.

In many of its uses, νά + verb is the equivalent of an infinitive in modern Western European languages. The lack of an infinitive, which is periodically lamented by Greek writers, makes it impossible for a verb to be used without at least an implied subject: the complete impersonality of reference found in an infinitive cannot be achieved in MG, the best approximation being the use of the second person singular (which is potentially ambiguous) or of κανείς 'one'. Consider this traditional translation of the famous line from *Hamlet*:

(1) Νά ζεῖ κανείς ἢ νά μή ζεῖ, ἰδού ἡ ἀπορία 'should one live or should one die, behold the question' (Vik. 1882: 82).

On the other hand, the flexibility and versatility which νά puts at the speaker's disposal provide a degree of compensation for the lack of the infinitive. Quite apart from the ease with which one can convey subtle distinctions of mood by means of νά and the fact that a verb after νά usually displays aspectual differentiation (something lacking, for instance, from the French infinitive), this particle also facilitates such syntactical switches as changes of person, thus making for conciseness of expression:

(2) θέλω νά πάω 'I want to go' (lit. 'I-want to I-go'): cf. F *je veux aller*;

(3) θέλω νά πᾶς 'I want you to go' (lit. 'I-want to you-go'): cf. F *je veux que tu ailles.*

While in the latter example English demands the insertion of the second subject ('you') and French needs to use a completely different construction from the first, MG simply alters the person ending of the second verb.

9.4.2.1 Νά + main verb

9.4.2.1.1 Commands and exhortations

As well as being employed in third-person equivalents of the imperative, νά + verb may be used as an alternative to the imperative in the second person, and, with the first person, to express an offer to do something:

(1) (3rd person) ὁ Γιῶργος νά ἔρθει στό τηλέφωνο 'Let George come to the telephone' (cf. imperative, ἔλα Γιῶργο στό τηλέφωνο 'come to the telephone, George');

(2) (2nd person) νά φύγεις αὔριο, ὄχι σήμερα 'you should leave tomorrow, not today' (cf. imperative, φύγε αὔριο . . ., which is more abrupt);

(3) (1st person) λύσε με καί νά σοῦ δείξω τό θησαυρό 'untie me and let me show you [or 'I'll show you'] the treasure.'

Deliberative questions in the first person (eliciting a yes/no answer) may also be expressed in the same way:

(4) νά σοῦ δείξω τό θησαυρό; 'shall/should I show you the treasure?' (i.e. 'do you want me to . . .?');

(5) νά τά ποῦμε [sc. τά κάλαντα]; 'should we sing [the carols]?' (said by children at Christmas when a householder opens the door to them).

In all the above examples, the perfective non-past is used. The imperfective non-past is used when the reference is to habitual or progressive action; and the imperfective past when reference is to the past. An example of the latter is (6):

(6) Τά ἤθελες; Νά μοῦ τό 'λεγες. 'Did you want them? You should have told me.'

9.4.2.1.2 Wishes and curses

With non-past forms, νά may be used to express a wish or a curse referring to future time; with the imperfective past, it may express one referring to past or present (and therefore incapable of fulfilment); in this case νά is often preceded by ἄχ:

(1) νά 'σαι καλά 'bless you' (lit. 'may you be well');
(2) νά ζήσει [τό παιδί σου] 'may [your child] live' (said as a polite formula to a parent);
(3) φύγε καί νά μή σέ ξαναδῶ! 'go away and never let me see you again!';
(4) ἄ νά χαθεῖς, βλαμμένε! 'get lost, you idiot!';
(5) νά 'σουνα μπροστά! 'if only you'd been there!';
(6) μόνο νά μήν ἀργοῦσες πάντοτε 'I only wish you weren't always late';
(7) ἄχ, νά μποροῦσα νά φύγω! 'oh, if only I could leave!'

9.4.2.1.3 Exclamations

In an exclamation (often of protest or indignation) νά may be followed by any finite verb form, depending on temporal reference. Such an exclamation is often expressed interrogatively.

(1) καί νά σκεφτεῖ κανείς πώς τόν μεγάλωσα ἐγώ! 'and to think [lit. 'one should think'] I raised him myself!';
(2) Νά ἔρχεται ὁ Μίκης νά μέ δεῖ; Ἀπίστευτο. 'Mikis is coming to see me? Incredible!';
(3) τόσες μέρες καί νά μήν τό σκέφτηκα! 'so many days [have gone by] and I haven't thought about it!' (Hesse 1980: 76).

9.4.2.1.4 Narrative νά

The imperfective non-past is sometimes used with νά in narratives in order to give dramatic effect to the description of a progressive or iterative action in the past:

(1) ἅμα τ᾽ ἄκουσε ἡ Μαρία, νά κλαίει, νά φωνάζει, νά τραβάει τά μαλλιά της 'as soon as Mary heard it, she began to cry and shout and tear her hair' (Tzartzanos 1963: 192).

9.4.2.2 Νά + subordinate verb

9.4.2.2.1 Νά as a subordinating particle with a verb

The most frequent uses of *νά* are in constructions of the type Verb + *νά* + Verb. These uses are those which correspond to most uses of the infinitive in certain other European languages. Among them, the most usual functions are those in which the first verb has, loosely, the sense of necessity, ability, or volition.

It is important to distinguish between *νά*-clauses that are the subjects of verbs and those that act as objects. As has been seen (2.4.1), impersonal verbs may have *νά*-clauses as their subjects; these verbs include πρέπει, μπορεῖ (but not personal μπορῶ), and the copula εἶναι with a neuter adjective. In the following subsections, most of the uses of *νά* which will be examined are as an introductive of object-clauses.

(a) μπορῶ and πρέπει (dynamic, obligative, and epistemic
    constructions)

In the imperfective, μπορῶ indicates potential ability, while in the perfective it implies achievement of this potential. Additionally, in the third person singular of the imperfective (normally non-past), μπορεῖ may be used in an epistemic sense to denote a possibility (see 2.4.1 and, for examples, 9.2 (6)–(9)).

(1) θά μπορούσαμε νά πᾶμε, ἀλλά . . . 'we could have gone, but . . .';

(2) [δέν] μπορέσαμε νά δοῦμε τήν παράσταση 'we were [not] able to see the performance' (for the paratactic alternative to the positive version of such a sentence, see 7.2 (14)).

Πρέπει, which exists only in the third person and only in the imperfective, denotes necessity, obligation (whether fulfilled or not), or probability (inference):

(3) ἔπρεπε νά σ᾽ τό πῶ (a) 'I had to tell you'; (b) 'I should have told you';

(4) ὁ Ταμανάκιας θά 'πρεπε νά εἶχε ἀρχίσει νά ψήνεται 'Tama-
nakias must [by then] have begun being roasted' (Ioa. 1976:
234) (epistemic sense: alternatively, ὁ Τ. θά εἶχε ἀρχίσει).

In sense (a) of example (3), an alternative might be to replace ἔπρεπε
with ἀναγκάστηκα 'I was forced'; in (b), the fact that the obligation was
unfulfilled could be stressed by saying νά σ' τό εἶχα πεῖ, and/or by
placing θά before ἔπρεπε. An alternative (colloquial) method of indicating an unfulfilled obligation is to place κανονικά (lit. 'ordinarily')
before ἔπρεπε. Note that the negative δέν ἔπρεπε νά σ' τό πῶ can mean
only 'I shouldn't have told you.'

There are of course other verbs or verbal phrases (followed by νά)
which denote ability or inability, obligation or necessity. One of the
ways of expressing obligation is by ἔχω νά 'I have to':

(5) ἔχω νά καθαρίσω τό σπίτι 'I have to clean the house.'

(b) Volitive and other uses
In a large number of uses loosely termed *volitive*, νά may replace
a direct object of the main verb (e.g. θέλω φαΐ 'I want food', θέλω
νά φάω 'I want to eat'). Such is the case with a number of verbs such
as θέλω 'I want', ζητῶ 'I ask', δέχομαι 'I agree (to do something)',
συμβουλεύω 'I advise', and ἀπαγορεύω 'I forbid'. Some of these demand
that both main and subordinate verbs be in the same person, others that
the persons be different, while yet others entail no such restrictions.
A clear example of a νά-clause as equivalent to a direct object is one
with κάνω such as the following:

(6) δέ θά κάνουν τίποτα ἄλλο παρά νά δεχτοῦν τό σχέδιο 'they'll
do nothing but accept the plan.'

With some volitive verbs, however (e.g. προσπαθῶ 'I try', ἑτοιμάζομαι
'I get ready', and verbs of motion), which cannot take the sort of
direct object which might replace the νά-clause, their relationship with
the main verb is more difficult to define. Generally the main verbs
contain some sense of being willing (or unwilling) to do something, or
of wanting someone to act (or preventing them from acting) in some
way. With some volitive verbs, the person or thing which the subject
of the main verb wants to perform the action of the subordinate verb
may appear either as the explicit object of the main verb or as the
explicit subject of the subordinate verb.

Normally, volitive verbs may be followed by any finite verb form but the perfective past. In expressions of fervent wishes or potential (contingent) situations, the imperfective past is often used after νά, especially when the head verb is in the same tense (cf. 9.4.2.1.2):

(7) ἄχ, νά 'ταν νά ξανάκανα τή ζωή μου! 'oh, if only I could live [lit. 'make'] my life over again!' (Kaz. 1965: 525);

(8) θά προτιμοῦσα νά ἐρχόσουνα αὔριο παρά σήμερα 'I'd prefer/ have preferred you to come tomorrow rather than today' (future reference in second verb: cf. θά προτιμοῦσα νά εἶχες φύγει χθές 'I would have preferred you to leave yesterday; I would prefer you to have left yesterday');

(9) [καί νά εἶχα,] δέν πρόκειται νά ὑπέγραφα '[even if I had,] I wouldn't sign' (for δέ θά ὑπέγραφα or δέ θά ἐπρόκειτο νά ὑπογράψω) (T 2 Aug. 1979, 37).

After certain verbs, νά + imperfective non-past is roughly equivalent to a present participle. Such verbs include βαριέμαι 'I'm bored', κουράζομαι 'I get tired', χαίρομαι 'I'm glad', and λυπᾶμαι 'I'm sorry':

(10) βαρέθηκα νά περιμένω 'I'[ve] got fed up waiting';

(11) λυπᾶμαι νά σᾶς ἀκούσω νά μιλᾶτε ἔτσι 'I'm sorry to hear you talking like this' (cf. 8.1.3.1).

Another use of νά which could be classed as volitive is that indicating destination after verbs of motion:

(12) τί ἦρθες νά κάνεις ἐδῶ; 'what did you come to do here?'

(c) Νά after verbs of perception
When a νά-clause is governed by a verb of perception it is usually an object complement. In such cases the object of the main verb (which must be stated) normally becomes the subject of the subordinate verb:

(13) δέν τόν εἴδαμε νά περνάει τό δρόμο 'we didn't see him cross the road'

((13) does not specify whether he crossed or not: cf. δέν τόν εἴδαμε πού πέρασε τό δρόμο, which implies that he did; and cf. 9.2 (15) and (16)). When that which is perceived is expressed not by a clitic pronoun but by a noun, the noun may figure either as the explicit object of the main verb or as the explicit subject of the subordinate verb:

(14a) νιώθαμε τήν ἄνοιξη νά ἔρχεται } 'we felt the spring coming'.
(14b) νιώθαμε νά ἔρχεται ἡ ἄνοιξη }

(d) Νά after verbs of saying etc.

Νά is used to convert an imperative into reported speech:

(15) προχωρῆστε! 'go ahead' → τούς εἶπε νά προχωρήσουν '(s)he told them to go ahead.'

Νά is also used after λές/λέτε 'do you think?', and certain other verbs (especially in the negative), such as πιστεύω 'I believe', θυμᾶμαι 'I remember', φαντάζομαι 'I imagine', and ξέρω 'I know':

(16) λές νά ἔρθει αὔριο; 'do you think (s)he'll come tomorrow?';
(17) δέν πιστεύω νά κάνω λάθος 'I don't think I'm mistaken';
(18) δέ θυμᾶμαι νά τόν εἶδα ποτέ 'I don't remember ever having seen him';
(19) δέ φαντάζομαι νά βρεῖς καμιά δυσκολία 'I don't imagine you'll find any difficulty.'

Except in the case of λές/λέτε, νά after the above verbs can be replaced by ὅτι/πώς (followed by θά if reference is to future time). The construction with νά implies that the possibility of the situation denoted by the subordinated verb being true is even more remote.

9.4.2.2.2 Νά after interrogatives and certain other words

Interrogative pronouns and adverbs may be followed by νά to form a question which bears the sense of 'I wonder . . .' The verb may be in the perfective/imperfective past or imperfective non-past for real situations in the past or present; or in the perfective/imperfective non-past or imperfective past for unreal situations in which reference is timeless or to the past:

(1) πότε νά ἔφυγε ἄραγε; 'when can/could (s)he have left, I wonder?';
(2) ποῦ νά πήγαινε ἄραγε; 'where can/could (s)he have been going, I wonder?';
(3) γιατί νά ἔρχεται στή Θεσσαλονίκη; 'why should (s)he be coming [or 'come' (habitually)] to Salonica?';
(4) πῶς νά μήν τόν ἀγαπήσω; 'how can I help loving him?' (lit. 'how may I not love him?');
(5) ποιός νά σηκώνεται κάθε πρωί στίς πέντε; 'who's going to get up at five every morning?' (or, 'who can it be that gets up . . .?');
(6) τί νά ἔκανα; 'what could I do/have done?'

There is also a narrative use of such a construction:

(7) μπαίνω στό σπίτι καί τί νά δῶ; . . . 'I went [lit. 'go'] into the house and what should I see? . . .'

Such interrogative clauses may also be governed by a verb:

(8) δέν ἔχω   } τί νά κάνω { 'I have nothing to do';
    δέν ξέρω   'I don't know what to do.'

There are certain other words which, as in examples (1)–(6), may govern νά without the presence of a verb other than the one in the νά-clause. These are: μακάρι, ἄντε, ἴσως, καλά, παρά λίγο, and τό πολύ-πολύ.

Μακάρι is used to express a wish: it may be used with any verb form, but is most often found with the imperfective past:

(9) μακάρι νά ἤξερα 'I wish I knew.'

῎Αντε 'come on' is especially used in SMG with νά + perfective non-past in one particular construction which expresses contemptuous disbelief in the possibility that an occurrence could happen in the future:

(10) ἄντε τώρα νά μποῦν αὐτοί στό πνεῦμα τό ἀρχαῖο τό ἑλληνικό! 'I'd like to see them [the Turks] entering into the ancient Greek spirit!' (Kazazis 1975: 162).

᾽Ακόμα νά is used with the perfective non-past to mean 'not yet':

(11) ἀκόμα νά περάσει τό λεωφορεῖο; 'hasn't the bus come by yet?'

Although ἴσως 'perhaps' may act as subjunctive marker on its own (see 9.4.4.2), and may combine with θά, it has an epistemic sense ('maybe') or a conditional sense (14) when followed by νά and any finite verb form. Whereas ἴσως alone is not often negated (when it is, it is followed by δέν), ἴσως νά may readily be negated by μήν:

(12) ἴσως νά ἦρθε 'maybe (s)he came/has come';
(13) ἴσως νά μή βρεθοῦμε πάλι 'maybe we won't meet up again';
(14) ἄλλοι, στή θέση του, ἴσως νά τίναζαν τά μυαλά τους στόν ἀέρα 'others, in his position, would perhaps have blown their brains out' (Kar. n.d.: I 227).

Καλά is used with νά + perfective non-past (irrespective of temporal reference) in the stereotyped phrase:

(15) καλά νά πάθεις 'it served/serves/will serve you right.'

Παρά λίγο 'nearly, almost' is followed by νά + perfective non-past or imperfective past:

(16) παρά λίγο νά πνιγοῦμε/πνιγόμαστε 'we nearly drowned.'

Τό πολύ-πολύ 'at the most' is normally used with νά + perfective non-past:

(17) ἐκείνην, τό πολύ-πολύ νά τήν ἀπασχολήσει ἕνα τηλεφώνημα τοῦ ἀντρός [= ἄντρα] της 'the most that would occupy her would be a phone-call from her husband (Koum. 1978: 55).

Similar to such constructions are those in which νά is preceded by an adjective, where a copula can be understood as having been deleted:

(18) [εἶναι] δυνατόν νά μή συμβεῖ ποτέ 'it's possible it will never happen';
(19) [εἶναι] πιθανόν νά περάσανε κιόλας 'it's probable they've already come by';
(20) [εἶναι] σπάνιο ν' ἀκούσεις τέτοιο πράγμα 'it's rare to hear such a thing.'

9.4.2.2.3 Νά governed by a clause

There is such a wide variety of different uses of νά governed by a whole clause (the νά-clause being an adverbial clause) that there is not enough space to deal with each one in detail. We shall confine ourselves to attempting to show the range of its functions by providing just a few examples of each of the main types of construction, namely conditional and concessive clauses and clauses of time and manner.

(a) Νά as a conditional or concessive conjunction

When used as a conditional conjunction, νά often gives the verb a slightly different nuance from the more neutral ἄν 'if'. There may be an emotional colouring (cf. νά as a subjunctive marker expressing wishes: 9.4.2.1.2):

(1) θά 'ταν ἀλλιῶς νά μ' ἔβλεπε μέ τή στολή μου 'if [only] she could see me in my uniform, it would be different.'

On the other hand, νά may be the equivalent of the concessive 'even if' (alternatively expressed by κι ἄν). Here νά is usually used with καί, which then appears as the first word in the clause (or second if the clause is introduced by another conjunction). Often in such constructions a special emphasis is placed on a particular phrase (the focus of the condition), which then stands between καί and νά and is given heavy stress in speech:

(2) μά καί ν' ἀρνηθεῖ ὁ Κωστής νά κάνει τή δωρεά, δέν θά χαλάσω τό γάμο 'but even if Kostis refuses to make the bequest, I shan't dissolve the marriage' (Kar. n.d.: I 172);

(3) καί τεράστια προίκα νά μοῦ 'φερνες, πάλι δέ θά σ' ἔπαιρνα 'even if you brought me a *huge* dowry, I still wouldn't marry [lit. 'take'] you.'

(b) Νά in clauses of time or manner

Νά may be used to introduce clauses of time (instead of, e.g., ὅταν 'when') or clauses of manner (instead of, e.g., μέ τό νά 'by'). In particular instances it is difficult, if not impossible, to distinguish whether it is time or manner which is being conveyed. In many cases in which the subject of the two verbs is the same, the νά-clause could be replaced by a present participle:

(4) νά ἀκούω ἔτσι τά ἀναφιλητά της, μοῦ ἐρχόντανε καί μένα δάκρυα στά μάτια 'to hear her sobbing [lit. 'sobs'] like that, tears came to my eyes too' (Hesse 1980: 115);

(5) δέ θά χάσουν τίποτα νά περιμένουν 'they'll lose nothing by waiting' (manner or condition);

(6) κάθισε πολλή ὥρα νά κλαίει '(s)he sat for a long time weeping' (alternatively κλαίγοντας 'weeping' or κι ἔκλαιγε 'and wept').

9.4.2.2.4 Νά governed by a noun or an adjective

Most uses of νά governed by nouns are equivalent to relative or result clauses (it is not always possible to distinguish which). With others, the noun in question is the equivalent of a verb in volitive or other use; while with yet others it is difficult to categorize the precise semantic function of the νά-clause.

(1) δέν εἶμαι γυναίκα νά φοβηθῶ τά ὄνειρα.

(1) may mean one of the following: (a) spoken by a woman, with no pause after γυναίκα: 'I'm not [the sort of] woman to be afraid of dreams' (relative); (b) spoken by a man, with a pause (comma) after γυναίκα: 'I'm not a woman, so that I'm not afraid of dreams' (result).

(2) τό τραῖνο, εὐτυχῶς, δέν εἶναι αὐτοκίνητο νά τό σταματοῦν, ὅπου θέλουν καί νά μαγαρίζουν 'a train, fortunately, isn't a car, for people to stop wherever they want and foul [the place]' (Ioa. 1976: 255) (result).

In its volitive uses, the *νά*-clause may explain the precise reference of the noun (which is often deverbal):

(3) *βγῆκε διαταγή νά γυρίσουμε στά σπίτια μας* 'an order was issued, [that is to say] that we should return to our homes' (cf. *μᾶς διατάξανε* 'they ordered us').

In such cases, the noun is often the subject or object of some commonly used verb such as *ἔχω* 'I have', *δίνω* 'I give', *κάνω* 'I make':

(4) *ἔχετε τήν καλοσύνη νά κλείσετε τήν πόρτα;* 'would you be so kind as to close the door?'

The situations in which *νά* is governed by an adjective are not very different:

(5) *ἤμουν ἔτοιμος νά σοῦ τό δώσω* 'I was ready/about to give it to you' (cf. *εἶχα ἐτοιμαστεῖ . . .* 'I had prepared myself . . .');
(6) [*ἦταν μιά ἐμπειρία*] *ἀνεπίδεχτη νά μεταβιβασθεῖ διδαχτικά στούς συνανθρώπους μου* '[it was an experience which was] unsusceptible of being conveyed educatively to my fellowmen' (Kar. n.d.: II 56).

9.4.2.2.5 *Νά governed by a preposition*

Νά may be governed by certain prepositions, each of the resulting combinations constituting a compound subordinating conjunction. These prepositions are *ἀντί, γιά, μέχρι, σάν*, and *χωρίς* (or *δίχως*). Other prepositions may not combine directly with *νά*. (*Πρίν*, which is sometimes found in combination with *νά*, is perhaps better seen as a conjunction than as a preposition in such circumstances, and it will be dealt with in the appropriate place: see 9.4.2.2.6).

In many cases, the *νά*-clause after a preposition may be seen as the development of a noun phrase into a clause. Since this does not usually hold true of *γιά νά*, and since this particular combination is the most frequently used, it will be dealt with separately, before the others.

(a) *Γιά νά*

This combination differs syntactically from the others in that the two elements may never be separated, whereas it is possible for, e.g., a subject noun phrase to be inserted between another preposition and *νά*.

The most common function of *γιά νά* is as an introductive to final clauses ('in order that'). The final clause is a special kind of volitive clause without volition being expressed explicitly in the main clause.

The origin of γιά νά as a development of γιά + noun phrase may be seen clearly in the following (cf. Tzartzanos 1963: 139):

(1) πῆγε | γιά | νερό '(s)he went for water';
(2) πῆγε | νά φέρει νερό '(s)he went to fetch water';
(1 + 2) πῆγε | γιά | νά φέρει νερό '(s)he went in order to fetch water.'

As has already been mentioned, verbs of motion may be followed by simple νά to indicate *destination*; while *purpose* is more likely to be expressed by γιά νά.

A second important function of γιά νά is as an introductive to result clauses, in which the combination acts instead of some other introductive such as ὥστε νά 'with the result that'. This may be observed especially when the main verb is negative:

(3) δέν ἔχω ἄμεση ἐμπειρία γιά νά μπορῶ νά σᾶς μιλήσω ὑπεύθυνα 'I don't have [any] immediate experience [of the subject] so as to be able to talk to you authoritatively' (i.e. 'with the result that I am unable') (*N* 10 Oct. 1979).

A special kind of result clause is that in which γιά νά is governed by an adjective preceded by πολύ (which has the sense of 'too'):

(4) οἱ περισσότεροι [ἦταν] πολύ φανταχτεροί γιά νά εἶναι ὡραῖοι 'most of them [were] too showy to be handsome' (Koum. 1970: 17) (contrast ἀρκετά φανταχτεροί γιά νά . . . 'showy enough to . . .').

The correspondence between such a construction as (5) (where πολύ is used without an adjective) and the equivalent with ὥστε νά (6) is conveniently illustrated in the following examples, taken from the same page of the same novel:

(5) ὁ Κωστῆς μ' ἀγαπάει πολύ, γιά νά τολμήσει νά σκεφθεῖ συνειδητά κάτι τέτοιο 'Kostis loves me too much to dare to think such a thing consciously' (i.e. 'he doesn't dare');
(6) εἶναι πολύ ἔξυπνος κι αὐτοκυριαρχημένος, ὥστε νά μήν παρουσιάσει, δίχως λόγο, τήν ἀπόκρυφη σκέψη του 'he's very clever and self-controlled, so that he won't reveal his innermost thought without reason' (or, 'he's too clever . . . to reveal . . .') (Kar. n.d.: II 64).

Note how in (6) a negative is necessary, both in Greek and in English, in the second clause if the 'too'/πολύ γιά νά-construction is not used.

In the above examples of result clauses introduced by γιά νά, the situation denoted by the subordinate verb does not occur in reality. There is another type of result clause in which the subordinate verb refers to a real situation. This type may be divided into two categories: (i) where the γιά νά-clause states the consequence (or perhaps simply the sequel) of the main clause (7); and (ii) where the γιά νά-clause expresses a real situation which has led the speaker to an inference stated in the main clause (8):

(7) ἔφυγαν γιά τή Γαλλία, γιά νά μή γυρίσουν πιά 'they left for France, never to return again';

(8) κάτι θά 'παθε ὁ Μῆτσος, γιά νά κάνει ἔτσι 'something must have happened to Mitsos for him to act like this.'

Γιά νά is used not only to express intention or result, but also cause; in (9) γιά νά is equivalent to γιατί 'because' or ἐπειδή/ἀφοῦ 'since':

(9) — Αὐτή ἐδῶ εἶναι ἀνύπαντρη; — Ἀνύπαντρη. Γιά νά μήν ἔχω λεφτά. Γαμπροί ἔρχονται, ἀλλά δέν ἔχω λεφτά. ' "This [girl] here is unmarried?" "[Yes,] unmarried. Because I haven't got any money. Prospective husbands come, but I haven't got any money." '

Finally, traces of γιά νά replacing γιά + noun phrase may be found when the combination is governed by a noun, or by some other word such as ὅσο:

(10) δέν ὑπάρχουν πιά ἄλλα περιθώρια γιά νά χειροτερέψει ἡ κατάσταση 'there is no more room [lit. 'there are no more margins'] for the situation to get worse' (K 23 Dec. 1980) (cf. περιθώρια γιά τήν ἐπιδείνωση 'room for deterioration'; but also, in same article: δέν ὑπάρχουν ἄλλωστε καί περιθώρια νά γίνουν τά πράγματα διαφορετικά 'besides, there is no room for things to happen otherwise', without γιά);

(11) ὅσο γιά νά μεταδώσουμε τίς σκέψεις μας, δέν ὑπάρχει πρόβλημα 'as for conveying our ideas, there's no problem' (cf. ὅσο γιά τή μετάδοση . . . 'as for the conveying . . .').

(b) Other prepositions governing νά

When followed by νά, the prepositions ἀντί, δίχως, and χωρίς are normally used with non-past verb forms:

(12) ἀντί νά τό κάνει ὁ Σωτήρης, τό 'κανε ἡ Γιώτα 'instead of Sotiris doing it, Yota did it';

(13) δέ θά πουλήσω τό σπίτι χωρίς/δίχως νά σέ εἰδοποιήσω
'I won't sell the house without informing you.'

Σάν νά is used to introduce comparative clauses. It is hardly ever followed by the perfective non-past. When the comparison is unreal, the imperfective past is normally used, although the imperfective non-past is sometimes used for present reference:

(14) φοροῦσε τή στολή του σάν νά ἦταν ἀληθινός στρατηγός 'he wore his uniform as if he was a real general' (cf. σάν ἀληθινός στρατηγός 'like a real general').

When σάν νά introduces an epistemic (inferential) clause (which may be a main clause, as in (16)), it may be followed by any verb form except the perfective non-past, according to the temporal reference:

(15) ξαφνικά σταμάτησε, σάν κάτι νά θυμήθηκε 'suddenly (s)he stopped, as if (s)he [had] remembered something';

(16) σάν ν' ἀκούω τή φωνή του '[it's] as if I can hear his voice', or 'I fancy I can hear his voice.'

Μέχρι is often converted into a conjunction by the addition of νά or πού. Whereas μέχρι πού is used to refer to completed events in the past, μέχρι νά may refer to present or future time; it may also refer to past time when its meaning is 'by the time that' or 'until such time as' rather than simply 'until' (i.e. when in the μέχρι-clause the speaker's viewpoint is situated at some point during, not after, the action; see also 3.3.1.4):

(17) ἔφτασε τό παιδί πέντε χρονῶν μέχρι νά μᾶς ποῦν ὅτι εἶναι αὐτιστικό 'the child [had] reached five years of age by the time they told us it was autistic' (T 25 May 1982, 100);

(18) καθίσαμε ἐκεῖ μέχρι νά περάσει ἡ μπόρα 'we sat there until [such time as] the storm should pass' (the focus of narration is situated during the storm; μέχρι πού πέρασε would mean 'until it passed', the speaker's standpoint being situated after the storm was over; cf. also the use of πρίν, 9.2).

9.4.2.2.6 Νά governed by a conjunction

Certain conjunctions may be followed by νά. Some (πρίν/προτοῦ 'before') need never be used with νά but are often found with it; certain temporal conjunctions (e.g. ὥσπου, ἕως ὅτου 'until') combine with νά when reference is to future time; universal relatives may optionally be followed by καί νά (or κι ἄν); the relatives πού and ὅπου and the result conjunction ὥστε take on a more conditional or potential sense with νά (see also 8.4); and νά converts the conjunction παρά from a noun-phrase connective to a clause connective.

Whether πρίν/προτοῦ is followed by νά is a matter of idiolectal preference. The conjunction without νά appears to be more standard:

(1) ὁ Μάνος χτύπησε στήν πόρτα μου πρίν [νά] ξημερώσει 'Manos knocked on my door before dawn [lit. 'before it dawned'].'

Several conjunctions meaning 'until' combine with νά in the same circumstances as have been specified for μέχρι νά above (9.4.2.2.5):

(2) τέλειωσε ἡ δουλειά ὥσπου νά πεῖς κίμινο 'the job was finished in a trice [lit. 'by the time you could say "cumin" ']';
(3) ἅμα κατέβει κάτω ὁ σφουγγαράς, γιατρεύεται, ὅσο νά ξανανέβει 'as soon as the sponge-diver goes down, he's cured—until [such time as] he comes up again' (Hesse 1980: 107).

(For ὅσο without νά see 8.2.4.2.)

When καί νά (or κι ἄν) is used with a universal relative, the latter's sense becomes either concessive or more universal:

(4) ὅσο καί νά τρέξω, δέ θά τόν φτάσω 'however much I run, I won't catch up with him';
(5) ὅ,τι καί νά πεῖς, εἶναι καλός ρήτορας 'whatever you might say, he's a good orator.'

The sense of the καί νά is 'absolutely (whoever, etc.)' or 'no matter (who, etc.)'. In addition, ὅπου and ὅσο are often used in special senses with νά:

(6) ὅπου νά 'ναι 'any time now';
(7) ὅσο νά 'ναι 'for all that; at all events'.

Followed immediately by νά, πού (relative or otherwise) takes on a sense of result ('such that'), expressing not so much an actual result as a potential result. In such senses πού may often be preceded by τόσος 'so much', τέτοιος 'such', or ἔτσι 'in such a way':

(8) θά πρέπει ἡ κυβέρνηση νά λάβει ὁπωσδήποτε μέτρα ἔτσι πού νά λυθεῖ τό πρόβλημα 'the government will definitely have to take measures such that the problem will be solved' (cf. πού introducing result clauses, 8.1.3.3).

Such a construction is often found when the main clause has a volitive, negative, or interrogative force:

(9) θέλω μιά δακτυλογράφο πού νά ξέρει ἀγγλικά 'I want a typist who knows English';

(10) μήπως ὑπάρχει κανένας ἐδῶ πού νά ξέρει γερμανικά; 'is there anyone here who knows German?'

The relative ὅπου is used in an analogous way:

(11) δέν ὑπάρχει γήπεδο τῆς Εὐρώπης, ὅπου νά ἀγωνίστηκε ἀγγλική ὁμάδα καί νά μήν ἔγιναν φοβερά ἐπεισόδια 'there isn't a football ground in Europe where an English team has played and [where] there haven't been frightful incidents' (T 21 Oct. 1982, 115).

Πού νά is also occasionally found as the introductive to an adverbial concessive clause:

(12) ἐγώ δέν τόν παίρνω αὐτόν, πού νά μέ κάνει χρυσή 'I'm not taking him [as a husband], even if he showers me with money [lit. 'he makes me golden']' (Tzartzanos 1963: 209).

When the conjunction παρά 'than' (not to be confused with the preposition παρά 'in spite of') combines with νά, the νά is actually governed by some word in the main clause:

(13) προτιμῶ νά φύγω παρά νά μείνω ἐδῶ χωρίς ἐσένα 'I prefer to leave than to stay here without you' (the verb προτιμῶ governs both the νά-clauses) (Hesse 1980: 98).

After a negative verb, παρά in the sense of 'except' may also combine with νά in cases such as the following:

(14) ἄλλο δέν ἔχει στό νοῦ της παρά νά παίξει καί νά γελᾶ 'she has nothing in mind but to play and laugh';

(15) δέν κάνω ἄλλο παρά νά ἐμποδίζω τό ἄδικο 'the only thing I'm doing is to prevent injustice' (lit. 'I'm doing nothing but to prevent . . .').

9.4.2.2.7 Νά preceded by the definite article

When preceded by the definite article, a νά-clause is clearly a noun clause. The article may be governed by a preposition (particularly, but not exclusively, one of those which cannot combine directly with νά: (1-2)); the article may even be in the genitive, governed by another noun, but it is always singular (3–4). Also, the article is normally present when a νά-clause (especially one which acts as the subject of the main verb) stands before the main clause (5).

(1) πῶς μποροῦν οἱ γονεῖς νά κατευθύνουνε τά παιδιά στό ν' ἀρκοῦν-ται στίς ἐπιδόσεις τῶν ἱκανοτήτων τους; 'how can parents direct [their] children towards being content with the performance [which is suited to] their abilities?';

(2) ἤξερε ἀπ' ὅλα, ἀπ' τό νά γιάνει τίς πληγές τῶν λαβωμένων ὥς τό διάβασμα τῶν ἀστεριῶν '(s)he knew everything, from heal-ing the wounds of the injured to reading the stars';

(3) ἡ αἴσθηση τοῦ νά εἶμαι Ἕλληνας 'my feeling of being Greek';

(4) τό ν' ἀφήσεις τόν πλησίον σου νά πεθάνει εἶναι μεγάλη ἁμαρτία 'to leave one's neighbour to die is a great sin.'

In (3), τοῦ could be omitted.

9.4.3 USES OF ΑΣ

The particle ἄς has two chief functions: (a) hortative or permissive, and (b) concessive.

In its hortative sense, ἄς is normally used only with the first or third person, and expresses an injunction on the speaker's part which is rather more a wish or desire than if νά were used in the same context (in which the expression would contain more of a sense of obligation):

(1) ἄς πᾶμε κι ἐμεῖς 'do let's go too';

(2) ἄς μήν ἔρθουν, ἀφοῦ δέ θέλουν 'let them not come, since they don't want [to].'

In (2), the ἄς-clause has a permissive sense ('I allow them not to come'), while νά instead of ἄς would convert the sense into something like, 'I order them not to come.'

When ἄς is followed by the imperfective past, it may be used with any person; here it expresses an unfulfilled wish:

(3) ἄς μοῦ τό 'λεγες! 'if only you'd told me!' (cf. 9.4.2.1.1 (6), with a similar meaning).

In its concessive sense ('even though'), ἄς is always immediately preceded by κι (= καί). In such cases, the ἄς-clause, which expresses a situation that is felt to be more real than if καί νά were to be used, is used together with another clause:

(4) ἔλα στό πάρτυ μας, κι ἄς φέρεις καί τόν ἄντρα σου! 'come to our party, even if you do bring your husband!';

(5) ἡ Σακοράφα ἔκανε πολύ καλά στούς 'Αγῶνες, κι ἄς μήν πῆρε χρυσό 'Sakorapha did very well in the Games, even if she didn't win a gold [medal].'

In (4), the origin of the concessive sense in a hortative/permissive construction is obvious. As can be seen from (5), concessive ἄς may be followed by a perfective past if the situation expressed is a real one.

9.4.4 OTHER SUBJUNCTIVE MARKERS

Having examined the functions of ϑά, νά, and ἄς, it remains to survey briefly the other subjunctive markers. They can conveniently be divided into the following groups: μή (and μήπως); ἴσως; ἄν and other conditional conjunctions; temporal conjunctions; and relatives.

9.4.4.1 Μή (and μήπως)

In addition to its role as a simple negative marker after νά and ἄς (and elsewhere: see 7.3), μή also acts as a subjunctive marker in main clauses and as a subordinating conjunction (in the latter function it may alternate with μήπως).

In a main clause, μή converts the verb into a negative imperative (if followed by the second person) or a negative hortative (if followed by other persons):

(1) μή φεύγεις 'don't go away' (negative of φύγε);

(2) μήν ξεχνᾱμε πώς . . . 'let's not forget that . . .' (= νά/ἄς μή);

(3) μή σέ νοιάξει 'don't let it worry you' (= νά μή).

As a subordinator, μή may be treated under two heads, according to whether it is governed by a verb or equivalent phrase denoting fear (in which case it is less often used than μήπως), or whether it is governed by some other verb or phrase (in which case μήπως is far less common). In all cases, the μή-clause may be negated by δέν. Semantically, the uses of μή/μήπως are quite various.

After expressions of fearing, the subordinate clause expresses what the subject of the main verb is afraid of. The perfective non-past is used to denote a situation posterior to the time of the main verb; the imperfective non-past indicates a situation contemporaneous with it; past tenses denote a situation anterior to it.

(4) ἔτρεμαν μή καί τό ἀνακαλύψει κανένας καθηγητής 'they were

afraid [lit. 'they trembled'] that some teacher might discover it' (*T* 18 Feb. 1982, 19);

(5) τό 'σκασε ἀπό φόβο μήν τό χτυπήσουν 'he ran off, for fear he might be beaten';

(6) φοβήϑηκα μήπως τόν ἔπιασε ὁ διάβολος καί μέ σκοτώσει 'I became afraid the devil might have got into him and he might kill me.'

After expressions of fearing, μή/μήπως may alternate with ὅτι/πώς: when ὅτι/πώς is used, the situation feared is perceived by the subject as being more real (here future reference is expressed by ϑά + the appropriate verb form). In sentences in which both verbs have the same subject and the sense is not that the subject fears the occurrence of the situation expressed in the subordinate clause but that (s)he is too afraid to perform the action of the second verb, φοβᾶμαι νά is used.

When not governed by an expression of fearing, μή(πως) may have two quite opposite senses of purpose, one negative (7), the other positive (8). The former is more normal; but only the context can distinguish between them:

(7) ἔφυγα, μήπως τυχόν κολλήσω καμιά ἡπατίτιδα 'I left, lest I might by chance catch (some) hepatitis (or other)';

(8) ϑά ἀρχίσω νά παρατηρῶ τά γύρωϑέ μου συμβαίνοντα, μήπως ἀπό αὐτά συμπεράνω τήν ὕπαρξη μιᾶς ϑέσης 'I shall begin to observe what's happening around me, in case I might [be able to] deduce from them the existence of a position' (i.e. 'so that I *might*') (Kar. n.d.: I 140).

Note in (6) how easily the verb may change its subject from one μή(πως)-clause to another: a second μή(πως) is, as usual, deleted before the second verb. Compare the following example of simultaneous change of grammatical subject and a switch from negative to positive:

(9) φοβᾶται μήπως ὁ Κωστής δέν πάει καί μείνει ἔρημος ἐκεῖ '[Andrew] is afraid Kostis might not go and he [Andrew] might stay there all alone' (Sid. 1959: 130).

One of two additional expressions is sometimes added to μή(πως)-clauses: the verb τυχαίνει 'it happens' (10) and the adverb τυχόν 'by chance' (7):

(10) κοίταξε μήν τύχει κι ἦρϑανε 'look [to see] whether they might happen to have come.'

In addition to these uses, μήπως (and, far less often, μή) may be used to introduce a direct question: it is especially useful in that declarative sentences in MG may normally become interrogative simply by a change of intonation (or, in the orthography, by a question mark). Thus μήπως may signal to the hearer/reader from the outset that the sentence expresses a question. Nevertheless, the fact that in this function μήπως is not normally a subjunctive marker is shown by the possibility of placing it at the end of a sentence:

(11a) μήπως θά 'ρθεις;
(11b) θά 'ρθεις μήπως; } 'are you going to come?'

9.4.4.2 Ἴσως

Ἴσως 'perhaps' may syntactically be either an adverb (followed by νά or θά) or a subjunctive marker on its own. The basic determining factor is the temporal reference of the utterance.

For present reference, ἴσως is followed by νά + imperfective non-past. For future reference it normally governs a verb in the perfective non-past, but may be used with νά or θά. For past reference it may govern a verb in the past or be used with νά + past, its use with θά + past being reserved for an epistemic sense (for further examples see 9.4.2.2.2):

(1) ἴσως ἔρθουν 'perhaps they'll come' (optionally with νά/θά);
(2) ἴσως (νά) ἦρθαν 'perhaps they've come';
(3) ἴσως θά ἦρθαν 'perhaps they'll have come [by now]' (inference).

It may also be used, without θά, in the apodosis of conditional sentences:

(4) ἴσως τόν ἔπειθα ἄν . . . 'perhaps I would have persuaded/convinced him if . . .'

9.4.4.3 Conditional conjunctions

Apart from ἄν 'if', there are other introductives to the protases of conditional sentences with similar meanings: ἐάν (a *katharevousa* borrowing which is not approved by most demoticists but is sometimes used to place special emphasis on the remoteness of the possibility), ἄμα (not considered correct by grammarians as a conditional conjunction, but very frequent in less educated speech), ἔτσι καί (a colloquial alternative, also not favoured by grammarians; it often implies some sort of threat), σέ περίπτωση πού (lit. 'in case that') (normally with future reference),

and εἴτε . . . εἴτε . . . ('whether . . . or': also ἤ . . . ἤ . . . in the same
meaning). The use of ἄν 'whether' in reported speech and of ἄν καί
'although' does not concern us here, since they are not subjunctive
markers.

As far as verb forms are concerned, conditional sentences may be
divided loosely into *factual* and *counter-factual*. Factual constructions
(including sentences which refer to the future as long as the situations
which they denote are seen as capable of fulfilment) may employ any
verb form, according to the aspect and temporal reference required
(although for the future, the conditional conjunction is normally used
with the perfective non-past alone, without ϑά (4)); counter-factual
constructions (including those which refer to the future but whose
situations are seen as less likely to occur) may employ the imperfective
past (preceded by ϑά in the apodosis), irrespective of temporal reference
(7), although the perfect past may be found in either the protasis (6)
or the apodosis (5), or both, for past reference. It is of course possible
for the protasis and apodosis to have different temporal references;
but each of the examples given below preserves the same temporal
reference for both parts.

(a) Factual
   (1) Past: ἄν γύρισε σπίτι χϑές, τότε διάβασε κιόλας τό γράμμα
        μας 'if (s)he returned home yesterday, then (s)he's already
        read our letter';
   (2) Present (progressive): ἄν ταξιδεύει μέ τέτοιον καιρό, τόν λυπᾶ-
        μαι 'if he's travelling in weather like this, I pity him';
   (3) Present (timeless): ἄν (or ἅμα) βρῶ μανιτάρια, τά τηγανίζω
        ἀμέσως 'if I find mushrooms, I fry them immediately' (ἄν
        = ὅποτε 'whenever');
   (4) Future: ἄν (or ἔτσι καί) τό μάϑει ὁ ἄντρας μου, ϑά μέ σκο-
        τώσει 'if my husband finds out, he'll kill me.'

(Factual conditions of the past (1) and progressive present (2) types
are a frequent stylistic alternative to causal or result clauses.)

(b) Counter-factual
   (5) Past only: ἄν ὁ Γιῶργος δέν ζοῦσε κάτω ἀπό τό νόμο τῆς
        ποιητικῆς ἔκφρασης, ϑά εἶχε αὐτοκτονήσει ἤ ϑά εἶχε σκοτω-
        ϑεῖ γιά μιά ἰδέα 'if George had not lived under the law of
        poetic expression, he would have committed suicide or been
        killed for an idea' (Tsa. 1973: 68);

(6) Past only: ἄν ὁ Χίτλερ τόν εἶχε ἀκούσει, δέ θά γινόντουσαν 'if Hitler had listened to him, [these things] wouldn't have happened' (Sef. 1973: 160);

(7) Past, present, or future: ἄν (or ἐάν) ἔπαιρνα ἄλλη γυναίκα, θά 'παιρνα καί προίκα 'if I'd married another wife, I'd also have got a dowry', or 'if I married another wife, I'd also get a dowry.'

Ἄν is sometimes reinforced by having κι placed before it ('even if'). Κι ἄν is also frequently used after universal relatives to increase their scope or to give them a concessive sense (see 8.2.1 and 8.2.2).

Although ἄν, and the other conditional conjunctions mentioned above, are regularly negated by δέν, there is an alternative conjunction ἐκτός ἄν 'unless', normally used only if the protasis follows the apodosis:

(8a) ἄν δέ βρέξει αὔριο θά πᾶμε ἐκδρομή 'if it doesn't rain tomorrow we'll go on an excursion';

(8b) θά πᾶμε ἐκδρομή αὔριο, ἐκτός ἄν βρέξει 'we'll go on an excursion tomorrow, unless it rains.'

A protasis is sometimes found without an apodosis in various interrogative and exclamatory constructions:

(9) ἄν πηγαίναμε νά τόν δοῦμε; '[what] if we went to see him?';

(10) ἄν εἶναι δυνατόν! 'is it possible?' (lit. 'if it's possible': usually said of a situation of which one disapproves);

(11) ἄν ἤξερες πόσο σ' ἀγαπάω! 'if [only] you knew how much I love you!'

In a conditional sentence, two or more alternative protases may be expressed by means of clauses beginning with ἄν and linked by ἤ 'or'. If there are two or more conditions, all of which must be fulfilled, the first clause begins with ἄν but subsequent clauses simply follow a coordinating καί. When there are two mutually exclusive protases, εἴτε . . . εἴτε . . . (or, less commonly, ἤ . . . ἤ . . .) 'whether . . . or . . .' is used:

(12) ἄν δεῖς τήν Ἑλένη ἤ ἄν τῆς μιλήσης στό τηλέφωνο, πές της ὅτι δέ θά 'ρθω 'if you see Helen or speak to her on the phone, tell her I won't be coming';

(13) ἐάν μιά μητέρα ἔρθει καί μᾶς πεῖ ὅτι ἀνησυχεῖ γιά τό παιδί

της, τί πρέπει νά κάνουμε; 'if a mother comes and tells us she's worried about her child, what should we do?';

(14) εἴτε τοῦ γράψεις εἴτε πᾶς νά τόν δεῖς, δέ θά σοῦ δώσει τήν ἀπάντηση πού θέλεις 'whether you write to him or go and see him, he won't give you the answer you want.'

9.4.4.4 Temporal conjunctions

As far as verbal syntax is concerned, temporal conjunctions may be divided into those (πρίν and προτοῦ) which are followed only by the perfective non-past, and those (the rest) which are followed by a past tense if reference is to past time, a perfective (or perfect) non-past with or without θά if the reference is to future time, and either an imperfective non-past or a perfective (or perfect) non-past if the reference is to the present or is general, according to whether or not there is temporal coincidence. Thus πρίν and προτοῦ are always subjunctive markers, while the others may or may not be, depending on syntactical context. (For words meaning 'until', which are not as straightforward as other temporal conjunctions, see 9.4.2.2.5 and 9.4.2.2.6; examples of πρίν-clauses have been given in 9.2.)

The other temporal conjunctions include ἅμα 'when', ἀφοῦ 'after' (but note that in its causal sense, 'because, since', ἀφοῦ is not a subjunctive marker), μόλις 'as soon as', ὅταν and σάν 'when'. Of these, ἀφοῦ, μόλις, and ὅταν are the most frequently used in SMG. It is clear that while ἀφοῦ and μόλις, by the nature of their meanings, do not allow temporal coincidence, the others may or may not display it, according to context. In addition, certain other conjunctions might be included, such as ἐφόσον 'as long as; provided that' and the *katharevousa* colloquialism ἅπαξ καί 'once', which form clauses in the same way as ὅταν and ἀφοῦ/μόλις respectively.

These examples show how ὅταν affects the following verb:

(1) ὅταν μοῦ μίλησε, κατάλαβα πῶς εἶχε δίκιο 'when (s)he spoke [= had spoken] to me, I realized (s)he was right';

(2) ὅταν μοῦ μιλοῦσε, κατάλαβα πῶς εἶχε δίκιο 'when [= while] (s)he was talking to me, I realized (s)he was right';

(3) ὅταν μοῦ μιλοῦσε, καταλάβαινα πῶς εἶχε δίκιο 'when (s)he used to talk to me, I realized (s)he was right';

(4) ὅταν βράσει, τό σουρώνει 'when it boils [= has boiled] she strains it' (either iterative or historic present);

(5) ὅταν βράζει, τό σουρώνει 'when [= while] it's boiling, she strains it' (Kahane and Kahane 1958: 457);

(6) ὅταν [θά] τελειώσουνε θά σηκωθοῦν καί θά φύγουνε 'when they finish [= have finished] they'll get up and leave.'

When ἀφοῦ or μόλις is used, constructions such as (5) are unlikely, since these conjunctions can only express non-coincidence. Nevertheless, while the imperfective is excluded after ἀφοῦ and μόλις in present and future reference, it may be used in past reference when the expression of iterativeness overrules the expression of non-coincidence (8):

(7) ἀφοῦ ἔφαγε, πῆγε περίπατο 'after (s)he ate [= had eaten], (s)he went for a walk' (single action);

(8) ἀφοῦ ἔτρωγε, πήγαινε περίπατο 'after (s)he had eaten, (s)he used to go for a walk' (habitual action);

(9) ἀφοῦ φάει, πάει περίπατο 'after (s)he eats [= has eaten] (s)he goes for a walk';

(10) ἀφοῦ φάει, θά πάει περίπατο 'after (s)he eats [= has eaten] (s)he will go for a walk' (single action).

Thus while πρίν and προτοῦ entail maximum neutralization of tense (and even aspectual) distinctions, and ὅταν causes almost minimal neutralization, ἀφοῦ stands somewhere between the two on the scale of neutralization (cf. 9.2).

9.4.4.5 Universal relatives

The universal relatives are those which correspond to the English relatives in '-ever' (see 8.2 ff.). Any of these may be followed by καί νά or κι ἄν to emphasize their universality.

As far as verbal aspect is concerned, these universal relatives behave in a similar way to the temporal conjunctions of the ὅταν variety. In other words, they are regularly followed by a perfective form if there is no temporal coincidence between the actions denoted by the main and subordinate verbs, but by an imperfective if there is coincidence. Nevertheless, universal relatives are frequently used with an imperfective, even where there is no coincidence, when the habitual nature of the action is stressed; and, conversely, even when the action of the subordinate verb is iterative, a perfective is often found when the all-embracing or universal nature of the conjunction is emphasized (for examples of these relatives used as subjunctive markers, see 3.2.3.4.1 (12)-(17)).

There is a particular elliptical use of these conjunctions in which no main clause governs the relative clause: here the perfective non-past is almost always used:

(1) τρέχανε ὅλοι πίσω ἀπό τό λεωφορεῖο καί ὅποιος προλάβει 'they all ran after the bus and whoever could catch it [caught it]';

(2) ἁπλῶστε ἐμπρός τά μπράτσα καί ὅπου φτάσουν 'stretch forth your arms and [take] whatever they reach' (both Hesse 1980: 113).

With those conjunctions that may or may not have a universal meaning (such as ὅ,τι), a different construction is used according to their semantic function. Compare the following examples:

(3) πιστέψτε με, ὅ,τι θά πῶ εἶναι ἀλήθεια 'believe me, what I'm about to say is [the] truth';

(4) ὅ,τι κι ἄν πεῖς θά εἶναι ψέματα 'whatever you say will be lies.'

In (3), since reference is to a particular statement that the speaker is about to make, the verb cannot be simply in the perfective non-past, but must be preceded by θά to give it particular future reference. In (4), the perfective non-past is used, with optional reinforcing particles (κι ἄν), to indicate that the speaker does not have any particular object of the verb 'say' in mind. Such conjunctions are therefore subjunctive markers in themselves only when they are used in an indefinite or universal (or potential) sense.

10

VOCABULARY

10.1 GENERAL CHARACTERISTICS

Two striking characteristics of the MG vocabulary are its size, and the length of its words.

There are a number of reasons why the vocabulary of MG is large. One of these is the high degree of synonymy, due to the varied origins of SMG, namely the dialects and *katharevousa*. In the case of words for the same concept from different dialects, one of these has usually become predominant, leading to the disappearance of the others from everyday usage, but not necessarily from literary writing: e.g. προσόψι (< AG πρός 'towards' + ὄψις 'face') and πεσκίρι (< T *peşkir*) 'towel' have yielded to πετσέτα (< It. *pezzetta*), while λάμα (< It. *lama*) 'razor-blade' has given way to ξυραφάκι (< ξυράφι 'razor' + -άκι). Nevertheless, Greek writers have often seen literature partly as a repository for non-standard words and phrases and (especially in the late nineteenth and early twentieth centuries) have added to these dialectal elements words of their own making (chiefly compounds). It is unfortunate that lexicographers of MG have largely ignored the wealth of non-standard words used by poets and fiction-writers.

With respect to the opposition between words which have entered SMG from the popular tradition and those which have been introduced via *katharevousa*, there is often an exact synonymy, each word sometimes being used to gloss the other in a dictionary: e.g. D ἀλέτρι and K ἄροτρο(ν) 'plough'. Often there is a stylistic difference (or difference of register) between the popular and learned member of a pair of doublets. For example, someone talking or writing today about the Greek War of Independence and attempting to project himself into the spirit of the period will talk of weapons as ἄρματα (< L *arma*), while an objective historian might use ὅπλα (AG). Again, 'bones' to a cook will be κόκκαλα (D), but ὀστᾶ (K) to a doctor. Often, where two words, one belonging to D and the other to K, were originally synonyms, the second has taken on a figurative meaning, or is used only in certain collocations: thus σπίτι (D) is 'house' for most purposes, but οἶκος, which is K for 'house', is normally used in SMG to mean '(commercial) firm'; also compare τό ἄσπρο σπίτι 'the white house', with ὁ Λευκός Οἶκος 'the White House (in Washington)'. The last is an example of a widespread phenomenon in SMG: the reluctance to use an everyday word in a figurative sense which has been imported from a Western European language. Thus, the 'arm' of a person is χέρι or μπράτσο (< Ven. *brazzo*), but the 'pick-up arm' of a record-player is βραχίονας (K βραχίων 'arm'); the 'ceiling' of a house is ταβάνι (< T *tavan*), but the 'ceiling' of, for example, a wage increase is πλαφόν (< F *plafond*); and while 'hole' is τρύπα (D), 'black hole (astron.)' is μαύρη ὀπή (AG ὀπή 'hole'). This may be a sign that MG is a healthy language: it often resists using an imported figurative meaning, preferring instead to use a completely different word (from a foreign language or from K) for this meaning. In some cases, one of a pair of roughly synonymous words is unmarked, or neutral, while the other is slightly or highly pejorative: e.g. κεφαλαιοκρατία (K) and καπιταλισμός (D) 'capitalism', the latter being the pejorative term.

Another factor underlying the large size of the MG vocabulary is the great ease with which derivatives may be formed, and especially the fact that many nouns require a corresponding denominal adjective. For the construction that corresponds to English or German Noun + Noun (*class struggle, Klassenkampf*) or French Noun + *de* + Noun (*lutte de classes*), MG usually prefers Adjective + Noun (ταξικός ἀγώνας: ταξικός < τάξη 'class'; cf. R *klássovaya borbá*). More examples of such formations are given later (see also 4.6 ff.). Nevertheless, MG does have other ways of joining concepts, such as the compound word in which the head-word appears second (e.g. γραφομηχανή 'typewriter', modelled on G *Schreibmaschine*) or first (πονοκέφαλος 'headache'), or the two-word collocation in which the headword appears first, and the second word is in the genitive (e.g. κρασί ποιότητος, modelled on F *vin de qualité*).

A further factor is the wealth of diminutive and augmentative endings (chiefly of nouns), which have already been examined (4.6.1).

Genuine MG words may end only in a limited number of sounds (either a vowel, or a vowel + /s/ or /n/). Furthermore, there is a rather restricted number of phonemes in the language, and these may combine only in a limited number of sequences. Despite these restrictions, the chief classes of words (nouns, adjectives, verbs) have to indicate, by their endings and sometimes by prefixation, their multiple relationships both with their referents and with other words in the clause (e.g. number, gender, case, aspect, voice, tense). In view of the combination of these factors, MG words tend to be rather long: this is also due to the fact that there are few root-words in the language, most words being derivatives of AG words, whether these words exist in the language today or not. Far from there having been any drastic reduction in the length of words since Classical times (such as that which occurred between Latin and French, for instance), MG tend on average to be longer than AG words.

Monosyllables are few in SMG, the most common word length being two or three syllables. Words of up to eight or nine syllables are not infrequent: e.g. πετρελαιοπαραγωγός 'oil-producer' (8), Παπαδημητρακόπουλος (surname) (8), δημοσιοϋπαλληλικός 'of civil servants' (9), οἰκονομικοκοινωνικός 'socio-economic' (9).

Whereas there are many monosyllables among the so-called 'grammatical words' in MG (the definite article, the clitic pronouns, καί 'and', τί 'what' (interrogative), πού 'who' (relative), etc.), others are disyllabic (γιατί 'why', πότε 'when' (interrogative), ὅταν 'when' (relative), ἀλλά 'but'). There are no monosyllabic adjectives, and only four monosyllabic nouns (γιός 'son', νοῦς 'mind', γῆ 'earth', and φῶς 'light'—if one excepts γειά 'health', which is used only in certain set phrases). The only other *lexical* (as opposed to *grammatical*) monosyllables are certain forms (chiefly non-past perfectives) of a few common verbs. Nevertheless, it is possible to form a sentence consisting solely of monosyllables: e.g. πῶς δέ θά πᾶς νά τούς τό πεῖς; 'why [lit. 'how'] won't you go and tell them (it)?' (Mirambel 1953: 66).

Finally, the importance of the ending in MG makes it impossible to form curtailed versions of long words in popular use: contrast E *[aero]-plane*, *[omni]bus*, *demo[nstration]*, *pram [perambulator]*, etc., or F *manif[estation]*, *dactylo[graphe]*, *frigo [frigidaire]*, etc. Although MG may take over certain ready-made abbreviated words from French (such as μετρό 'underground railway' < F *métro[politain]*, or πορνό 'pornography/-ic' < F *porno[graphique]*), there are only two truly abbreviated words in SMG, namely προκάτ 'prefab' (noun and adjective < προκατασκευασμένος 'prefabricated' (formed by analogy with E *prefab*) and τό δίς 'a billion (1,000 million)' (usually of drachmas) < δισεκατομμύριο. (In addition, there are acronyms and stump compounds, mentioned in 10.3.5, and certain slang abbreviations, such as ἀνθύπας for ἀνθυπασπιστής 'regimental sergeant major', which do not belong to the standard language.)

10.2 ORIGINS OF THE MG VOCABULARY

Another striking characteristic of the MG vocabulary is the overwhelming preponderance of words of AG origin. Five different categories of such words might be distinguished:

(i) Words which have remained unchanged in the language since ancient times (unchanged, that is, in orthography, since almost all have slightly altered phonologically): these include most of the grammatical words such as καί, τί, πῶς, and ποῦ, but also many basic nouns and other words, such as ἄνθρωπος 'person, man', θάλασσα 'sea', οὐρανός 'sky', μητέρα 'mother', πατέρα 'father' (acc. sing.) (the last two are identical to the accusative, but not to the nominative, singular in AG);

(ii) Words which have altered slightly in morphology: e.g. παιδί 'child' (< παῖς, root παιδ-), τραπέζι 'table' (< τράπεζα);

(iii) Words which fell out of ordinary use but have been reintroduced more or less unchanged into the modern language (internal borrowings), such as βουλή 'parliament', πολίτης 'citizen', στοά 'arcade' (it is of course not always possible to define what is meant by the phrase 'fell out of use', since a large number of ancient words were kept half-alive by the learned tradition, even though the common people were ignorant of them);

(iv) Derivatives of AG words which have passed through the popular tradition, such as νερό 'water' (< AG νεαρόν [ὕδωρ] 'fresh [water]'), παίρνω 'I take' (< AG ἐπαίρω 'I raise'), παράθυρο 'window' (< AG παρά 'next to' + θύρα 'door'), πάω 'I go' (< AG ὑπάγω 'I lead under; I go on'); and

(v) Derivatives of AG words which have been coined in modern times, e.g. λεωφορεῖο 'bus' (< Attic λεώς 'people' + root φερ/φορ- 'carry'), πολιτισμός 'culture, civilization' (< πολίτης).

Another division cuts across categories (i) to (iii), namely, whether the word has undergone some semantic change or not.

Van Dijk-Wittop Koning (1963: 100–4) has made the following calculations on the basis of three written MG texts. Out of 1,148 different words found, 324 are AG words that have remained in continuous use and unchanged in form and meaning; another 191 have undergone morphological or semantic change, or both (e.g. ὀλίγος → λίγος 'little', πίπτω → πέφτω 'I fall', τίθημι → θέτω 'I place'; δουλεύω 'I am a slave' → 'I work', κράτος 'strength' → 'state'); 129 are AG words whose use has been revived in modern times; a further 202 words manifested themselves in written Greek between the fourth century BC and the fourth century AD (all derivatives of AG words: e.g. συνεχίζω 'I continue', ἐνέργεια 'action', ἀκατάπαυστος 'incessant'); while the rest consist mainly of MG popular or learned derivatives of AG words: only fifty loanwords were found in this corpus.

The proportion of loanwords to words of Greek origin (like that of AG derivatives of popular origin to AG derivatives of learned origin) varies according to register: it is quite possible to write whole pages on certain abstract or scholarly topics without using a single loanword, whereas everyday conversation abounds in them. Indeed, some of the most basic nouns are of foreign origin (the vast majority of loanwords are nouns), such as πόρτα 'door' (< L *porta*), σπίτι 'house' (< L *hospitium*), τζάκι 'hearth' (< T *ocak*), and even a few grammatical words such as μά 'but' (< It. *ma*). In addition, there are many loanwords which are so much a feature of MG that they help to give it its special character: e.g. γλέντι 'party; merrymaking' (ult. < T *eğlendi*), κέφι 'mood; high spirits' (< T *keyif*). There are loanwords for denoting family and social relationships, such as κουμπάρος 'best man; godfather' (< It. *compare*) and μπατζανάκης 'brother-in-law' (see 10.4.1: < T *bacanak*), and some exclamations: e.g. ἀμάν! 'alas!, oh dear!' (< T *aman*), γούρι! 'good luck!' (said when someone accidentally breaks a glass or piece of crockery: < T *uğur*), and μπράβο! 'well done!' (< It. *bravo*).

Since many scientific and other technical terms in Western European languages are themselves of Greek origin, MG has found little difficulty in reconstituting their 'original' Greek form: thus F *anécdote* has become ἀνέκδοτο (as in ἕνα σόκω ἀνέκδοτο 'a dirty joke'!), G *Leukämie* is λευχαιμία (the German word is in fact an erroneous formation, which has been corrected in the Greek), F *nécrologie* 'obituary' is νεκρολογία, and E *telephone* is τηλέφωνο. Some of the words of AG origin which were borrowed by MG from other languages were indeed AG words themselves which had fallen out of use in the Greek language.

Great efforts have been made by Greek academics and journalists, especially in the nineteenth century, to find suitable Greek translations of Western European concepts, instead of simply importing loanwords. Quite apart from the nationalist ideology which urged that all traces of non-Hellenic culture should be effaced, there were two valid linguistic reasons for avoiding the wholesale introduction of loanwords: one was that MG nouns, adjectives and verbs require inflectional endings, and another that, owing to the limited range of MG phonology, most words from French, German, or English, if used in MG, would have either to change beyond recognition in order to become susceptible of being pronounced and spelled by Greeks, or to alter the phonology and orthography of the MG language. (French, German, and English sounds such as [ʃ], [ʒ], [w], [h], [œ], [y], etc., do not exist in spoken MG, nor can they be indicated in the orthography. (The fact that the existence of some of these sounds in Turkish did not prevent a large number of loanwords being adopted by MG from Turkish is irrelevant, since these words entered the Greek language by a natural and gradual process of assimilation, not through wholesale importation by the intelligentsia.) There was also a positive advantage in using Greek roots in order to coin words for new concepts, namely that the resulting words were likely to be more readily comprehensible and therefore more widely acceptable than actual loanwords.

Examples of calques or loan translations based on Western European languages abound: σιδηρόδρομος 'railway' (< AG σίδηρος 'iron' + MG δρόμος 'road': most probably based on G *Eisenbahn*), ἀλεξικέραυνος 'lightning-conductor' (< AG ἀλέξω 'I ward off' + κεραυνός 'thunder-bolt': based on F *paratonnerre* or It. *parafulmine*), βραχυκύκλωμα 'short circuit' (< AG βραχύς 'short' + MG κύκλωμα 'circuit'), διεθνής 'international' (< δια- 'inter-' + ἔθνος 'nation'), ἐντομοκτόνο 'insecticide' (< ἔντομο 'insect' + AG -κτόνος 'killing'), ἐντυπωσιάζω 'impress' (< post-Classical ἐντύπωσις 'impression' + -ιάζω: based on F *impressionner*), οὐρανοξύστης 'skyscraper' (< οὐρανός + AG ξύω 'I scrape'), ὑλισμός 'materialism' (< ὕλη 'matter'), ὑπαρξισμός 'existentialism' (< ὕπαρξη 'existence'). There are also semi-calques (based on a foreign word, part of which is of Greek and part of non-Greek origin), such as αὐτοκίνητο 'automobile' (< αὐτο- 'self-' + κινητός 'mobile'), γραφειοκρατία 'bureaucracy' (< γραφεῖο 'office; desk' + -κρατία 'ruling'), τηλεόραση 'television' (< τηλε- 'far' + ὅραση 'vision').

As has already been said, however, since the beginning of the nine-teenth century a large number of words have been revived from AG, or invented, in order to translate foreign concepts without adhering closely to the form of the relevant foreign words. The intelligentsia of the nineteenth century was responsible for successfully introducing thousands of such words into everyday Greek, an achievement for which they have received scant acknowledgement in recent times. Revivals from AG include the following (most of the dates in brackets after certain words are those given for their first use in Koumanoudis' (1900) invaluable collection of neologisms):

    ἀλληλογραφία (lit. 'mutual writing'): AG 'the writing of amoebaean poems'; MG 'correspondence' (*c.*1800);

θερμοκρασία (lit. 'hot-mixing'): AG 'mixing of hot drink'; MG 'temperature' (1812);

ὑπάλληλος: AG 'subordinate' (adj.); MG 'employee, clerk' (noun);

ὑπουργός: AG 'serving' (adj.); MG 'minister' (noun) (1824), formerly μνίστρος;

βιομήχανος: AG 'clever at getting a living' (adj.); MG 'industrialist' (noun) (before 1840);

ταχυδρόμος (lit. 'fast running'): AG 'courier'; MG 'postman' (1833);

τελωνεῖο (revived from post-Classical Greek with the same meaning): 'customs house' (before 1840), replacing κουμέρκι (< L commercium);

ἀεροπόρος: AG 'traversing the air' (adj.); MG 'airman' (noun) (early twentieth century).

New coinages included the following:

λαθρεμπόριο 'smuggling' (1809: < AG λάθρα 'by stealth' + MG ἐμπόριο 'trade'), formerly κοντραμπάντο;

ζαχαροπλαστεῖο 'pâtisserie' (1810: < ζάχαρη 'sugar' + πλαστ- 'mould');

πανεπιστήμιο 'university' (1810s: cf. AG πανεπιστήμων 'all-knowing');

δημοσιογράφος 'journalist' (1826: < δημόσιος 'public' + -γράφος 'writing');

πρωτοβουλία 'initiative' (1871: < πρῶτος 'first' + AG βουλή 'wish, will');

ποδήλατο 'bicycle' (1890: < ποδ- 'foot; leg' + AG ἐλαύνω 'drive');

πολυβόλο 'machine-gun' (< AG adj. πολυβόλος '(of catapult) throwing many missiles');

θερμοσίφωνο 'water-heater' (1898: < θερμός 'hot' + AG σίφων 'tube').

It is notable that most of the words coined in order to render modern European concepts since 1800 have been based on AG roots, including some that are not used in the demotic vocabulary. Very few have been based on demotic roots (a notable example is τροχόσπιτο 'caravan', < τροχός 'wheel' + σπίτι 'house'). Still today the process of forming new words based on AG roots (whether by loan-translation or not) continues apace, and the ability of the Greek language to form new words is still very much alive.

Nevertheless, a surging tide of new loanwords has been sweeping over Greece during the present century, the chief donor languages being French and English: the latter is close to superseding French as the chief source of loanwords today. As in other countries, intellectuals constantly bemoan, and attempt to resist, this tide, but it seems that, with the constant advances in technology and in other fields where English is the chief language of communication, Greece can do little but accept a large number of loanwords which may never be either assimilated phonologically and morphologically or translated into its own language. The problems lie not so much with those loanwords which are (often as a result of pure accident) fully declinable in MG (e.g. ἐξτρεμιστής 'extremist', κάμερα 'cine-camera', κουλτούρα 'culture', μαρίνα '(yachting) marina', μπουλντόζα 'bulldozer', νετρόνιο 'neutron' (< F neutron), πλουραλισμός 'pluralism', σοσιαλισμός 'socialism'), as with indeclinable nouns and adjectives (verbs must inflect in MG), many of which contain un-Greek combinations of sounds, especially at their ends. Linguists and others are fighting a losing battle to translate foreign loanwords which have already become well entrenched. While ἠλεκτρονικός ὑπολογιστής 'computer' (lit. 'electronic calculator'), despite its length, is sometimes used instead of κομπιοῦτερ (the diminutive κομπιουτεράκι is firmly established as 'pocket calculator'), the proposed translations of some other words (such as ἀγορατεχνική for μάρκετιγκ 'marketing' or χειραγώγηση for μάνατζμεντ 'management', suggested by Tsopanakis (1979: 485-6), or ἐμπορευματοκιβώτιο for κονταίηνερ 'container') will surely go the way of many nineteenth-century attempts at Hellenizing already familiar concepts (e.g. περισκελίς for παντελόνι 'trousers', or λαιμοδέτης for γραβάτα 'tie', which sound as ridiculous today as when they were invented).

French still acts as the chief donor of words connected with *haute couture*. It is significant that even such an apparently basic word as μπλέ 'blue' should be from French (< *bleu*); many words for subtle shades of colour are also of French origin, presumably because they are connected with fashion: e.g. μπλέ σιέλ 'sky-blue' (< *bleu ciel*), μπλέ μαρέν (*sic*) 'navy blue' (< *bleu marine*), μαρόν 'chestnut' (< *marron*) (side by side with the native καστανός), μώβ 'mauve', ρόζ 'pink' (< *rose*), μπέζ 'beige', καφέ 'brown' (< *café*), λιλά 'lilac' (< *lilas*), etc. There are other adjectives, such as ἀσορτί 'matching' (< *assorti*), καρό 'check' (< *carreau*), ντέ-πιές 'two-piece' (< *deux-pièces*), and ὀξυζενέ 'peroxided' (< *oxygéné*), but it is chiefly as nouns that French words appear in Greek fashion pages: τό καλσόν 'tights' (<

caleçon), ἡ κολεξιόν '(fashion) collection', τό μαγιό 'bathing-costume' (< *maillot*), τό μαννεκέν 'mannequin, model', ὁ/ἡ μοντελίστ 'dress designer' (< *modéliste*), τό μπλού-τζήν 'jeans' (< *blue-jean* < E), τό μπόρ 'rim (of hat)' (< *bord*), τό παλτό 'coat' (<*paletot*), ἡ περμανάντ 'perm' (< *permanante*), τό σεσουάρ 'hair-dryer' (< *séchoir*), τό σμόκιν 'dinner-jacket' (<*smoking* < E).

It is not uncommon on the fashion pages of Greek magazines to find captions to photographs such as the following:

(1) μακό πενιέ γκαζέ μερσεριζέ μπλούζα ριγέ σέ μπλέ καί ἄσπρο μέ τιράντες 'gauze-like mercerized sleeveless combed-cotton blouse striped in blue and white with shoulder-straps' (*T* 24 June 1982, 106).

The following French loanwords are used in this example: *peigné, gazé, mercerisé, blouse,* and *bleu*; τιράντα is from It. *tirante* (masc., with different meaning). But perhaps the most interesting word here is ριγέ, which is a conflation of F *rayé* with MG ρίγα 'stripe' (< It. *riga*); or perhaps even ρίγα + suffix -έ. This suffix is common enough in words of French origin to have become a Greek suffix in its own right: thus there is a type of apple called μπανανέ (< μπανάνα 'banana' + -έ), and there are slang versions of some words with this ending (e.g. τζαμπέ 'free, without paying', < τζάμπα < T *caba*).

Another area in which loanwords from French are prominent is the motor car: e.g. τό ἀμπραγιάζ 'clutch' (< *embrayage*), τό καπό 'bonnet' (< *capot*), τό καρμπυρατέρ 'carburetter' (< *carburateur*), τό λεβιέ 'gear-lever' (< *levier*), τό μπουζί 'sparking-plug' (<*bougie*), τό παρμπρίζ 'windscreen' (< *pare-brise*), τό πόρτ-μπαγκάζ 'boot' (< *porte-bagages*), ἡ σαμπρέλα (declinable) 'inner tube' (<*chambre à air*), ὁ σοφέρ 'driver' (< *chauffeur*); there are also verbs (fully inflected, with the suffix -άρω < It. -*are*) such as μαρσάρω 'I rev up' (< *marcher* 'I run (of engine)'), ντεραπάρω 'I skid' (< *déraper*), ροντάρω 'I run in (engine)' (< *roder*).

Finally, French loanwords figure prominently in the areas of entertainment and the arts: ἡ ἀτραξιόν 'attraction (special number in cabaret etc.)', ἡ γκαλερί 'art gallery' (< *galerie*), ὁ ἰμπρεσιονισμός (declinable) 'impressionism', ναΐφ 'naïve (of painter or painting)' (< *naïf*), ἡ πρεμιέρα 'première' (declinable), τό ρεσιτάλ 'recital' (<*récital*), τό σουξέ 'success (i.e. successful song etc.)' (< *succès*), ἡ τουρνέ '(concert) tour' (< *tournée*), τό φεστιβάλ 'festival'. Apart from such examples, French loanwords appear in sport, cuisine, science, technology, and in fields of more abstract thought.

Loanwords first began to enter MG in significant numbers from English in the realm of sport (especially football). Although ποδό-σφαιρο (calqued on E *football*) has replaced φουτμπόλ (the stress suggests that this latter entered Greek via French) as the name of the game, the following words are constantly on the lips of most Greek males: ἄουτ 'out', τό γκόλ 'goal', ὁ γκολκῆπερ 'goalkeeper', τό κόρνερ 'corner (-kick)', ὁ λάινσμαν 'linesman' (also ἐπόπτης), ὄφ-σάιτ 'off-side', τό πέναλτυ 'penalty', ὁ ρέφερη(ς) 'referee' (also διαιτητής), ὁ σέντερ-φόρ 'centre-forward', τό σκόρ 'score', σουτάρω 'I shoot', οἱ τρίπλες 'dribbling' (conflation of *dribble* with τριπλός 'triple'), and τό φάουλ 'foul'. Outside football, there are the names of various sports (e.g. τό βόλεϋ 'volley-ball', τό γκόλφ 'golf', τό μπάσκετ 'basket-ball', τό τένις 'tennis'), and certain terms used in these and other games: τό ἀουτσάιντερ 'outsider' (contrast τό φαβορί 'favourite' < F *favori*), τό νόκ-ἄουτ 'knock-out', τό ρίγκ '(boxing) ring', ὁ τζόκεϋ 'jockey'.

The other main area in which English plays a leading role as donor language is the world of entertainment: τό γουέστερν 'Western (film)' (also τό καουμπόικο < *cowboy*), τό θρίλλερ 'thriller', ὁ κλόουν 'clown', τό κόμικ(ς) 'comic (book)', τό μιούζικαλ 'musical (show)', τό μπέστ-σέλλερ 'best-seller', τό σήριαλ '(television) serial', ὁ/ἡ στάρ 'star', τό στριπτήζ 'striptease', τό σώου 'show', τό τζιούκ-μπόξ 'juke-box', τό τρανζίστορ 'transistor radio'.

A number of English words have entered the world of business, and especially shipping: e.g. τό λόκ-ἄουτ 'lock-out', τό τάνκερ 'tanker (ship)'. Fashion, leisure, and travel have their share too of English loan-words: e.g. τό μαίηκ-ἄπ 'make-up' (also τό μακιγιάζ < F *maquillage*), τό μπαγκαλόου '(holiday) bungalow', τό μπόρντιγκ-κάρντ 'boarding-card', (τό) σή-θρού 'see-through' (noun and adjective), τά σόρτς 'shorts', τό σπρέυ 'aerosol spray', τό τσάρτερ 'charter (flight etc.)'. Anglo-American cuisine is popular among young Greeks, who are fond of τά ντόνατς 'doughnuts', τά τσίπς 'potato crisps' (US 'potato chips'), and τά χάμ-πουργκερ 'hamburgers'; but τά κρακεράκια 'cream crackers' and τό μπέικον 'bacon' have been known for longer; and τό μίξερ 'food mixer' and τό μπλέντερ 'food blender' are firmly entrenched in Greek kitchens.

Finally, English has supplied some common words used in various walks of life: e.g. τό σέρβις '(motor-car) service', τά σλάιτς '(photo) slides', τό σουπερμάρκετ 'supermarket', τό τέστ 'test (of intelligence, or medical)', τό τσέκ-ἄπ '(medical) check-up', τό χιοῦμορ 'humour', and τό χώλ 'hall (of house or flat)'. Two other words have become very widely used: σόρρυ 'sorry' (e.g. σόρρυ πού σέ στενοχώρησα 'sorry to have upset you') and φούλ '(adj.) full; (noun) full speed; (adv.) flat out, at full speed', which is used in a variety of idiomatic ways (also verb φουλάρω 'I fill up; I sprint; I cause (machine) to work flat out').

German, which has provided the model for a large number of loan-translations in MG (e.g. κοσμοθεωρία 'world-view' < Weltanschauung, κοσμοϊστορικός 'of world importance' < welthistorisch), has been the source of very few loanwords (e.g. τό κράχ '(financial) crash' <Krach, τό λάιτ-μοτίβ 'leitmotiv', and τό προτσές 'process' <Prozess (normally διαδικασία)). It is not clear why there should be so few German loan-words in MG.

Italian has continued to provide a number of loanwords since the early nineteenth century, but on a far smaller scale than before. Many of these are used in the performing arts: e.g. ὁ κομπάρσος 'walking-on part' (< comparsa), τό κουαρτέτο 'quartet' (< quartetto), τό μπαλέτο 'ballet' (< balletto), τό ντεμπούτο 'début (< debutto < F début), τό παλκοσένικο 'stage' (<palcoscenico), ἡ πρόβα τζενεράλε 'dress rehearsal' (< prova generale), τό σενάριο 'scenario', τό φινάλε 'finale'. Most of these (but not φινάλε) are fully declinable.

Some trade names (Greek and foreign) have become normal words for certain types of product, even when the actual product in question is not made by the manufacturer specified: e.g. τό ἀφρολέξ 'foam rubber', τό κρίς-κράφτ 'speedboat' (< Chris Craft), ὁ λευκοπλάστης 'sticking plaster' (< Leukoplast), τό μπίκ 'ballpoint pen' (< Bic), τό νοβοπάν 'hardboard' (< Novopan), ἡ ριπολίνη 'gloss paint' (< Ripolin), τό φελιζόλ 'polystyrene'.

Sometimes a word of foreign origin has entered the language even when a word already existed for the same concept. In such cases, the loanword has either superseded the old one or pushed it into a lower register. Thus τό μπανιερό 'bathing costume' has given way to μαγιό, τό ρωγοβύζι 'baby's bottle' to τό μπιμπερό (< F biberon), and τό φτιασίδι 'make-up' to μακιγιάζ (which is in turn giving way to μέικ-άπ). On the other hand, τό σκαμνί 'stool' is now reserved for a lowly kind of stool, while τό (ἐ)σκαμπό (< F escabeau) refers to a fashionable stool which might adorn one's drawing-room. Two curious examples of displacement are the words for 'henna' and 'hashish': the older Greek words entered the language from Turkish (ἡ κινά < T kına, and τό χασίσι < T haşiş). Both these words became tainted, the former because of its associations with the cosmetic habits of Turks and Arabs, the latter because of its associations with the underworld. Now that 'respect-able' people may talk about drugs with impunity, 'hashish' is τό χασίς (indeclinable, < F *haschische*, or E), and now that henna has begun to be imported into Greece from the West, it is now called ἡ χέννα (presumably < E).

10.3 WORD-FORMATION

Word-formation in MG occurs through the addition of a prefix or suffix (in either case, with or without changing the part of speech of the base-word), or by the compounding of two or more roots into one. The grammatical category (part of speech) of a word cannot normally be altered without a prefix or suffix (usually the latter) being added.

The only examples of words changing their category without the addition of affixes (prefixes or suffixes) are provided by various types of substantivization. In the first, a word that normally belongs to another category may become a noun: e.g. πιστεύω 'I believe' → τό πιστεύω 'the creed'; ἐγώ 'I' → τό ἐγώ 'the ego'; σήμερα (adverb) 'today' → τό σήμερα (οἱ Ἕλληνες τοῦ σήμερα 'the Greeks of today'). In the second, an adjective becomes a noun through the omission of a noun which it modifies (although it is not always possible to specify which noun has been deleted). This is different from another kind of substantivization of an adjective, in which any adjective can play the role of a noun temporarily and in a particular context (see 4.2: in addition, some neuter adjectives may be substantivized as abstract nouns, e.g. τό πεζικό 'infantry', or τό ἡλεχτρικό 'electricity'). Some of the substantivized adjectives which concern us here have been inherited from AG (the omitted noun appears in square brackets): e.g. ἡ γραμματική [τέχνη] 'grammar' (in full: 'the art of letters), ἡ εὐθεία [γραμμή] 'straight line'. Others have entered the language since Classical times: ἡ ταχεία [ἀμαξοστοιχία] 'fast train, express', ἡ Τρίτη [ἡμέρα] 'Tuesday', ὁ ὑδραυλικός [τεχνίτης?] 'plumber'.

Adjectives with nouns omitted are frequently used in contemporary Greek: usually the relevant noun may optionally be specified. Some examples are the following: τό βραδινό [φαγητό] 'dinner (evening meal)', ἡ δημοτική [γλώσσα] 'the demotic language', τό δημοτικό [σχολεῖο] 'primary school', ὁ ἐμφύλιος [πόλεμος] 'the [Greek] civil war', ὁ ἠλεκτρικός [σιδηρόδρομος] 'the [Athens] Metro', τό μονοτονικό [σύστημα] 'the single-accent system', ἡ Νομική [Σχολή] 'the Law Faculty', ὁ τελικός [ἀγώνας] 'the final (in sports)', τό τετραγωνικό [μέτρο] 'square metre'. There are many neuter singular forms in which a noun such as πρόβλημα 'problem' or ζήτημα 'question' is understood: τό κυπριακό 'the Cyprus question', τό μεσ[ο]ανατολικό 'the Middle East problem'. In some neuter plurals, γεγονότα 'events' is understood: τά Δεκεμβριανά 'the events of December 1944'. Some substantivized adjectives may stand for more than one phrase: ἡ λαϊκή [γλῶσσα] 'slang', or [ἀγορά] 'weekly open market'; ἡ πρώτη [παράσταση] 'first performance, première', or [ταχύτητα] 'first gear'.

The formation of words by means of prefixes and suffixes is not always a simple matter, and may involve changes of stem or of stress. To take two examples with the privative prefix ἀ-, the opposite of φυσικός 'natural' is ἀφύσικος (change of stress) and the opposite of δίκαιος 'just' is ἄδικος (change of stem and stress).

The number of affixes used in forming words in MG is considerable. Since a comprehensive account of word-formation appears in Triandaphyllidis (1941: 115–79), it would be vain to attempt a full coverage of this vast subject here. We shall confine ourselves to examining some of those affixes which are most productive today, and some typical modern compounds. In our discussion of affixes we shall treat only those which cannot stand as words on their own (i.e. those which are bound forms), consigning free forms to our examination of compounds.

If we compare Triandaphyllidis's list of affixes with those which are productive today, our conclusion is that, despite the revival of various ancient affixes, the repertoire is nowadays rather less rich than it has been in the past. The fact is that many of the traditional demotic affixes have fallen out of active use.

10.3.1 SUFFIXATION

Some examples of word-formation by suffixes have already been given in the chapters on morphology, namely diminutives and augmentatives (4.6.1), feminines of masculine nouns referring to persons (4.6.2), and nouns and adjectives derived from verbs (5.2.7). The aim in this section is to give some modern examples of word-formation using typial suffixes. While Triandaphyllidis's examples illustrate traditional formations, we shall for the most part avoid the kinds of example which he provides.

(a) The largest group of suffixes consists of those which produce nouns. Of these, the majority convert nouns into other nouns (the examples given below exclude augmentative, diminutive, and feminine formations):

(i)　Nouns referring to persons:

-άς (masc.): τυρόπιτα 'cheese pie' → τυροπιτάς 'cheese-pie maker/seller';

-αδόρος (masc.) (< Ven. -ador; added especially to words of Romance origin): κομπίνα 'trick, racket' (< F combine) → κομπιναδόρος 'trickster' (also from verbs: μαρκάρω 'mark' (< It. marcare) → μαρκαδόρος 'marker (pen)');

-(ι)άρης (masc.) (< L -arius): κουλτούρα 'culture' (< F culture) → κουλτουριάρης 'culture-vulture' (fem. -ιάρα, adj. -ιάρικος);

-ίας (masc.): ἀντίρρηση 'objection' → ἀντιρρησίας 'conscientious objector';

-ίστας (masc.) (< F -iste or It. -ista, both ult. < AG -ιστής): κιθάρα 'guitar' → κιθαρίστας 'guitarist' (cf. It. chitarrista; also κιθαριστής) and many other words for instrumentalists; ἄρση βαρῶν 'weight-lifting' → ἀρσιβαρίστας 'weight-lifter', and other athletes (also from verbs: γράφω 'I write' → γραφίστας 'graphic artist'; based on F graphiste);

-τζής (masc.) (< T -ci): γλυκά 'sweet cakes' → γλυκατζής '(man) who has a sweet tooth' (fem. -τζού); μπετά 'concrete' (colloquial plural of μπετό(ν) < F béton) → μπετατζής 'concreter';

(ii)　Nouns referring to objects:

-άρα (fem.) (see also 4.6.1): δύο 'two' → δυάρα 'a two (in dice or cards)';

-άρι (neuter): δυάρι 'two-roomed flat'; δώδεκα 'twelve' → δωδεκάρια 'twelve-point type'; σαρανταπέντε 'forty-five' → σαρανταπεντάρι '.45 pistol';

-ιέρα (fem.) (< F -ière or It. -iera): σαμπάνια 'champagne' (< F) → σαμπανιέρα 'champagne bucket'; ψωμί 'bread' → ψωμιέρα 'bread-basket';

(iii)　Nouns referring to places:

-(α)ρία (fem.) (< It. -(e)ria): πίτσα 'pizza' (< It.) → πιτσαρία 'pizzeria';

-δικο (neuter) (usually from nouns in -άς or -τζής): ἕτοιμα [ρούχα] 'ready-made [clothes]' → ἐτοιματζής → ἐτοιματζήδικα 'reach-me-downs'; τυροπιτάς → τυροπιτάδικο 'cheese-pie shop';

(iv) Nouns referring to abstract concepts:

-ιά (fem.): κεφάλι 'head' → κεφαλιά 'header (in football)'; μπάλα 'ball' (< It. *palla* or F *balle*) → μπαλιά 'kick (in football)';

-ισμός (masc.) (properly from verbs in -ίζω + -μός): στρουθοκάμηλος 'ostrich' → στρουθοκαμηλισμός 'ostrich mentality'; έτσι θέλω 'that's how I want it' → ετσιθελισμός 'selfish and arbitrary behaviour'; καθώς πρέπει 'comme il faut' → καθωσπρεπισμός '(excessive) respectability' (also οι διάφοροι -ισμοί 'the various -isms');

-(ι)λίκι (neuter) (< T -lik): αρχηγός 'leader' → αρχηγιλίκι 'the post of leader';

-λογία (fem.): ανέκδοτο 'joke, anecdote' → ανεκδοτολογία 'the telling of anecdotes'; φήμες 'rumours' → φημολογία 'the various rumours (on a certain subject)'.

(b) There are a few suffixes which convert verbs into nouns (see also 5.2.7):

(i) Persons: -τής (masc.): αναλύω 'I analyse' → αναλυτής 'analyst'; επενδύω 'I invest' → επενδυτής 'investor' (contrast K επενδύτης 'overcoat');

(ii) Implements: -τήρας (masc.): αναπνέω 'I breathe' → αναπνευστήρας 'snorkel'; ανάπτω (K) 'I light' → αναπτήρας 'lighter'; ανεμίζω 'expose to the air' → ανεμιστήρας 'fan, ventilator';

(iii) Place: -τήριο (neuter): εκθέτω 'I exhibit' → εκθετήριο 'exhibition hall';

(iv) Abstract: -μα (neuter): γιγαντώνομαι 'I become gigantic' → γιγάντωμα '(action of) becoming gigantic'; διαλέγω 'I choose' → διάλεγμα '(action of) choosing'.

There are also a couple of endings which convert adjectives into (usually abstract) nouns:

-ούρα (fem.) (< L -ura): λαϊκός 'of the people' → λαϊκούρα 'the plebs';

-τητα (fem.): ιδιαίτερος 'particular' → ιδιαιτερότητα 'specificity, particularity' (= F *particularité*); συντροφικός 'of comrades' → συντροφικότητα 'comradeship'.

(c) There is a number of suffixes forming adjectives, either from nouns or from verbs. The base-word is usually a noun:

-άτος (< L -atus): σικ 'chic' (<F) → σικάτος (same meaning); φρέσκος

'fresh' (< It. *fresco*) → φρεσκάτος '(of person) looking/feeling fresh';

-ειδής: φασίστας 'fascist' (< It. *fascista*) → φασιστοειδής 'fascist-like' (lit. 'fascistoid');

-ένιος (base-words denote materials): κοντραπλακέ 'plywood' (< F *contre-plaqué*) → κοντραπλακένιος 'plywood (adj.)'; λαμαρίνα 'sheet metal' (< Ven. *lamarin*) → λαμαρινένιος 'made of sheet metal';

-ι(α)κός (by far the most productive adjectival ending): Αἴολος 'Aeolus (ancient god of the winds)' → αἰολική ἐνέργεια 'wind-power'; ἀνάπτυξη 'development' → ἀναπτυξιακό πρόγραμμα 'development programme'; εἰρηνευτής 'peacemaker' → εἰρηνευτική δύναμη 'peace-keeping force'; κοινότητα 'community' → κοινοτική νομοθεσία '[EEC] community legislation';

-ίστικος (base-words usually denote persons): διανοούμενος 'intellectual' → διανοουμενίστικος 'of intellectuals (pejorative)'; μπεμπέ 'baby' (< F *bébé*) → μπεμπεδίστικα 'baby-talk';

-οῦχος (lit. 'possessing'): γήπεδο 'football pitch' → γηπεδοῦχος 'home team'; κύπελλο 'cup' → κυπελλοῦχος 'cup-holder' (both substantivized).

(d) A couple of suffixes convert verbs to adjectives (see also 5.2.7 and 5.5.2):

-τέος (referring to an action which must be carried out on the noun): μεταρρυθμίζω 'reform' → μεταρρυθμιστέος 'which must be reformed';

-ιμος (= susceptible of having the relevant action carried out on it): ἐξάγω 'I export' → ἐξαγώγιμος 'exportable'; κατοικῶ 'I inhabit' → κατοικήσιμος 'inhabitable' (≠ ἀκατοίκητος 'uninhabited'); συνεννοοῦμαι 'reach an understanding' → συνεννοήσιμος 'understanding, co-operative'.

(e) Lastly, a few suffixes (all of them highly productive) convert nouns or adjectives into verbs:

-άρω (< It. *-are*): γυαλόχαρτο 'sandpaper' → γυαλοχαρτάρω 'I sandpaper'; κοστούμι 'suit' (< It. *costume*) → κοστουμαρισμένος 'wearing a suit'; μπίς or μπίζ 'encore!' (< F or It. *bis*) → μπιζάρω 'I encore' (cf. F *bisser* and It. *bissare*); πρόστιμο 'fine' → προστιμάρω 'I fine'; τζίρος 'turnover' (< It. *giro*) → τζιράρει δυό ἐκατομμύρια 'it has a turnover of two million';

-ίζω: κόμμα '(political) party' → κομματισμένος 'belonging to a party';
-ποιώ (and noun -ποίηση) (this has become the verbal formant *par excellence* in recent years, superseding most others, a fact bewailed by many Greeks): άνοσος 'immune' → ἀνοσοποιώ 'immunize'; Κύπριος 'Cypriot' → ἡ κυπριοποίηση τῆς Ἐθνικῆς Φρουρᾶς 'the Cypriotization of the National Guard'; ποινικός 'penal' → ἀποποινικοποιήθηκε ἡ μοιχεία 'adultery has been decriminalized';
-ώνω: γραβάτα 'tie' (< It. *cravatta*) → γραβατωμένος 'wearing a tie'; φθόριο 'fluoride' → φθοριώνω 'I fluoride (water supply)'.

Sometimes a suffix that is itself derived from a word should nevertheless be seen as a suffix proper, since it existed as a suffix in AG and it may not be associated in speakers' minds with the word with which it is etymologically connected. Such is the case with -λογία above (< λόγος 'word'), and even with -οῦχος (< ἔχω 'I have, possess'). There are other such suffixes, such as -κρατῶ and -κρατία (< AG κράτος 'power': e.g. ἀνδροκρατία 'dominance of society by males').

10.3.2 PREFIXATION

Prefixes too may be divided into those which are derived from existing words and those which are not: the latter include AG words which are not used in SMG, or which as prefixes have different senses from those in which they are used as words in SMG.

The majority of prefixes proper used in SMG are AG prepositions. These will be examined in alphabetical order.

ἀνα- (attached to verbs and nouns: 're-'): γόμωση 'stuffing' → ἀναγόμωση 'retread (of tyre)'; παλ(α)ιώνω 'make/grow old' → ἀναπαλαιώνω 'restore (building)';

ἀντι- (attached to nouns and adjectives: 'un-' or 'anti-'): ἐπιστημονικός 'scientific, scholarly' → ἀντιεπιστημονικός 'unscientific, unscholarly'; ἐπιχείρημα 'argument' → ἀντεπιχείρημα 'counterargument'; ἡλιακός 'solar' → ἀντιηλιακό φίλτρο 'filter against sunburn'; κλέπτης (K) 'thief' → ἀντικλεπτικός χαρτοφύλακας 'anti-theft briefcase';

ἀπο- (attached to verbs: 'de-, dis-'): μαγνητίζω 'I magnetize' → ἀπομαγνητίζω 'I demagnetize';

δια- (converts nouns to adjectives: 'inter-'): πολιτισμός 'culture' → διαπολιτισμικός 'cross-cultural'; ὑπουργός 'minister' → διϋπουργική ἐπιτροπή 'interministerial committee';

ἐκ- (converts adjectives to verbs, often in conjunction with -ίζω:

'-ize'): δημοκράτης 'democrat' → ἐκδημοκρατίζω 'democratize';
δυτικός 'western' → ἐκδυτικίζω 'westernize';

ἐν- (converts nouns to adjectives: 'containing'; converts nouns to
verbs: 'in-, en-'): ὄργανο 'instrument, organ' → ἐνόργανη χημεία
'organic chemistry', ἐνόργανη γυμναστική 'apparatus gymnastics';
σῶμα 'body' → ἐνσωματώνω 'embody';

ἐπανα- (attached to verbs: 're-'): προσδιορίζω 'define' → ἐπανα-
προσδιορίζω 're-define';

μετα- (traditionally attached to verbs: 'trans-'; now especially converts nouns to adjectives: 'post-'; also attached to nouns: 'meta-'):
ἐμφύλιος [πόλεμος] 'civil war' → ἡ μετεμφυλιακή Ἑλλάδα 'post-
Civil War Greece'; γλώσσα 'language' → μεταγλώσσα 'metalanguage';

παρα- (attached to nouns; modern formations probably based on F
para-: 'beside, para-'): παιδεία 'education' → ἡ παραπαιδεία 'the
unofficial (private) education system'; φεστιβάλ 'festival' → οἱ
παραφεστιβαλικές ἐκδηλώσεις 'fringe events';

προ- (converts nouns to adjectives: 'pre-'): σεισμός 'earthquake' →
ἡ προσεισμική Ζάκυνθος 'Zakynthos as it was before the [1953]
earthquake';

συν- (attached to nouns and adjectives: 'co(n)-'): παραγωγή 'production' → συμπαραγωγή 'co-production';

ὑπερ- (attached to any class of word: 'super-, over-, hyper-, trans-,
inter-'): ἀστικός 'urban' → ὑπεραστικός 'trunk (call)' (cf. F.
interurbain); Ἀτλαντικός 'Atlantic' → ὑπερατλαντικός 'trans-
atlantic'; εὐαίσθητος 'sensitive' → ὑπερευαίσθητος 'hypersensitive';
ἦχος 'sound' → ὑπερηχητικός 'supersonic'; καλύπτω 'I cover' →
ὑπερκαλύπτονται οἱ ἀνάγκες τῆς ἀγορᾶς 'the market needs are
more than covered';

ὑπο- (attached to any class of word: 'sub-, under-'): ἀπασχόληση
'employment' → ὑποαπασχόληση 'under-employment'; βαθμός
'grade' → ὑποβαθμίζω 'degrade, debase' (a vogue word dis-
approved of by many commentators); ἐπιτροπή 'committee' →
ὑποεπιτροπή 'subcommittee'.

A number of other prefixes (mostly of AG origin) are widely used in
SMG. The most productive of these include the following:

ἀ- (attached to adjectives and nouns: 'un-'): χτυπάω 'I beat' →
ἀχτύπητος 'unbeatable' (see also 5.5.2);

ἀρχι- (attached to nouns: 'arch-, chief'): βομβιστής 'bomber (person)'
→ ἀρχιβομβιστής 'arch-bomber';

αὐτο- (mostly attached to verbs: see 3.1.2.2): ἐξόριστος 'exile'
(person)' → αὐτοεξόριστος 'self-exile';

δυσ- (mostly attached to nouns; the opposite of εὐ-: 'dys-, mal-'):
λειτουργία 'function' → δυσλειτουργία 'malfunction' (see also
5.5.2);

ἐξω- (mostly attached to adjectives: 'extra-'): συζυγικός 'conjugal' →
ἐξωσυζυγικός 'extra-marital'; σχολικός 'of school' → ἐξωσχολικός
'out of school' (adj.: = F extra-scolaire);

εὐ- (forms chiefly adjectives: 'eu-, well, easily'): ἐπηρεάζω 'I influence' → εὐεπηρέαστος 'easily influenced';

Εὐρω- (attached to nouns: < E and F Euro-): Εὐρωβουλευτής
'Euro-MP'; Εὐρωκοινοβούλιο 'European Parliament';

ἡμι- (attached to nouns and adjectives: 'semi-'): διατροφή 'board
(food)' → ἡμιδιατροφή 'half-board';

ξε- (attached to verbs: 'de-, un-'): ζαλίζομαι 'I (begin to) feel dizzy' →
ξεζαλίζομαι 'I (begin to) recover from dizziness'; χέρι 'arm, hand'
→ ξεχεριάστηκα 'my arms are practically dropping off (through
heavy lifting etc.)' (genuine demotic prefix);

παν- (attached to nouns and adjectives: 'pan-, very'): ἄσχημος 'ugly'
→ πανάσχημος 'very ugly';

τηλε- (attached to nouns and adjectives: 'remote; tele- (concerning
telephones or television)'): κατευθύνω 'control' → τηλεκατευ-
θυνόμενος 'remote-controlled'; θεατής 'spectator' → τηλεθεατής
'television viewer' (cf. F téléspectateur).

Like some suffixes, some prefixes are derived from existing words,
but have special meanings. These include: ἀξιο-, '-worthy' (σημειώνω
'I note' → ἀξιοσημείωτος 'noteworthy'), κρυπτο- 'crypto-' (κρυπτοχουν-
τικός 'clandestine supporter of the junta'), μεγαλο- 'big' (μεγαλοεπιχει-
ρηματίας 'big businessman'), μικρο- 'small, petty, micro-' (μικροομάδα
'small group'), μονο- 'uni-, single' (μονόπατος 'single-storeyed'), νεο- 'neo-'
(νεοχουντικός 'latter-day supporter of the junta'), πολυ- 'multi-, much-,
poly-' (πολυεκατομμυριοῦχος 'multi-millionaire', πολυφωτογραφημένος
'much-photographed'), and φιλο- 'pro-' (φιλοκυβερνητικός 'pro-
government'; also suffix -φιλος: τουρκόφιλος 'pro-Turkish'). Especially
worth noting are some prefixes expressing opprobrium: βρωμο- (βρω-
μόκαιρος 'filthy weather'), κωλο- (κωλότοπος 'bloody awful place'),
παλιο- (παλιοκομμούνι 'bloody Commie'), πουστο- (πουστόκαιρος

'bloody awful weather'), and ψευτο- (ψευτοπολυτέλειες 'phoney luxuries').

10.3.3 COMPOUNDING

Traditional demotic was rich in compound words, which were used especially in oral poetry. Greek poets of the nineteenth and early twentieth centuries were eager to exploit to the full both the wealth of existing compounds and the ease with which new compounds could be formed. Much compounding still takes place, but, as has been mentioned (10.2), recent compounds tend to be based more on the learned than on the demotic tradition (for literary compounds, see also 11.1.2.1).

An attempt will be made here to classify some of the chief ways in which compounding takes place in the present state of the language. These can be classed under three heads, according to whether (a) the base-words belong to the same part of speech, each playing the same grammatical role; (b) one of the base-words modifies the other; or (c) one of the base-words is a verb and the other is its subject or direct object.

(a) When two or more words of the same part of speech are compounded, they may be nouns, adjectives, adverbs, or verbs. If each base-word plays the same grammatical role in the compound, the compound belongs to the same part of speech as each of the base-words:

N + N → N: ἀπογειοπροσγειώσεις 'take-offs and landings'; χαρτο-
     φάκελλα 'notepaper and envelopes';
A + A → A: ἀσπρόμαυρος '(of film etc.) black and white'; ὀπτικο-
     ακουστικός 'audio-visual';
V + V → V: κατοικοεδρεύω 'I live and work (at)'.

There are also a few indeclinable nouns derived from singular imperative forms: e.g. τό ἄρπα-κόλλα 'hurried and botched job/work' (ἀρπάζω 'I snatch' + κολλάω 'I stick').

(b) When one of the base-words modifies the other, the possible relationships between them are various. In most cases, the second base-word is modified by the first. In (N + N → N) compounds, in which A represents the first base-word and B the second, the compound means 'B of A', 'B made of A', 'B as of A', 'B for A', or 'B like A':

νοοτροπία 'mentality' (< νούς 'mind' + τροπ- 'turn': B of A);
πετρελαιοκηλίδα 'oil-slick' (< πετρέλαιο 'oil' + κηλίδα 'stain': B
     made of A);

βατραχοπέδιλα 'flippers (for swimming)' (< βάτραχος 'frog' + πέδιλο 'sandal': B as of A);

ὠτοασπίδες 'ear-plugs' (< AG ὠτ- 'ear' + MG ἀσπίδα 'shield': B for A);

βατραχάνθρωπος 'frogman' (modelled on English: B like A).

There are many other types of combination under this head (where one of the base-words is a verb and the other a noun, the latter appears to stand in an adverbial relationship to the former):

A + N → N: σαπιοκάραβο 'old hulk' (< σάπιο καράβι 'rotten ship');

A + N → A: χαμηλόμισθος 'low-paid' (< χαμηλός μισθός 'low wages');

N + V → V: ἀγγλοφέρνω v.i. 'imitate the English' (< Ἄγγλος 'English-man' + φέρνω 'I bring'); λογοκρίνω v.t. 'I censor' (< λόγος 'word' + κρίνω 'I judge'; also derivative λογοκριτής 'censor'); πολιτο-γραφῶ v.t. 'I naturalize' (< πολίτης 'citizen' + γραφ- 'write');

N + V → N: δακτυλογράφος 'typist' (< AG δάκτυλος 'finger' + γραφ-, or F dactylographe);

N + V → A: δακτυλόγραφος 'typewritten' (here the verb has a passive rather than an active sense);

Adv. + V → V: καθαρογράφω v.t. 'I make a fair copy of' (< καθαρά 'clearly' + γράφω);

Adv. + V → N: πολύγραφος 'duplicating machine' (< πολύ 'much' + γραφ-);

Adv. + V → A: πολυγράφος '(of writer) prolific' (active meaning); δυσκολοκατάκτητος 'difficult to master' (< δύσκολα 'with diffi-culty' + κατακτῶ 'I conquer': passive meaning).

There are also a very few compounds in which the second element modifies the first:

N + N → N: τσικλόφουσκα 'bubble-gum' (< τσίκλα 'chewing-gum' + φούσκα 'bubble') (τσίκλα (also τσίχλα by erroneous assimilation with τσίχλα 'thrush') is the singular of an originally plural τσίκλες < 'Chiclets' (brand name) or Sp. chicle).

Finally, there are some adjectival formations in which the first base-word (A) is an adjective, the second (B) a verb, and the sense of the compound is 'A to be B'ed':

A + V → A: ἑτοιμοπαράδοτος 'ready to be delivered/for delivery' (< ἕτοιμος 'ready' + παραδίδω 'I deliver').

(c) In the last category are compounds formed from a verb and a noun, the latter being the subject or direct object of the former. When the noun is the verb's subject, it may precede or follow the verb:

N + V → N: ἡλιοβασίλεμα 'sunset' (< ἥλιος 'sun' + βασιλεύω 'I set');
V + N → N: ραπτομηχανή 'sewing-machine' (< K ράπτω 'I sew' + μηχανή 'machine').

Similarly, when the noun is the direct object it may also come first or second:

N + V → V: ἀφισοκολλῶ 'I stick posters (on walls)' (< ἀφίσα 'poster' + κολλῶ 'I stick');
N + V → N: πολεοδομία 'town-planning' (< πόλη 'town' + δομῶ 'I construct');
N + V → A: πετρελαιοπαραγωγός (adj. and noun) 'oil producing/-er' (πετρέλαιο 'oil' + παράγω 'I produce');
V + N → A: σπαραξικάρδιος 'heart-rending' (< σπαράσσω 'I tear apart' + καρδιά 'heart').

In the examples given above, the derivation has sometimes been specified rather abitrarily, and it is possible to see some of these words as being derived in a different way (e.g. πετρελαιοπαραγωγός < πετρέλαιο + παραγωγός 'producer'). Some words may be seen as derivatives of non-existent compounds: one example above is ἡλιοβασίλεμα, which may be seen as deriving either from ἥλιος + βασίλεμα 'setting' or from a non-existent verb *ἡλιοβασιλεύω; similarly, παλαιοημερολογίτης 'old-calendrist' may be said to come either from παλαιό ἡμερολόγιο 'old calendar' + -ίτης or from a non-existent form *παλαιοημερολόγιο, while μεγαλοϊδεάτης 'supporter of the *Megali Idea* [the nineteenth-century irredentist ideology]' may derive from Μεγάλη Ἰδέα 'Great Idea' or from *Μεγαλοϊδέα.

10.3.4 LOOSE COMPOUNDS BY APPOSITION

The last few decades have seen a huge increase in the use of loose compounds consisting of two words (almost always nouns), normally united by a hyphen, such as παιδί-θαῦμα 'child prodigy'. Semantically, these expressions may mean either 'A which is also B' (i.e. the two base-words are grammatically equivalent), or 'A which is like B'. Some set phrases in which a noun is placed appositively after another noun, which it qualifies, existed in traditional demotic (e.g. παιδί μάλαμα 'first-rate child/lad' (lit. 'child-gold'), or θάλασσα λάδι 'completely calm sea' (lit. 'sea oil')). Most of these are of the 'A which is like B' variety, and are usually written without a hyphen. In addition, there is the phrase κίνδυνος θάνατος 'deadly danger' (lit. 'danger death', with both words in the nominative), which appears on signs at electrical installations etc., and is constructed in a different way.

More recent formations, which are found frequently, particularly in journalism but also in everyday speech, are often based on French: such formations are condemned by Triandaphyllidis (1941: 177-8) as being alien to the spirit of the Greek language. The earliest of these can easily be traced back to their French origins: e.g. λέξη-κλειδί 'key-word' (*mot clé*), ἀπάτη-μαμμούθ 'mammoth fraud' (*imposture mammouth*); and the second element of such compounds (κλειδί, μαμμούθ, also ἔκπληξη 'surprise' and ἀστραπή 'lightning') may be freely added to a wide range of nouns. Other compounds may however be coined *ad hoc*, using practically any pair of nouns.

Morphologically, when the first word is in an oblique case or in the plural, the second may or may not follow it in case and number. It is difficult to establish a criterion as to whether or not the second base-word is to inflect; it seems, however, that more formal usage prefers to have both words inflected (as occurs in French for number), but that the second element is less likely to indicate an oblique case than it is to appear in the plural.

Examples: ἕνα γκόλ-ἀστραπή 'a lightning goal' (cf. F compounds in -*éclair*), ἡ οἰκογένεια-πρότυπο 'the model family', μιά ὁμάδα-ἀσανσέρ 'a team that has shot up to the top of the league' (lit. 'team-lift') (*T* 27 Sept. 1979, 35), ἡ ἔκρηξη-τίναξη τοῦ μότορσιπ 'the explosion [and] blowing up of the motor-yacht' (*T* 11 Oct. 1979, 15), μιά συνέντευξη-ἐξομολόγηση 'a confessional interview' (lit. 'an interview-confession'), ὁ ὑπουργός-ἀναπληρωτής συντονισμοῦ 'the deputy minister of co-ordination', οἱ παῖκτες-κλειδιά (pl.) 'the key players', οἱ συνεπιβάτες-φρουροί του (pl.) 'the bodyguards who drove with him' (lit. 'the fellow passengers-guards of-him'), τῆς δεσποινίδος-θαῦμα (lit. 'of-the miss-wonder': the first noun is in the genitive, the second in the nom./acc.), ἡ εἰκόνα τῆς μάνας-σκλάβας (both gen.) 'the picture of the mother [as a] slave', δυό παραστάσεις-σκάνδαλο 'two scandalous productions' (the second noun is singular) (*T* 4 Dec. 1980, cover), τίς χρονολογίες-σταθμούς (both acc. pl.) 'the dates [which are/were] milestones'.

Syntactically, the second base-word may govern, or be governed by, another word or phrase. Such constructions are especially frowned upon by grammarians. Examples: τῶν χωρῶν-μελῶν (or -μέλη) τῆς

EOK 'of the member-countries of the EEC', ἡ μάνα-προαγωγός τῶν τριῶν ἀνήλικων κοριτσιῶν 'the mother of the under-age girls, who was also their procuress' (lit. 'the mother-procuress of . . .') (T 29 Nov. 1979, 20), ὁ ἔμπορος-ἐκπρόσωπος τῶν παραγωγῶν 'the merchant [who is also the] representative of the producers', μιά φυλακή-πρώην σχολεῖο 'a prison which was formerly a school' (R 12 Jan. 1982).

In many instances, the second word could be replaced by an adjective (e.g. ἀστραπιαῖο ταξίδι 'a lightning trip' for ταξίδι-ἀστραπή, or σκανδαλώδεις παραστάσεις for παραστάσεις-σκάνδαλο above). It seems to be especially in such instances that the second word is uninflected.

In the writing of some journalists, such loose compounds are often overused:

(1) Μέ μιά ἀνάλυση-ντοκουμέντο, πού καταγράφει στό χρονικό ὅριο μιᾶς νύχτας τή 'γυναίκα: σύμβολο-πειραματόζωο' μέσα ἀπό τά σύγχρονα ρεύματα 'τέχνης' καί 'πολιτικῆς', ὁ νέος Σαλονικιός σκηνοθέτης Σ.Β. ἐπιχειρεῖ ἀπ' τήν καινούρια του ταινία-'ψυχογράφημα' [. . .] νά δώσει τό ἀληθινό πρόσωπο τῆς σύγχρονης γυναίκας 'With an *analysis-cum-documentary* which records during the time limit of one night the '*woman: symbol and guinea-pig*' through the modern currents of 'art' and 'politics', the young Salonican director S.V. attempts through his new *film-cum-psychological portrait* [. . .] to convey the true face of modern woman' (N 8 Sept. 1980) (my underlinings).

(Here the phrase γυναίκα: σύμβολο-πειραματόζωο is perhaps an example of a triple compound!)

Lastly, there are other types of combination in which two words are joined by a hyphen but which are formed in a different way, in that the two nouns do not have the same referent. Examples include: ὁ νόμος προσφορά-ζήτηση (nom.) 'the law of supply and demand', πύραυλος ἐδάφους-ἀέρας (gen.) 'ground-to-air missile', and ἡ σχέση δασκάλου-μαθητῆ (gen.) 'the teacher–pupil relationship'.

10.3.5 ACRONYMS AND STUMP COMPOUNDS

The use of acronyms and *stump compounds* has become prevalent in Greece, particularly since the inter-war period, under the influence of the practice in various countries (especially the Soviet Union). An acronym consists of the initial letters of a phrase which are pronounced together as a word; stump compounds are similar, except that they involve the use of initial syllables. Such words are extremely frequent in popular use, so much so that many have formed derivatives. The gender of the acronym is almost always that of the head-word of the full phrase.

Among the most common acronyms and stump compounds are the following: ὁ ΟΤΕ (pronounced *oté*) = Ὀργανισμός Τηλεπικοινωνιῶν Ἑλλάδος 'Telecommunications Organization of Greece'; ὁ ΕΟΤ (*eót*) = Ἐθνικός Ὀργανισμός Τουρισμοῦ 'National Tourist Organization'; ἡ ΔΕΗ (*deí*) = Δημόσια Ἐπιχείρηση Ἠλεκτρισμοῦ 'Public Electricity Enterprise'; ἡ ΕΡΤ = Ἑλληνική Ραδιοφωνία-Τηλεόραση 'Greek Radio and Television'; τό ΠΑΣΟΚ (*pasók*) = Πανελλήνιο Σοσιαλιστικό Κόμμα 'Panhellenic Socialist Movement' (also adjective πασοκικός and noun Πασοκτζής 'PASOK supporter'); τό ΠΡΟ-ΠΟ (*propó*) = Προγνωστικό Ποδοσφαίρου 'football pools' (also τό προ-ποτζήδικο 'shop that acts as football pools agency'); ἡ ΚΝΕ = Κομμουνιστική Νεολαία Ἑλλάδας 'Communist Youth [Movement] of Greece' (also ὁ Κνίτης 'member of KNE'); ΕΒΓΑ (*énga*) = Ἑλληνική Βιομηχανία Γάλακτος 'Greek Milk Industry' (suppliers of milk and ice cream; also ὁ Ἕβγας 'one who runs a shop selling milk etc.'). Some acronyms actually consist of the initials of non-Greek words: e.g. τό ΝΑΤΟ (*náto*) = 'North Atlantic Treaty Organization'; ἡ ΣΙΑ (*sía*) = 'Central Intelligence Agency'; ἡ ΟΠΕΚ (*opék*) = 'Organization of Petroleum Exporting Countries'. Sometimes an acronym is formed from the *names* of the initial letters (either the official or the popular names: see 1.2): e.g. τό ΙΧ (*jotaxí*) 'private car' (from the now obsolete classification of such vehicles as Ἰδιωτικῆς Χρήσεως 'of private use'; also ὁ γιωταχής 'private motorist'); τό ΚΚΕ (*kapakapaépsilon* or *kukué*) = Κομμουνιστικό Κόμμα Ἑλλάδας 'Communist Party of Greece' (also ὁ Κουκουές 'member of the KKE' and ὁ κουκουεδοπόλεμος 'the war against the KKE (i.e. the Civil War)'); ἡ TV (*tiví*) = 'television' (also diminutive ἡ τουβούλα).

10.4 SEMANTIC CHARACTERISTICS

When one considers that the MG language has been widely and consistently used and developed for the purposes of communication on subjects outside the rural domain only since the early nineteenth century, it is remarkable how successfully it can cope with the requirements of the modern world. If one leaves aside such special fields as computer science, MG has managed, using chiefly the diachronic resources of the Greek language and a remarkably small number of foreign loanwords, to keep abreast with the advances in the various areas of science and culture. Nevertheless, the normal speech of educated Greeks tends not to contain either as many scientific terms (whether used in a technical or a figurative sense) or as many literary allusions as that of English-speakers of a similar educational level. This may be due to the lower popular awareness of literature and science in Greece.

10.4.1 SEMANTIC FIELDS

Many concepts which had words attached to them in traditional demotic have disappeared from today's SMG, and one frequently hears educated Greeks lamenting the paucity of colourful words and expressions in the speech of urban people in comparison with that of the traditional peasant. The chief cause of the disappearance of such colourful elements is most probably the traditional insistence in Greek schools that demotic words were to be avoided, and the consequent social stigma that attached to anyone who used words or forms which were not generally considered correct. Literary writers have often attempted to preserve such words and expressions in their work. Anyone who reads MG literature is struck by the number of non-standard words used: and some of these words have equivalents in English which are quite normal. A familiar example is ἀφουγκράζομαι 'I listen to', found in various forms in the dialects and in literature, which has now been excised from SMG, with the result that ἀκούω has to cover both 'I hear' and 'I listen to'. Another example found in literature and clearly widespread in the dialects is κρουνελιάζω 'I trickle' (again, the verb has various forms), which in SMG can be rendered only by τρέχω 'I run' or κυλάω 'I roll', both of which existed side by side with κρουνελιάζω in the dialects and in the traditional literary language. One result of this impoverishment is that many Greeks find it difficult to read their own literature.

There are naturally certain concepts which are difficult to translate into MG, just as there are MG concepts which cannot properly be rendered in other languages. There is, for example, no MG word for 'privacy', the nearest equivalent (μοναξιά 'loneliness') having a necessarily negative sense.

There are few basic colour terms in SMG. The 'prime' colours (linguistically speaking) are κόκκινος 'red', κίτρινος 'yellow', and πράσινος 'green', all three characteristically derivatives of nouns for fruits or vegetables, namely AG κόκκος ' "kermesberry" ' (actually an insect, but formerly believed to be a fruit), κίτρο 'citrus', and πράσο 'leek'.

There are two traditional words for 'blue' in use today, namely γαλά-
ζιος and γαλανός (both derived from γάλα 'milk'), but these are
reserved for light blue, the darker shades being denoted by μπλέ (< F
bleu), which can also be used for 'blue' in a general sense. It is indicative
that there are verbal derivatives of the other chief colour adjectives
(meaning 'I am/make/become' the relevant colour), but not of the
words for 'blue': ἀσπρίζω '. . . white', μαυρίζω '. . . black', κοκκινίζω
'. . . red', κιτρινίζω/κιτρινιάζω '. . . yellow', and πρασινίζω '. . . green',
but not *γαλανίζω or *γαλανιάζω '. . . blue' (the verb μπλαβίζω
μπλάβος 'blue' < Ven. *blavo*, has a much more restricted meaning).

As has been mentioned, French words have been taken over into
Greek to cover the various nuances of colour, sometimes superseding
native Greek words (especially denominal adjectives in -ής, of which
there were a large number: σταχτής 'grey' < στάχτη 'ash', οὐρανής
'sky-blue' < οὐρανός 'sky', θαλασσής 'sea-blue' < θάλασσα 'sea',
τριανταφυλλής 'pink' < τριαντάφυλλο 'rose', etc.). Each of the three
'prime' colours (with the addition of 'black' and 'white') has to cover
a wide range of shades: κόκκινος, for instance, is applied to meat that
has been well browned by roasting or grilling; 'brown bread' is μαῦρο
ψωμί, and the verb used to mean 'I go brown (in the sun)' is μαυρίζω.

By contrast, there is a relatively large number of words for family
relationships, the most interesting of which concern relationships by
marriage. The use of some of these words differs according to whether
one is looking into or outside one's own family. Thus when a man
marries, he becomes the γαμπρός (also 'bridegroom') of his wife's
brothers and sisters and of her parents; similarly, a woman is the
νύφη (also 'bride') of her husband's siblings and parents. In these cases
the members of the wife's family (in the first case) or the husband's
family (in the second) are looking outwards to someone who has
married into their family. On the other hand, the γαμπρός or νύφη,
looking inwards into his/her spouse's family, calls his/her spouse's
sister κουνιάδα and his/her spouse's brother κουνιάδος. There is a separate pair of words for father-/mother-in-law (πεθερός/πεθερά), even
though the same word is used for son-in-law as for brother-in-law (looking outwards), and for daughter-in-law as for sister-in-law (again looking
outwards). Additionally, the husbands of two sisters are called μπατζα-
νάκηδες in relation to each other; the wives of two brothers are συν-
νυφάδες; and the fathers of a married couple are συμπέθεροι. This
complex vocabulary reflects the importance attached to the relative
family roles by Greek society.

Partly no doubt because of the inaccuracy and inadequate coverage of lexicography in Greece, and because of the low level of linguistic education, borderlines between concepts in MG often appear relatively blurred to the foreign observer. There is a tendency for Greeks not to feel a necessity to be specific or even accurate when naming concepts. Many non-Greeks have been amused or frustrated when they have asked a Greek townsman or peasant the name of a particular kind of flower, only to be told that it is called λουλούδι 'flower' or perhaps λουλουδάκι 'little flower'; and the owner of a small restaurant, when asked what food is available, will often include κρέας 'meat' in the list of dishes, and will have to be questioned further to specify which animal has provided this meat. There are some widespread confusions about the meanings of certain words: a prime example is τόξο 'bow', which is widely used to refer also to an *arrow* (properly βέλος) on road signs (the confusion is even enshrined in the Greek highway code, and I have heard the 'wrong' word used in conversation by one of the leading Greek poets). Similarly, λάμπα φθορίου (φθόριο 'fluorine, fluoride') is often said for λάμπα φθορισμού 'fluorescent light' (e.g. Douk. 1979: 23), and φίλντισι 'ivory' is popularly used also for σεντέφι 'mother-of-pearl'.

10.4.2 POLYSEMY AND SYNONYMY

There is a high degree of polysemy in SMG. Some instances existed in traditional demotic (e.g. πόδι 'foot; leg', χέρι 'hand; arm'); some are due to a traditional demotic word having dropped out of the standard language without being replaced, its meaning being taken over by an already existing word (e.g. ἀκούω: see 10.4.1); and others are due to new meanings, imported from Western Europe, being added to existing words.

Some examples are the following: ἀναλογία 'proportion; analogy'; ἀστικός 'urban; bourgeois; civil (code)'; ἄτομο 'individual; atom'; δημοτικός 'primary (school, education); demotic (language); folk (song); of a town council'; καλάμι 'reed; stem (esp. of cereals); fishing rod; shin-bone'; λάστιχο 'rubber; elastic; tyre; elastic band; (child's) catapult'; μέτρο 'measure; metre'; πολίτης 'citizen; civilian'; σύλληψη 'conception (biological or abstract); arrest, capture'; συμφωνία 'agreement; symphony'; σύνταξη 'compilation; pension; syntax'; ὑπερβολή 'exaggeration; hyperbole; hyperbola'; ὑπόθεση 'supposition; hypothesis; affair; business; plot (of novel etc.)'.

Some generalizations may be made about certain of the above

examples. In some instances (e.g. συμφωνία) there are two meanings, for each of which English or French has a separate word, one from Latin, the other from Greek (see further, 10.4.3). In others (e.g. λάστιχο) the word for a substance is also used for various objects made of that substance (this is perhaps another manifestation of the unspecific character of the MG vocabulary); the meanings of λάστιχο may be supplemented if one bears in mind that the plural λάστιχα can mean 'galoshes', and the diminutive λαστιχάκι means 'washer (esp. in plumbing)'; similarly, the diminutive καλαμάκι is 'drinking-straw' and 'piece of split cane on which *souvlaki* is grilled'; also, ξύλο is 'wood; piece of wood; stick; beating', and the diminutive ξυλαράκι is 'stick (for lollipop)'. There is also a number of adjectives that have become substantivized, the substantives then giving rise to adjectives that have the same form as the original adjectives: e.g. φύση 'nature' → φυσικός 'natural' → ἡ φυσική [τέχνη] 'physics' → φυσικός 'physical (of physics)' and even ὁ φυσικός 'physicist'. Other examples of such 'semantic derivatives' of substantivized adjectives are given by Lypourlis (1977): e.g. ἀριστερός 'left; left-wing'; διαμαρτυρόμενος 'protesting; Protestant'; καθολικός 'universal; Catholic'; ἐσωτερικός 'inner, interior; domestic'; σκεπτικός 'thoughful; sceptical'; τακτικός 'regular; tactical'.

Such polysemy can sometimes cause real confusion in the reader's mind, as when, for instance, a literary critic is discussing the ἀστικό μυθιστόρημα, by which it is not clear whether (s)he means the 'urban' or the 'bourgeois' novel.

On the other hand, endings may serve to differentiate various shades of meaning: e.g. τό βελόνι 'sewing or knitting needle' and τό βελονάκι 'crochet needle', as well as the augmentative ἡ βελονάρα 'huge needle'; and there are also compounds denoting needles used for knitting various articles (καλτσοβελόνα for socks, φανελοβελόνα for vests, and so on).

As has been said (10.1), there is a large amount of synonymy in MG. In some pairs of synonyms there is no difference in meaning or use, one of the words being substitutable for the other in all contexts and all registers: e.g. σκαλί or σκαλοπάτι 'step, stair; rung'. In other pairs, one member may be replaced by the other in certain linguistic contexts: thus, while in the literal meaning of κοστίζει and στοιχίζει 'it costs' the latter belongs more to K than does the former, the verbs are freely interchangeable in the figurative expression μοῦ κόστισε or μοῦ στοίχισε 'it was a great blow to me.' In a large number of cases, however, the difference is a matter of register, one of the pair originating from D and the other from K: in most such cases the D word is the more frequently used in informal speech and literature, while the K equivalent (which may also be used in more formal speech) is the one generally found in more official writing. Examples of these (the first word is of D, the second of K origin) are: ἄσπρος and λευκός 'white', λεφτά and χρήματα 'money', ρόδα and τροχός 'wheel', σίγουρος and βέβαιος 'sure, certain', σοφέρ and ὁδηγός 'driver', ταβάνι and ὁροφή 'ceiling', τριαντάφυλλο and ρόδο 'rose' (the latter is also poetic), and φτάνει and ἀρκεῖ 'it's enough/ sufficient'. In some cases the synonymous words are equally demotic, one being neutral (and therefore usable in most registers) and the other reserved for colloquial speech; examples (with the neutral member first) include χτυπάω and βαράω 'I hit, strike, beat', κρατάω and βαστάω 'I hold; I keep', and δραχμή and φράγκο 'drachma'. With regard to the last pair, however, the derivative δίφραγκο is the neutral word for 'two-drachma piece', while δίδραχμο is reserved for more official usage. Lastly, the use of some synonyms seems to be a matter of individual style, in other words, personal preference: e.g. τό πῆρα χαμπάρι and τό πῆρα εἴδηση 'I got wind of it', or ἄκρη and μπάντα 'side, edge', together with the idiom βάζω λεφτά στήν ἄκρη/μπάντα 'I put money aside' (nevertheless, μπάντα has a more restricted meaning than ἄκρη since, unlike the former, the latter can also mean 'end').

10.4.3 PROBLEMS OF THE MG VOCABULARY

One problem of the MG vocabulary has already been alluded to: this is caused by the perfectly laudable convention that, as far as possible, neologisms are coined from exclusively Greek roots. This means, as we have seen, that sometimes a single Greek word has to cover at least two quite different meanings, for which English or French possesses two separate words, one from Latin and the other from Greek.

It has been suggested by at least one historian that the lack of distinction in MG between 'democracy' and 'republic' (both δημοκρατία) has contributed to the political turmoils of Greece. In fact, the two concepts may be distinguished by the addition of the adjective ἀβασί-λευτη (< βασιλεύω 'I reign') for 'republic', but the fact is that this distinction is not normally made; and, in reality, it is quite possible to have an undemocratic republic! The clumsiness of the full phrase for 'republic' is evident when one wants to talk about 'republicans': one author talks of οἱ Δημοκρατικοί — τῆς Ἀβασίλευτης (lit. 'the Demo-crats—of the unreigned [Democracy]') (Chr. 1976: 62). When referring to US politics, Greeks talk about οἱ Ρεπουμπλικανοί to distinguish them from οἱ Δημοκρατικοί, but the former word is not used with reference to other countries: for instance, the Irish Republican Army is 'Ιρλανδικός Δημοκρατικός Στρατός (which suggests 'Democratic' and is not normally associated in the Greek speaker's mind with the Irish *Republic*); and the German Democratic Republic is ἡ Λαϊκή Δημοκρατία τῆς Γερμανίας 'People's Republic of Germany' (which is not strictly correct).

There are problems in distinguishing between 'political' and 'civil rights' (both πολιτικά δικαιώματα). But there are also rather amusing confusions inherent in the double meanings of ἀτομικός 'individual; atomic' and ἐνέργεια 'action; energy', in that ἀτομική ἐνέργεια may mean 'individual action' or 'atomic energy'; and a 'personal nuclear shelter' is ἀτομικό(!) πυρηνικό καταφύγιο.

Especially problematic are various scientific and technical terms which Western European languages have coined on the basis of Greek roots. When the Greeks want to talk about such concepts, they often find that the word concerned already means something quite different in their own language. Thus κυβερνητικός 'governmental' has to take on the meaning 'cybernetic', παραδειγματικός 'exemplary' has to do for 'paradigmatic', and συνταγματικός 'constitutional' for 'syntagmatic' (both these new meanings concern linguistics), and, in philosophy and science, it is difficult, if not impossible, to translate 'stochastic' (cf. στοχαστικός 'judicious'), 'axiomatic' (cf. ἀξιωματικός (noun) 'officer; (adj.) official'), and many other terms.

Sometimes foreign technical terms of Greek origin have been successfully translated using other roots: e.g. γνωσιολογία 'epistemology' (< γνώση 'knowledge'; cf. ἐπιστήμη 'science'), and σημασιολογία 'semantics' (< σημασία 'meaning'; cf. G *Semasiologie*, but σημαντικός 'significant'). But often writers, especially those translating hurriedly, use the 'wrong' Greek word (i.e. ἐπιστημολογία, properly 'philosophy of science', for γνωσιολογία, or σημαντικός for σημασιολογικός), thus causing further confusion. Hence writers often feel the need to gloss a technical term (or the technical use of a term) by placing its French, English, or German equivalent in brackets after it.

11

STYLE AND IDIOM

11.1 GENERAL STYLISTIC CHARACTERISTICS

The culture of modern Greece is still to a larger extent an oral one than
are those of northern European countries. Greeks spend little time on
their own: they are usually either working together, eating together,
walking together, or at least talking together with their friends or
extended families. They spend a considerable time discussing and
arguing about various topics, and in telling stories (usually humorous).
Greeks talk a lot, and effusiveness is a highly valued and sometimes
obligatory component of behaviour between people. Few spend much
time in the solitary activity of reading, and, even on crowded com-
muter trains or buses, they are usually ready to express their opinions
to complete strangers. The advent of the telephone, radio, and television in this century has only served to consolidate the oral basis of
the culture.

With Greeks, among others, in mind, Tannen (1980a) has attempted
to define the linguistic difference which separates oral from literate
cultures: 'What has been called "oral tradition" is language use which
emphasizes shared knowledge or the relationship between communicator
and audience; what has been called "literate" emphasizes decontextual-
ized content or downplays communicator/audience interaction' (326).
In oral cultures, when telling stories, people tend to point up the story
by non-linguistic means (gestures, facial expression, etc.); in more
literate societies they tend to underline their points more explicitly,
that is, verbally: all the information they are communicating is part
of a text, not a combination of text and context (ibid. 336).

Elsewhere (1980b: 84) Tannen writes that while educated members
of American and some western European societies have conventionalized literate rhetorical strategies for oral use in many public situations,
this is not true to such an extent of Greeks; that is, for oral purposes
Greeks tend to use a 'restricted code' rather than an 'elaborated code'
(Bernstein 1970), and their conversational style is likely to be very

different from their written. Indeed, people are often laughed at in Greece for using in their speech linguistic elements which are felt to belong more to written styles.

Until 1974, most of the non-literary reading that was done (newspapers, text-books, instruction manuals, etc.) was of texts written in *katharevousa*: thus a SMG prose style suitable for abstract but precise writing has been slow to evolve; but it is significant that it is literary writers who have been chiefly responsible for its development, whether in literary essays (such as those of Seferis) or in ἐπιφυλλίδες (*feuilletons*) in the daily press. On the other hand, the reading of poetry has been a favourite and highly valued activity among a significantly large group of educated Greeks, and books of poetry often appear near the top of the lists of best-sellers. The concrete expression of the MG language and the vagueness of its semantic boundaries (see 10.4.1) have contributed to make it an eminently suitable language for poetry. Another factor contributing to the success of poetry in Greece is perhaps the relative indirectness (the use of hints instead of direct expression) which has been observed in Greek conversational style (e.g. by Tannen, 1981).

Anyone who has attempted to translate from a language such as English or French into MG will have been struck by the difficulties of conveying abstract yet precise concepts in that language. (The absence of an infinitive, which means that every verb must have at least an implicit subject, has already been remarked on: 9.4.2.)

Mirambel (1959), with many decades of work on MG language and literature behind him, makes some perceptive generalizations about the 'spirit' of the MG language. He talks, for instance, of the 'concrete' nature of MG, which prefers 'the image to the concept' (409). As examples of this, he points to expressive compound adjectives, which are 'motivated' (in the Saussurean sense: i.e. their meaning is clear to see): λιγομίλητος 'taciturn' (lit. 'little-speaking'), πολυάριθμος 'numerous' (lit. 'much-number'), ἕνα πολυσέλιδο βιβλίο 'a voluminous [lit. 'many-paged'] book' (404). One could add compound nouns such as μαχαιροπήρουνα 'cutlery' (lit. 'knives–forks', but including spoons too).

Conscious of the problems involved in writing about abstract matters in MG, Mirambel says:

Le traducteur d'une langue occidentale en grec moderne, aussi bien que le technicien hellène lui-même, se trouvent en présence du problème d'expression 'précise' (c'est-à-dire non équivoque et aisément identifiable), 'immédiate' (c'est-à-dire adaptée aux besoins sans cesse accrus de la pensée scientifique, du développement des techniques, et qui ne souffrent pas du retard), 'impersonnelle' (c'est-à-dire communicable et compréhensible en toute occasion, et fixée autant qu'il est possible). (410)

There is, however, a positive corollary of this: 'On peut, semble-t-il, parler ici du caractère particulièrement humain de cette langue, en ce sens que la personnalité de l'individu apparaît sans cesse dans l'usage qu'il en fait, ce qui suppose une part de variabilité dans l'expression' (ibid.). The πολυτυπία of MG, which has already been alluded to (4.8), provides ample opportunity for stylistic choice, even though the very existence of alternative forms often leads to individual styles being based simply on phonological and morphological variants rather than on more subtle choices, such as synonyms, length of phrases and sentences, etc.

Mirambel contrasts AG and MG style in the following terms:

Alors que l'effort de la pensée grecque antique avait consisté à faire entrer la réalité dans les schèmes construits par l'esprit de façon à ramener le réel à des principes intellectuelles, le grec démotique d'aujourd'hui exprime de préférence la réalité telle qu'elle apparaît à l'observateur 'vivant' plutôt que 'pensant'. (428)

Mirambel cites the use of parataxis (which avoids the rationalization of cause and effect) as evidence of this tendency in MG. He concludes that: 'Le style néo-grec est caractérisé par l'intensité dans l'expression plutôt que par la représentation objective' (432).

The fact that MG has few periphrastic forms of the verb, and has no separate word for 'of' makes it sometimes more concise than English or French: e.g. τρῶς;—'Are you eating?'—'[Est-ce que] tu manges?' When the language is handled by a competent poet, the conciseness it can achieve is remarkable, as witness the following extract from a poem by Seferis (1969: 302–3) and its (inevitably longer) English translation:

> Λίγες οἱ νύχτες μέ φεγγάρι πού μ' ἄρεσαν.
> Τ' ἀλφαβητάρι τῶν ἄστρων πού συλλαβίζεις
> ὅπως τό φέρει ὁ κόπος τῆς τελειωμένης μέρας
> καί βγάζεις ἄλλα νοήματα κι ἄλλες ἐλπίδες,
> πιό καθαρά μπορεῖς νά τό διαβάσεις.

> Few are the moonlit nights that I've cared for:
> the alphabet of the stars—which you spell out
> as much as your fatigue at the day's end allows
> and from which you gather other meanings and
>   other hopes—
> you can then read more clearly.

Here the Greek is more compact in words than the English (35 to 45), although in syllables the proportions are nearly reversed (66 to 54). Typically, words have to be inserted in English to make semantic and syntactical connections clearer ('are' and 'have' in line 1, 'from which' line 4, and 'then' in line 5); and it is still not as obvious as it is in the Greek that 'the alphabet' is the direct object of 'read'.

11.1.1 SPOKEN STYLES

A striking feature of MG oral style is the use of 'obligatory situational formulas' (Tannen and Öztek 1981). There is a large number of such formulas (though considerably fewer than in Turkish), which have a ritualistic nature and are uttered automatically, though not without genuine feeling. These formulas, which generally express wishes, are used in a variety of particular circumstances. Thus, apart from καλά Χριστούγεννα 'happy Christmas', καλό Πάσχα 'happy Easter', and καλή χρονιά 'happy [New] Year', there are also χρόνια πολλά (lit. 'many years', said on namedays and other festivals), καλό μήνα and καλή βδομάδα (said at the beginning of the month and week respectively); beside καλησπέρα 'good evening' (when meeting), there is also καλό βράδι 'have a good evening' (when parting), and beside καληνύχτα 'goodnight', there is also καλό ξημέρωμα (lit. 'good dawning': said when parting in the early hours of the morning); as well as καλή όρεξη 'bon appétit' (said to someone eating or about to eat), there are γειά στά χέρια σου! (lit. 'health to your hands!', said to the person who has prepared the meal) and καλή χώνεψη (lit. 'good digestion', said to someone who has just had a meal); beside καλή επιτυχία 'good luck' (e.g. in examinations), there is καλά αποτελέσματα (lit. 'good results', said after the examinations have taken place but before the results are known); and there are various other expressions, such as καλῶς ἤρθατε 'welcome', to which the reply is καλῶς σᾶς βρήκαμε (lit. 'well we have found you'), καλορίζικο (lit. 'well-rooted', said to one who is moving house), μέ γειά ('with health', to one who is wearing a new item of clothing), and καλή λευτεριά (lit. 'good liberty', to an expectant mother).

One particular characteristic of MG spoken style is the very frequent use of interrogative sentences as rhetorical questions ((1)-(3)), often as responses to other questions ((4)-(5)):

(1) τί λές; 'you don't say' (in its non-sarcastic meaning) (lit. 'what are you saying?');

(2) τί νά κάνουμε; (usually untranslatable: sometimes 'what can we do?' (lit. 'what should we do?');

(3) θά 'θελα νά διαβάζω ἕνα σωρό βιβλία, μά πού καιρός γιά τέτοια πράγματα; 'I'd like to read a whole load of books, but there's no time [lit. 'where time'] for such things';

(4) — Θέλεις νά ἔρθεις; — Πῶς δέ θέλω; or simply πῶς; ' "Do you want to come?" "Of course I do [lit. 'how do I not want?']" ';

(5) — Τί ἔχετε νά φᾶμε; — Καί τί δέν ἔχουμε; ' "What have you got for us to eat?" "Anything you like [lit. 'And what haven't we got?']" '

Sarcastic exclamation is also frequent: e.g. μᾶς φώτισες! (lit. 'you enlightened us') 'you don't say' (sarcastic: also μάγος εἶσαι; (lit. 'are you [a] magician?')), or καλά τά κατάφερες! 'you've really messed things up!' (also, more literally, 'you've managed things well').

Another characteristic of MG style (written as well as oral), which is a consequence of the syntactical make-up of the language, is the narrower range of possibilities of ellipsis than there are, for instance, in English. Thus, a verb has to be repeated in MG when in English an auxiliary or the pro-form *do* can be used:

(6) θά φάω ψάρια ἄν θά φᾶς κι ἐσύ 'I'll eat fish if you *will* (too)';

(7) ἔγινα μέλος ἀφοῦ ἔγινε αὐτή 'I became [a] member after she *did*.'

Perhaps connected with this (as also with the display of enthusiasm and effusiveness in expression which is valued in the culture) is the tendency to echo words or phrases from a yes/no question in an answer, with or without using ναί 'yes' or ὄχι 'no':

(8) — Θά πᾶς; — Θά πάω. ' "Will you go?" "[Yes], (I will go)" ';

(9) — Κέρδισες; — Ὄχι, δέν κέρδισα. ' "Did you win?" "No, I didn't (win)." '

On the other hand, verbless sentences are far more common in Greek than in English, and are perfectly acceptable in written styles. Indeed, some idioms depend on this facility: e.g. τά μάτια σου τέσσερα 'keep your eyes skinned' (lit. 'your eyes four'), or ὁ Παῦλος τό βιολί του 'Paul kept harping on the same tune' (lit. 'Paul his violin').

On the whole, Greeks tend to be eloquent, but many of them need to use 'fillers' which have little or no semantic content, such as νά ποῦμε (normally unstressed) 'let's say', κατάλαβες; 'do you understand?', ξέρεις 'you know', βλέπεις 'you see', and ἔτσι (lit. 'thus', used when the speaker is trying to think especially of an abstract noun or an adjective), but also ἔ, ἔμ, ἄ, τσ, μ, which are used generally while the speaker is hesitating. Such fillers are of course normally banished from written styles. Apart from the filler ἔ, which is unstressed in speech, there are two kinds of stressed ἔ: (a), with falling intonation and preceded by a glottal stop, implying optimistic resignation; and (b), with rising intonation, meaning either 'What did you say?' or 'What do you say to that?' (Waring 1976: 318–19). Other words which also belong exclusively to spoken styles are ἀμέ (optionally preceded by ναί) 'yes' and μπά 'no; I don't think so' (and with a wide range of other meanings according to intonation).

Perhaps connected with the indirectness of MG oral styles (mentioned in 11.1) is the highly idiomatic nature of colloquial Greek speech, in contrast to the sometimes monotonous literalness of much non-literary writing. Andriotis (1976: 515) provides some striking examples of idiomatic phrases which express the speaker's attitude to what is being talked about and which would be excluded from formal written styles. Some of these examples (slightly adapted) are: καρφί δέν τοῦ καίγεται 'he doesn't give a damn' (lit. 'nail not of-him is-burned', expressing disapproval: cf. the less expressive δέν ἐνδιαφέρεται 'he's not interested'), ποιός τή χάρη σου! 'you lucky thing!' (lit. 'who your grace', expressing envy: cf. εἶσαι τυχερός 'you're lucky'), ἔχει γοῦστο νά 'ρθει! 'it would be just [my etc.] luck if (s)he came' (lit. 'it-has taste to (s)he-come', expressing apprehension: cf. ἐλπίζω νά μήν ἔρθει 'I hope (s)he doesn't come'), μέ γειά σου, μέ χαρά σου 'do what you like for all I care' (lit. 'with your health, with your joy', expressing indifference: cf. ὅπως θέλεις 'as you like').

There are also more or less derogatory alternatives for certain words, where the neutral terms are more likely to be found in written styles: e.g. τσίτσιδος 'starkers' for γυμνός 'naked', κυρά 'missus' for κυρία 'lady; Mrs; Madam', μπάσταρδος 'bastard' for νόθος 'illegitimate', μοῦτρα or μούρη 'mug' for πρόσωπο 'face', μάπα 'bonce' for κεφάλι 'head', ἀρίδες, ξερά, or ξεράδια for πόδια 'feet; legs' (the last two may also stand for χέρια 'hands; arms'), γκουβέρνο for κυβέρνηση 'government', and πόστο or ὀφίτσιο for θέση 'position' (especially, 'plum/ cushy job in the civil service'). It is noticeable that in some instances the derogatory term is a loanword, while the neutral term is of AG origin.

The use of such slang vocabulary is quite common, even among educated people, in their informal speech. MG slang (λαϊκή), which owes much to the low-life characters of pre-war Athens (μάγκες), consists of a large number of words, almost all of which conform with normal MG phonology and morphology, and there are no particular syntactical features which distinguish λαϊκή from SMG. A number of slang words have entered the vocabulary of SMG (partly perhaps as a result of compulsory military service), such as those given in the previous paragraph. As is to be expected, there is a wealth of slang words and phrases with sexual meanings, some of the most characteristic being the following: μαλάκας 'wanker, jerk' (a familiar and often affectionate form of address among young males), πούστης (used metaphorically as 'bugger' is in English, but literally denoting the 'female' partner in a homosexual relationship; the 'male' partner is κωλομπαράς); and γκόμενος and γκόμενα 'lover', or simply '(handsome) lad' and '(beautiful) girl' respectively. Other commonly used slang words include ἡ κούρσα '(de luxe) car' (= αὐτοκίνητο), ἡ λυπητερή 'the bill' (= λογαριασμός), ἡ μάσα 'grub' (= φαΐ 'food'), ὁ μπόμπιρας 'shortie' (= κοντός 'short'), ὁ πιτσιρίκος 'nipper' (= παιδί 'boy'), and ὁ ψηλέας 'tall guy' (= ψηλός). A thorough list of the vocabulary of λαϊκή, much of which is of Turkish, Italian, French, and English origin, is to be found in Dangitsis (1967).

The only other kind of special language to be found until recently in Athens is καλιαρντά, the jargon of homosexuals (see Petropoulos 1971). Again, the grammar is Greek, but many of the words are of French, Italian, English, and even Romany origin. Very few of these words are normally used in SMG, exceptions being τό τεκνό '(younger) boyfriend; handsome lad' and its derivative ἡ τεκνατζού 'woman who has a younger lover or lovers'. In very recent years, however, a new slang has been developing among young people, especially those who are involved in drugs: many of the words used are of English (US) origin, including τό φρικιό ' "freak" ' (i.e. drug-taker).

Apart from these, there is also a children's jargon (κορακίστικα, lit. 'the ravens' language'), which consists of normal Greek but with the syllable ke inserted before every syllable.

Lastly, a few words should be said about the incidence of 'learnedisms' (Kazazis 1979) in the speech of educated Greeks. Kazazis has studied the use of forms and expressions belonging to AG, koine or katharevousa in the novel Τό τρίτο στεφάνι (1962) by K. Tachtsis, in which the narrator is a middle-class Athenian woman (born soon after 1900) who completed high school but did not attend university. The language in which Τό τρίτο στεφάνι is written is generally agreed to be representative of the speech of such a person. Some of the features of this kind of language are simply morphological deviations from SMG: others (which concern us more here) consist of more or less fixed phrases which the author (though not the narrator) no doubt sees as clichés.

Since the Bible (particularly the New Testament) is normally known in its earliest Greek version, and the liturgy and other ecclesiastical writings are all in Byzantine Greek, expressions taken from these texts are in a form of the language often far removed from SMG. Kazazis finds in Tachtsis's novel many proverbial sayings of Christian origin, such as τό μέν πνεῦμα πρόθυμο(ν), ἀλλ' ἡ σάρξ ἀσθενής 'the spirit is willing, but the flesh is weak', ἄλλαι αἱ βουλαί ἀνθρώπων, ἄλλα ὁ Θεός κελεύει 'man proposes, God disposes', ἀπολωλός πρόβατο 'lost sheep', ψυχῇ τε καί σώματι 'body and soul' (adverbial), ὅταν ὁ ἀλέκτωρ ἐφώνησε τρίς 'when the cock crew thrice'; he also quotes other archaic phrases which are not necessarily ecclesiastical, such as εἰρήσθω ἐν παρόδῳ 'it should be said in passing', ὀλίγου δεῖ καί . . . 'nearly', ἄνω ποταμῶν 'incredible', κόρη ὀφθαλμοῦ 'apple of [my etc.] eye', τί ἐστί . . .; 'what is . . .?', τό διέλυαν εἰς τά ἐξ ὧν συνετέθη 'they were breaking it down into its constituent parts', πνέω τά λοίσθια 'I breathe my last.' He also finds in the same novel several examples of legal phrases which belong to katharevousa: e.g. διάταγμα περί ἐθελουσίας ἐξόδου τῶν παλαιῶν ὑπαλλήλων 'decree concerning voluntary retirement of long-standing employees', ἐπεδείξατο μετάνοιαν καί ἀρίστην διαγωγήν 'he showed repentance and excellent behaviour', κεκλεισμένων τῶν θυρῶν 'in camera'; but also other katharevousa expressions, such as μία ὡραία πρωία 'one fine day', ἐπ' οὐδενί λόγῳ 'on no account', ἀφ' ἑνός . . . ἀφ' ἑτέρου 'on the one hand . . . on the other . . .'. One could easily add other archaic expressions which are used frequently in speech, such as ἤ οὔ; (from the New Testament: as in ἔρχεσαι ἤ οὔ; 'are you coming or not?'), ἐκ τῶν ὧν οὐκ ἄνευ 'sine qua non', τό ἄκρον ἄωτον 'the last word, the ultimate', or τρόπος τοῦ λέγειν 'in a manner of speaking'.

Some of the above expressions contain not only non-standard lexical items, but morphological and syntactical categories which do not appear in SMG, such as the dative case, the infinitive, the aorist middle tense, the perfect participle, and the third person of the imperative, as well as other grammatical features which are different from those of the standard language. In addition to these expressions, there is a large number of collocations consisting of preposition + noun, some examples of which have been given in 6.2.6.

Some of these expressions are normally said only with comic intention (at least nowadays), while others are spoken in all seriousness. There is, however, a tendency for most proverbial expressions, whether of popular or of learned origin, to be avoided by educated people, who tend to find them amusing when uttered seriously (and sometimes incorrectly) by the less educated.

Clearly the subject of style (like those of vocabulary and idiom) is inexhaustible, and one can do no more than mention a small number of striking characteristics.

11.1.2 WRITTEN STYLES

Since the late nineteenth century there has been a wide chasm between literary and non-literary styles in Greek, literature being composed in demotic and other writing in *katharevousa*. Until recently the demotic of literature often displayed an attempt to approximate to the speech of the uneducated peasant; and even though, on the one hand, the language of literature has gradually been brought closer to the spoken language of the educated, while, on the other, the language of journalism, of the administration, of science, etc., has in its turn moved away from K, there is still a gap between literary and non-literary styles. The lack of common ground in Greece between literature and science is striking: scientists do not normally allow themselves to write in either an elegant or an everyday style, while novelists have avoided the kind of analytical, expository writing that forms an important element of much of English and French fiction. Indeed, according to Andriotis (1976: 532–3), scientific writing should not possess 'style' at all (by which he presumably means *personal* style). The same writer expresses his objection to the use of the popular names of plants in botanical treatises (ibid. 529): in fact, it is the scientific names (not even the Latin ones, which are accepted world-wide, but pseudo-AG ones) that are taught in natural history in Greece, so that the popular names of certain phenomena of nature are in danger of dying out. In Greece there is as yet no use of colloquial language in scientific terminology as there is in Anglo-American science (e.g. 'hairy spheres' in mathematics (topology)). It is noticeable that even demoticists are unwilling to use everyday terms in scientific discourse, since they have too much of a familiar, homely ring about them (or simply sound vulgar, like ἡ γαϊδούρα 'she-donkey', for which a writer on veterinary medicine will use the AG ἡ ὄνος). These writers will often use a word which does not follow a demotic declension in preference to an everyday word (e.g. βαρύ ὕδωρ 'heavy water' for *βαρύ νερό); and a doctor is likely to prefer τό ἧπαρ to τό συκώτι for 'liver', particularly perhaps because the latter is redolent of the kitchen. (For interesting discussions of the problems of writing about science in demotic, see Techni 1976, and *Provlimata* 1977.)

The gap between bellettristic and other styles is thus obvious to see. Prose fiction has traditionally tended to be written in short, colloquial and idiomatic sentences, with a high incidence of proverbial and metaphorical language; journalism and other non-literary writing has tended to be literal, flat, colourless, and highly complex in syntax. The difference is also detectable at the levels of morphology and phonology, and a writer who writes (and says) τῆς κυβερνήσεως 'of the government' or προσεκτικά 'carefully' outside literary discourse will normally write τῆς κυβέρνησης and προσεχτικά in a poem or novel. Indeed, it is at these levels that 'style' is usually talked about by Greek readers, who often concentrate so much on such niceties that they seem unaware of far more interesting stylistic differences.

One of the unfortunate results of MG diglossia, with the consequent polarization of styles between the *faux-naïf* hyper-demotic and the impersonal but turgid, has been that it is impossible to base one's usage on that of the 'best authors', as is usually the case in standard European languages. In their enthusiasm to promote the language of the people at the expense of the official K, literary writers have tended until recently to flaunt with defiance precisely those words and forms which are most at variance with official usage. Their desire to enshrine in their works forms of MG which they saw as being in danger of extinction under the pressure of education and the press led them to employ dialect features, vulgarisms, and sometimes quite arbitrary coinages, many of which were (and are) alien to the linguistic sense of the majority of educated Greeks.

Thus it is difficult to find a Greek literary writer whose language and style can stand as a model. The author who comes to mind most often in this context is G. Seferis, whose essays on poetry, language, and culture are among the finest examples of MG style: but even Seferis, if one examines his language closely, produces sentences which are clumsy or even ungrammatical (for instance, by using the present participle in an idiosyncratic manner, probably under French or English influence); and he sometimes uses forms which mark him as an extreme demoticist. It is certainly difficult to find prose *fiction* written in a style on which a Greek can model his own writing; so that one is limited to the work of Seferis and a few other literary critics and essayists. If one looks elsewhere (at journalism, for instance), one finds the most heterogeneous types of writing, much of which clumsily preserves many of the forms and structures of K.

It is nevertheless inevitable that the style of much non-bellettristic writing should be to some extent based on K, since the style of K itself was to a significant degree modelled on written French, and was thus a vehicle through which MG could enter the so-called European *Sprachbund* and take on many additional characteristics of 'Standard Average European'. Some elements of the impersonal style developed by K are clearly suitable for administrative documents, although readers of the Greek press have reason to lament the fear of metaphor from which many journalists seem to suffer. Traditionally, along with K, Greek children were taught the importance of κυριολεξία ('literalness'); and exhortations to avoid figurative language seem to have led some writers to adopt the annoying habit of placing inverted commas around any expression which is felt to be colloquial or metaphorical. For example:

(1) Εἴκοσι τέσσερις αἰῶνες ὁ Φίλιππος 'κοιμόταν' κάτω ἀπό τά χωράφια τῆς Βεργίνας. [. . .] Ἕνα μεσημέρι, πρίν 15 μέρες ὁ κασμάς τοῦ πεισματάρη ἀρχαιολόγου 'βρῆκε' τό ταβάνι τοῦ τάφου! 'For twenty-four centuries [King] Philip had been "sleeping" under the fields of Vergina. [. . .] One afternoon, a fortnight ago, the pickaxe of the dogged archaeologist "hit upon" the ceiling of the tomb!' (*T* 1 Dec. 1977, 101).

Greek journalistic and official writing also suffers from an overuse of *nominal style* (see 'substantivitis', 11.1.2.2) and of passive constructions, which are intended to give an effect of impersonality. In both journalistic and other non-literary styles, however, writers attempt to avoid repetition through the use of periphrases, including personifications such as ἡ Θέμις (the ancient goddess of justice) for 'justice' or 'the legal profession', hackneyed metaphors such as τό ὑγρό στοιχεῖο 'the liquid element' (= 'the sea') or τό μαῦρο χρυσό 'black gold' (= 'oil'), and sobriquets and metonymic appellations, as when a journalist writing about a football team calls it by its name, Ὀλυμπιακός, in the first sentence, then goes on to refer to it in the second and third sentences as ἡ πειραϊκή ὁμάδα 'the Piraeus team' and οἱ ἐρυθρόλευκοι 'the red-and-whites' respectively.

It is in fact in the sporting newspapers and in the sports pages of the press in general that journalists seem to permit themselves to indulge in figurative language, and it is no wonder that such writing is read with far greater enthusiasm than are the dull and basically uninformative columns of news and comment on current events. Thus the players of Παναθηναϊκός (or ΠΑΟ) are οἱ Πράσινοι 'the Greens', while their supporters are οἱ φίλοι τοῦ τριφυλλιοῦ 'friends of the clover' (after the team's emblem); AEK is ὁ Δικέφαλος 'the Double-headed [eagle]' (the Byzantine eagle which serves as its badge) or ὁ κιτρινόμαυρος ἀετός 'the yellow-and-black eagle'; and, amid the colourful use of the technical terminology of football, of augmentatives, appositional compounds (of the type mentioned in 10.3.4), and idiomatic expressions, one encounters metaphorical phrases such as the following:

(2) ἡ AEK ἔδωσε ρεσιτάλ, μέ σολίστ τόν X. 'AEK gave a recital, with X. [one of the leading players] as soloist' (*AI* 15 Sept. 1980);

(3) ἕνα ἐπιθετικό κρεσέντο τοῦ Παναθηναϊκοῦ στό τελευταῖο δεκάλεπτο τοῦ πρώτου μέρους 'an aggressive crescendo by Panathinaikos in the last ten minutes of the first movement' (*FD* 15 Sept. 1980);

(4) ὁ Ἡρακλῆς ἔπαιξε μέ τό ρόπαλό του τή λύρα τοῦ Ἀπόλλωνα 'Hercules played Apollo's lyre with his club' (Hercules and Apollo are both football teams) (quoted in *T* 25 Feb. 1982, 75)!

(For further details about the language of Greek football see Rotolo 1973.)

11.1.2.1 Literary styles

As has been said before, the language of literature since the end of the nineteenth century has usually stood at a considerable distance from K, and even from the ordinary spoken language of educated Greeks. The demoticist reaction against the official domination of K led to the use of many features which are non-standard according to the norms of present-day Greek. In their effort to recapture the time when their own speech was unadulterated by the influence of education, many writers used dialectal words and forms in their poetry and prose. Indeed, the language of prose fiction did not become distinguished from the language of poetry until rather recently, and many prose-writers used linguistic features which came to be seen as conventionally poetic. In the last decade of the nineteenth century and the first two of the twentieth it became almost *de rigueur*, particularly in poetry, to employ linguistic features marked as poetic, whether these were lexical items (e.g. τό ἄτι 'steed' for ἄλογο 'horse', ἀποσταίνω for κουράζομαι 'I get tired', κοτῶ for τολμῶ 'I dare', or διαφεντεύω for προστατεύω 'I defend', and especially compound words, e.g. γλυκοχαράζει 'it begins to dawn (sweetly)', or morphological variants (e.g. πέλαγο for πέλαγος 'open sea', or παραθύρι for παράθυρο 'window'). Such features became so conventionalized that their use was taken by lesser writers as being a sure recipe for good poetry, and much poor verse was written because writers believed that such features were all that was needed. There was also a tendency among early demoticists, especially in prose, to take K words and adapt them to D phonology (e.g. διεύτυση for διεύθυνση 'address', or βνωμοσύνη for εὐγνωμοσύνη 'gratitude'), an attempt which has been resisted by SMG.

A reaction to such tendencies came in the poetry of Cavafy and Karyotakis, who freely used K elements alongside D. But the real revolution occurred during the 1930s, when poets such as Seferis began using a variety of the language which, without straying far from the demotic, avoided those linguistic elements which had become poetic clichés and which were outside the standard language as it had by then developed. Nevertheless, extremes persisted in literature, Kazantzakis (justifiably) feeling the need to append a glossary of 3000 unusual words to his hyper-demotic epic poem Ὀδύσεια (1938), and, at the other extreme, the surrealist Embirikos using K in the prose-poems of his collection Ὑψικάμινος (1935), which were allegedly composed by means of 'automatic writing'. This use of K in literature by Embirikos and others served two purposes: it was a reaction against the folksy demotic of earlier writing, but it also undermined convention through writing about taboo subjects (such as sexual pleasure) in a variety of the language which was highly euphemistic and was normally used for administrative and scientific purposes.

K is sometimes used outside literature for comic purposes. From 1979 to 1983 the weekly magazine *Tachydromos* published the strip-cartoon *Blanche Épiphanie*, in which the narrative and dialogue (translated from the French) appeared in a K which suited the historical setting (about 1900) but contrasted amusingly with the sexual misadventures of the heroine. There are occasionally whole articles in such popular magazines which are written in K for comic effect, chiefly because their style is in striking contrast with the often scurrilous or at least trifling nature of their content. Such styles perhaps owe as much to Embirikos as they do to memories of the time when all non-literary prose was written in K.

Since the Second World War, the language of literature has come much closer to SMG, culminating in Tachtsis's Τό τρίτο στεφάνι (already mentioned in 11.1.1), which faithfully captures the spoken style of a certain type of Athenian woman. Nevertheless, some writers, such as Kazantzakis and Prevelakis, continued to use the 'popular style' in their novels, which teem with linguistic features that are dialectal, or at least obsolete in the speech of urban Athenians.

In poetry, of course, more liberties may be taken than in prose, and the work of Elytis, particularly Τό ἄξιον ἐστί (1959), contains a large number of non-standard features which are not so much dialectal elements as coinages by the poet himself. Some of these are compound words or other derivatives which Elytis generally forms from AG rather than D roots: these include ἡλιοπότης 'sun-drinker', Ἐρεβοκτόνος 'erebus-slayer', οὐρανοσύνη 'sky-ness', χιμαιροποίκιλτος 'adorned with chimaeras', and νησιωτίζω v.t. 'I island'. Elytis also employs non-standard morphology and syntax. Like other MG poets he sometimes uses normally intransitive verbs with direct objects. An example from another of his poems is:

(1) καί μιά σημαία πλατάγιζε ψηλά γῆ καί νερό 'and a flag on high was flapping earth and water' (Ely. 1971: 9):

although πλαταγίζω may have a direct object when it has a human subject (πλαταγίζω τή γλώσσα μου 'I click my tongue'), the verb is normally intransitive when its subject is σημαία. Elytis is sometimes idiosyncratic in his use of participles, as in:

(2) Ὁ νικήσαντας τόν Ἅδη καί τόν Ἔρωτα σώσαντας 'He who has conquered Hades and saved Love' (Ely. 1974: 115):

here the ancient aorist active participles νικήσας and σώσας have been given a demotic ending (cf. SMG present active paticiples νικώντας and σώζοντας), but have also been substantivized with the addition of the definite article, a process which does not take place with active participles in SMG.

Despite the possibility of such poetic licence, it is impossible to write Greek (as it is possible to write English) in such a way as to leave it uncertain whether certain words are nouns or verbs; even in the most Surrealistic of Greek poetry there is a strong element of logic, in that it is almost always clear which is the subject and which the direct object of a given verb, and other syntactical connections are usually equally unambiguous (e.g. adjectives have to agree with their nouns etc.), since every noun, adjective, and verb has a suffix which indicates its connection with other elements in the phrase.

The use of specially coined compound words in literature, which was a frequent phenomenon in nineteenth-century poetry as well as in that of Elytis and other modern poets, represents an attempt to form new metaphors by condensing the meaning of a whole phrase into a single word. And just as in everyday language the compound noun ἀσπρό-ρουχα 'underclothes' does not mean precisely the same as the phrase from which it has been formed (ἄσπρα ροῦχα 'white clothes': underclothes are not always white, nor are all white clothes underclothes!), so in poetry Elytis's χρυσεγέρτης (ἄνεμος) (1974: 130) '(the wind) which raises gold' (a reference to golden dust in the sun) has a different resonance from a more analytical phrase, especially since this particular compound is reminiscent of an adjective applied to Christ by the Church Fathers (νεκρεγέρτης 'He who raises the dead'). Thus, analysed in full, the phrase χρυσεγέρτης ἄνεμος means 'the wind which raises golden dust just as Christ raises the dead'.

To finish this section, let us look at three complex sentences which show how literary demotic, as developed over the past hundred years, has become capable of moving away from 'popular' conversational styles and of producing sentences which are both complex and precise in expression. In (3), which is taken from a piece of literary criticism, distinctions of aspect are employed to remove likely ambiguities:

> (3) Καί τόν ἔπλασε ἀπό τήν ἀρχή, δείχνοντάς τον νά ξαναβγαίνει στή ζωή τή σημερινή, αὐτός ὁ συμβολικά ἕτοιμος πάντα ν' ἀνασταθεῖ, νά παίρνει ἀνθρώπινο σχῆμα μέσα στό ἀττικό φῶς, ἀπό φάσμα νά γίνεται ἄνθρωπος. 'And [Palamas] created [Ascraeus] from the beginning, showing this [man who was] always symbolically ready to be resurrected emerging again into contemporary life, taking on human form in the Attic light, and changing from a spectre into a man' (Karandonis, *NE* 73 (1963): 468).

The clumsy English rendering does not do justice to the Greek, which, with its use of νά, makes the connections between clauses absolutely clear, and indicates by its use of aspects that only ν' ἀνασταθεῖ (perfective) depends on ἕτοιμος, while all the other νά-clauses (in which the verbs are in the imperfective) are governed by δείχνοντάς τον.

Despite his use of non-standard elements, Kazantzakis could be

a fine stylist, as is shown in (4) and (5) by the way in which he arranges
the order of constituents to achieve the greatest possible impact:

(4) Ἔνας ἄνθρωπος, ὅταν, ὕστερα ἀπό πολλά χρόνια ἀγώνα καί
περιπλάνηση στήν ξενιτιά, γυρίσει στήν πατρίδα κι ἀκουμπήσει
στίς πατρικές πέτρες καί σβαρνίσει γύρα του μέ τή ματιά τά
γνώριμα πυκνοκατοικημένα ἀπό ντόπια πνέματα καί παιδικές
θύμησες καί νεανικές λαχτάρες τοπία, τόν κόβει ξαφνικός
κρύος ἱδρώτας. 'When a man returns to his homeland after
many years of struggling and wandering in foreign parts; when
he touches his native [lit. 'paternal'] stones and surveys the
familiar landscape [which is] thickly populated with local
spirits, childhood memories and youthful yearnings, he feels
a sudden chill come over him [lit. 'sudden cold sweat cuts him']'
(Kaz. 1965: 524).

Here a powerful effect is achieved through the delay between ἔνας
ἄνθρωπος, placed at the very beginning of the sentence and interpreted
by the reader as the subject of a main verb, and the verb whose subject
it is. In the event, the main verb turns out to have a different subject
(ξαφνικός κρύος ἱδρώτας), while ἄνθρωπος is reduced to the object
pronoun τόν. Quite apart from the grammatical surprise of the anacolouthon (which is in fact not uncommon in spoken Greek: see 2.2.6),
the fact that 'man', which is the subject of three active verbs in the subordinate clauses, suddenly becomes the object of the main verb indicates
what a shock it is to return home. The delay between apparent subject
and main verb is achieved by the interpolation of a complex series of
three clauses depending on ὅταν, the first interrupted by a long adverbial phrase introduced by ὕστερα ἀπό and the third lengthened by
the interpolation (by hyperbaton: see 6.1.1) of an adverbial phrase
introduced by ἀπό between the adjectival participle πυκνοκατοικημένα
and the noun τοπία.

The effect of (5) is again achieved through postponement, this time
of the subject:

(5) Κι ἔνα βράδι ἦρθε καί κουλουριάστηκε στήν πλώρα, ντυμένος
σάν κι ἐμᾶς, μέ προβιές ἀλεπούς, μέ μυτερό γαλάζο σκοῦφο μέ
κόκκινη φούντα, μέ κάτασπρα γένια, μέ τό πρόσωπο, τό στῆθος,
τά μπράτσα, τά μεριά χαρακωμένα μέ δεμένες πληγές καί μᾶς
χαμογελοῦσε μέ τρυφεράδα, ὁ Χάρος· καταλάβαμε, ξυγώναμε

πιά στήν ἄκρα τῆς πορείας. 'And one evening Charos [= personification of death] came and curled up in the bows [of our boat], dressed like us in fox-skins, wearing a pointed blue cap with a red tassel, with [a] snow-white beard, (with) his face, chest, arms, and thighs furrowed with scars; he smiled tenderly at us, and we realized that we had (now) been approaching the end of the journey' (Kaz. 1965: 588).

In the Greek, despite the fact that he is the subject of all the verbs before the semi-colon and is described in vivid detail, ὁ Χάρος is not named until immediately before the semicolon. The very structure of the sentence imitates the process which the 'we' of the discourse pass through, that is, the gradual realization that the old man is none other than Death himself.

11.1.2.2 'Genitivitis' and 'substantivitis'

Two of the chief targets of attack from demoticist grammarians are the overuse of the genitive and the overuse of abstract nouns (as opposed to verbs), which are characteristic of journalistic and bureaucratic styles: demoticists view these abuses as particularly clumsy relics of *katharevousa*. It is not difficult to find examples of such abuses, which in fact regularly co-occur in the same phrase: such phrases could indeed be made clearer and less objectionable were one or two of the nouns to be replaced by verbs. Such phrases as these are frequent:

(1) ἡ μονάδα βενζίνης, ὕψους ἐπενδύσεως τριάντα ἐκατομμυρίων δολλαρίων. 'the oil refinery, in which thirty million dollars have been invested . . .' (lit. 'the unit of-petrol, of-height of-investment of-thirty millions of-dollars') (T 4 Oct. 1979, 16):

the genitives appear to consist of one of quality or purpose (βενζίνης), two of measurement (ὕψους, ἐκατομμυρίων), one of figurative possession (ἐπενδύσεως), and one partitive genitive (δολλαρίων). It is even possible to find strings of genitives as long as that in the following example:

(2) τά ἄτοκα δάνεια θά χορηγηθοῦν ὑπό τόν ὅρο καταβολῆς τῶν τυχόν ὀφειλομένων μέχρι σήμερα (δεδουλευμένων) ἀποδοχῶν, τοῦ ἐπιδόματος ἑορτῶν καί τῶν ἀποδοχῶν τοῦ δευτέρου δεκαπενθημέρου τοῦ μηνός Δεκεμβρίου 'the interest-free loans will be issued on condition that any earned income owed up to the

present, plus holiday bonuses, and the income for the second fortnight in December are all paid' (lit. 'the interest-free loans will be-issued under the condition of-payment of-the by-any-chance owed until today (worked-for) income, of-the bonus of-festivals and of-the income of-the second fortnight of-the month of-December') (*K* 23 Dec. 1980).

The total of eight nouns in the genitive presents a complex pattern of dependence (which is further complicated by the hyperbaton, character-istic of *katharevousa*, consisting of an adverb, an adverbial phrase and two participles inserted between the article τῶν and the noun ἀπο-δοχῶν).

11.2 IDIOM

We have already mentioned that, outside *belles-lettres*, MG written styles tend to be rather unidiomatic. The same cannot be said either of colloquial or of literary styles. On the other hand, educated people may sometimes adopt an approximation of a written style when speaking in a formal context, and their speech then tends to become literal and un-idiomatic. The fact is that there is a tendency for urban people to avoid linguistic features which might betray rural origins. The disappearance of proverbial expressions has already been referred to.

In less formal situations, however, educated urban people use a large amount of idiomatic language (some examples are given in 11.1.1 as well as elsewhere in this book), although many of the idioms concerned may employ a small repertoire of words. A type of idiomatic expres-sion frequently found in the contemporary spoken language is one that consists of a verb used with a clitic object pronoun which has no referent in the linguistic or situational context. Thus the clitic pronoun appears to stand for a deleted noun that may or may not be identifiable. Examples of widely used traditional phrases include the following: τό βάζω στά πόδια 'I take to my heels' (lit. 'I put it to the feet/legs'), τά βάζω μέ . . . 'I pick a quarrel with . . .' (lit. 'I put them with . . .'), τά βγάζω πέρα 'I manage' (lit. 'I take them out beyond'), φτηνά τή γλύτωσα 'I got off lightly' (lit. 'cheaply I escaped/saved it': sc. τή ζωή '[my] life'?), τά καταφέρνω 'I manage it', τήν ἔπαθα 'I copped it' (lit. 'I suffered it': sc. τή δουλειά 'the business'?), τήν πάτησα 'I've put my foot in it' (lit. 'I trod on it': sc. τήν πεπονόφλουδα 'the melon-skin'?), τό ρίχνω σέ . . . 'I indulge immoderately in . . .' (lit. 'I throw it to . . .'), μοῦ τήν ἔφτιαξε '(s)he played a trick on me' (lit. '(s)he fixed it of-me': sc. τή δουλειά?).

Some verbs may be constructed with different pronouns in different meanings: e.g. κοπανάω 'I beat, pound'—τά κοπανάω 'I drink' (sc. τά ποτήρια 'the glasses'?), τήν κοπανάω 'I make off', and μή μοῦ τό κοπανᾶς 'don't rub it in' (in the last, τό may in fact be seen as referring to the point that the other speaker has been making). In some similar expressions the pronoun could be construed as referring either to some specific idea or to a following clause, with a noun after the verb in apposition to the pronoun: e.g. τό βάξω πεῖσμα νά . . . 'I'm firmly resolved to . . .' (lit. 'I put it obstinacy to . . .'), τό πάω στοίχημα [πώς] . . . 'I bet . . .' (lit. 'I go wager [that] . . .'), and τό παίρνω ἀπόφαση 'I accept the inevitable' (lit. 'I take it decision'). The following idioms appear to be of more recent origin: τή βγάζω (μέ) 'I get by (with)', τή βρίσκω (μέ) 'I get a kick (out of)', and μοῦ τή σπάει '(s)he gets on my nerves' (also μοῦ τή δίνει, with the same meaning or with a contrary sense: '(s)he excites me').

Colloquial MG speech teems with idioms (or metaphorical usages) based on a few common verbs. A selection of these is given below, with (where appropriate) synonymous equivalents in parentheses.

1. βάζω 'I put'; also 'I put on (clothes)' (φοράω), 'I serve with (at table)' (with indirect object of person), 'I get (person to do something)', 'I lay (table)' (στρώνω), 'I impose (tax)'; (perfective passive + νά) 'I set about (doing something)'; (πενήντα) καί βάλε '(fifty) and more', τῆς ἔβαλα καλό βαθμό 'I gave her a good mark (at school)', βάλαμε δύο γκόλ 'we scored two goals', βάζω τά δυνατά μου 'I do my best', βάζω τό κεφάλι μου 'I stake my life', βάζω νερό στό κρασί μου 'I moderate my views/tone', βάζω στοίχημα 'I lay a wager' (στοιχηματίζω), βάζω ὑποψηφιότητα 'I stand for office', βάζω τίς φωνές 'I start shouting' (φωνάζω), βάζω φωτιά σέ 'I set fire to', δέν τό βάζει κάτω '(s)he won't give up', τόν βάλανε μέσα 'they put him away' (τόν φυλάκισαν 'they imprisoned him'), βάζω μπρός v.t. 'I start up (engine).'

2. βγάζω 'I take out/off'; also 'I extract', 'I put out (leaves, shoots, etc.)', 'I give off (smoke, smell)', 'I publish' (ἐκδίδω), 'I elect', 'I produce' (παράγω), 'I earn' (κερδίζω), 'I make out (meaning, writing)', 'I dislocate (arm)'; ποῦ βγάζει αὐτός ὁ δρόμος; 'where does this road lead?', τόν βγάλανε Γιάννη 'they named him John', βγάζω κάτι στήν ἀγορά 'I put something on the market', τόν βγάλανε ἀπ' τή μέση 'they got him out of the way', τό βγάλανε στό σφυρί 'they auctioned it',

βγάζω τά ἀπωθημένα μου 'I give vent to my frustrations', βγάζω τό ἄχτι μου 'I let off steam', βγάζω γλώσσα 'I answer cheekily', βγάζω δίσκο 'I pass the hat round', τόν βγάλανε λάδι 'he was acquitted' (τόν ἀθώωσαν), τοῦ βγάλανε λάδι 'they drove him hard', βγάζω τό λαρύγγι μου 'I shout myself hoarse', βγάζω λόγο 'I make a speech', βγάζω ὄνομα 'I become well known', μοῦ 'βγαλε τήν πίστη '(s)he gave me a hard time', βγάζω τό φίδι ἀπ' τήν τρύπα 'I pull the chestnuts out of the fire', τόν βγάλανε ψεύτη 'he was proved a liar', βγάζω τό ψωμί μου 'I earn my living.'

3. ἔχω 'I have, possess'; (impersonal) 'there is/are, there was/were'; τί ἔχεις; 'what's the matter with you?', πόσο ἔχει; 'how much is it (does it cost)?', πόσες ἔχει σήμερα ὁ μήνας; 'what date is it today?', ἔχω δίκιο 'I'm right', ἔχω δουλειά 'I'm busy', ἔχω δυό μέρες νά τόν δῶ 'I haven't seen him for two days', τί τόν ἔχεις; 'what relationship is he to you?', αὐτός ἔχει τό Θεό μπάρμπα 'he has powerful connections' (lit. 'he has God [as his] uncle'), δέν τόν ἔχω σέ μεγάλη ὑπόληψη 'I don't regard him very highly', δέν τό 'χει τίποτα νά . . . '(s)he thinks nothing of . . .', τό ἔχω σέ καλό 'I think it lucky', ἔχω καλύτερα νά . . . 'I prefer to . . .', τήν ἔχω καλά 'I'm sitting pretty', τά ἔχουμε καλά 'we're on good terms', τά ἔχω μαζί της 'I'm having an affair with her', τά ἔχει τετρακόσα '(s)he has his/her head screwed on the right way', δέν ἔχει νά κάνει 'it makes no difference', δέν ἔχει σημασία 'it's not important', τό ἔχω πῶς καί πῶς 'I look after it very carefully', τόν ἔχουνε ὤπα-ὤπα 'they make a fuss of him.'

4. κάνω 'I do'; also 'I make (bed)' (στρώνω), 'I give (a present)' (προσφέρω); (with πώς) 'I pretend (to/that)'; (with νά) 'I make (as if) to'; τί κανεις; 'what are you doing?; how are you?', πόσο κάνει; 'how much does it come to?', κάνε γρήγορα! 'hurry!', μήν κάνεις ἔτσι! 'don't go on like that!', δέν κάνει (νά) 'it doesn't do (to)', δέ μοῦ κάνει 'it doesn't suit me; it's not what I want', τό ἴδιο μοῦ κάνει 'it's all the same to me', ἔκανε δυό ἀγόρια 'she had (gave birth to) two boys', ἔκανα στήν Ἀθήνα 'I spent some time in Athens', ἔκανα μῆνες νά πάω 'I didn't go for months', κάνω τό γύρο (+ gen.) 'I tour, go round', κάνει ζέστη 'it's hot (of weather)', τά κάνω θάλασσα 'I make a mess of things', μοῦ ἔκανε καλό 'it did me good', μέ ἔκανε καλά '(s)he/it cured me', κάνω τοῦ κεφαλιοῦ μου 'I go my own way', κάνω μάθημα 'I'm having/giving a lesson', κάνω μπάνιο 'I have a bath; I go for a swim', κάνει νερά 'it's leaking', κάνω ὑπομονή 'I'm patient', κάνω φτερά 'I vanish' (ἐξαφανίζομαι), κάνω χωρίς . . . 'I do without . . .', κάνω στήν ἄκρη v.t. and v.i. 'I move aside.'

5. παίρνω 'I take; I receive'; also 'I buy', 'I assume, take on (an appearance, etc.)', 'I earn', 'I have (a drink)', 'I marry', 'I contain, hold'; (with νά) 'I begin'; τόν παίρνω 'I take a nap', μέ πῆρε ὁ ὕπνος 'I fell asleep', τήν πῆραν τά κλάματα/γέλια 'she burst out crying/laughing', τόν πῆρε ὁ καρκίνος 'he died of cancer', μέ πῆρε ἀπό κακό μάτι '(s)he took a dislike to me', μέ πῆρε ἀπό συμπάθεια '(s)he took a liking to me', θά σέ πάρω (τηλέφωνο) 'I'll phone you', τόν πῆραν στό ψιλό/μεξέ 'they made fun of him', τόν πῆρες στό λαιμό σου 'you were the cause of his misfortune', τόν πῆρε τό μάτι μου 'I caught sight of him', δέ μᾶς παίρνει ἡ ὥρα 'we haven't got time', παίρνω ἀέρα 'I become cheeky', πῆρε ὁ νούς του ἀέρα 'he's got too big for his boots', παίρνω τήν κάτω βόλτα 'I run to seed', παίρνω τά βουνά 'I take to the hills', παίρνω κουράγιο 'I take courage', παίρνω ὅρκο (πώς) 'I swear', παίρνω σβάρνα v.t. 'I make the round of', πῆρε φωτιά 'it caught fire', τό παίρνω ἀπάνω μου 'I give myself airs', παίρνω ἀπάνω μου 'I recover (in health)', τόν παίρνω ἀπό πίσω/κοντά 'I follow him closely', δέν παίρνει ἀπό λόγια '(s)he won't listen to reason', τό παιδί δέν πῆρε ἀπό μένα 'the child doesn't take after me', παίρνω μπρός v.i. 'I start up/off', πάρε-δῶσε 'dealings'.

6. πάω/πηγαίνω 'I go; I take (convey)', 'I bet, stake'; also (with νά) '[I'm] nearly . . .'; (usually third person) 'it/they suit(s)/fit(s)'; πάει αὐτός 'he's finished/done for/dead', πάει νά πεῖ (or παναπεῖ) 'it means; in other words', πῶς (τά) πᾶς; 'how are you doing?', τά πᾶμε καλά 'we get on well [with each other]', ποῦ τό πᾶς; 'what are you getting at?', πᾶνε δέκα χρόνια ἀπό τότε 'ten years have passed since then' (πέρασαν), αὐτό πάει πολύ! 'that's too much, that's going too far', πῆγε ἔξη ἡ ὥρα 'it's just six o'clock', οἱ ντομάτες πῆγαν 40 τό κιλό 'tomatoes (have) reached 40 a kilo', πῆγε ἀπό (καρδιά etc.) '(s)he died of (a heart attack etc.)', πάω γιά (πρόεδρος) 'I'm standing for (president)', πάω γιά ὕπνο 'I go to bed', πάει γυρεύοντας '(s)he's asking for trouble', ἡ γλώσσα τους πάει ροδάνι 'they talk nineteen to the dozen', πάει ρολόι 'it's going like clockwork', τό ρολόι πάει μπροστά/πίσω 'the watch/clock is fast/slow', πάει χαμένο 'it's wasted.'

7. πιάνω 'I catch, seize'; also (v.t.) 'I occupy, take possession of', '(of fever, anger, etc.) I overcome (someone)', 'I begin (conversation, job)'; (v.i.) 'I put in (of ship)', 'I germinate (of seed)', 'I stick (of label etc.)', 'I catch on (of fashion)', 'I come off (of joke etc.)', 'I burn, catch (of food, saucepan, firewood)', 'I come on, break out (of rain, wind, cold, fire, etc.)'; (passive) 'I am paralysed', (pl.) 'we quarrel; we come to blows', τί σ' ἔπιασε; 'what's got into you?', μ' ἔπιασε τό

κεφάλι μου 'I've got a headache', μέ πιάνει ἡ θάλασσα 'I get seasick', πιάνω τά ἔξοδά μου 'I cover my expenses', πιάνει τόπο 'it takes up space; it comes in useful', ἔπιασα φιλίες μαζί τους 'I made friends with them', πιάστηκε ἡ φωνή μου 'I lost my voice', πιάστηκα πάνω του 'I leant on him.'

8. τρώω 'I eat'; also 'I spend, consume, squander', 'I eat away, wear away/out, fray', 'I worry, nag', 'I beat, get the better of', 'I suffer, undergo'; (passive) 'I am edible', 'I grumble', (with νά) 'I'm madly keen to', (plural) 'we quarrel'; ἡ σκουριά τρώει τό σίδερο 'rust corrodes iron', τό ποτάμι ἔφαγε τό χωράφι 'the river ate into the field', μέ τρώει . . . 'my . . . itches', τόν τρώει ἡ μύτη του 'he's asking for trouble', φάγαμε δυό γκόλ 'we had two goals scored against us', τίς φάγαμε 'we came a cropper', τόν φάγανε λάχανο 'he was done in (= killed)', δέν τρώω ἄχερα/πίτουρα 'I'm no fool', ἔφαγε μιά κλωτσιά στόν πισινό 'he got a kick in the backside', τρώω τόν κόσμο (νά) 'I search everywhere (to)', τρώει τίς λέξεις '(s)he mumbles when (s)he speaks', τρώω τά νύχια μου 'I bite my nails', τρώω ξύλο 'I get a hiding', τρώω τόν περίδρομο or τρώω τοῦ σκασμοῦ 'I eat fit to burst', ἔφαγε φύσημα '(s)he was given the boot; (s)he was transferred elsewhere.'

9. φέρνω 'I bring; I fetch'; also 'I bring on/about'; (passive) 'I behave'; μιά πού τό 'φερε ὁ λόγος 'by the way', ὁ λόγος τό φέρνει 'in a manner of speaking', φέρνω ἀντιρρήσεις 'I raise objections', τά φέρνω βόλτα 'I make ends meet', τόν φέρνω βόλτα 'I get round him', φέρνω ἕνα παράδειγμα 'I produce/bring forward an example', φέρνω γύρω v.t. 'I go round', ποῦ φέρνει αὐτός ὁ δρόμος; 'where does this road lead?', τό χρῶμα φέρνει πρός τό καφέ 'the colour is brownish', φέρνεται ἄσχημα στά παιδιά του 'he treats his children badly.'

While many of these collocations or figurative uses of verbs have close parallels in Turkish and in other Balkan languages (the same is true of many of the situational formulas given in 11.1.1: for Greek-Turkish parallels see Newton 1962), idioms which belong more to written styles tend often to be based on Western European languages (especially French). There is little point in supplying a large number of examples (a list of Gallicisms is given in Papadopoulos 1930); but it is noticeable, especially in the political commentary columns of the Greek press, that much use is made of (sometimes inaccurate) translations of foreign turns of phrase (which nowadays are often English). Some examples are the following:

(1a)   τό ζήτημα τοῦ NATO εἶναι ἁπλῶς ἡ κορυφή τοῦ παγόβουνου 'the question of NATO is simply the tip of the iceberg' (*T* 20 Sept. 1979, 12);

(1b) ἡ ὁρατή πλευρά τοῦ παγόβουνου (lit. 'the visible side of the iceberg');

(2a) μιά ἀλυσιδωτή ἀντίδραση 'a chain reaction';

(2b) εἶχε ἀλυσιδωτές ἐπιπτώσεις σέ . . . (lit. 'it had chain effects on . . .');

(2c) μιά σειρά ἀλυσιδωτῶν ἀντιδράσεων (lit. 'a series of chain reactions': the writer presumably intended to render 'a chain reaction') (*T* 10 May 1979, 84);

(3) μέσα στά καθήκοντα τοῦ κ. Χ. θά εἶναι καί ἐκεῖνο τοῦ ξεκαθαρίσματος τῆς αἰτίας γιά τήν ὁποία παραιτήθηκε τό Διοικητικό Συμβούλιο 'among Mr X's duties will be *that of clarifying* the cause of the Board of Directors' resignation' (for τό ξεκαθάρισμα) (*T* 2 July 1981, 50);

(4) θά 'θελα νά ἀπολογηθῶ στό ἀκροατήριο γιατί πολύ λίγα γνωρίζω γιά . . . 'I'd like to *apologize* to the audience because I know very little about . . .' (for νά ζητήσω συγνώμη ἀπό τό ἀκροατήριο) (*Prov.* 1977: 119).

All these would be felt by most speakers of Greek to be un-Greek turns of phrase. Indeed, I have been unable to find a Greek (other than those who know English well) who can tell me the meaning of (1a) and (1b). Although the above phrases were taken from articles or talks written or given in Greek, they clearly originated in other pieces hurriedly translated from English or some other foreign language.

APPENDIX I
TABLES OF INFLECTION

NOUNS

1M parisyllabic

S	N	κλέφτ-η-ς
	VAG	κλέφτ-η
P	NVA	κλέφτ-ες
	G	κλεφτ-ών

1F parisyllabic

S	NVA	θάλασσ-α
	G	θάλασσ-α-ς
P	NVA	θάλασσ-ες
	G	θαλασσ-ών

1M imparisyllabic

S	N	καφ-έ-ς
	VAG	καφ-έ
P	NVA	καφ-έ-δ-ες
	G	καφ-έ-δ-ων

1F imparisyllabic

S	NVA	γιαγι-ά
	G	γιαγι-ᾶ-ς
P	NVA	γιαγι-ά-δ-ες
	G	γιαγι-ά-δ-ων

1Ma (-éas)

S	N	συγγραφ-έ-α-ς
	VAG	συγγραφ-έ-α
P	NVA	συγγραφ-εῖς
	G	συγγραφ-έ-ων

1Fa

S	NVA	κυβέρνησ-η
	G	κυβέρνησ-η-ς
P	NVA	κυβερνήσ-εις
	G	κυβερνήσ-ε-ων

1Ma (-ís)

S	N	συγγεν-ή-ς
	VAG	συγγεν-ή
P	NVA	συγγεν-εῖς
	G	συγγεν-ών

2A

S	N	άνθρωπ-ο-ς
	V	άνθρωπ-ε
	A	άνθρωπ-ο
	G	ανθρώπ-ου
P	NV	άνθρωπ-οι
	A	ανθρώπ-ους
	G	ανθρώπ-ων

2B

S	NVA	δωμάτι-ο
	G	δωματί-ου
P	NVA	δωμάτι-α
	G	δωματί-ων

2C

S	NVA	παιδί
	G	παιδι-ού
S	NVA	παιδι-ά
	G	παιδι-ών

3A

S	NVA	όνομα
	G	ονόμα-τ-ος
P	NVA	ονόμα-τ-α
	G	ονομά-τ-ων

3B

S	NVA	έδαφ-ος
	G	εδάφ-ους
P	NVA	εδάφ-η
	G	εδαφ-ών

ADJECTIVES

2A–2B–1F (a)

		M	N	F
S	N	νόστιμ-ο-ς		
	V	νόστιμ-ε	νόστιμ-ο	νόστιμ-η
	A	νόστιμ-ο		
	G	νόστιμ-ου		νόστιμ-η-ς
P	NV	νόστιμ-οι		
	A	νόστιμ-ους	νόστιμ-α	νόστιμ-ες
	G	νόστιμ-ων		

2A–2B–1F (b)

		M	N	F
S	N	ἄξι-ο-ς		
	V	ἄξι-ε	ἄξι-ο	ἄξι-α
	A	ἄξι-ο		
	G	ἄξι-ου		ἄξι-α-ς
P	NV	ἄξι-οι		
	A	ἄξι-ους	ἄξι-α	ἄξι-ες
	G	ἄξι-ων		

—2C–1F

		M	N	F
S	N	βαθύ-ς	βαθύ	βαθι-ά
	A	βαθύ		
	G	(βαθι-ού/βαθύ)		βαθι-ᾱ-ς
P	N	βαθι-οί		
	A	βαθι-ούς	βαθι-ά	βαθι-ές
	G	βαθι-ῶν		

1M–2B–1F

		M	N	F
S	N	ζηλιάρ-η-ς	ζηλιάρ-ικ-ο	ζηλιάρ-α
	VA			
	G	ζηλιάρ-η	ζηλιάρ-ικ-ου	ζηλιάρ-α-ς
P	NVA	ζηλιάρ-η-δ-ες	ζηλιάρ-ικ-α	ζηλιάρ-ες
	G	ζηλιάρ-η-δ-ων	ζηλιάρ-ικ-ων	—

(1Ma–3B)

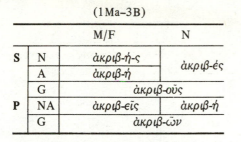

		M/F	N
S	N	ἀκριβ-ή-ς	ἀκριβ-ές
	A	ἀκριβ-ή	
	G	ἀκριβ-οῦς	
P	NA	ἀκριβ-εῖς	ἀκριβ-ή
	G	ἀκριβ-ῶν	

πολύς

		M	N	F
S	N	πολύ-ς	πολύ	πολλ-ή
	A	πολύ		
	G	(πολύ/πολλ-οῦ)		πολλ-ῆ-ς
P	N	πολλ-οί	πολλ-ά	πολλ-ές
	A	πολλ-ούς		
	G	πολλ-ῶν		

-on

		M	N	F
S	N	ἐνδιαφέρ-ων	ἐνδιαφέρ-ον	ἐνδιαφέρ-ουσ-α
	A	ἐνδιαφέρ-ον-τα		
	G	ἐνδιαφέρ-ον-τος		ἐνδιαφέρ-ουσ-α-ς
P	NA	ἐνδιαφέρ-ον-τες	ἐνδιαφέρον-τα	ἐνδιαφέρ-ουσ-ες
	G	ἐνδιαφερ-όν-των		(ἐνδιαφερ-ουσ-ῶν)

ARTICLES AND NUMERALS

Definite article

		M	N	F
S	N	ὁ	τό	ἡ
	A	τό(ν)		τή(ν)
	G	τοῦ		τῆς
P	N	οἱ	τά	οἱ
	A	τούς		τίς
	G	τῶν		

Indefinite article and 'one'

		M	N	F
S	N	ἕνας	ἕνα	μιά
	A	ἕνα(ν)		μιά(ν)
	G	ἑνός		μιᾶς

		'three'				'four'	
		M/F	N			M/F	N
P	NA	τρεῖς	τρία	P	NA	τέσσερις	τέσσερα
	G		τριῶν		G		τεσσάρων

VERBS

ACTIVE

Imperfective non-past

		1	2a	2b(i)	2b(ii)
S	1	δέν-ω	θεωρ-ῶ	ἀγαπ-άω/-ῶ	διασπ-ῶ
	2	δέν-εις	θεωρ-εῖς	ἀγαπ-ᾶς	διασπ-ᾶς
	3	δέν-ει	θεωρ-εῖ	ἀγαπ-άει/-ᾶ	διασπ-ᾶ
P	1	δέν-ουμε/-ομε	θεωρ-οῦμε	ἀγαπ-ᾶμε/-οῦμε	διασπ-οῦμε
	2	δέν-ετε	θεωρ-εῖτε	ἀγαπ-ᾶτε	διασπ-ᾶτε
	3	δέν-ουν(ε)	θεωρ-οῦν(ε)	ἀγαπ-ᾶνε/-οῦν(ε)	διασπ-οῦν

Imperfective imperative

	1	2a	2b(i)	2b(ii)
S	δέν-ε	(θεώρ-ει)	ἀγάπ-α	—
P	δέν-ετε	θεωρ-εῖτε	ἀγαπ-ᾶτε	—

Present participle

1 δέν-οντας   2a θεωρ-ώντας   2b(i) ἀγαπ-ώντας   2b(ii) διασπ-ώντας

Imperfective past

		1	2a and 2b(ii)	2b(i)
S	1	ἔ-δεν-α	θεωρ-οῦσ-α, διασπ-οῦσ-α	ἀγαπ-οῦσ-α/ἀγάπ-αγ-α
	2	ἔ-δεν-ες	(then endings as for 1)	(then endings as for 1)
	3	ἔ-δεν-ε		
P	1	δέν-αμε		
	2	δέν-ατε		
	3	ἔ-δεν-αν/δέν-ανε		

Perfective non-past

		1	2a	2b(i)	2b(ii)
S	1	δέσ-ω	θεωρήσ-ω	ἀγαπήσ-ω	διασπάσ-ω
			(then endings as imperfective non-past of 1)		

Perfective past

		1	2a	2b(i)	2b(ii)
S	1	ἔ-δεσ-α	θεώρησ-α	ἀγάπησ-α	δι-έ-σπασ-α
			(then endings as imperfective past)		

Perfective imperative

	1	2a	2b(i)	2b(ii)
S	δέσ-ε	θεώρησ-ε	ἀγάπησ-ε	—
P	δέσ-τε	θεωρῆσ-τε	ἀγαπῆσ-τε	—

Perfect

1	2a	2b(i)	2b(ii)
ἔχω δέσ-ει	ἔχω θεωρήσ-ει	ἔχω ἀγαπήσ-ει	ἔχω διασπάσ-ει

PASSIVE

Imperfective non-past

		1	2a	2b(i)
S	1	δέν-ομαι/-ουμαι	θεωρ-οῦμαι	ἀγαπ-ιέμαι
	2	δέν-εσαι	θεωρ-εῖσαι	ἀγαπ-ιέσαι
	3	δέν-εται	θεωρ-εῖται	ἀγαπ-ιέται
P	1	δεν-όμαστε	θεωρ-ούμαστε	ἀγαπ-ιόμαστε
	2	δέν-εστε/-όσαστε	θεωρ-εῖστε	ἀγαπ-ιέστε/-ιόσαστε
	3	δέν-ονται	θεωρ-οῦνται	ἀγαπ-ιοῦνται

		2b(ii)	2c
S	1	διασπ-ῶμαι	θυμ-ᾶμαι
	2	διασπ-ᾶσαι	θυμ-ᾶσαι
	3	διασπ-ᾶται	θυμ-ᾶται
P	1	διασπ-όμαστε/-ώμεθα	θυμ-όμαστε
	2	διασπ-ᾶστε/-ᾶσθε	θυμ-ᾶστε/-όσαστε
	3	διασπ-ῶνται/-οῦνται	θυμ-οῦνται

		3a	3b	εἶμαι
S	1	συνίστ-αμαι	διατίθ-εμαι	εἶ-μαι
	2	συνίστ-ασαι	διατίθ-εσαι	εἶ-σαι
	3	συνίστ-αται	διατίθ-εται	εἶ-ναι
P	1	συνιστ-άμεθα	διατιθ-έμεθα	εἴ-μαστε
	2	συνίστ-ασθε	διατίθ-εσθε	εἶ-στε/εἴ-σαστε
	3	συνίστ-ανται	διατίθ-ενται	εἶ-ναι

Present participle

1 σχεδιαζ-όμενος[1] 2a θεωρ-ούμενος 2b(i) — 2b(ii) διασπ-ώμενος
3a συνιστ-άμενος 3b διατιθ-έμενος

Imperfective past

		1	2a
S	1	δεν-όμουν(α)	(θεωρ-ούμουν)
	2	δεν-όσουν(α)	(θεωρ-ούσουν)
	3	δεν-όταν(ε)	θεωρ-ούνταν/-εῖτο

[1] Since δένω does not happen to possess a present participle passive, the verb σχεδιάζω has been given instead.

P	1	δεν-όμαστε	(θεωρ-ούμαστε)	
	2	δεν-όσαστε	(θεωρ-ούσαστε)	
	3	δέν-ονταν/-όντουσαν	θεωρ-ούνταν/-ούντο	
		2b(i)	2c	
S	1	ἀγαπ-ιόμουν(α)	θυμ-όμουν(α)	
		(then with endings	(then with endings	
		as 1, but with -j-)	as 1)	
		3a	3b	εἶμαι
S	1			ἤμουν(α)
	2			ἤσουν(α)
	3	συνίστ-ατο	διατίθ-ετο	ἦταν/ἤτανε
P	1			ἤμαστε
	2			ἤσαστε
	3	συνίστ-αντο	διατίθ-εντο	ἦταν/ἤτανε/ἦσαν

Perfective non-past

1 δε-θ-ῶ	2a θεωρ-ηθ-ῶ	2b(i) ἀγαπ-ηθ-ῶ	2b(ii) διασπ-ασθ-ῶ
2c θυμ-ηθ-ῶ	3a συστ-ηθ-ῶ	3b διατε-θ-ῶ	

(then with endings as for imperfective non-past active of 2a)

Perfective past

1 δέ-θ-ηκ-α	2a θεωρ-ήθ-ηκ-α	2b(i) ἀγαπ-ήθ-ηκ-α
2b(ii) διασπ-άσθ-ηκ-α	2c θυμ-ήθ-ηκ-α	3a συστ-ήθ-ηκ-α
3b διατέ-θ-ηκ-α		

(then endings as imperfective past active of 1)

Perfective imperative

	1	2a	2b(i)
S	δέσ-ου	θεωρήσ-ου	ἀγαπήσ-ου
P	δε-θ-εῖτε	θεωρ-ηθ-εῖτε	ἀγαπ-ηθ-εῖτε
	2b(ii)	2c	
S	δισπάσ-ου	θυμήσ-ου	
P	διασπ-ασθ-εῖτε	θυμ-ηθ-εῖτε	

Perfect

1	2a	2b(i)	2b(ii)
ἔχω δε-θ-εῖ	ἔχω θεωρ-ηθ-εῖ	ἔχω ἀγαπ-ηθ-εῖ	ἔχω διασπ-ασθ-εῖ
2c	3a	3b	
ἔχω θυμ-ηθ-εῖ	ἔχω συστ-ηθ-εῖ	ἔχω διατε-θ-εῖ	

Past participle

1	2a	2b(i)	2b(ii)
δε-μένος	θεωρη-μένος	ἀγαπη-μένος	διασπασ-μένος

APPENDIX II
THE MONOTONIC SYSTEM

In 1982 the monotonic (single-accent) system was introduced by presidential decree into education and the civil service. Over the years several versions of the monotonic system have been proposed, and the one adopted by the Greek authorities may not be the most efficient. Its chief principles are as follows:

(a) the breathings are abolished;
(b) monosyllabic words are written without an accent;
(c) words of more than one syllable are written with an acute accent over the stressed vowel.

The exceptions to these rules are as follows:

(i) an accent is written over words which have become monosyllabic as a result of elision or prodelision (e.g. κόψ' το 'cut it' < κόψε; θα 'ρθώ 'I'll come': θαρθό); but it is not written when, as a result of prodelision, the stress is shifted on to the previous vowel (e.g. θα 'ρθω (θάρθο) for θα έρθω);

(ii) the following monosyllables take an accent: the disjunctive conjunction ή 'or' (cf. article η) and the interrogative adverbs πού and πώς (cf. relative pronoun που and conjunction πως);

(iii) a proclitic pronoun may be accented if in the context it might otherwise be mistaken for an enclitic (e.g. o πατέρας μού είπε 'the father said to me', but o πατέρας μου είπε 'my father said');

(iv) when an enclitic causes a stress shift in the previous word, an accent is written both over the syllable actually stressed and over that which would have been stressed but for the presence of the enclitic (e.g. o δάσκαλος 'the teacher', but o δάσκαλός μας 'our teacher').

These rules are by no means perfect (to (ii) one might want to add γιατί; 'why?' and γιατι 'because', ώς 'until' and ως 'as'), and they do not always make the written accent conform to the spoken stress (e.g. από χτες is actually stressed only on the last syllable: *apoxtés*).

The following (unconnected) sentences are a sample of the three chief versions of MG orthography: (a) traditional, (b) simplified, and (c) monotonic. Certain additional features of the traditional orthography have been tacitly included.

(a) TRADITIONAL

Ἀπὸ χτὲς οἱ δικοί του ἔλειπαν σὲ διήμερη ἐκδρομή. Μ' ὅλο ποὺ θἄθελε νὰ τὴν ἀράξῃ δίπλα στὸ μαγνητόφωνο, ἔπρεπε νὰ διαβάσῃ αὐτὲς τὶς μέρες. // Καταβλήθηκε προσπάθεια γιὰ νὰ προσαρμοστοῦν στὸ τυπικὸ τῆς δημοτικῆς οἱ λέξεις τῆς ἀρχαίας ποὺ χρησιμοποιεῖ.

(b) SIMPLIFIED

Ἀπό χτές οἱ δικοί του ἔλειπαν σέ διήμερη ἐκδρομή. Μόλο ποὺ θά 'θελε νά τήν ἀράξει δίπλα στό μαγνητόφωνο, ἔπρεπε νά διαβάσει αὐτές τίς μέρες. // Καταβλήθηκε προσπάθεια γιὰ νὰ προσαρμοστοῦν στὸ τυπικὸ τῆς δημοτικῆς οἱ λέξεις τῆς ἀρχαίας ποὺ χηρσιμοποιεῖ.

(c) MONOTONIC

Από χτες οι δικοί του έλειπαν σε διήμερη εκδρομή. Μόλο που θα 'θελε να την αράξει δίπλα στο μαγνητόφωνο, έπρεπε να διαβάσει αυτές τις μέρες. // Καταβλήθηκε προσπάθεια για να προσαρμοστούν στο τυπικό της δημοτικής οι λέξεις της αρχαίας που χρησιμοποιεί.

It can hardly be denied that a greater economy is achieved by the use of the monotonic system; for example, whereas for the traditional system the typesetter needed thirteen different alphas, according to the presence or absence of one of the two breathings, one of the three accents, and the so-called *iota subscript* (or a combination of two or three of these), only two alphas are required for the monotonic, viz. a and ά.

It will have been noticed that most of the spelling reforms concern only accents and breathings. For the rest, the orthography of MG retains the ancient spelling in words and roots of AG origin (as long as this does not conflict with the actual pronunciation), and the number of voices raised during the past two centuries in favour of so-called phonetic spelling, in which each sound would be always represented by the same letter, has been small. In particular, it has been extremely rare for the introduction of the Latin alphabet to be mooted. Bearing in mind that the Greek alphabet was the first properly phonetic (or phonemic) alphabet in the world, and that the letters of the present alphabet (at least the capitals) have remained in use unaltered since the fifth century BC, most Greeks seem prepared to tolerate the difficulties of the orthography as long as the alternative would threaten to cut the modern language off from its ancient origins. Similarly, there are few people who have tried to promote the complete abolition of accents; this despite the argument that accents are not placed on words written entirely in capitals, and that children have no difficulty in reading aloud phrases in comic books, which are printed in capitals.

Despite the introduction of the monotonic system, it seems unlikely that further spelling reforms will take place in the near future. Even though the spelling of certain sounds still causes difficulties for most Greeks, and there is still a measure of variation in orthographic usage, on the other hand there is no problem involved in reading words from the page.

BIBLIOGRAPHY

The following abbreviations are used in the bibliography:

BMGS   *Byzantine and Modern Greek Studies*
BSLP   *Bulletin de la Société de Linguistique de Paris*
EEPSPA   *Epistimoniki Epetiris Philosophikis Scholis Panepistimiou Athinon*
EEPSPT   *Epistimoniki Epetiris Philosophikis Scholis Penepistimiou Thessalonikis*
FL   *Foundations of Language*
FN   *Folia Neohellenica*
JL   *Journal of Linguistics*
K   *Kathimerini*
NE   *Nea Estia*
SSMG   *Scandinavian Studies in Modern Greek*

ALEXIOU, M. (1982), 'Diglossia in Greece', in *Standard Languages, Spoken and Written* (ed. W. Haas), pp. 156–92, Manchester University Press, Manchester.

ANAGNOSTOPOULOS (1922): Ἀναγνωστόπουλος, Γ., 'Περί τοῦ ἄρθρου', Ἀθηνᾶ 34.166–247.

ANDRIOTIS (1932): Ἀνδριώτης, Ν. Π., 'Ε. Γιανίδη, Γλωσσικά πάρεργα' (book review), *NE* 12.777–9.

— (1934), '῾Υπάρχει ὑποταχτική στή νέα ἑλληνική;', *NE* 15.445–50.

— (1957), 'Ἀντίστοιχα ἐκφραστικά μέσα τῆς ἀρχαίας καί τῆς νέας ῾Ελληνικῆς', ῾Ελληνικά 15.1–25.

— (1967), Ἐτυμολογικό λεξικό τῆς κοινῆς νεοελληνικῆς (2nd edn.), Salonica.

— (1976), Ἀντιχάρισμα στόν καθηγητή Νικόλαο Π. Ἀνδριώτη, Salonica.

— (1980), 'Νεοελληνικά παρατακτικά σύνθετα', ῾Ελληνικά 32.3–31.

ANGELOPOULOS, A. (1979), 'Population distribution of Greece today according to language, national consciousness and religion', *Balkan Studies* 20.123–32.

BABINIOTIS (1972): Μπαμπινιώτης, Γ., Τό ῥῆμα τῆς ῾Ελληνικῆς, Vivliothiki Sofias S. Saripolou, Athens.

— (1979a), 'A linguistic approach to the "Language Question" in Greece', *BMGS* 5.1–16.

— (1979b), Νεοελληνική Κοινή. Πέρα τῆς καθαρευούσης καί τῆς δημοτικῆς, Grigoris, Athens.

— and KONDOS (1967): Μπαμπινιώτης, Γ., Κοντός, Π., Συγχρονική γραμματική τῆς κοινῆς νέας ἑλληνικῆς. Θεωρία — Ἀσκήσεις, Athens.

BAKKER, W. F. (1965), 'The aspect of the imperative in Modern Greek', *Neophilologus* 49.89–103 and 203–10.

— (1970), 'The aspectual differences between the present and aorist subjunctives in Modern Greek', Έλληνικά 23.78–108.

— (1971), 'Some remarks on the use of relative pronouns in the Erotokritos', Κρητικά Χρονικά 23.309–21.

BARRI, N. (1981), 'Aoristic present, "subjunctive" and converters in Modern Greek', in *Studies Presented to Hans Jakov Polotsky* (ed. D. W. Young), pp. 1–20, Pirtle & Polson, Beacon Hill (Mass.).

BEN-MAYOR, I. (1980), 'The semantics of some modal constructions in Modern Greek: the modal auxiliaries and the particle *tha*', Doct. Diss., Oxford.

BENTOLILA, F. (1979), 'Projet d'une grammaire fonctionnelle du grec contemporain', *Actes du Vᵉ colloque international de linguistique fonctionnelle*, pp. 25–54, Paris.

BERNSTEIN, B. (1970), 'Social class, language and socialization', in Giglioli (1972), pp. 157–78.

BOUBOULIDIS (1946): Μπουμπουλίδης, Φ. Κ., Ή μετοχή στά νεοελληνικά, Athens.

BOURAS (1969): Μπούρας, Ν., Ύφολογικαί έπιδράσεις τής Άθηναϊκής Σχολής έπί τής συγχρόνου γλώσσης (Συμβολή είς τήν ίστορίαν τής Νέας Έλληνικής), Athens.

BROWNING, R. (1983), *Medieval and Modern Greek*, 2nd edn., Cambridge University Press, Cambridge.

CARATZAS, S. C. (1957–8), 'Die Entstehung der neugriechischen Literatursprache', *Glotta* 36.194–208.

CHRISTIDIS (1975): Χρηστίδης, Χ., Τό σύνταγμα τής Έλλάδας τής 9 Ίουνίου 1976: έπίσημο κείμενο καί μεταγραφή του στή δημοτική, Athens.

CHRISTIDIS (1982): Χριστίδης, Α.-Φ., ' Ότι/πως – που: επιλογή δεικτών συμπληρωμάτων στα νέα ελληνικά', in *Meletes* (1982), pp. 113–77.

CLAY, D. (1977), 'Influence of Greek on the speech of a Greek Gypsy community', *BMGS* 3.81–94.

CONTOSSOPOULOS: see KONDOSOPOULOS.

DANGITSIS (1967): Δαγκίτσης, Κ., Λεξικό τής λαϊκής, Vasiliou, Athens.

DORBARAKIS (1979): Δορμπαράκης, Π. Χ., 'Ή σωστή χρήση τής δημοτικής', *K* 21–22 Oct., 28 Oct., 4–5 Nov., 11–12 Nov., and 18–19 Nov. 1979.

EBBESEN, S. (1979), ' "Contract verbs" in Modern Greek', Έλληνικά 31.65–107.

EFSTATHIADIS, S. (1974), 'Tense and aspect in Greek and English', *EEPSPT* 13.37–71.

EIDENEIER, H. (1977), 'Hellenisch oder Romäisch? Zum Ursprung und gegenwärtigen Stand der neugriechischen Sprachfrage', *FN* 2.41–63.

EKLUND, B.-L. (1975), 'A tentative terminology of tense and aspect in Modern Greek', *FN* 1.39–43.

(1976), *Modern Greek: Verbal Aspect and Compound Nouns. Two Studies.* Kungl. Vetenskaps- och Vitterhets-Samhället, Gothenburg.

FERGUSON, C.A. (1959), 'Diglossia', *Word* 15.325–40.

GEORGACAS, D. J. (1958), 'Remarks and corrections on Pring's A Grammar of Modern Greek', *Orbis* 7.536–58.

GIGLIOLI, P. P. (ed.) (1972), *Language and Social Context*, Penguin, Harmondsworth.

GRAMMATIKI (1931): Γραμματική: Τύποι καί κανόνες τῆς κοινῶς ὁμιλουμένης νεοελληνικῆς. Μελέτη γραμμένη ἀπό 'Αθηναίους, Athens.

HADZIDAKIS (1905–7): Χατζιδάκις, Γ. Ν., Μεσαιωνικά καί νέα ἑλληνικά, 2 vols., Athens.

— (1909), Περί τῆς χρήσεως τῶν μέσων, τῶν μεταβατικῶν καί ἀμεταβάτων ρημάτων ἐν τῇ Νέα 'Ελληνικῇ, Athens.

— (1911), Φιλολογικαί μελέται, Athens.

— (1915), Σύντομος ἱστορία τῆς ἑλληνικῆς γλώσσης, Athens.

— (1927), 'Συμβολή εἰς τήν ἱστορίαν τῆς ἑλληνικῆς γλώσσης: Περί τῆς γενικῆς', 'Αθηνᾶ 39.56–72.

— (1928), 'Συμβολή εἰς τήν ἱστορίαν τῆς ἑλληνικῆς γλώσσης: Περί τῶν μετοχῶν', Πρακτικά τῆς 'Ακαδημίας 'Αθηνῶν 3. 634–45.

HALL, R. A., Jr. (1972), 'Pidgins and Creoles as standard languages', in Pride and Holmes (1972), pp. 142–53.

HAUGEN, E. (1966), 'Dialect, Language, Nation', in Pride and Holmes (1972), pp. 97–111.

HESSE, R. (1978), 'Γνῶθι σεαυτόν — Γνώρισε τόν ἑαυτό σου', *SSMG*, no. 2, pp. 53–64.

— (1980), *Syntax of the Modern Greek Verbal System: the use of the forms, particularly in combination with θα and να*, Museum Tusculanum Press, Copenhagen.

HORROCKS, G. (1980), 'The order of constituents in Modern Greek', unpublished paper delivered at the Philological Society, London, 7 Nov. 1980.

HOUSEHOLDER, F. W., Jr. (1962), 'Greek diglossia', *Georgetown Monographs* 15.109–32.

HOUSEHOLDER et al. (1964), Householder, F. W., Kazazis, K., and Koutsoudas, A., *Reference Grammar of Literary Dhimotiki*, Indiana University, Bloomington.

IKONOMOU (1933): Οἰκονόμου, Μ. Χ., Νεοελληνική γραμματική (τῆς κοινῆς νεοελληνικῆς), Athens.

JONES, A. B. (1966), 'Stress and intonation in Modern Greek', *Glotta* 44.254–62.

JOSEPH, B. (1980a), 'Linguistic universals and syntactic change', *Language* 56.345–70.

— (1980b), 'Recovery of information in relative clauses: evidence from Greek and Hebrew', *JL* 16.237–44.

KAHANE, H., and KAHANE, R. (1954), (Review of Seiler 1952), *Language* 30.115–23.

372   BIBLIOGRAPHY

KAHANE, H., and KAHANE, R. (1958), 'The tense system of Modern
Greek', in *Omagiu lui Iorgu Iordan cu Prilejul împlinirii a 70 de ani*,
pp. 453–74, Bucharest.
— — (1979), 'Decline and survival of Western prestige languages',
Language 55.183–98.
KAISSE, E. (1976), 'Stress melodies and a fast speech rule in Modern
Greek', in *Actes du 6ème congrès de l'Association linguistique du
nord-est* (ed. A. Ford *et al.*), pp. 165–76, Montreal.
KAKOURIOTIS, A. (1980), 'Raising in Modern Greek', *Lingua* 52.
157–77.
KAKRIDIS (1946): Κακριδῆς, I. Θ., 'Ο συγγραφέας τοῦ πρώτου νεοελληνικοῦ συντακτικοῦ, *NE* 40.922–8.
KATRANIDES, A. (1970), 'Co-occurrence restrictions of aspect and
tense in Modern Greek subjunctive constructions', in *Actes du Xe
congrès des linguistes*, vol. 2, pp. 859–64, Bucharest.
KAZAZIS, K. (1967), 'A case of ambiguity in Modern Greek', in
Languages and Areas: Studies Presented to George V. Bobrinskoy,
pp. 70–6, Chicago.
— (1970), 'The relative importance of parents and peers in first-
language acquisition: the case of some Constantinopolitan families
in Athens', *General Linguistics* 10.111–20.
— (1972), 'The status of Turkisms in the present-day Balkan languages',
in *Aspects of the Balkans: Continuity and Change* (ed. H. Birn-
baum and S. Vryonis), pp. 87–116, Mouton, The Hague/Paris.
— (1973), 'Ταχυδρόμος's Turkish lessons', in *Issues in Linguistics:
Papers in Honor of Henry and Renée Kahane* (ed. B. B. Kachru
et al.), pp. 394–408, University of Illinois Press, Urbana.
— (1975a), 'Greek reactions to an Ancient Greek primer for Turks',
Journal of Modern Philology 73.162–5.
— (1975b), 'On some aspects of linguistic Hellenocentrism', in *Proceed-
ings of the Eleventh International Congress of Linguists* (ed. L. Heil-
mann), pp. 1075–80. Mulino, Bologna.
— (1976a), 'Greek and Arvanitika in Corinthia', *Balkanistica* 3.42–51.
— (1976b), 'A superficially unusual feature of Greek diglossia', in
Papers from the Twelfth Regional Meeting, Chicago Linguistic
Society, pp. 369–75, Chicago.
— (1979), 'Learnedisms in Costas Taktsis's *Third Wedding*', *BMGS*
5.17–28.
— (1980), 'On Modern Greek ποι- "who?" ', in *Papers from the
Parasession Pronouns and Anaphora*, Chicago Linguistic Society,
pp. 251–7, Chicago.
— and PENTHEROUDAKIS, J. (1976), 'The reduplication of indefinite direct objects in Albanian and Modern Greek', *Language*
52.398–403.
KOLTSIDAS (1978): Κολτσίδας, A. M., Λεξικό τῆς πιάτσας: λέξεις
καί ἐκφράσεις τῆς καθημερωνῆς ζωῆς μέ εἰδική ἤ μεταφορική σημασία, Salonica.
KONDOSOPOULOS (1978): Contossopoulos, N. G., *L'Influence du*

français sur le grec: emprunts lexicaux et calques phraséologiques, Athens.
— (1981): Κοντοσόπουλος, Ν. Γ., Διάλεκτοι καί ίδιώματα τῆς νέας ἐλληνικῆς, Athens.
KOUMANOUDIS (1900): Κουμανούδης, Σ., Συναγωγή νέων λέξεων, Athens (reprint, Ermis, Athens 1980).
KOURMOULIS (1964-5): Κουρμούλης, Γ. Ι., 'Μορφολογικαί ἐξελίξεις τῆς ἐλληνικῆς γλώσσης', *EEPSPA* 15.9–22.
— (1967), Ἀντίστροφον λεξικόν τῆς νέας ἐλληνικῆς, Athens.
KOUTSOUDAS, A. (1962), *Verb Morphology of Modern Greek: A Descriptive Analysis*, Indiana University, Bloomington.
KRIARAS (1979): Κριαράς, Ε., Ἄρθρα καί σημειώματα ενός δημοτικιστή, Kollaros, Athens.
LABOV, W. (1970), 'The logic of non-standard English', in Giglioli (1972), pp. 179–215.
LAMBRIDI (1966): Λαμπρίδη, Ε., 'Ἡ γλώσσα μας', *NE* 80.1357–65, 1417–26.
LASCARATOU, C., and WARBURTON, I. P. (1981), 'The use of passive constructions in Modern Greek', *Mandatophoros*, no. 17 (June 1981), pp. 53–64.
LEXIKON (1933): Λεξικόν τῆς ἐλληνικῆς γλώσσης. Συνταχθέν ὑπό ἐπιτροπῆς φιλολόγων καί ἐπιστημόνων ἐπιμελείᾳ Γ. Ζευγώλη, Proia, Athens.
LYONS, J. (1968), *Introduction to Theoretical Linguistics*, Cambridge University Press, Cambridge.
LYPOURLIS (1977): Λυπουρλής, Δ. Δ., ''Επίθετα ἀπό οὐσιαστικοποιημένα ἐπίθετα', *EEPSPT* 16.97–166.
MAKRYMICHALOS (1961): Μακρυμίχαλος, Σ. Ι., 'Ένα πρόβλημα τῆς γραφομένης ἐλληνικῆς, Athens.
MALIKOUTI (1970?): Μαλικούτη, Α., Μετασχηματιστική μορφολογία τοῦ νεοελληνικοῦ ὀνόματος, Athens.
MATTHEWS, P. H. (1967), 'The main features of Modern Greek verb inflection', *FL* 3.262–84.
— (1974), *Morphology*, Cambridge University Press, Cambridge.
MEGAS (1925-7): Μέγας, Α. Ε., Ἱστορία τοῦ γλωσσικοῦ ζητήματος, 2 vols., Kollaros, Athens.
MELETES (1982): Μελέτες γιά τήν ἐλληνική γλώσσα, Konstandinidis, Salonica.
MESEVRINOS (1973): Μεσεβρινός, Η προδομένη γλώσσα, Lund/ Nicosia (reprint, Kedros, Athens 1974).
— (1978): Σωστη δημοτικη, Ta tetradia tou Riga, Salonica.
MIRAMBEL, A. (1932), 'Les Diverses valeurs de l'aspect verbal en grec moderne', *BSLP* 33.31–49.
— (1937), 'Les "États de langue" dans la Grèce actuelle', *Conférences de l'Institut de linguistique de l'Université de Paris*, 5.19–53.
— (1938a), 'Note de phonétique néo-hellénique: La contraction de *e* et de *i*', *BSLP* 39.133–4.

MIRAMBEL, A. (1938b), 'Note de syntaxe néo-hellénique: La valeur "moyenne" de quelques verbes', *BSLP* 39.135–6.
— (1939a), 'Remarque de phonétique néo-grecque: La quantité vocalique', *BSLP* 40.58–61.
— (1939b), 'Remarque de syntaxe néo-grecque: L'Emploi de l'article défini', *BSLP* 40.62–68.
— (1940), 'Note sur le suffixe diminutif -άκι en grec moderne', *BSLP* 41.89–91.
— (1942), 'De l'emploi de l'*aoriste* en grec moderne', *Transactions of the Philological Society*, 1942, pp. 15–39.
— (1946a), 'Le Groupe *ts* en grec moderne', *BSLP* 42.89–102.
— (1946b), 'Négation et mode en grec moderne', *BSLP* 43.57–66.
— (1950), 'L'Opposition de *ts* à *tz* en grec moderne', *BSLP* 46.58–68.
— (1952), 'Du caractère des chuintantes dans certains parlers néo-helléniques', *BSLP* 48.63–78.
— (1953), 'Monosyllabes en grec moderne', *BSLP* 49.52–66.
— (1956), 'Subordination et expression temporelle en grec moderne', *BSLP* 52.219–53.
— (1959), *La Langue grecque moderne: description et analyse*, Klincksieck, Paris.
— (1960), 'Participe et gérondif en grec médiéval et moderne', *BSLP* 56.46–79.
— (1964), 'Les Aspects psychologiques du purisme dans la Grèce moderne', *Journal de psychologie normale et pathologique*, 4 (October 1964), 405–36.
NAKAS (1981): Νάκας, Θ., 'Πώς χρησιμοποιεί τη μετοχή ο Σεφέρης', Τομές, no. 70 (March 1981), pp. 37–43.
NEA IKONOMIA (1965): 'Νέα Οἰκονομία', Σύντομες ὁδηγίες γιά τήν καλή χρήση τῆς δημοτικῆς, Melissa, Athens.
NEOELLINIKI (1976): Νεοελληνική γραμματική: Ἀναπροσαρμογή τῆς Μικρῆς νεοελληνικῆς γραμματικῆς τοῦ Μ. Τριανταφυλλίδη, Organismos Ekdoseos Didaktikon Vivlion, Athens.
NEWTON, B. E. (1961), 'The rephonemicization of Modern Greek', *Lingua* 10.275–84.
— (1962), 'Some Modern Greek–Turkish semantic parallelisms', *Glotta* 40.315–20.
— (1963), 'The grammatical integration of Italian and Turkish substantives into Modern Greek', *Word* 19.20–30.
— (1971), 'Postconsonantal yod', *Lingua* 26.132–70.
— (1972a), 'The dialect geography of Modern Greek passive inflections', *Glotta* 50.262–89.
— (1972b), *The Generative Interpretation of Dialect: A Study of Modern Greek Phonology*, Cambridge University Press, Cambridge.
— (1973a), 'The dialect geography of Modern Greek active inflections', *Glossa* (Burnaby, BC) 7.189–230.
— (1973b) (Review of Warburton 1970), *JL* 9.331–9.
— (1974–5), 'The dialect geography of Modern Greek oxytone imperfects', *Glotta* 52–3.301–12.

— (1979a), 'Habitual aspect in Ancient and Modern Greek', *BMGS* 5.29–42.

— (1979b), 'Scenarios, modality, and verbal aspect in Modern Greek', *Language* 55.139–67.

NEWTON, B. E., and VELOUDIS, I. (1980a), 'Intention, destination and Gͬeek verbal aspect', *Lingua* 52.269–84.

— — (1980b), 'Necessity, obligation and Modern Greek verbal aspect', *Lingua* 50.25–43.

NYMAN, N. (1981), 'Paradigms and transderivational constraints: stress and yod in Modern Greek', *JL* 17.231–46.

PAPADOPOULOS (1926): Παπαδόπουλος, Α. Α., Γραμματική τῶν βορείων ἰδιωμάτων τῆς ἑλληνικῆς γλώσσης, Athens.

— (1930), 'Οἱ γαλλισμοί τῆς ἑλληνικῆς γλώσσης', Ἀθηνᾶ 42.3–33.

PAPAS (1973): Παπάς, Κ. Ν., Γλωσσικό ζήτημα καί γλωσσική πραγματικότητα, Athens.

PERIDIS (1965): Περίδης, Μ., Ἡ ἑλληνική γλώσσα καί ἡ σημερινή μορφή της, Athens.

PETROPOULOS (1971): Πετρόπουλος, Η., Καλιαρντά, Digamma, Athens.

PETROUNIAS, E. (1978), 'The Modern Greek language and diglossia', in *The 'Past' in Medieval and Modern Greek Culture* (ed. S. Vryonis, Jr.), pp. 193–220, Undena Publications, Malibu.

PHILIPPAKI-WARBURTON: see WARBURTON.

PHOKAS (1978): Φωκάς, Ν., 'Εὐρωπληθυντικός καί ἑλληνική ἀγλωσσία', *K* 19 Oct. 1978.

PHORIS (1976): Φόρης, Β. Δ., 'Νομικά καί δημοτική', *K* 2, 3, and 6 July 1976.

— (1978), 'Ἡ θεωρία τῆς "συγχρονικῆς" ἑλληνικῆς γλώσσας', *K* 9 May 1978.

— (1979), 'Ἀναδρομή κι ἐπιδρομή', Τό Βῆμα, 18 Mar. 1979.

PHRANGOS (1972): Φράγκος, Χ. Π., Ἡ ἐπίδραση τῆς γλωσσικῆς μορφῆς τοῦ κειμένου στήν ἀνάγνωση τῶν μαθητῶν καί στήν κατανόηση, Yannina.

PRIDE, J. B., and HOLMES, J. (1972), *Sociolinguistics*, Penguin, Harmondsworth.

PRING, J. T. (1950), *A Grammar of Modern Greek on a Phonetic Basis*, University of London Press, London.

— (1965), *The Oxford Dictionary of Modern Greek (Greek–English)*, Oxford University Press, Oxford.

— (1981), *The Oxford Dictionary of Modern Greek (English–Greek)*, Oxford University Press, Oxford.

PROVLIMATA (1977): Προβλήματα μεταγλωττισμοῦ στή νεοελληνική γλώσσα, Vivliothiki Genikis Paideias, Athens.

QUIRK, R., and GREENBAUM, S. (1980), *A University Grammar of English*, Longman, London.

ROTOLO, V. (1973), *Il linguaggio calcistico in Grecia*, Quaderni del circolo semiologico siciliano, Palermo.

RUGE, H. (1969), *Zur Entstehung der neugriechischen Substantiv-deklination*, Acta Univ. Stockh., Stockholm.

— (1973), 'Imperfekt passiv im Neugriechischen: Ein Vergleich zwischen normativen Grammatik und Alltagssprache in Athen, Kavala und Istanbul', *Glotta* 51.142–59.

— (1975), 'Zum Passiv im Neugriechischen', *FN* 1.143–54.

— (1976), 'Phonetik', in Eideneier, H., *Sprachvergleich Griechisch–Deutsch*, pp. 13–29, Schwann, Düsseldorf.

SAPHARIKAS (1961): Σαφαρίκας, Α., Έρευνα ἐπί τοῦ λεξιλογίου τῶν Ἑλλήνων μαθητῶν, Athens.

SEILER, H. (1952), *L'Aspect et le temps dans le verbe néo-grec*, Les Belles Lettres, Paris.

SETATOS, M. (1971), 'Transformations of emotive meaning in Modern Greek *koine*', *Orbis* 20. 458–69.

— (1974): Σετάτος, Μ., Φωνολογία τῆς κοινῆς νεοελληνικῆς, Papazisis, Athens.

SOTIROPOULOS, D. (1972), *Noun Morphology of Modern Greek*, Mouton, The Hague/Paris.

STATHOPOULOU (1979): Σταθοπούλου, Α., Γιά τήν ἀκολουθία τῶν κυρίων ὅρων KP (κατηγορηματικό ρῆμα) – Υ (ὑποκείμενο) στίς δευτερεύουσες προτάσεις', *SSMG*, no. 3, pp. 28–34.

STAVROPOULOS, D. N., and HORNBY, A. S. (1977), *The Oxford English–Greek Learner's Dictionary*, Oxford University Press, Oxford.

STAVROU-SIPHAKI (1982): Σταύρου-Σηφάκη, Μ., Μεριστικές καί ψευδομεριστικές ὀνοματικές φράσεις στή νέα ἑλληνική, in *Meletes* (1982), pp. 79–111.

SWANSON, D. C. (1958), 'English loanwords in Modern Greek', *Word* 14.26–46.

TANNEN, D. (1980a), 'Implications of the oral/literate continuum for cross-cultural communication', in *Current Issues in Bilingual Education* (ed. J. E. Alatis), pp. 326–47, Georgetown University Press, Washington.

— (1980b), 'A comparative analysis of oral narrative strategies: Athenian Greek and American English', in *The Pear Stories: Cognitive and Linguistic Aspects of Narrative Production* (Advances in Discourse Processes, 3), pp. 51–87, Ablex, Norwood (NJ).

— (1981), 'Indirectness in discourse: ethnicity as conversational style', *Discourse Processes* 4.221–38.

— and ÖZTEK, P. C. (1981), ' "Health to our mouths": formulaic expressions in Turkish and Greek', in *Conversational Routine* (ed. F. Coulmas), pp. 37–54, Mouton, The Hague/Paris/New York.

TECHNI (1976): Τέχνη (Μακεδονική Καλλιτεχνική Ἑταιρεία), Προβλήματα τῆς δημοτικῆς γλώσσας, Salonica.

THAVORIS (1966): Θαβώρης, Α. Ι., Ὁ ἀπόλυτος ὑπερθετικός βαθμός μερικῶν ἐπιθέτων στή Νέα Ἑλληνική', Ἑλληνικά 19.16–47 and 254–95.

— (1969), Ούσιαστικά άπό έπίθετα (καί μετοχές) στή νέα έλληνική ('Ελληνικά: Παράρτημα 19), Salonica.

THEOPHANOPOULOU-KONDOU, D. (1972–3), 'Fast speech rules and some phonological processes of Modern Greek: A preliminary investigation', EEPSPA 23.372–90.

— (1980): Θεοφανοπούλου-Κοντού, Δ., Μέσα αύτοπαθή ρήματα τής νέας έλληνικής, in 'Μνήμη' Γεωργίου Ι. Κουρμούλη, Athens.

— (1982), Τά μέσα ρήματα τής νέας έλληνικής, in Meletes (1982), pp. 51–78.

THUMB, A. (1895), Handbuch der neugriechischen Volkssprache, Trübner, Strasbourg (revised edn. 1910).

TRIANDAPHYLLIDIS (1941): Τριανταφυλλίδης, Μ., Νεοελληνική γραμματική (τής Δημοτικής), Organismos Ekdoseos Scholikon Vivlion, Athens.

— (1949), Μικρή νεοελληνική γραμματική, Neoelliniki Vivliothiki, Athens.

TSOPANAKIS (1950): Τσοπανάκης, Α. Γ., 'Συμβολή στή ρύθμιση τού νεοελληνικού κλιτικού συστήματος', EEPSPT 6.243–80.

— (1976), 'Γραπτή καί προφορική δημοτική', NE, Christmas 1976, pp. 115–34.

— (1979), ''Ο Δημοτικισμός καί ή γλώσσα τού Βαλαωρίτη', NE, Christmas 1979, pp. 475–87.

— and DERVISOPOULOU, M. (1957): Τσοπανάκης, Α. Γ., Δερβισοπούλου, Μ., 'Τό κλιτικό μας σύστημα', EEPSPT 7.117–53.

TZARTZANOS (1932): Τζάρτζανος, Α., 'Δέν ύπάρχει ύποτακτική στή νέα έλληνική;', NE 12.826–7 (Response to Andriotis 1932).

— (1934), 'Κι όμως ύπάρχει!' NE 15.515–16 (Response to Andriotis 1934).

— (1935), 'Δημοτική καί νεοδημοτική: 'Η προσπάθεια ένός συλλόγου', Φιλολογικός Νέος Κόσμος, no. 2 (February 1935).

— (1946), Νεοελληνική σύνταξις (τής κοινής δημοτικής) (2nd edn.), Vol. 1, Organismos Ekdoseos Scholikon Vivlion, Athens.

— (1963), Νεοελληνική σύνταξις (τής κοινής δημοτικής) (2nd edn.), Vol. 2, Organismos Ekdoseos Didaktikon Vivlion, Athens.

VAN DIJK-WITTOP KONING, A. M. (1963), Die continuïtet van het Grieks, Tjeenk Willink, Zwolle.

VELOUDIS (1979): Βελούδης, Γ., 'Παρατηρήσεις πάνω στά γενικά χαρακτηριστικά τών δίπτυχων καί ψευδοδίπτυχων προτάσεων', EEPSPT 18 (1979), 39–56.

VELTSOS et al. (1979?): Βέλτσος, Γ., κ.ά. Γιά τή δημοτική γλώσσα, Grigoris, Athens.

VOSTANTZOGLOU (1962): Βοσταντζόγλου, Θ., 'Αντιλεξικόν ή όνομαστικόν τής νεοελληνικής γλώσσης (2nd edn.), Athens.

— (1967), 'Αναλυτικόν όρθογραφικόν λεξικόν τής νεοελληνικής γλώσσης, Athens.

WARBURTON, I. P. (1970a), 'Rules of accentuation in Classical and Modern Greek', Glotta 48.107–21.

WARBURTON, I. P. (1970b), *On the Verb in Modern Greek*, Indiana University, Bloomington.
— (1973), 'Modern Greek verb conjugation: Inflectional morphology in a transformational grammar', *Lingua* 32. 193–226.
— (1975), 'The passive in English and Greek', *FL* 13.563–78.
— (1976), 'On the boundaries of morphology and phonology: A case study from Modern Greek', *JL* 12.259–78.
— (1977a), 'The function of inflectional paradigms in synchronic and diachronic linguistic descriptions', in *Phonologica 1976* (ed. W. U. Dressler and O. E. Pfeiffer), pp. 53–8, Innsbruck.
— (1977b), 'Modern Greek clitic pronouns and the "surface structure constraints" hypothesis', *JL* 13.258–81.
— (1979): Φιλιππάκη–Warburton, I., ''Ο μετασχηματικός κανόνας τῆς ἀνύψωσης στά νέα ἑλληνικά', *EEPSPT* 18.489–526.
— (1980), 'Greek diglossia and the true aspects of the phonology of Common Modern Greek', *JL* 16.45–54.
— (1982), 'Προβλήματα σχετικά μέ τή σειρά τῶν ὅρων στίς ἑλληνικές προτάσεις', Γλωσσολογία 1.99–107.
WARING, H. (1976), 'The Intonation of Modern Greek', Doct. Diss., London.
— (1982), 'The investigation of Modern Greek intonation', *Mandatophoros*, no. 20 (November 1982), pp. 18–29.
YPOURGEIO (1977): Ὑπουργεῖο Προεδρίας Κυβερνήσεως, Ἡ νεοελληνική γλώσσα στή διοίκηση, Athens.
ZOUKIS (1934): Ζούκης, Γ., Συμβολή στή γραμματική τῆς νέας ἑλληνικῆς γλώσσας (Ἡ ὑποτακτική ἔγκλισις), Athens.

INDEX OF
GREEK WORDS

GENERAL INDEX